MULTIPLE CRITERIA DECISION MAKING IN INDUSTRY

STUDIES IN PRODUCTION AND ENGINEERING ECONOMICS

Edited by Professor R. W. Grubbström, Department of Production Economics, Linköping Institute of Technology, S-58182 Linköping, Sweden.

ELSEVIER SCIENCE PUBLISHERS B.V.
Sara Burgerhartstraat 25,
P.O. Box 211, 1000 AE Amsterdam, The Netherlands

Distributors for the United States and Canada:

ELSEVIER SCIENCE PUBLISHING COMPANY, INC.
655 Avenue of the Americas,
New York, NY 10010, U.S.A.

Library of Congress Cataloging-in-Publication Data

Tabucanon, Mario T.
    Multiple criteria decision making in industry / Mario T. Tabucanon.
        p.   cm. — (Studies in production and engineering economics; 8)
    Includes bibliographies and indexes.
    ISBN 0-444-70541-4 (U.S.)
    1. Decision-making.   I. Title. II. Series.
    T57.95.T32 1988
    658.4'03—dc19

                                            88-30200
                                              CIP

ISBN 0-444-70541-4 (Vol. 8)
ISBN 0-444-41963-2 (Series)

Printed in The Netherlands

STUDIES IN PRODUCTION AND ENGINEERING ECONOMICS, 8

MULTIPLE CRITERIA DECISION MAKING IN INDUSTRY

Mario T. Tabucanon

Division of Industrial Engineering and Management,
Asian Institute of Technology,
Bangkok, Thailand

ELSEVIER
AMSTERDAM – OXFORD – NEW YORK – TOKYO   1988

To my wife Monthip,
and children, Ray and Allan

PREFACE

During the last few decades, the world has witnessed the dramatic growth of Operations Research. From its humble beginning during World War II when OR techniques were used in logistical systems up to the present time, the field has grown by leaps and bounds - the number of specialists has multiplied, research publications have tremendously increased, and the number of OR tools and techniques developed has soared quantumly in many directions. Operations Research has grown remarkably to such an extent that its applicability is already inherent in problems confronting our daily lives.

Conspicuous in this disciplinary growth is the emergence of Multiple Criteria Decision Making (MCDM), choosing the "best" solution that would satisfy the conflicting criteria. In this area of OR, we have witnessed a stream of research publications in various journals, books and monographs. In fact, there have been books written as well as special issues of international journals published which are devoted solely to MCDM. It can be seen from these publications that many applications of MCDM theories are on decision making problems confronting industries. It is this state-of-the-art that has motivated the author to spend time and effort in putting together into one cover some theories of MCDM as well as their applications in industry.

The book is organized into seven chapters. The first four chapters deal with the fundamentals and theories of MCDM, the techniques in model building, and the procedures necessary to derive the solutions from the models. The remaining three chapters cover the various applications of MCDM models in industrial problems such as those mainly in production, and to some extent in personnel, finance, marketing, project, and other management-related problems of specific organizations. Chapter I is an overview of MCDM giving insights on its usefulness in many real life decision making situations. It also attempts to project the complicacy of MCDM in the light of conflicting objectives. The book moves on to Chapter II where the fundamentals of multicriterion optimization are discussed. It highlights the underlying foundations on which MCDM rests. In MCDM, the conflicting objectives may have varying degrees of importance to the decision maker. Chapter III discusses the forms in which degrees of importance are and can be measured and the way they are derived from the decision makers. Various MCDM techniques are presented in Chapter IV.

Applications start in Chapter V. In this chapter, an important beneficiary field, production management, is highlighted. Several applications of MCDM techniques, particularly in production planning, scheduling and control, are featured. Other applications in business management such as manpower, financial and marketing management are discussed in Chapter VI. Chapter VII deals with applications of MCDM techniques in other related, macro-level, areas in business and industry.

There is, however, no claim that the models and applications presented here cover all the published literatures in the field. The book is by no means exhaustive. However, the book attempts to feature representative documentations covering a wide spectrum of MCDM models and applications in industries. It is hoped that this book could provide the present and future managers, teachers, researchers, and other practitioners with the pertinent information and technical knowhow relevant to their daily decision making activities. The reader should have a solid background in optimization and mathematical programming, like linear programming to say the least, before they can appreciate this book.

I am pleased to take this opportunity to introduce to the reader, in a nutshell, a unique institute of technology - an academic setting where this book was written. Located in Thailand and governed by an international Board of Trustees, the Asian Institute of Technology (AIT) is the only graduate engineering university of its kind in the world. It is autonomous and independent and yet is supported by some 20 governments and many other funding agencies, foundations, corporations, and individuals. It is entirely international in its administration, faculty, student body and in all phases of its teaching programs. Situated on a 400-acre campus, 42 kilometers north of Bangkok, AIT's laboratories, library and teaching facilities are of an exceptionally high standard. The student body numbers over 600, all studying at postgraduate level. With few exceptions, AIT alumni remain and work in Asia.

I wish to extend my deepest gratitude to the following individuals for their assistance in preparing the manuscript: Mr. Lin Jia, Mrs. Lisa Tan Reyes, Mr. Ernesto T. Uy, and to my other former graduate students; the two secretaries of the AIT's Division of Industrial Engineering and Management, Mrs. Pornrachanee Chuawongse and Mrs. Sirithorn Natikool, and others whose names are not mentioned here but had also contributed towards the completion of this book. I would like to thank Dr. G. Lewis, Mr. Jun Gonzales, Mr. H. L. Tien and some other staff members of AIT's Regional Computer Center for their kind assistance in the printing of the final manuscript. Special thanks are due to Prof. R. W. Grubbström of Linköping Institute of Technology and to Drs.

Arie Jongejan of Elsevier for their support.

Finally, I would like to thank my wife, Monthip, for her support, patience and inspiration.

MARIO T. TABUCANON
Division of Industrial Engineering
and Management
Asian Institute of Technology
Bangkok, Thailand

CONTENTS

CHAPTER I

MULTIPLE CRITERIA DECISION MAKING – AN INTRODUCTION

1.1 MCDM - BALANCING A VARIETY OF NEEDS AND GOALS

The ability to make rational decisions is one of mankind's unique attributes. Man has continuously devised ways and means to enlarge his abilities
to cope with the growing complexity of his decision problems. Operations
Research, to cite an example, is one of the recent additions to man's arsenal
of software weaponry for overcoming decision making problems. Computer Technology is another discipline that provides impetus for widening man's elbowroom
in facing the complexities of decision making. Indeed, Operations Research and
Computer Technology, in addition to knowledge of economics, engineering and
sociology among other disciplines, enable him to face reality in a better
perspective.

A characteristic of most of the formal techniques that have been used for
decision making is the selection of the best alternative with respect to a
certain figure of merit. However, the nature of many decision problems has
changed considerably in recent years and serious doubts have been raised as to
the adequacy of many models and their solution techniques. A good example is
evinced by business firms which have now been compelled to incorporate not only
the classical economic objective of profit but also other non-economic yet
vital objectives of an organization. Fig. 1.1 illustrates graphically the
conceptual model of modern-age decision making faced with multiple objectives.
Some of these non-economic objectives are concerned with personnel, consumer
needs, societal needs, stockholders' interests, product quality, relations with
suppliers and distributors, compliance with government regulations, prestige,
etc. Several factors, such as shown in Fig. 1.2, affect the organization, thus
leading to multiplicity of objectives in decision making situations. Adding to
the complicacy is the fact that objectives are not only multiple but also
arranged in a hierarchy as illustrated in Fig. 1.3. On top of it, there must
be compatibility among the objectives of the different suborganizational
levels. For example, in a manufacturing organization, apart from its overall
objectives of profit and market share maximization, each department has specific objectives to achieve such as those shown in Table 1.1.

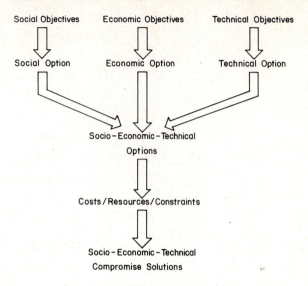

Fig. 1.1   A Conceptual Model of Modern Decision
Making in Industrial Systems Faced with
Three Kinds of Objectives

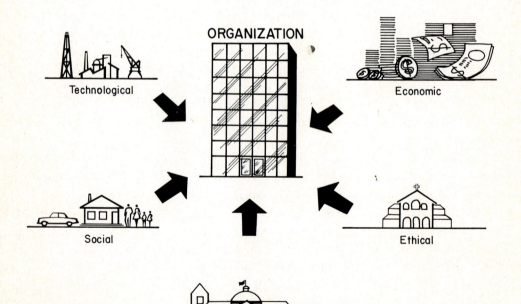

Fig. 1.2   Factors Affecting the Organization

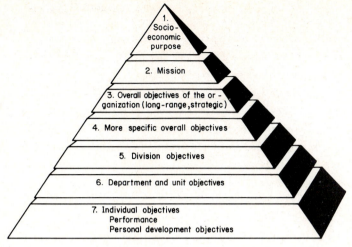

Fig. 1.3 Hierarchy of Objectives

Table 1.1 Multiple Objectives in a
Manufacturing Organization

Department	Objective(s)
1) Budget	- cost minimization.
2) Production	- production output maximization. - production time minimization.
3) Quality Control	- product quality maximization.
4) Personnel	- minimization of hiring and firing.
5) Marketing	- uninterrupted supply of products.

There are many cases of multiple criteria decision making situations in industrial systems: A business firm may wish to find the optimal allocation of products to the different market locations that will simultaneously provide for high profit and big market share; the firm may also wish to make a decision on the material allocations to the various production facilities at minimum manufacturing cost and maximum facility utilization; an employer trying to fill a vacancy will take into consideration the characteristics of the applicants when appraising their suitability to a job. On a macro scale, a national government may be interested in promoting "what type of industry" in "which region" in order to propel exports, maximize employment opportunities, and distribute income more evenly among the regions, depending upon the priorities of the government. In judging alternative locations of a large industrial project, the national government also has to consider the pros and cons of the economic and environmental state of development of a particular region, as well as the spill-over effects upon other regions. These and many more real life situations substantiate the fact that multiple criteria decision making is part of an organization's vital activities.

Computational expertise with the various quantitative techniques for management is a necessary but certainly not a sufficient requirement for making good decisions. Of paramount importance is the appropriateness of the method-ology and the suitability of the model used to represent reality. Many applic-ations of modeling in problems confronting management are mismatched with reality. They seem to advertently and explicitly express organizational aspir-ations in terms of only a single criterion which may be a misrepresentation of reality. Models that accommodate consideration of multiple objectives as a general case and that of a single objective as merely a special case are nowadays needed. In recent years, multiple criteria decision making method-ology has come into prominence, its tools and techniques have been developed and subsequently applied to a myriad of decision problems which are in great proportion related to industrial sector problems. With this development, it is extremely desirable for decision makers and analysts to keep abreast with the very dynamic state-of-the-art of multiple criteria decision making. As the next century unfolds, it will be satisfying to realize that the practice of multiple criteria decision making has become a norm rather than an exception.

1.2 DEFINITION OF MCDM

The process of decision making is the selection of an act or courses of action from among alternative acts or courses of actions such that it will produce optimal results under some criteria of optimization. This concise definition of decision making invokes further elaboration to a certain extent.

Before the problem can be considered well-defined, the set of alternatives and the set of criteria have to be known and established first; only then can the selection process commence. What makes multiple criteria decision making complex is the plurality of the criteria involved in the problem. In a single objective problem the selection process can be managed with relative ease even if there are a large number of alternatives. As a matter of fact, solution procedures for single criterion decision problems with several alternatives are widely available.   The degree of difficulty of decision making is far more sensitive with the number of criteria.

In decision analysis of complex systems, such terms as "multiple criteria", "multiple objectives", or "multiple attributes" are used to describe decision situations.   Often, these terms are used interchangeably. Certainly, there are no universal definitions of these terms.   Multiple criteria decision making (MCDM) has seemed to emerge as the accepted nomenclature for all models and techniques dealing with multiple objective decision making (MODM) or multiple attribute decision making (MADM).   These are the two brand categories of MCDM problems.   MODM methods are often used with reference to problems with large set of alternatives, while MADM methods are meant to select the best from a small explicit list of alternatives.   MODM, therefore, is a problem of design, and mathematical techniques of optimization are needed in solving it. On the other hand, MADM is a problem of choice and classical mathematical programming tools need not be used.

As an illustration, consider the problem of product mix in a manufacturing firm, i.e., the question of "what" and "how much" to produce in a multi-product establishment.   Management aspires for maximization of both profit and market share.   Clearly, this is an MODM problem.   There are only two criteria in the problem but the number of alternatives, subject to the firm's resource limitations, can be considered infinitely large especially if the products are mass produced.   On the other hand, the case of MADM can be illustrated by considering a problem of selecting the best system of production such as the type of production technology to be used from among a realistically small number of alternatives.   Assume that there are three criteria of selection, namely, profitability, employment generation, and use of indigenous materials.

In the subsequent chapters of this book, emphasis is given to multiobjective decision making.   Hence, "multicriterion" and "multiobjective" are terms used interchangeably.

1.3   CONFLICTING CRITERIA

A necessary condition of MCDM is the presence of more than one criterion. The sufficient condition is that the criteria must be conflicting in nature. In summary, the following definition can be stated: A problem can be considered as that of MCDM if and only if there appears at least two conflicting criteria and there are at least two alternative solutions.

Criteria are said to be in conflict if the full satisfaction of one will result in impairing or precluding the full satisfaction of the other(s). In precise terms, criteria are considered to be "strictly" conflicting if the increase in satisfaction of one results in a decrease in satisfaction of the other. The sufficient condition of MCDM, however, does not necessarily stipulate "strictly" conflicting criteria.

Conflict may arise due to intrapersonal and interpersonal reasons. A consumer purchasing a car is often confronted with conflicting criteria caused intrapersonally. For example he may wish to have a cheap, comfortable, fuel-efficient, and luxurious car. Usually no single car model can satisfy all these criteria. A similar situation is in the case of an industrial executive trying to fill up a general managerial position in his company. On the other hand, a family looking for a house to reside is a typical example where conflicts of criteria may be due to interpersonal reasons. The working father may prefer a house near his workplace; the mother may wish to have one near the market and near the school for the children.

In the context of multiattribute decision making, if $A(a_1, a_2, \ldots, a_n)$ represent the different available decision alternatives and $C(c_1, c_2, \ldots, c_m)$ the set of criteria, then a decision matrix can be formulated as shown in Fig. 1.4, where the entries v_{ij} represent the value of the different alternatives with respect to the criteria. Assuming that in Fig. 1.4 the criteria are maximizing in nature, conflict for all the m criteria subject to the n alternatives can only be said to be true if all the alternatives in the matrix are nondominating among each other. An alternative is said to be dominated by another if all its elements in the row are either equal or less (for at least one element) than the corresponding elements of another.   In Fig. 1.5(a) the criteria are nonconflicting since a_2 is dominated by a_1 and a_1 can be selected with full satisfaction of both criteria. On the other hand, Fig. 1.5(b) represents a decision making situation with conflicting criteria. Selection of a_1 will not satisfy c_1 since $v_{21} > v_{11}$ (150 > 100), and selection of a_2 will not satisfy c_2 since $v_{12} > v_{22}$ (200 > 170).

$$
\begin{array}{c|ccccc}
 & c_1 & c_2 & \cdot\ \cdot & c_j & \cdot\ \cdot & c_m \\
\hline
a_1 & v_{11} & v_{12} & \cdot\ \cdot\ \cdot & \cdot\ \cdot & v_{1m} \\
a_2 & v_{21} & v_{22} & \cdot\ \cdot\ \cdot & \cdot\ \cdot & v_{2m} \\
\cdot & \cdot & \cdot & & & \cdot \\
a_i & \cdot & \cdot & v_{ij} & & \cdot \\
\cdot & \cdot & \cdot & & & \cdot \\
a_n & v_{n1} & v_{n2} & \cdot\ \cdot\ \cdot\ \cdot & \cdot\ \cdot & v_{nm}
\end{array}
$$

Fig. 1.4   Decision Matrix for MADM

	c_1	c_2
a_1	100	200
a_2	90	150

(a) Nonconflicting Criteria

	c_1	c_2
a_1	100	200
a_2	150	170

(b) Conflicting Criteria

Fig. 1.5   Examples of Decision Matrices with Nonconflicting
and Conflicting Criteria

In the framework of multiobjective decision making, conflicting and nonconflicting criteria can be illustrated as shown in Fig. 1.6. Fig. 1.6(a) shows two objective functions whose full achievements are made possible with a single solution, whereas Fig. 1.6(b) shows a situation in which full satisfaction of the objectives are achieved by two different solutions.

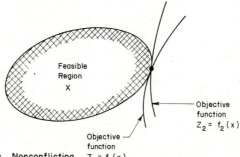

(a) Objective Functions Nonconflicting

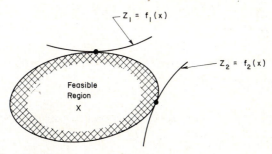

(b) Conflicting Objective Functions

Fig. 1.6   Biobjective Optimization Problems with
Nonconflicting and Conflicting Objectives (Criteria)

In view of the conflicting nature of the criteria involved in MCDM, choosing the "best" alternative is indeed a difficult task for the decision maker. Consequently there is a need for methods to systematically resolve the conflicts among criteria (or objectives) in order to reach acceptable compromises and come up with satisfying (or often termed as "satisficing") solutions.

1.4 DEFINITIONS: ATTRIBUTES, OBJECTIVES, GOALS, CRITERIA

It seems imperative to clarify at this early stage the differences among the commonly and yet interchangeably used words in MCDM, namely "attributes", "objectives", "goals" and "criteria". "Attributes" are characteristics used to describe a thing. They can be objective traits such as age, wealth, height, weight, number of employees, volume of production, or they can be subjective traits such as prestige, goodwill, and beauty. "Objectives" are aspirations that also indicate directions of improvement of selected attributes such as maximize profit, minimize losses, etc. The limits of achievements of these objectives are defined by the constraints. While "objectives" are aspirations without the decision maker specifying their levels, "goals" are aspirations with given "a priori" levels of attributes desired. For example, the statement "To meet the sales quota of 10 tons for each product" means that the sales goal is 10 tons and this level has been prespecified. "Criteria" are measures, rules, and standards that guide decision making. All those attributes, objectives or goals, which have been judged relevant in a given decision situation are criteria.

REVIEW QUESTIONS

1. Differentiate Multiple Objective Decision Making from Multiple Attribute Decision Making.

2. Why do objectives have to be conflicting in MCDM? Explain the concept of conflicting objectives?

3. Using the MCDM terminology, differentiate the following: Attributes, Objectives, Goals, and Criteria.

4. Describe the difficulties that you will encounter when solving a multiobjective decision making problem as compared to a single objective decision making problem.

5. What are the different elements that constitute an MCDM problem?

6. Describe various situations in industry concerning MCDM.

CHAPTER II

FUNDAMENTALS OF MULTICRITERION OPTIMIZATION

2.1 FORMULATION

In precise terms, multiobjective optimization is not purely a maximizing or minimizing problem. It is a peculiar mixture of several conflicting maximum or minimum problems which boils down to that of "satisficing" (meaning, attaining a satisfactory solution) these conflicting objectives. This kind of problem is nowhere dealt with in classical mathematics. Rather, it exists as a new brand of mathematical programming in the mixed objective and subjective modes.

A number of techniques on multiobjective optimization have been developed. Some are too simplified; others invoke lots of assumptions; quite a number possess mathematical rigor but tend to unfortunately lose individual or organizational preferences and values. Despite all these shortcomings, the state-of-the-art still exhibits certain appealing features. It is more flexible in approaching complex problems, and it absorbs the existing single-objective methodology as a special case.

A general constrained optimization problem is defined as a problem of optimizing (maximizing or minimizing) a function $f(x)$ subject to the con-straints $g_1(x) \leq b_1$, $g_2(x) \leq b_2$, ..., $g_m(x) \leq b_m$, where x is a vector of n nonnegative real numbers. When there are k objectives to be optimized simul-taneously, one thus encounters a multiobjective optimization problem which can be formulated in the following form:

$$\text{Maximize:} \quad z_\ell = f_\ell(x) \quad , \quad \ell = 1, 2, \ldots, k \tag{2.1}$$

Subject to:

$$g_i(x) \leq b_i \quad , \quad i = 1, 2, \ldots, m \tag{2.2}$$

$$x \geq 0 \tag{2.3}$$

It is always possible to express the objective functions in their "maximize" form since a minimization problem can always be transformed to a maximization problem by proper sign manipulations. Likewise for the constraints, "greater thans" and "equals" are always convertible to their equivalent "less thans".

The matrix version of the above model can be conveniently written as:

Maximize: Z = CX   (2.4)

Subject to:

$$AX \leq B \qquad (2.5)$$

$$X \geq 0 \qquad (2.6)$$

where Z, X and B are $k \times 1$, $n \times 1$, and $m \times 1$ matrices, respectively; C is a $k \times n$ matrix; and A is an $m \times n$ matrix.

In multicriterion optimization, the concept of a unique optimum no longer holds for it is impossible to simultaneously maximize all the conflicting objectives. In other words, the increase in any one of the objectives will decrease the others. Optimality is thus replaced by the concept of "satisfic-ing" or of best compromise solution, which depends on the decision maker's preferences with respect to the objectives. The availability of explicit information on the decision maker's preferences of the objectives may vary from obscurity to complete familiarity depending upon the type of model used.

Another important aspect with regard to multicriterion optimization problems is that several tacit assumptions are made in the formulation of such problems. These include the following:

(i)   Multiple objectives do in fact exist and that this is the best way to formulate the problem in question;

(ii)   Multiple objectives cannot be collapsed into one another and the problem reformulated in a simpler formulation;

(iii) No important objectives deemed relevant at the time of formulation have been omitted.

Thus the model builder should ensure that these assumptions are satisfied whenever an attempt is made to formulate a problem as a multicriterion optimiz-ation problem.

2.2 CONCEPT OF OPTIMAL AND EFFICIENT SOLUTIONS

An optimal solution in the classical sense is one which attains the maximum value of all the objectives simultaneously. The solution x^* is optimal to the problem defined if and only if $x^* \in S$ and $f_\ell(x^*) \geq f_\ell(x)$ for all ℓ and for all $x \in S$, where S is the feasible region. In general, there is no optimal solution to a multiobjective problem. Optimality is not an illusion, only when the objectives are nonconflicting. Therefore, one must be satisfied with obtaining efficient solutions.

An efficient solution (also called: noninferior solution or Pareto optimal solution) is one in which no increase can be obtained in any of the objectives without causing a simultaneous decrease in at least one of the objectives. The solution x^* is efficient to the problem defined if and only if there does not exist any $x \in S$ such that $f_\ell(x) \geq f_\ell(x^*)$ for all ℓ and $f_\ell(x) > f_\ell(x^*)$ for at least one ℓ. This solution is obviously not unique. Graphically, this is illustrated in Fig. 2.1. Any "point" in the shaded portion is superior (meaning, yielding a better solution) than point 0. It can be observed that the set of efficient points is the segment ab.

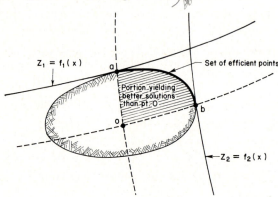

Fig. 2.1 Illustration on Concept of Efficiency

In most cases, the determination of the efficient set of solutions is not sufficient; one must choose a decision which is by some definition "best". Thus, additional criterion (or criteria) must be introduced to distinguish the "best" of the efficient solutions. Some authors retain the term "optimal" for this "best" solution. The term "compromise" solution is adopted in this book to avoid ambiguity and to reflect the operating procedures of the tools and techniques to be introduced later.

A slightly restricted definition of efficiency that eliminates efficient points of a certain anomalous type and lends itself to more satisfactory characterization is called "proper" efficiency. x^* is said to be a proper efficient solution if it is efficient and there exists a scalar $M > 0$ such that for each ℓ, $f_\ell(x) > f_\ell(x^*)$ and

$$\frac{f_\ell(x) - f_\ell(x^*)}{f_h(x^*) - f_h(x)} \leq M \quad , \quad \ell \neq h \tag{2.7}$$

for some h such that $f_h(x) < f_h(x^*)$.

An efficient point that is not properly efficient is said to be "improperly" efficient.   Thus for x^* to be improperly efficient means that to every scalar $M > 0$ (no matter how large) there is a point $x \in S$ and an ℓ such that $f_\ell(x) > f_\ell(x^*)$ and

$$\frac{f_\ell(x) - f_\ell(x^*)}{f_h(x^*) - f_h(x)} > M \tag{2.8}$$

for all h such that $f_h(x) < f_h(x^*)$.

Example 2.1

Consider the following biobjective problem confronting the management of a firm.   Find the efficient points to this problem.

$$\begin{aligned}
\text{Maximize} \quad & z_1 = -2\,x_1 + x_2 \\
\text{Maximize} \quad & z_2 = 2\,x_1 + x_2
\end{aligned}$$

Subject to:

$$\begin{aligned}
-x_1 + x_2 &\le 1 \\
x_1 + x_2 &\le 7 \\
x_1 &\le 5 \\
x_2 &\le 3 \\
x_1,\ x_2 &\ge 0
\end{aligned}$$

The solution to the problem is illustrated in Fig. 2.2 where the efficient points are those along the periphery of the convex set points $(0,1)$, $(2,3)$, $(4,3)$ and $(5,2)$.

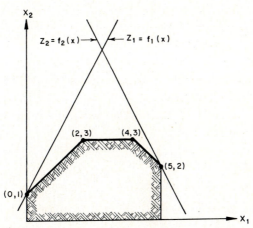

Fig. 2.2   Efficient Points of the Problem

2.3 CONCEPT OF IDEAL SOLUTIONS

Due to the conflicting nature of the objectives in multiobjective optimization, it is not at all possible to achieve the individual optimum of each
objective by a single solution.   Each objective function has its own "ideal"
solution which is different for all other objectives.   Hence, using one of the
"ideals" as the solution for the multiobjective problem would only mean that
one objective achieves its individual optimum while all the rest only achieve
partial satisfaction with respect to their individual optima.   The matrix, or
generally known as "payoff" matrix, shown in Fig. 2.3 helps to clarify this
phenomenon.   The diagonal of the matrix constitutes individual optimal values
of the k objective functions.   The x^{h*}'s are the individual optimal solutions
and each of these are used to determine the values of other individual objective functions, thus the payoff matrix is developed.

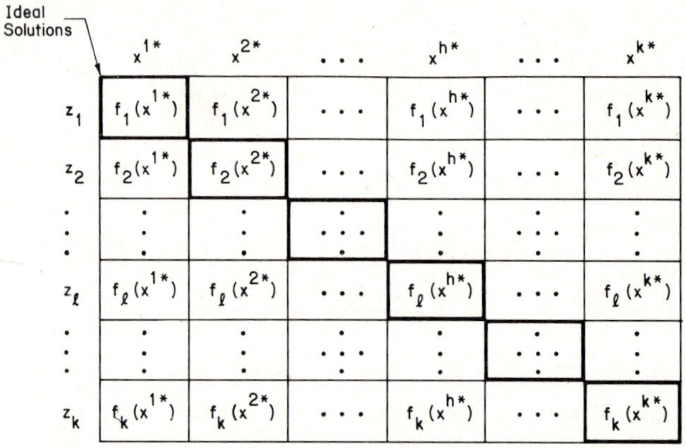

Fig. 2.3 Payoff Matrix

Example 2.2

Construct the payoff matrix of the MCDM problem given below:

$$\text{Maximize} \quad z_1 = -x_1 + 3x_2$$
$$\text{Maximize} \quad z_2 = 2x_1 + x_2$$
$$\text{Maximize} \quad z_3 = -2x_1 + x_2$$

Subject to:

$$-x_1 + x_2 \leq 1$$
$$x_1 + x_2 \leq 7$$
$$x_1 \leq 5$$
$$x_2 \leq 3$$
$$x_1, x_2 \geq 0$$

The individual optimal solutions are as follows (see Fig. 2.4):

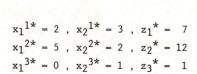

$$x_1^{1*} = 2 \ , \ x_2^{1*} = 3 \ , \ z_1^{*} = 7$$
$$x_1^{2*} = 5 \ , \ x_2^{2*} = 2 \ , \ z_2^{*} = 12$$
$$x_1^{3*} = 0 \ , \ x_2^{3*} = 1 \ , \ z_3^{*} = 1$$

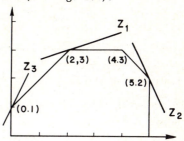

And the payoff matrix is shown in Fig. 2.5.   Fig. 2.4 Graphical Solution

	x^{1*}	x^{2*}	x^{3*}
z_1	7	1	3
z_2	7	12	1
z_3	-1	-8	1

Fig. 2.5 Payoff Table of the Problem

REVIEW QUESTIONS

1. Comment on the concept of optimality in MCDM.

2. Is the following statement an acceptable definition of nondominance? "A solution is nondominated if, and only if, there is no other feasible solution which would lead to an improvement in at least one criterion without simultaneously degrading at least one other criterion". Why?

3. Which of the following problems is an MODM problem? Give your reason.
    (i) Max. $z_1 = x_1 + x_2$, Max. $z_2 = 2x_1 + x_2$; s.t. $0 \le x_1 \le 5$ & $0 \le x_2 \le 7$.
    (ii) Max. $z_1 = x_1 + x_2$, Max. $z_2 = x_1 + x_2$; s.t. $0 \le x_1 \le 5$ & $0 \le x_2 \le 6$.

4. Why are we only interested in finding the efficient points?

5. Consider the following biobjective LP formulation:

    Maximize $z_1 = 3 \ x_1 + \ x_2$
    Maximize $z_2 = \ x_1 + 2 \ x_2$
    Subject to:

$$x_1 + x_2 \leq 7$$
$$x_1 \qquad \leq 5$$
$$x_2 \leq 5$$
$$x_1 , x_2 \geq 0$$

Show graphically the set of efficient solutions.

6.   Consider the following problem:

      Maximize $z_1 = -x_1 + 2 x_2$

      Maximize $z_2 = 2 x_1 + x_2$

      Subject to:

$$-x_1 + 3 x_2 \leq 21$$
$$x_1 + 3 x_2 \leq 27$$
$$4 x_1 + 3 x_2 \leq 45$$
$$3 x_1 + x_2 \leq 30$$
$$x_1 , \quad x_2 \geq 0$$

(a)   Find and show the set of all efficient solutions graphically.

(b)   If the two objectives are combined linearly and then the problem is solved by the simplex method, what would be the compromise solution?

7.   Consider the following graphical problem representation: There are five objective functions maximized over X.   Their respective slopes and individual maxima are graphically displayed.

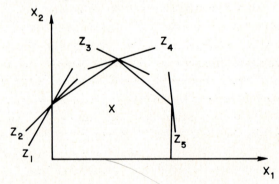

(a)   Show on the graph the set of efficient points.

(b)   How would the "shape" of the efficient set change if you would delete objectives z_2 and z_3?   What will happen to the set if you delete z_4 or z_5?   If you delete z_1?

CHAPTER III

IMPORTANCE OF CRITERIA

3.1 INTRODUCTION

Every multicriterion decision problem involves conflicting objectives that may be of varying importance to the decision maker. Some objectives can be of overriding importance while some are considered to be less significant than others. This relativity in importance can be conceptualized in several ways. It may be that: (1) all objectives are indispensable and no tradeoff is possible - this is the case of no solution; (2) all are indispensable up to some limiting value, but beyond that limit additional quantities for all objectives are of little or no value; (3) all are indispensable up to some limiting value and beyond that value, tradeoff is possible albeit the tradeoff rate may be variable; (4) some objectives are indispensable, but others can be traded-off infinitely, and (5) all objectives are dispensable, all can be traded-off although some may be more important than others. This listing of possibilities are arranged in the order decreasing degree of difficulty in terms of finding the solution. It is in the backdrop of the last possibility mentioned that most multicriterion decision techniques are developed.

In assessing degrees of importance of multiple criteria, there are methods which depend entirely on judgement of people. Techniques in this category may involve either a single individual or a group of people. In general, for group techniques, members would consist of experts or specially knowledgeable individuals, possibly including some of the responsible decision makers.

Opinion measurement includes a variety of methods used either to extract information from a single individual or to accumulate input from a number of persons who are often experts in an area of interest. The simplest of these methods is the single expert opinion. Surveys and panels using experts provide a better way of opinion measurement. The advantage of a group over an individual opinion is that it brings a broad range of information, skill and experience into analysis. However, there could be some problems in using expert groups viz., time consuming, dominance of authoritative figures, persuasiveness that could set the direction of discussion, bandwagon effect, problems of face saving, and group bias due to interest.

3.2 SCALES OF MEASUREMENT

In many situations, ranking of the objects or ideas based on a set of criteria is required. For example, the academic performance of students in a class are ranked based on their grade point average. In the context of multiple criteria optimization, ranking has a major role to play. The analyst needs to know the relative importance of each of the criteria.

Relative importance of criteria may be expressed in terms of "priority" or "weight". "Priority" refers to the case where the criteria are ordered according to importance and unless the higher level criterion is taken into consideration, the next one does not come into play. In other cases, "weights" are attached to differentiate the relative importance of several criteria with the same priority. If one criterion gets 60% weightage and the other gets 40%, the former is more important than the other by a ratio of 1.5:1.0. There are other variations in dealing with the questions of priority and weight for solving a multiple criteria problem.

Nominal Scales. These scales are least restrictive as well as least informative of all. The numbers serve merely as labels. For example, workers in production lines are given numbers to serve only the purpose of identification. These have nothing to do with the relative properties of the workers.

Ordinal Scales. These are purely ranking scales. One has to distinguish between elements according to a single criterion. For example, a person may be able to rank a group of product brands according to taste. He can say that brand A is No. 1 or best, brand B is No. 2 or second best, brand C is No. 3 and so on. However, mere ranking in this method does not indicate the difference of preference in magnitude. The difference between the preferences on brands A and B and that between brands B and C are not known directly from the ordinal measurement.

Interval Scales. These have constant units of measurement. A very common example is the Fahrenheit scale of temperature measurement. The zero point of Fahrenheit scale is not natural. An object A at $50^{o}F$ and another object B at $100^{o}F$ would not say that B is twice as hot as A, but it can be said that B is hotter than A by $50^{o}F$.

Ratio Scales. Measurements of length, weight, volume, speed, height are examples of ratio scales. These have a natural zero and a constant unit of measurement. For example, if production volume of brand A is 100 tons and brand B is 200 tons, then B is heavier than A (ordinal), B is 100 tons more than A (interval), and B is twice the weight of A (ratio). Obviously, the ratio scales provide the most information of all. The ordinal scale provides more information than the nominal scale but less than the interval scale. Loosely termed, the nominal and ordinal scales are categorical or qualitative scales while the interval and ratio scales are quantitative scales of measurement.

In multiple criteria decision making, the ranking of the various criteria is necessary and the criterion for ranking is based on the deemed "importance" of the objectives. In that respect, nominal scales provide too little information, therefore the use of ordinal, interval and ratio scales are sufficient for the purpose.

Ordinal scales, as the name suggests, provide ordinal ranking where the exact difference between the importance of the criteria are not known while the interval and ratio scales reveal the exact numerical degree of importance. The cardinal ranking or weight-attached ranking can be obtained directly from interval scales or through conversion of measurements in an ordinal scale. When importance has to be measured subjectively, ordinal scales are primarily used.

A significant aspect of evaluating criteria is the fact that there are usually more than one person involved in the assessment. This normally results to different rankings based on each individual's judgement; however, there are methods for synthesizing differing judgements.

3.3 CONCEPT OF WEIGHTS

The association of a relative numerical degree of importance to each criterion is imperative in MCDM. Weights can be derived from both ordinal and cardinal ranks. Let w_ℓ ($\ell=1,2,...k$) be the weight associated with criteria ℓ ($\ell=1,2,...k$). For convenience in mathematical manipulations, it is, by and large, suggested the weights be normalized to 1.0, which means that the following relationships among w_ℓ's must hold true:

$$0 < w_\ell < 1 \tag{3.1}$$

and
$$\sum_{\ell=1}^{n} w_\ell = 1 \tag{3.2}$$

The expression $w_\ell > w_h$ denotes that criterion ℓ is more important than criterion h, and $w_\ell = w_h$ indicates equal importance between them.

3.4 ASSESSING THE MULTIPLE CRITERIA

One of the main concerns for the analyst of a multicriterion decision making problem is to know which objective is more important and how much more. In this section, several methods of indicating importances are discussed and in these method, the judgement of experts are incorporated.

3.4.1 RANKING

Each judge is asked to place a numerical rank for each criterion, the most valuable in the situation being indicated by rank 1, the next to most valuable by rank 2, and so on. These raw ranks are transformed into converted ranks such that raw rank 1 becomes converted rank m-1 where m is the number of criteria, raw rank 2 becomes converted rank m-2 and so on up to raw rank m which becomes converted rank 0. These ranks are manipulated as follows:

$$R_\ell = \sum_{j=1}^{n} R_{\ell j} \tag{3.3}$$

where, R_ℓ = sum of the converted ranks across judges for each criterion ℓ;

$\quad\quad\quad R_{\ell j}$ = converted rank assigned to criterion ℓ by judge j;

$\quad\quad\quad$ n   = the number of judges.

The weights are determined by,

$$w_\ell = R_\ell \ / \ \sum_{\ell=1}^{m} R_\ell \tag{3.4}$$

where, w_ℓ = composite weight of criterion ℓ across all judges.

Since each judge produces only a set of integers, it is not possible to develop a set of weights for each judge; only the weights for the composite of all the judges' ranks can be obtained. This ranking method is simple and least time-consuming for the judges.

Example 3.1

Suppose that 20 judges or decision makers were asked to rank three criteria and the results are given below. The weight corresponding to each criterion is calculated as follows:

| | Rank | | |
Criteria	1	2	3
z_1	10	10	0
z_2	6	8	6
z_3	4	6	10

$$\sum_{\ell=1}^{3} R_\ell = [(10)(2) + (10)(1) + 0] + [(6)(2) + (8)(1) + 0]$$
$$+ [(4)(2) + (6)(1) + 0]$$

$$w_1 = [(10)(2) + (10)(1) + 0] / \sum_{\ell=1}^{3} R_\ell = 0.47$$

$$w_2 = [(6)(2) + (8)(1) + 0] / \sum_{\ell=1}^{3} R_\ell = 0.31$$

$$w_3 = [(4)(2) + (6)(1) + 0] / \sum_{\ell=1}^{3} R_\ell = 0.22$$

Notice that the summation of all weights equals 1.

3.4.2 RATING

The criteria are presented to each of the judges who are requested to give ratings for each criterion. The rating values are usually continuous ranging from 0.0 to a higher limit of 10.0 or 100.00. More than one criterion can have the same rating. The lower limit of 0.0 indicates no importance of the objective while the higher limit refers to the value of maximum possible importance.

The weights are derived from the raw ratings in the following manner:

$$w_{\ell j} = \rho_{\ell j} / \sum_{\ell=1}^{m} \rho_{\ell j} \qquad (3.5)$$

$$w_\ell = \sum_{j=1}^{n} w_{\ell j} / (\sum_{j=1}^{n} \sum_{\ell=1}^{m} w_{\ell j}) \qquad (3.6)$$

where, $w_{\ell j}$ = weights computed for criterion ℓ by judge j;

$\rho_{\ell j}$ = rating by judge j to criterion ℓ.

3.4.3 PAIRED COMPARISON

All the paired comparison methods are the same in principle in the sense that every judge compares each criterion with all other criteria to indicate his preference. For example, if A and B are two criteria, a judge would say whether A is more important than B or conversely. The number of times each criterion is chosen over the other criteria is tabulated for each judge and then added together to determine the total number of times each criterion is chosen over all other criteria. The weights are derived using the following formula:

$$f_{\ell j} = \sum_{\ell'=1}^{m-1} f_{(\ell/\ell')j} \tag{3.7}$$

$$w_{\ell j} = f_{\ell j} / J \tag{3.8}$$

where,

$f_{\ell j}$ = frequency of choice of criterion ℓ over all other criteria by judge j;
$f_{(\ell/\ell')j}$ = frequency of choice of criterion ℓ over criterion ℓ' by judge j;
J = total number of comparisons made.

The composite weight (w_ℓ) can be determined using equation 3.6.

Example 3.2

Consider criteria A, B, C, D and E and suppose that a pairwise comparison has been made with the following results.

1. A > B		6. B > D	
2. A > C		7. B < E	
3. A > D		8. C > D	
4. A > E		9. C < E	
5. B < C		10. D < E	

The sign ">" means "more preferred than" and "<" means "less preferred than". Revise the listing so that they all have the same preference sign yielding a new list below.

1. A > B		6. B > D	
2. A > C		7. E > B	
3. A > D		8. C > D	
4. A > E		9. E > C	
5. C > B		10. E > D	

From the above table, ranks are assigned and scores are given below.

Rank r	Criterion	n-r
1	A	4
2	E	3
3	C	2
4	B	1
5	D	0

n = the number of criteria

Should there be inconsistencies in the decisions of the judges causing intransitivity, e.g. to say that A > B, B > C, and then to also say that C > A would be inconsistent causing intransitivity of preference since the correct order of preference should be A > C, then the judges should be asked to make the comparison again.

Another version of paired comparison can be explained in the following fashion. Assign weights by comparing criteria two at a time, until all possible combinations are exhausted. At each pairwise comparison, three final results are possible: (1) the first is preferred over the second, (2) the second is preferred over the first, or (3) the two have equal preference. Corresponding numerical values for each of the above results are: (1) 1 for the first and 0 for the second, (2) 1 for the second and 0 for the first, and (3) 1 for both criteria.

The above formulation can be put in a sample matrix form as follows:

Criterion	Decisions 1	2	3	4	5	6	Preference Values	Criterion Rating
1	P_{12}	P_{13}	P_{14}				$P_{12}+P_{13}+P_{14}$	$(P_{12}+P_{13}+P_{14})/P$
2	P_{21}			P_{23}	P_{24}		$P_{21}+P_{23}+P_{24}$	$(P_{21}+P_{23}+P_{24})/P$
3		P_{31}		P_{32}		P_{34}	$P_{31}+P_{32}+P_{34}$	$(P_{31}+P_{32}+P_{34})/P$
4			P_{41}		P_{42}	P_{43}	$P_{41}+P_{42}+P_{43}$	$(P_{41}+P_{42}+P_{43})/P$
Total							P	1

3.4.4 SUCCESSIVE COMPARISONS

This method is rather difficult and time consuming on the part of the judges. However, it has the merit of self-correction by the judges of their own ranking. This method is very similar to rating. A judge proceeds as follows:

a)   Rank all the criteria in order of preference as in the ranking
     method;

b)   Assign tentatively the value (V_1) 1.0 to the most important criteri-
     on, and other values (V_i) between 0 and 1 to the other criteria in
     order of importance;

c)   Decide whether the criterion with the value 1.0 is more important
     than all other criteria combined.   If so, increase V_1 until it
     becomes greater than the sum of all subsequent V_i's, i. e.,

$$V_1 > \sum_{i=2}^{n} V_i \qquad\qquad V_1 > \sum_{\ell=2}^{m} V_\ell$$

     If not, adjust V_1, if necessary, so that it becomes less than the sum
     of all subsequent V_i's, i. e.,

$$V_1 < \sum_{i=2}^{n} V_i \qquad\qquad V_1 < \sum_{\ell=2}^{m} V_\ell$$

d)   Decide whether the second most important criterion with value V_2 is
     more than all lower-valued criteria and proceed as in step c above;

e)   Continue until (n-1) criteria have been evaluated in this manner.

With the use of equations 3.5 and 3.6 as for the rating cases, the weights
for the different criteria are calculated.   This method is often considered the
most accurate in measuring weights.

3.4.5 DELPHI TECHNIQUE

An advanced method for opinion measurement, called the Delphi technique,
has a degree of scientific respectability and acceptance not enjoyed by other
similar techniques.   The Delphi procedure is characterized by the following
features which distinguish it from the other group opinion measurement techniques:

(i) Anonymity.   During a Delphi sequence, the group members are not made
known to each other.   The interaction of the group members is handled in a
completely anonymous fashion, through the use of questionnaires.   This avoids
the possibility of identifying a specific opinion with a particular person.   As
a result, the originator of an opinion can change his mind without publicly
admitting that he has done so.

(ii)   Interaction with Controlled Feedback.   The individual or agency
carrying out the interaction extracts from the questionnaires only those pieces
of information that are relevant to the issue, and presents these to the group.

The primary effect of this controlled feedback is to prevent the group from taking on its own goals and objectives.

(iii)   Statistical Group Response.   The Delphi procedure, instead of presenting a majority view point, presents a statistical response which includes the opinion of the entire group. On a single question, for instance, the group response may be presented in terms of a median and the two quartiles. In this way each opinion within the group is taken into account in the median and the spread of opinion is shown by the size of the interquartile range.

The iteration of goal Delphi rounds is illustrated below (Fig. 3.1):

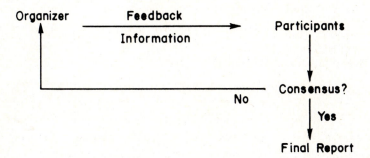

Fig. 3.1 The Delphi Process

The basic features of Delphi technique makes it more advantageous in the sense that no member of the panel of experts can exert undue influence over other members. When the judges live distances apart and it becomes prohibitive to bring them together for committee meetings, Delphi can serve well. A careful selection of the panel will make it possible to incorporate the opinions of all the parties affected by the decision. If a judge happens to overlook some aspect of the problem, he will most probably be apprised thereof through the feedback of others' opinions.

The most outstanding problem in implementing the Delphi technique involves the selection of the experts. Specifically, these are: (1) the identification of experts, and (2) the selection of the panel. It has been suggested that respondents should be of high level of responsibility. Top management people may have a broad view of the organization but they may not have time to answer questionnaires, so a tradeoff should be made. Delphi is a rather time-consuming technique and unless the organizer functions very carefully and efficiently, the whole exercise will prove futile.

3.5 CONCEPT OF TRADEOFFS

Degrees of importance of criteria can also be represented by tradeoffs. This approach gives more emphasis on the relative value of criterion increments than it is with their absolute values. Economists dubbed the concept as the marginal rate of substitution -- it means to say that for two objectives, how many units of criterion z_1 are necessary to replace a unit of criterion z_2, or vice versa. Two methods by which tradeoffs can be obtained from a decision making group are briefly discussed below.

(1) First, the decision maker is asked to provide the local marginal rates of substitution (or tradeoffs) with each of the criteria at any solution point. The question to be asked is that "what change Δ_1 in the first criterion (reference criterion) compensates for a change Δ_j in the jth criterion, with all others remaining at their current values?"

(2) The second method is of graphical or direct-choice nature. The decision maker is asked to express his tradeoff between any two criteria at a reference point. The tradeoff between any two criteria is determined by the amount of change in one criterion required to offset a small change in another. For example, see Fig. 3.2. Let A be the present operating point. If the value of z_1 for a new operating point B is z_1^B, which is one unit less than z_1^A, what value of z_j that the new operating point B must have in order for the decision maker to be indifferent between points A and B? The decision maker is asked to express his value of z_j by plotting the point B on the dotted line of the graph.

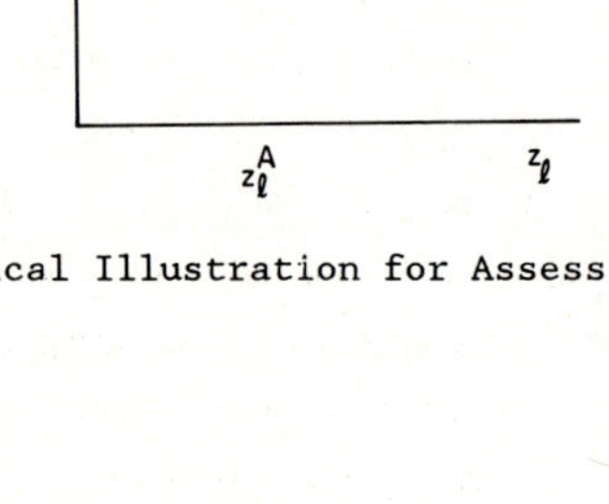

Fig. 3.2 Graphical Illustration for Assessing Tradeoffs

REVIEW QUESTIONS

1. Differentiate the following terms: priority vs. weight; weight vs. tradeoff; ordinal vs. cardinal ranking.

2.   Three objectives (A, B and C) are ranked by three judges in the following manner:

Judge I	Judge II	Judge III
A > B	A < B	A > B
A > C	A > C	A > C
B > C	B > C	B > C

Determine the overall ranking assuming that the judgements are weighted equally.

3.   Consider the Cafeteria as a decision problem in your personal life involving multiple criteria.   The five most important criteria for this problem, as you may see them, could be the following:

z_1 - Quality of food
z_2 - Quantity of food
z_3 - Sanitation
z_4 - Price
z_5 - Quality of the environment

(a)   Using the method of paired comparison, rank them by ordinal scaling.

(b)   Suppose that some 5% of the costumer population were interviewed and that they were asked to rank the above criteria.   The summary of the responses are given below:

Rank Criteria	1	2	3	4	5
z_1	8	5	4	8	5
z_2	10	5	5	8	2
z_3	15	3	1	10	1
z_4	9	6	3	8	4
z_5	6	6	6	6	6

Determine the weights of the criteria.

4.   List ten most important criteria you would consider in selecting the next

president or head of your organization. Using the methods of paired comparison, rank these criteria in an ordinal scale.

REFERENCES

1.   Aczél, J. and C. Alsina, 1986.   On Synthesis of Judgements.   Socio-Economic Planning Sciences, 20:333-340.

2.   Aczél, J. and C. Alsina, 1987.   Synthesizing Judgments: A Functional Equations Approach. Mathematical Modelling, 9:311-320.

3.   Ali, I., W. D. Cook, and M. Kress, 1986.   Ordinal Ranking and Intensity of Preference: A Linear Programming Approach.   Management Science, 32:1642-1647.

4.   Arrow, K. J. and H. Raynaud, 1986.   Social Choice and Multicriterion Decision Making.   The MIT Press.

5.   Bana e Costa, C. A., 1986.   A Multicriteria Decision Aid Methodology to Deal with Conflicting Situations on the Weight.   European Journal of Operational Research, 26:22-34.

6.   Barron, F. H., 1987.   Influence of Missing Attributes on Selecting a Best Multiattributed Alternative.   Decision sciences, 18:178-193.

7.   Barzilai, J., W. D. Cook, and B. Golany, 1987.   Consistent Weights for Judgments Matrices of the Relative Importance of alternatives.   Operations Research Letters, 6:131-134.

8.   Belton, V., 1986.   A Comparison of the Analytic Hierarchy Process and a Simple Multi-attribute Value Function.   European Journal of Operational Research, 26:7-21.

9.   Bouyssou, D., 1986.   Some Remarks on the Notion of Compensation in MCDM. European Journal of Operational Research, 26:150-160.

10.   Brownlow, S. A. and S. R. Watson, 1987.   Structuring Multi-Attribute Value Hierarchies.   Journal of the Operational Research Society, 38:309-318.

11.   Canada, J. R. and J. A. White, Jr., 1980.   Capital Investment Decision Analysis for Management and Engineering.   Prentice-Hall.

12.   Churchman, C. W. and R. L. Ackoff, 1954.   An Approximate Measure of Value. Operations Research, 2:172-181.

13.   Crawford, G. B., 1987.   The Geometric Mean Procedure for Estimating the Scale of a Judgment Matrix.   Mathematical Modelling, 9:327-334.

14.   Debreu, G., 1960.   Topological Methods in Cardinal Utility Theory. In K. J. Arrow, S. Karlin and P. Suppes (Editors), Mathematical Methods in Social Sciences, Stanford University Press, California.

15.   Dennis, S. Y., 1987.   A Probabilistic Model for the Assignment of Priorit-

ies in Hierarchically Structured Decision Problems. Mathematical Modelling, 9:335-344.

16. Dessouky, M. I., M. Ghiassi, and W. J. Davis, 1986. Estimates of the Minimum Nondominated Criterion Values in Multiple-Criteria Decision-Making. Engineering costs and Production Economics, 10:95-104.

17. Easton, A., 1973. Complex Managerial Decision Involving Multiple Objectives. Wiley, New York.

18. Eckenrode, R. T., 1965. Weighting Multiple Criteria. Management Science, 12:180-192.

19. Epstein, B. J. and W. R. King, 1982. An Experimental Study of the Value of Information. Omega, 10:249-258.

20. Farmer, T. A., 1987. Testing the Robustness of Multiattribute Utility Theory in an Applied Setting. Decision Sciences, 18:178-193.

21. Fichtner, J., 1986. On Deriving Priority Vectors from Matrices of Pairwise Comparisons. Socio-Economic Planning Sciences, 20:341-346.

22. Fischer, G. W., N. Damodaran, K. B. Laskey, and D. Lincoln, 1987. Preferences for Proxy Attributes. Management Science, 33:198-214.

23. Fischer, G. W., M. S. Kamlet, S. E. Fienberg, and D. Schkade, 1986. Risk Preferences for Gains and Losses in Multiple Objective Decision Making. Management Science, 32:1065-1086.

24. Fishburn, P. C., 1964. Decision and Value Theory. Wiley, New York, pp. 36-44 and 333-366.

25. Fishburn, P. C., 1967. Methods of Estimating Additive Utilities. Management Science, 13:435-453.

26. Foreman, E. H., 1987. Relative vs. Absolute Worth. Mathematical Modelling, 9:195-202.

27. Gass, S. I., 1986. A Process for Determining Priorities and Weights for Large-Scale Linear Goal Programmes. Journal of the Operational Research Society, 37:779-786.

28. Gass, S. I., 1987. The Setting of Weights in Linear Goal-Programming Problems. Computers & Operations Research, 14:227-230.

29. Golden, B. L. and E. A. Wasil, 1987. Ranking Outstanding Sports Records. Interfaces, 17:32-34.

30. Górecki, H. and A. M. Skulimowski, 1986. A Joint Consideration of Multiple Reference Points in Multicriteria Decision Making. Foundations of Control Engineering, 11:81-94.

31. Harker, P. T., 1987. Alternative Modes of Questioning in the Analytic Hierarchy Process. Mathematical Modelling, 9:353-360.

32. Helmer, O., 1966. The Delphi Method for Systematizing Judgements About the Future. University of California at Los Angeles.

33. Hindle, D., 1975. An Efficient Procedure for Differential Weighting of
     Committee Members' Subjective Estimates. Operational Research Quarterly,
     26:759-762.

34. Isermann, H. and R. E. Steuer, 1988. Computational Experience Concerning
     Payoff Tables and Minimum Criterion Values Over the Efficient Set.
     European Journal of Operational Research, 33:91-97.

35. Keeney, R. L., and H. Raiffa, 1976. Decisions with Multiple Objectives:
     Preferences and Value Tradeoffs. Wiley, New York.

36. Khairullah, Z. Y. and S. Zionts, 1987. An Approach for Preference Ranking
     of Alternatives. European Journal of Operational Research, 28:329-342.

37. Knoll, A. L. and A. Engelberg, 1978. Weighting Multiple Objectives - The
     Churchman-Ackoff Technique Revisited. Computers and Operations Research,
     5:165-177.

38. Koksalan, M., M. H. Karwan and S. Zionts, 1983. Approaches for Discrete
     Alternative Multiple Criteria Problems for Different Types of Criteria,
     Working Paper No. 572, School of Management, State University of New York
     at Buffalo.

39. Koksalan, M., M. H. Karwan and S. Zionts, 1983. An Improved Method for
     Solving Multiple Criteria Problems Involving Discrete Alternatives,
     Working Paper No. 558, School Of Management, State University of New York
     at Buffalo.

40. Koksalan, M., M. H. Karwan and S. Zionts, 1983. An Approach for Solving
     Discrete Alternative Multiple Criteria Problems Involving Ordinal Criter-
     ia, Working Paper No. 571, School of Management, State University of New
     York at Buffalo.

41. Korhonen, P., J. Wallenius and S. Zionts, 1981. Some Theory and a Method
     for Solving the Discrete Multiple Criteria Problem, Working Paper No. 498,
     School of Management, State University of New York at Buffalo.

42. Krovák, J., 1987. Ranking Alternatives - Comparison of Different Methods
     Based on Binary Comparison Matrices. European Journal of Operational
     Research, 32:86-95.

43. Lee, S. M. and J. P. Shim, 1986. Interactive Goal Programming on the
     Microcomputer to Establish Priorities for Small Business. Journal of the
     Operational Research Society, 37:571-578.

44. Mareschal, B., 1988. Weight Stability Intervals in Multicriterion
     Decision Aid. European Journal of Operational Research, 33:54-64.

45. Ovchinnikov, S. V. and V. M. Ozernoy, 1988. Using fuzzy binary Relations
     for Identifying Noninferior Decision Alternatives. Fuzzy Sets and
     Systems, 25:21-32.

46. Phillips, N. V., 1987. A weighting Function for Pre-Emptive Multi-

Criteria Assignment Problems. Journal of the Operational Research Society, 38:797-802.

47. Pliskin, J. S. and D. Dori, 1982. Ranking Alternative Warehouse Area Assignments: A Multiattribute Approach. IIE Transactions, 14:19-26.

48. Rivett, P., 1977. Multidimensional Scaling for Multiobjective Policies. Omega, 5:367-379.

49. Saaty, T. L., 1980. The Analytical Hierarchy Process. McGraw-Hill, New York.

50. Saaty, T. L., 1982. Decision Making for Leaders. Wadsworth, Inc.

51. Saaty, T. L., 1986. Exploring Optimization Through Hierarchies and Ratio Scales. Socio-Economic Planning Sciences, 20:355-360.

52. Saaty, T. L., 1987. Decision Making, New Information, Ranking and Structure. Mathematical Modelling, 8:125-132.

53. Saaty, T. L., 1987. Rank Generation, Preservation, and Reversal in the Analytic Hierarchy Decision Process. Decision Sciences, 18:157-177.

54. Saaty, T. L. and L. G. Vargas, 1982. The Logic of Priorities. Kluwernijhoff Publishing, Boston.

55. Saaty, T. L. and L. G. Vargas, 1987. Uncertainty and Rank Order in the Analytic Hierarchy Process. European Journal of Operational Research, 32:107-117.

56. Siskos, J., 1982. A Way to Deal With Fuzzy Preferences in Multicriteria Decision Problems. European Journal of Operations Research, 10:314-324.

57. Solymosi, T. and J. Dombi, 1986. A Method for Determining the Weights of Criteria: The Centralized Weights. European Journal of Operational Research, 26:35-41.

58. Stillwell, W. G., D. von Winterfeldt, and R. S. John, 1987. Comparing Hierarchical and Nonhierarchical Weighting Methods for Eliciting Multi-attribute Value Models. Management Science, 33:442-450.

59. Tabucanon, M. T., 1986. Multiple-Criteria Decision-Making: Balancing a Variety of Needs and Goals. Engineering Costs and Production Economics, 10:85-88.

60. Takeda, E., K. O. Cogger, and P. L. Yu, 1987. Estimating Criterion Weights Using Eigenvectors: A Comparative Study. European Journal of Operational Research, 29:360-369.

61. Tiwari, R. N., S. Dharmar, and J. R. Rao. Priority Structure in Fuzzy Goal Programming. Fuzzy Sets and Systems, 19:251-260.

62. Vargas, L. G., 1987. Preference Relations, Transitivity and the Reciprocal Property. Mathematical Modelling, 8:154-156.

63. Vargas, L. G., 1987. Priority Theory and Utility Theory. Mathematical Modelling, 9:381-386.

64. Von Neumann, J. and O. Morgenstern, 1953. Theory of Games and Economic Behavior, 3rd Edition, Princeton University Press, p. 641.

65. Werezberger, E., 1981. Multiobjective Linear Programming with Partial Ranking of Objectives. Socio-Economic Planning Science, 15:331-339.

66. Wiedeman, P., 1978. Planning With Multiple Objectives. Omega, 6:427-432.

67. Zahedi, F., 1986. Group Consensus Function Estimation When Preferences Are Uncertain. Operations Research, 34:883-894.

CHAPTER IV

TECHNIQUES

4.1 INTRODUCTION

The use of models in multiple criteria decision making in industry is extremely advisable. Models offer a number of advantages to the decision maker. To mention some, models assist logical organization of ideas; they lead to improved system understanding; they illustrate need for detail and relevance; they expedite speed of analysis; they provide framework for testing modifications; they give ease to manipulate than the actual system itself; they permit varying degree of control over system behavior; and they offer lesser cost of experimentation than direct work with the actual system.

There are several ways in classifying the different models to multiobjective optimization. Adulbhan and Tabucanon (1980), for example, classified the different techniques into three main approaches. Such classification was based on the way the initial multiobjective problem is transformed into a mathematically manageable format. These approaches are: conversion of secondary objectives to constraints; development of a single combined objective function; and treatment of all objectives as constraints.

Hwang, Masud, Paidy and Yoon (1982), on the other hand, made up a different classification. They based their grouping of techniques according to the stage at which information from the decision maker is needed by the analyst. The classification is mainly divided into four approaches: no articulation of preference information; "a priori" articulation of preference information; progressive articulation of preference information; and "a posteriori" articulation of preference information.

Some of those who also published survey papers on multiobjective optimization are Roy (1971), Hwang and Masud (1979), Johnsen (1968), Cochrane and Zeleny (1973), Leitmann and Marzollo (1975), and Starr and Zeleny (1977). There are basically three principles according to which multiobjective optimization methods can be classified, namely, the nature of the input, the throughput, and the output.

In this chapter, existing methods of multiobjective optimization are presented based on the following classification: Single objective approach; Unified objective functions approach; Goal programming approach; Interactive approach; Compromise programming approach; ELECTRE approach; Parametric approach; and De Novo programming approach.

Despite the considerable diversity in MCDM models, there are some general features which are shared by all, viz.:   (i)   The decision maker faces a certain choice problem;   (ii) The decision maker is assisted by an analyst (person/machine) who has the task of providing scientific assistance;   (iii) The decision maker evaluates the alternatives by means of a certain set of criteria he wishes to achieve;   (iv) The analyst has at his disposal informa- tion about the instruments to realize the criteria as well as the impacts of the decision instruments on the criteria;   (v)   The criteria and instruments have been operationally defined; the objectives are at least ordinally measura- ble.

4.2   SINGLE OBJECTIVE APPROACH

A somewhat primitive way of handling multiobjective optimization problems is by optimizing one objective (the most important one) and convert the remaining (k-1) objectives as constraints.   This is done by specifying a maximum (for minimization) or minimum (for maximization) level of attainment for each of the secondary objectives.   The multiobjective problem is then converted to a single objective optimization problem, that is

$$\text{Maximize} \qquad z_1 = f_1(x) \tag{4.1}$$

Subject to

$$g_i(x) \leq b_i \ , \ i = 1,2,\ldots,m \text{ (original constraints)} \tag{4.2}$$

$$f_\ell(x) \geq z'_\ell, \ \ell = 2,3,\ldots,k \text{ (additional constraints)} \tag{4.3}$$

$$x \geq 0$$

where the z_ℓ's are the specified minimum levels of attainment allowed of the remaining objectives.   It is assumed in the above formulation that all objec- tives are of maximizing nature.   The limiting values may be obtained by expressing them as percentages of their individual optima (z_ℓ^*).   Although this method is practical, there are certain cases where the approach gives no defined feasible region after the introduction of the (k-1) additional con- straints.   This null set phenomenon can be illustrated in Fig. 4.1.

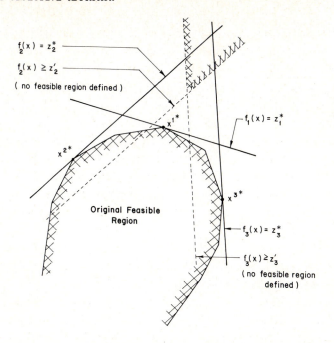

Fig. 4.1   A Case of Nonexisting Feasible Region after
Introduction of Secondary Objectives as Constraints

4.3   UNIFYING OBJECTIVE FUNCTIONS APPROACH

4.3.1   GLOBAL CRITERION METHOD

This method develops a global objective function which is made up of the sum of the deviations of the values of the individual objective functions from their respective ideal values as a ratio to that of the ideal values.   Thus, from the original k objective functions, a single function is formulated and the problem tantamounts to solving a single objective optimization.   The modified problem is:

$$\text{Minimize} \qquad F = \sum_{\ell=1}^{k} \left[\frac{f_\ell(x^*) - f_\ell(x)}{f_\ell(x^*)} \right]^p \qquad (4.4)$$

Subject to

$$g_i(x) \leq 0 , \qquad i = 1, 2, \ldots, m \qquad (4.5)$$

$$x \geq 0$$

where $f_\ell(x^*)$ is the value of objective function ℓ at its individual optimum x^*,

$f_\ell(x)$ is the function itself, p is an integer valued exponent that serves to reflect the importance of the objectives, and g_i is the function of constraint i.

Since the individual terms in the global objective function are expressed in ratios which are necessarily dimensionless, it follows that one does not have to worry regarding the problem of dimensional consistency. The "best" solution chosen for the problem differs greatly according to the value of p chosen. Setting p=1 implies that equal importance is given to all deviations, while p=2 implies that these deviations are weighted proportionately with the largest deviation having the largest weight. Setting p > 2 means that more and more weight is given to the largest of the deviations. There is, however, a tradeoff associated with this functional behavior that one must decide. It may sound realistic to set p=1, but the degree of difficulty that one will encounter in optimizing the global function increases since this will involve exponential order of the decision variables. If one wants to shun this difficulty, p=1 may still be a good choice. If the original k-objective problem is linear, the modified problem will still be linear for p=1.

This technique is particularly appealing in situations where the decision maker is not closely accessible to the analyst. Except for the value of p, explicit information on the relative importance of the objectives is not necessary. Moreover, there is also less subjectivity involved in the process.

Example 4.1

A factory produces products I and II. Product I is manufactured 2 hours and 1 hour in machines A and B, respectively. Product II is manufactured 3 hours in machine A and 4 hours in machine B. Both machines are available for 12 hours. The prices for products I and II are 0.8 and 2 dollars per kilogram, respectively. The manager of the factory wants to maximize both total revenue and total output.

Formulation:

$$\text{Maximize} \quad f_1(x) = 0.8\, x_1 + 2\, x_2$$
$$f_2(x) = x_1 + x_2$$

Subject to

$$2\, x_1 + 3\, x_2 \leq 12$$
$$x_1 + 4\, x_2 \leq 12$$
$$x_1, \; x_2 \geq 0$$

where x_1, x_2 = respective amounts of products I and II produced.

Step 1 - Obtain the individual ideal solutions:

Max. $f_1(x) = 0.8 x_1 + 2 x_2$ subject to $x \in X$ where X is the feasible set of constraints is a LP problem whose ideal solution is $x_1^{1*} = 2.4$, $x_2^{1*} = 2.4$, $f_1(x_1^*) = 6.72$, at point B in Fig. 4.2.

Max. $f_2(x) = x_1 + x_2$ subject to $x \in X$ is another LP problem whose ideal solution is $x_1^{2*} = 6$, $x_2^{2*} = 0$, $f_2(x_2^*) = 6$, at point C in Fig. 4.2.

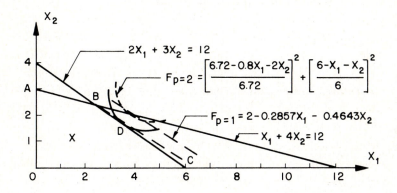

Fig. 4.2   Illustration of the Method of Global Criterion
For Two variables with p=1 and p=2 in the Decision
Variable Space for the Numerical Example

Step 2 - Construct a payoff table:

	x^{1*}	x^{2*}
$f_1(x)$	6.72	4.8
$f_2(x)$	4.8	6

Step 3 - Obtain the preferred solution:

Case 1: p = 1

$$\underset{x \in X}{\text{Minimize}} \quad F_{p=1} = \left[\frac{6.72 - (0.8\ x_1 + 2\ x_2)}{6.72} \right] + \left[\frac{6 - x_1 - x_2}{6} \right]$$

$$= 2 - 0.2857\ x_1 - 0.4643\ x_2$$

It is a LP problem.   The solution is at point C again:

$$x_1^{**} = 6, \quad x_2^{**} = 0 \quad f_1^{**} = 4.8, \quad f_2^{**} = 6$$

It can be seen that when p =1, the "preferred" solution may still be one of the individual optimal solutions which is incorrect.   This is clearly a weakness of the technique.   However, one major advantage of the technique is that the problem remains a LP problem.

Case 2: p = 2

$$\text{Minimize}_{x \in X} \quad F_{p=1} = \left[\frac{6.72 - (0.8 \ x_1 + 2 \ x_2)}{6.72} \right]^2 + \left[\frac{6 - x_1 - x_2}{6} \right]^2$$

This is a nonlinear programming problem.   The solution is at point D in Fig. 4.2:

$$x_1^{**} = 3.58, \ x_2^{**} = 1.61, \ f_1^{**} = 6.09, \ f_2^{**} = 5.19$$

4.3.2 UTILITY FUNCTION METHOD

The utility function method converts the multiobjective optimization problem into a single objective problem in the following form:

$$\text{Maximize} \quad z = F \ [f_1(x), \ f_2(x), \ \ldots \ , \ f_k(x)] \quad\quad (4.6)$$
$$\text{Subject to}$$
$$g_i(x) \leq 0 , \quad\quad i = 1,2,\ldots,m \quad\quad (4.7)$$
$$x \geq 0$$

where F is the utility function of the multiple objectives, representing the decision maker's preferences.   If F is properly determined, the solutions obtained will ensure the decision maker's satisfaction.   However, the determination of F can also be extremely difficult.

F can be of many forms.   The most common form assumes that the decision maker's utility function is additively separable with respect to the objectives.   Thus the additive utility function method converts the objective functions into one of the following form:

$$\text{Maximize} \quad z = \sum_{j=1}^{k} F_j[f_j(x)] \quad\quad (4.8)$$

F_j is used in the same manner as attaching a weight to each objective function. Thus, the problem is transformed into the following:

$$\text{Maximize} \quad z = \sum_{j=1}^{k} w_j \, f_j(x) \quad\quad\quad (4.9)$$

where w_j indicates the relative importance of objective j, and this is determined "a priori".

4.3.3 MINIMUM DEVIATION METHOD

The minimum deviation method is applicable when the analyst has partial information of the objectives -- that is, the optimal values of the objectives are known but their relative importance is not known. It aims at finding the best compromise solution which minimizes the sum of individual objective's fractional deviations. The fractional deviation of an objective refers to a ratio between the deviation of a value of that objective from its individual optimal solution and its maximum deviation. The maximum deviation of an objective is obtained from the difference between its individual optimal solution and its least desirable solution, which corresponds to the individual optimal solution of one of the other objectives.

1) Develop a Payoff Table

For each objective function, its optimal value is first determined subject to the original set of constraints. The values of other objective functions which correspond to the individual optimum are then calculated. After this is done for all objectives, a payoff table can then be formed as shown in Fig. 4.3. Column j corresponds to the solution vector x^{j*}, which optimizes the jth objective, $f_j(x)$. $f_i{}^j$ is the corresponding value taken on by the objective $f_i(x)$ when $f_j(x)$ reaches its individual optimum value $f_j{}^*$. The individual optimum value of each objective function is on the diagonal elements of the payoff table (i.e., when i=j).

Let x^* denote the ideal solution, which gives the k vector of the optimum value of each objective function. Thus

$$F^*(x^*) = [f_1{}^*, f_2{}^*, \ldots, f_k{}^*] \quad\quad\quad (4.10)$$

is the ideal objective vector. This vector can not be obtained unless all objective functions are not conflicting.

	x^{1*}	x^{2*}	...	x^{j*}	...	x^{k*}
z_1	f_1^*	f_1^2	...	f_1^j	...	f_1^k
z_2	f_2^1	f_2^*	...	f_2^j	...	f_2^k
$\vdots$	$\vdots$	$\vdots$		$\vdots$		$\vdots$
z_i	f_i^1	f_i^2	...	f_i^j	...	f_i^k
$\vdots$	$\vdots$	$\vdots$		$\vdots$		$\vdots$
z_k	f_k^1	f_k^2	...	f_k^j	...	f_k^*

Fig. 4.3   Payoff Table

2)   Computational Procedure

The best compromise solution is defined as the solution that will give the minimum of the sum of the fractional deviation of all objectives.   The fractional deviation of each of the objectives is expressed as a fraction of its maximum deviation.   This is necessary for the following reasons:

(a)   The objectives may be   different in units of measurement.   The fractional conversion will help eliminate the effect of the dimension differences in computation.

(b)   In the event of any   significant   difference in magnitude of the objective functions, the total deviation in absolute terms will be dominated by the objective which has a greater magnitude.   The fractional term will help normalize the magnitude of each objective.

(c)   It helps to avoid the   difficulty when the individual optimum of an objective is very small or close to zero.

Let f_{j*} be the least desirable objective value of $f_j(x)$.   The minimum deviation problem is formulated as follows:

$$\text{Minimize:} \qquad Z_o = \sum_{j=1}^{k} \left[\frac{f_j^* - f_j(x)}{f_j^* - f_{j*}} \right] \tag{4.11}$$

$$\text{Subject to:} \quad x \in X \tag{4.12}$$

The denominator $(f_j^* - f_{j*})$ in (4.11) gives the normalization of each objective.   Thus the term $[(f_j^* - f_j(x)]/[f_j^* - f_j)]$ is expressed as a fractional deviation of the objective $f_j(x)$. The idea of the minimization of Z_0 in (4.11) can be shown by geometrical interpretation in a simple multiple objective linear programming of two objectives with two variables as shown in Fig. 4.4. In the figure shown, $f_1(x)$ and $f_2(x)$ are to be optimized.

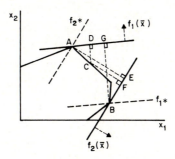

Fig. 4.4 Geometric Interpretation of the
Minimum Deviation Approach

Points A and B give the individual solution of objectives $f_1(x)$ and $f_2(x)$, respectively. The magnitude $(f_j^* - f_{j*})$ can be represented by the length of BG and AE, respectively for j=1 and j=2. If C is any point which is the candidate for the best compromise solution, then the length of CD and CF represent the magnitude of $(f_1^* - f_1(x))$ and $(f_2^* - f_2(x))$, respectively. The objective function Z_0 in (4.11) is the minimization of (CD/BG + CF/AE). (4.11) can be rearranged as follows:

$$\text{Minimize:} \qquad Z_0 = \sum_{j=1}^{k} \left[\frac{f_j^* - f_j(x)}{f_j^* - f_{j*}} \right] \qquad\qquad (4.13)$$

$$\text{or:} \qquad Z_0 = \sum_{j=1}^{k} w_j [f_j^* - f_j(x)] \qquad\qquad (4.14)$$

where

$$w_j = \frac{1}{f_j^* - f_{j*}}$$

Thus, the objective function becomes:

$$\text{Minimize:} \qquad Z_0 = \sum_{j=1}^{k} w_j [f_j^* - f_j(x)] \qquad\qquad (4.18)$$

It may become apparent that the physical meaning of the minimum deviation method is to place a weight on the multiple objective $f_j(x)$ which is inversely proportional to its maximum deviation. Two numerical examples are provided for illustrations.

Example 4.2

$$\text{Maximize:} \quad f_1(x) = -2x_1 + x_2$$
$$\text{Maximize:} \quad f_2(x) = 3x_1 - x_2$$
$$\text{Subject to:} \quad -x_1 + x_2 \le 1$$
$$x_1 + x_2 \le 7$$
$$x_1 \quad \le 5$$
$$x_2 \quad \le 3$$
$$x_1, x_2 \ge 0$$

A geometric representation is shown in Fig. 4.5.

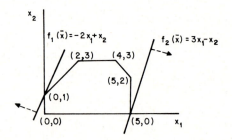

Fig. 4.5   Geometric Interpretation of Example 4.2

It is found that

$$f_1^* = 1 \qquad\qquad , \quad f_2^* = 15$$
$$x^{1*} = (0, 1) \qquad , \quad x^{2*} = (5, 0)$$
$$f_2^1 = -1 \qquad\qquad , \quad f_1^2 = -10$$

The payoff table is developed as shown below.

	x^{1*}	x^{2*}
$f_1(x)$	1	-10
$f_2(x)$	-1	15

The ideal objective vector is $F^*(x^*) = (1, 15)$.   Thus, the problem is to:

$$\text{Minimize: } Z_o = \left[\frac{1 - (-2x_1 + x_2)}{1 - (-10)} \right] + \left[\frac{15 - (3x_1 - x_2)}{15 - (-1)} \right]$$

$$= \frac{181}{176} - \frac{x_1}{176} - \frac{5x_2}{176}$$

Subject to the original constraints.

The solution obtained is minimum $Z_o = 162/176$ and $x^{**} = (4, 3)$.   The best compromise solution is $F^{**}(x^{**}) = (-5, 9)$.

Example 4.3

Minimize $f_1(x) = (x_1 - 2)^2 + (x_2 - 1)^2$
Maximize $f_2(x) = x_1^2 + x_1x_2 + 2x_2^2$
Subject to $0.1 \leq x_1 \leq 2.5$
              $0.1 \leq x_2 \leq 2.0$
              $x_1x_2 \leq 3.0$

A geometric interpretation of the problem is shown in Fig. 4.6.

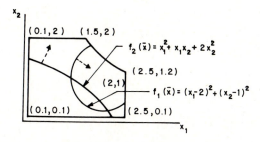

Fig. 4.6   Geometric Interpretation of Example 4.3

The following individual optimal solutions are determined:

$f_1^* = 0.0$, $f_2^* = 13.25$
$x^{1*} = (2, 1)$, $x^{2*} = (1.5, 2)$
$f_2^1 = 8.0$, $f_1^2 = 1.25$

The payoff table is developed as shown below.

$$
\begin{array}{c|cc}
 & x_1{}^* & x_2{}^* \\
\hline
f_1(x) & 0.0 & 1.25 \\
f_2(x) & 8.0 & 13.25 \\
\end{array}
$$

The ideal objective vector is $F^*(x^*) = (0.0, 13.25)$.   Therefore, the problem is to

$$
\text{Minimize} \quad Z_o = \left[\frac{0.0 - [(x_1 - 2)^2 + (x_2 - 1)^2]}{0.0 - 1.25} \right]
$$

$$
+ \left[\frac{13.25 - [x_1{}^2 - x_1 x_2 + 2x_2{}^2]}{13.25 - 8.0} \right]
$$

Subject to the original constraints.

The solution obtained is

$$
\text{Minimum} \qquad Z_o = 0.44
$$
$$
x^{**} = (2.37, 1.26)
$$

Hence, the best compromise solution is

$$
F^{**}(x^{**}) = [0.205, 11.78]
$$
$$
x^{**} = (2.37, 1.36)
$$

4.3.4   COMPROMISE CONSTRAINT METHOD

4.3.4.1   Bicriterion Linear Programming

This method was developed by Tabucanon (1977) and it starts with the following lemma.

Lemma 1.   If $f_1(x)$ and $f_2(x)$ are two objective functions whose feasible maxima are $z_1{}^*$ and $z_2{}^*$, respectively, and if the functions move toward the feasible region (that is, both functions decrease in

numerical value simultaneously), then the equation of the locus of
the point or region of intersection of the functions has the following form:

$$\alpha_2[f_1(x)-z_1{}^*] - \alpha_1[f_2(x)-z_2{}^*]=0 \qquad\qquad (4.16)$$

where α_1 and α_2 are the rates at which the respective functions are
moving.

   Proof.   Introduce a dummy variable, say t (which may be interpreted as
time).   If α_1 and α_2 are the rates of change of the objective functions, then
the following differential equations can be formulated:

$$df_1(x) / dt = \alpha_1 \qquad\qquad (4.17)$$
$$df_2(x) / dt = \alpha_2 \qquad\qquad (4.18)$$

General solutions of the differential equations are

$$f_1(x) = \alpha_1 t + k_1 \qquad\qquad (4.19)$$
$$f_2(x) = \alpha_2 t + k_2 \qquad\qquad (4.20)$$

where k_1 and k_2 are constants of integration.
   Initially (t=0), $f_1(x)$ and $f_2(x)$ are equal to their respective maximum,
$z_1{}^*$ and $z_2{}^*$.   Thus the particular solutions could be derived, as follows:

$$f_1(x) = \alpha_1 t + z_1{}^* \qquad\qquad (4.21)$$
$$f_2(x) = \alpha_2 t + z_2{}^* \qquad\qquad (4.22)$$

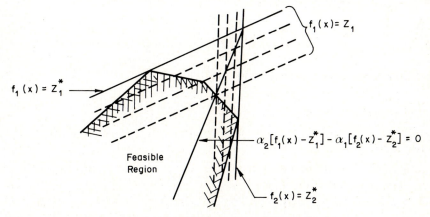

Fig. 4.7   Illustration of Lemma 1

To obtain the desired equation of the locus is to eliminate the dummy variable t by equating its identities obtained using (4.21) and (4.22); hence

$$\alpha_2[f_1(x)-z_1{}^*] - \alpha_1[f_2(x)-z_2{}^*] = 0 \quad \text{Q.E.D.} \tag{4.23}$$

A depiction of Lemma 1 and its proof is in Fig. 4.7.

Lemma 2. Suppose objectives z_1 and z_2 have utility values of β_1 and β_2 respectively, then the single objective equivalent of the two objectives, z, is given by the sum of the products of the utility and the objective, i.e.

$$z = \beta_1 f_1(x) + \beta_2 f_2(x) \tag{4.24}$$

The lemma's graphical representation can be illustrated as in Fig. 4.8.

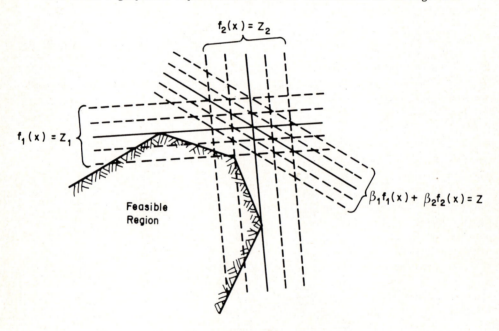

Fig. 4.8   Illustration of Lemma 2

Method of Solution

Consider the following bicriterion linear programming problem.

$$\text{Maximize} \qquad z_1 = \sum_{j=1}^{n} c_{1j}x_j \tag{4.25}$$

$$z_2 = \sum_{j=1}^{n} c_{2j}x_j \qquad (4.26)$$

Subject to:

$$\sum_{j=1}^{n} a_{ij}x_j \le b_i , \qquad i = 1, 2, \ldots, m \qquad (4.27)$$

$$x_j \ge 0 , \qquad \text{for all } j.$$

Referring to Lemma 1, α_1 and α_2 are in fact related to the weights w_1 and w_2. An objective with a bigger weight should descend from its maximum at a slower rate than the objective with a smaller weight; or in mathematical terms,

$$\alpha_1 \propto 1 / w_1 \qquad \text{and} \qquad \alpha_2 \propto 1 / w_2 \qquad (4.28)$$

where $\propto$ is a notation of proportionality. Thus equation (4.19) now becomes

$$w_1[f_1(x) - z_1^*] - w_2[f_2(x) - z_2^*] = 0 \qquad (4.29)$$

To examine the role of equation (4.29) let us again see an example shown in Fig. 4.9.

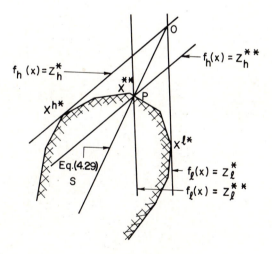

Fig. 4.9 Geometric Illustration of
The Role of Equation 4.29

The point or region common to both objectives is '0'. Had this laid within the feasible region this would have been the best compromise. Since it does not, both objectives have to move towards the feasible region until their common point is feasible. In other words, the point where the "plane" 'OP' first touches the region (at 'P') is the maximum feasible compromise. It is no coincidence that all points in the "plane" described by equation (4.29) are fair compromises; the maximum feasible compromise has the label of being the "optimal" solution. Due to the compromising character of equation (4.29) it is labelled as "compromise constraint", to be added to the original set of constraints, thus forcing the two objectives to settle down to take 'P'.

Granting that all coefficients of the compromise constraint are known, variations of the weights of objectives (between 0 and 1) generates a "pencil" of planes. In geometry a "pencil" of planes refers to planes having a common point of concurrency. Consider Fig. 4.10 for illustration. When $w_1=1$ and $w_2=0$, the compromise constraint passes through point x^{1*} or it has exactly the same equation as that of objective z_1 at its individual optimal condition. As w_1 decreases and w_2 increases in values, the compromise constraint swings to the right (as shown in Fig. 4.10) with a pivot point at 'O'. A "pencil" of planes is thus developed until such a point where $w_1=0$ and $w_2=1$. At this condition, the compromise constraint passes through point x^{2*}, thus assuming the same equation as that of objective z_2 at its individual optimal condition.

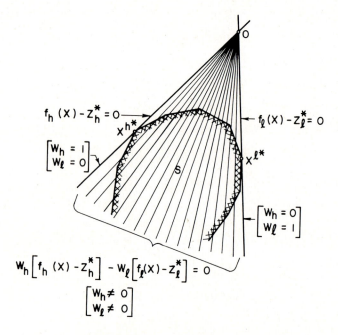

Fig. 4.10   "Pencil" of Planes Generated by
Variations of Weights

What is achieved, so far, is the creation of a new feasible region resulting from the compromise. Three objective functions are now available, the third one defined by equation (4.24) and which, when transformed into function of weights, becomes ($\beta_1 \propto w_1$ and $\beta_2 \propto w_2$)

$$z = w_1 f_1(x) + w_2 f_2(x) \tag{4.30}$$

Using any of the three known objective functions yield the same solution.

Ultimately, the development of the single objective equivalent of the two objective problem is accomplished. But another problem still persists -- the coefficients of objective functions are of differing magnitudes. When the coefficients of one objective function are so big compared with those of the other, the former objective dominating the latter arises. For example, if the coefficients of $f_1(x)$ are so big compared with those of $f_2(x)$ that the absolute value of the expression $[f_1(x) - z_1^*]$ is very large than that of the expression $[f_2(x) - z_2^*]$, then the compromise constraint will be unfairly dominated by the objective z_1. It is the role of the model builder to eliminate this dominating character of one objective. The weights are assumed to have been adjusted by the model builder. In other words, the preference values originally given by top managers are adjusted in the light of the model builders' knowledge of the mathematical traits -- magnitudes of coefficients in particular -- of the objective functions. In order to eliminate the effect of dominance, it is necessary first to convert the objective functions into their "normal" forms before obtaining the compromise constraint and the "supergoal" z.

Maximize any one of :

$$z_1 = \sum_{j=1}^{n} c_{1j} x_j \tag{4.31}$$

$$z_2 = \sum_{j=1}^{n} c_{2j} x_j \tag{4.32}$$

$$z = \frac{w_1}{\sqrt{(\sum_{j=1}^{n} c_{1j}^2)}} \sum_{j=1}^{n} c_{1j} x_j + \frac{w_2}{\sqrt{(\sum_{j=1}^{n} c_{2j}^2)}} \sum_{j=1}^{n} c_{2j} x_j \tag{4.33}$$

Subject to:

$$\sum_{j=1}^{n} a_{ij}x_j \le b_i \ , \qquad i = 1,2,\ldots,m \tag{4.34}$$

$$\frac{w_1}{(\sum_{j=1}^{n} c_{1j}{}^2)} \ [\ \sum_{j=1}^{n} c_{1j}x_j - z_1{}^* \ ] \ - \ \frac{w_2}{(\sum_{j=1}^{n} c_{2j}{}^2)} \ [\ \sum_{j=1}^{n} c_{2j}x_j - z_2{}^* \ ] \ = \ 0 \tag{4.35}$$

$$x_j \ge 0 \ , \qquad\qquad j=1,2,\ldots,n.$$

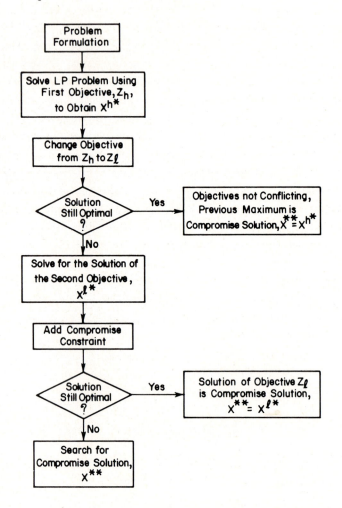

Fig. 4.11   A Flowchart for Biobjective
Linear Programming Procedure

The procedure has three sets of single objective linear programming problems, viz. LP using z_1 to get z_1^*, LP using z_2 to get z_2^*, LP using either z_1, z_2, or z with added compromise constraint to get the final solution. However, the three sets do not constitute, completely, three different problems. The first two share the same set of constraints while the third one may use the same objective although with an added new equality constraint. Without having to solve three series of new problems, the whole procedure of solving a bicriterion problem could be viewed as a parametric programming problem (involving postoptimality analysis) with the following sequence of changes in the system: change in objective function and adding a new constraint.

In other words, the procedure starts by first solving z_1 to obtain its maximum z_1^*. Without starting a completely new LP problem, change the objective z_1 to z_2, check for optimality of the previous solution, and if it is destroyed, continue to search for the new optimum, which eventually obtains z_2^*. At this stage, develop the compromise constraint, then add it to the original set. Again, the addition of this new constraint does not constitute the formulation of a completely new problem but a continuation of the previous one. Check for feasibility again and depart from the previous optimal tableau to find the optimal solution if optimality is destroyed. This is precisely the type of situation where the dual simplex method should be used to progress to a feasible optimal solution. The whole solution procedure is described in the flowchart of Fig. 4.11.

Example 4.4

Solve the following two-objective linear programming problem.

Maximize: $z_1 = -2 x_1 + x_2$, $w_1 = 0.6$

$z_2 = 2 x_1 + x_2$, $w_2 = 0.4$

Subject to:

$$- x_1 + x_2 \leq 1$$
$$x_1 + x_2 \leq 7$$
$$x_1 \qquad \leq 5$$
$$x_2 \leq 3$$
$$x_1 , x_2 \geq 0$$

Tableau 1 (Initial for objective z_1):

	x_1	x_2	x_3	x_4	x_5	x_6	RHS
x_3	-1.0	1.0	1.0	0.0	0.0	0.0	1.0
x_4	1.0	1.0	0.0	1.0	0.0	0.0	7.0
x_5	1.0	0.0	0.0	0.0	1.0	0.0	5.0
x_6	0.0	1.0	0.0	0.0	0.0	1.0	3.0
z_1	-2.0	1.0	0.0	0.0	0.0	0.0	0.0

Tableau 2 (Final for objective z_1):

	x_1	x_2	x_3	x_4	x_5	x_6	RHS
x_2	-1.0	1.0	1.0	0.0	0.0	0.0	1.0
x_4	2.0	0.0	-1.0	1.0	0.0	0.0	6.0
x_5	1.0	0.0	0.0	0.0	1.0	0.0	5.0
x_6	1.0	0.0	-1.0	0.0	0.0	1.0	2.0
z_1	-1.0	0.0	-1.0	0.0	0.0	0.0	1.0

Tableau 2 reveals optimality at $x_1^{1*} = 0$ and $x_2^{1*} = 1$ [or $x^{1*} = (0, 1)$] with $z_1^* = 1$.   The process is continued with z_1 changed to z_2 as the new objective function.   According to the principle of postoptimality analysis, in the objective row of Tableau 2, the coefficient of x_1 (-1) will be increased by 4 ($c_{21} - c_{11}$); in other words, it will assume a value of 3, which is nonnegative and therefore the previous solution is now nonoptimal.   This result substantiates that objectives z_1 and z_2 are conflicting.   Since optimality is destroyed, it therefore becomes necessary to make x_1 an entering basic variable and then continue with the simplex algorithm.   The optimal tableau for objective z_2 is presented below:

Tableau 3 (Final for z_2):

	x_1	x_2	x_3	x_4	x_5	x_6	RHS
x_3	0.0	0.0	1.0	-1.0	2.0	0.0	4.0
x_2	0.0	1.0	0.0	1.0	-1.0	0.0	2.0
x_1	1.0	0.0	0.0	1.0	1.0	0.0	5.0
x_6	0.0	0.0	0.0	-1.0	1.0	1.0	1.0
z_2	0.0	0.0	0.0	-1.0	-1.0	0.0	12.0

From tableau 3, the following conditions of optimality are obtained:

$$x_1^{2*} = 5, \quad x_2^{2*} = 2 \quad \text{and} \quad z_2^* = 12.$$

Now comes the last stage -- progressing towards a compromise solution. Development of the compromise constraint is presented as follows:

$$0.6[-2x_1 + x_2 - 1] - 0.4[\ 2x_1 + x_2 - 12] + (\sigma_{12}^- - \sigma_{12}^+) = 0$$
Or, $\quad -2x_1 + 0.2x_2 + \sigma_{12}^- - \sigma_{12}^+ = -4.2$

The compromise constraint can only eliminate previous feasible solutions, so that optimal solution (i.e., for z_2^*) must either decrease or remain unchanged. Obviously, a decrease in the previous optimum is certain. Since the previous optimal solution does not satisfy the compromise constraint, a departure towards optimality is necessary with this added compromise constraint and objective function of $z_2 = 2x_1 + x_2 - \sigma_{12}^- - \sigma_{12}^+$. The final tableau (Tableau 4) giving the compromise solution is presented as follows:

Tableau 4 (Compromise solution):

	x_1	x_2	σ_{12}^-	σ_{12}^+	x_3	x_4	x_5	x_6	x_7	RHS
x_1	1.0	0.0	1.0	-1.0	1.0	0.0	0.0	0.0	0.1	2.4
x_4	0.0	0.0	1.0	-1.0	1.0	1.0	0.0	0.0	-0.9	0.4
x_5	0.0	0.0	-1.0	1.0	-1.0	0.0	1.0	0.0	-1.1	1.6
x_6	0.0	0.0	-1.0	1.0	-1.0	0.0	0.0	1.0	-0.1	2.6
x_2	0.0	1.0	0.0	0.0	0.0	0.0	0.0	0.0	1.0	3.0
z_2	0.0	0.0	-3.0	-1.0	0.0	0.0	0.0	0.0	-1.2	7.8

The compromise solution obtained from tableau 4 is: $x_1^{**} = 2.4$, $x_2^{**} = 3$ with objective values of $z_1^{**} = -1.8$ and $z_2^{**} = 7.8$; deviational variables, σ_{12}^{-} and σ_{12}^{+}, are both equal to zero. The value of the sum of weighted objectives at compromise solution is $z^{**} = 2.04$. The extents of relaxation of objectives z_1 and z_2 are 2.8 [i.e., 1-(-1.8)] and 4.2 [i.e., 12-7.8] respectively, making their ratio (2.8/4.2 = 0.67) equals the inverse of the ratio of their corresponding weights (0.4/0.6 = 0.67). Fig. 4.12 illustrates the example.

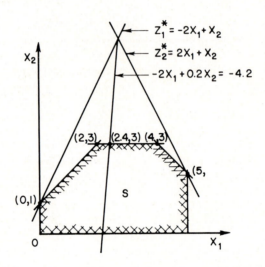

Fig. 4.12   Graphical Version of Example 4.4

Example 4.5

Suppose that management is aiming at two objectives of a firm in a competitive business environment -- maximization of profit and maximization of sales revenue. The problem is on the production of two types of capital goods requiring three types of resource. Unit profits, unit revenues, production parameters and objective weights are known. The mathematical formulation of the problem is as follows:

Maximize: $z_1 = 21x_1 + 5x_2$, $w_1 = 0.7$ (sales revenue in $1,000)

              $z_2 = x_1 + 4x_2$, $w_2 = 0.3$ (profit in $1,000)

Subject to:

$x_1 \leq 50$ (availability of resource type 1)

$x_2 \leq 60$ (availability of resource type 2)

$x_1 + x_2 \leq 70$ (availability of resource type 3)

$x_1 , x_2 \geq 0$

where z_1 is sales revenue in thousand dollars per year, z_2 is profit in thousand dollars per year, x_1 is the amount of product type 1 produced per year, and x_2 is the amount of product type 2 produced per year. The values of $w_1 = 0.7$ and $w_2 = 0.3$ are the weights attached by management to sales revenue and profit objectives.

It can be seen that sales revenue and profit objectives are conflicting. Sales revenue objective has more preference to x_1 than x_2, as governed by the unit prices -- \$21,000 for product type 1 while only \$5,000 for product type 2. However, x_2 is more preferred than x_1 for the profit objective. This is because the profit for a unit of product type 2 sold is \$4,000 while for product type 1, the unit profit is only \$1,000.

Individual optimal solutions are: $z_1^* = \$1,150,000$ at $x_1^{1*} = 50$, $x_2^{1*} = 20$; and $z_2^* = \$250,000$ at $x_1^{2*} = 10$, $x_2^{2*} = 60$. The compromise constraint is:

$$0.7[21x_1 + 5x_2 - 1,150] - 0.3[x_1 + 4x_2 - 250] + (\sigma_{12}^- - \sigma_{12}^+) = 0$$
$$\text{Or,} \quad 14.4x_1 - 2.3x_2 + \sigma_{12}^- - \sigma_{12}^+ = 730$$

The compromise solution is at $x_1^{**} = 47.02$ and $x_2^{**} = 22.98$ with $z_1^{**} = \$1,102,320$, $z_2^{**} = \$138,940$ and $z^{**} = \$813,306$. Deviational variables, σ_{12}^- and σ_{12}^+, are both zero. The graphical representation of the problem and its solution is shown in Fig. 4.13.

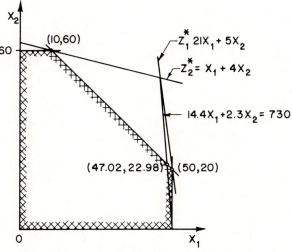

Fig. 4.13 Graphical Version of Example 4.5

As to what management has really done in finding the above compromise solution is something to be clarified. The extents at which the objectives relax from their respective individual maximum are inversely proportional to the weights attached to the objectives.   Thus, the ratios

$$\frac{w_2}{w_1} = \frac{0.3}{0.7} \quad \text{and} \quad \frac{f_1(x^{**}) - z_1^*}{f_2(x^{**}) - z_2^*} = \frac{1,102,320 - 1,150,000}{138,940 - 250,000}$$

have equal values of 0.428

The rates of relaxation are evaluated as follows:

$$\theta_1 = (1/0.7) \cdot 1,000 \quad \text{and} \quad \theta_2 = (1/0.3) \cdot 1,000$$

with values $\theta_1 = \$30,800$ and $\theta_2 = \$13,700$.   For every relaxation of $\$30,800$ of sales revenue, management relaxes $\$13,700$ of profit.

4.3.4.2 The Case of Multiple Objective Functions

What has been discussed so far is a biobjective case where a zero value on the left hand side of the compromise constraint in its standard form is attained.   By and large, especially for problem with more than two objectives, this zero value of the compromise constraint is not necessarily attained.   This section introduces a generalized technique.

The general formulation of the single objective equivalent problem of a multiobjective optimization problem using the technique is as follows:

Maximize:
$$z = \sum_{\ell=1}^{k} w_\ell f_\ell(x) - \sum_{h \neq \ell} (\sigma_{h\ell}^- + \sigma_{h\ell}^+) \tag{4.36}$$

$$h = 1, 2, \ldots, k;$$

$$\ell = 1, 2, \ldots, k$$

Subject to:
$$w_\ell[f_\ell(x) - z_\ell^*] - w_h[f_h(x) - z_h^*] + (\sigma_{h\ell}^- - \sigma_{h\ell}^+) = 0 \tag{4.37}$$

$$h = 1, 2, \ldots, k;$$

$$\ell = 1, 2, \ldots, k;$$

$$h \neq \ell$$

$$\sum_{j=1}^{n} a_{ij} x_j \leq b_i \qquad i = 1, 2, \ldots, m; \tag{4.38}$$

$$x_j, \sigma_{h\ell}^-, \sigma_{h\ell}^+ \geq 0 \qquad j = 1, 2, \ldots, n; \tag{4.39}$$

$$h = 1, 2, \ldots, k;$$

$$\ell = 1, 2, \ldots, k;$$

$$h \neq \ell$$

The introduction of variables $\sigma_{h\ell}^{-}$ and $\sigma_{h\ell}^{+}$ is necessary to account for the nonzero value on the left hand side of the compromise constraint in its standard form. Variable $\sigma_{h\ell}^{-}$ refers to negative deviation while $\sigma_{h\ell}^{+}$ represents the positive deviation from the supposed to be "zero value" of the compromise constraint developed between objectives z_h and z_ℓ. In other words, $\sigma_{h\ell}^{-}$ is nonzero when the left hand side of the compromise constraint is negative; $\sigma_{h\ell}^{+}$ is nonzero when the value is positive for the said constraint; and "ideal" condition is achieved when $\sigma_{h\ell}^{-}$ and $\sigma_{h\ell}^{+}$ are both zero.

On one hand, management has to aspire for a closest adherence to the compromise constraint. Thus, the expression $(\sigma_{h\ell}^{-} + \sigma_{h\ell}^{+})$ has to be minimized which then leads to mutual exclusiveness of $\sigma_{h\ell}^{-}$ and $\sigma_{h\ell}^{+}$. For example, a negative deviation of 3 from 0 calls for values of $\sigma_{h\ell}^{-} = 3$ and $\sigma_{h\ell}^{+} = 0$ to minimize their summation, rather than having, say values of $\sigma_{h\ell}^{-} = 6$ and $\sigma_{h\ell}^{+} = 3$ or $\sigma_{h\ell}^{-} = 4$ and $\sigma_{h\ell}^{+} = 1$. Likewise, a positive deviation of 3 has to have values of $\sigma_{h\ell}^{-} = 0$ and $\sigma_{h\ell}^{+} = 3$ instead of having other combinations.

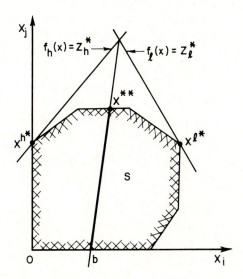

Fig. 4.14   Graphical Illustration of the Host
Of Compromise Solutions Derived by
Minimizing $(\sigma_{h\ell}^{-} + \sigma_{h\ell}^{+})$

On the other hand, management seeks for maximum feasible value of the objective functions. Minimization of $(\sigma_{h\ell}^{-} + \sigma_{h\ell}^{+})$ alone will not suffice as

it will merely lead to a host of solutions for the biobjective case and an
inferior solution for more than two objective case.   In Fig. 4.14, the host of
solutions is depicted by line (or surface) $'x^{**}b'$, the trace of the compromise
constraint.   In Fig. 4.15, the possible compromise solution apparently lies
within the shaded region (S'). Obviously, this is an inferior solution. It is
therefore necessary to introduce the concept of efficiency in order to derive a
unique and efficient solution.   The most logical way of doing this is to avail
of the maximization of the weighted sum of all objectives, thus coming up with
an objective function, equation (4.36), composed basically of two parts --
weighted sum of all objective functions and summation of all deviational
variables.   The negative sign preceeding the second part symbolizes the
minimization effort for the deviational variables. It is assumed that management gives equal preferences to both parts of the generalized objective
function. Otherwise, appropriate preference values have to be prefixed in both
parts of the function.

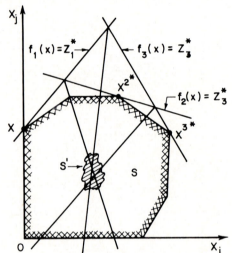

Fig. 4.15 Graphical Illustration of a Possible
Inferior Compromise Solution Derived by
Minimizing $(\sigma_{h\ell}^{-} + \sigma_{h\ell}^{+})$

So far, the objective function has been assumed to have equal preferences
given to both the summation of weighted objectives and summation of deviational
variable parts of the objective function. To be more general, let w' represent
the preference value (not necessarily 0.5) given to $\sum w_{\ell} f_{\ell}(x)$, $\ell=1,2,\ldots,k$; and
(1 - w') be the one given to $\sum (\sigma_{h\ell}^{-} + \sigma_{h\ell}^{+})$; h = 1,2,\ldots,k; $\ell = 1,2,\ldots,k$. The
objective function is replaced by the following:

$$z = w'[\sum_{\ell=1}^{k} w_\ell f_\ell(x)] - (1 - w')[\sum_{h \neq \ell} (\sigma_{h\ell}^- + \sigma_{h\ell}^+)] \qquad (4.40)$$

$$h = 1, 2, \ldots, k$$
$$\ell = 1, 2, \ldots, k$$

Example 4.6

Solve the following-three objective linear programming problem:

Maximize: $z_1 = -x_1 + 3x_2$, $w_1 = 0.1$

$z_2 = 2x_1 + x_2$, $w_2 = 0.3$

$z_3 = -2x_1 + x_2$, $w_3 = 0.6$

Subject to: $-x_1 + x_2 \leq 1$

$x_1 + x_2 \leq 7$

$x_1 \leq 5$

$x_2 \leq 3$

$x_1 , x_2 \geq 0$

The simplex algorithm yields the following individual optimal solutions:

$$x_1^{1*} = 2 , \qquad x_2^{1*} = 3 , \qquad z_1^* = 7$$
$$x_1^{2*} = 5 , \qquad x_2^{2*} = 2 , \qquad z_2^* = 12$$
$$x_1^{3*} = 0 , \qquad x_2^{3*} = 1 , \qquad z_3^* = 1$$

The three compromise constraints are derived as follows:

(i)   For z_1 and z_2 --

$$0.1 \left[\frac{7 - (-x_1 + 3x_2)}{\sqrt{(-1)^2 + (3)^2}} \right] - 0.3 \left[\frac{12 - (2x_1 + x_2)}{\sqrt{(2)^2 + (1)^2}} \right] + (\sigma_{12}^- - \sigma_{12}^+) = 0$$

Or, $0.3 x_1 + 0.039 x_2 + \sigma_{12}^- - \sigma_{12}^+ = 1.388$

(ii)   For z_2 and z_3 --

$$0.3 \left[\frac{12 - (2x_1 + x_2)}{\sqrt{(2)^2 + (1)^2}} \right] - 0.6 \left[\frac{1 - (-2x_1 + x_2)}{\sqrt{(-2)^2 + (1)^2}} \right] + (\sigma_{23}^- - \sigma_{23}^+) = 0$$

Or, $-6 x_1 + x_2 + \sigma_{23}^- - \sigma_{23}^+ = -10$

(iii)   For z_1 and z_3 --

$$0.1 \left[\frac{7 - (-x_1 + 3x_2)}{\sqrt{(-1)^2 + (3)^2}} \right] - 0.6 \left[\frac{1 - (-2x_1 + x_2)}{\sqrt{(-2)^2 + (1)^2}} \right] + (\sigma_{31}^- - \sigma_{31}^+) = 0$$

Or, $-0.504\, x_1 + 0.173\, x_2 + \sigma_{31}^- - \sigma_{31}^+ = 0.0465$

The required objective function is derived as follows:

$$z = 0.1 \left[\frac{-x_1 + 3x_2}{\sqrt{(-1)^2 + (3)^2}} \right] + 0.3 \left[\frac{2x_1 + x_2}{\sqrt{(2)^2 + (1)^2}} \right] + 0.6 \left[\frac{-2x_1 + x_2}{\sqrt{(-2)^2 + (1)^2}} \right]$$

$$- [\sigma_{12}^- + \sigma_{12}^+ + \sigma_{23}^- + \sigma_{23}^+ + \sigma_{31}^- + \sigma_{31}^+]$$

Or, $z = -0.3x_1 + 0.497x_2 - \sigma_{12}^- - \sigma_{12}^+ - \sigma_{23}^- - \sigma_{23}^+ - \sigma_{31}^- - \sigma_{31}^+$

In summary, the equivalent single objective problem of the original three objective linear programming problem is as follows:

Maximize:
$$z = -0.3x_1 + 0.497x_2 - \sigma_{12}^- - \sigma_{12}^+ - \sigma_{23}^- - \sigma_{23}^+ - \sigma_{31}^- - \sigma_{31}^+$$
Subject to:

$$
\begin{aligned}
0.3x_1 + 0.039x_2 + \sigma_{12}^- - \sigma_{12}^+ \quad\quad\quad\quad\quad\quad &= 1.388 \\
-6x_1 + \quad x_2 \quad\quad\quad\quad + \sigma_{23}^- - \sigma_{23}^+ \quad\quad\quad &= -10 \\
-0.504x_1 + 0.173x_2 \quad\quad\quad\quad\quad\quad + \sigma_{31}^- - \sigma_{31}^+ &= 0.0465 \\
-x_1 + \quad x_2 \quad\quad\quad\quad\quad\quad\quad\quad\quad\quad &\leq 1 \\
x_1 + \quad x_2 \quad\quad\quad\quad\quad\quad\quad\quad\quad\quad &\leq 7 \\
x_1 \quad\quad\quad\quad\quad\quad\quad\quad\quad\quad\quad\quad\quad &\leq 5 \\
x_2 \quad\quad\quad\quad\quad\quad\quad\quad\quad\quad\quad &\leq 3 \\
x_1, x_2, \sigma_{12}^-, \sigma_{12}^+, \sigma_{23}^-, \sigma_{23}^+, \sigma_{31}^-, \sigma_{31}^+ \quad\quad\quad &\geq 0
\end{aligned}
$$

The resulting compromise solution has the objective values of $z_1^{**} = 6.83$, $z_2^{**} = 7.34$ and $z_3^{**} = -1.34$ at $x_1^{**} = 2.17$ and $x_2^{**} = 3$. Fig. 4.16 shows the graphical version of the problem and its solution.

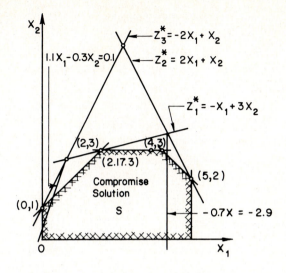

Fig. 4.16   Graphical Version of Example 4.6

4.4   GOAL PROGRAMMING APPROACH

4.4.1   FORMULATION

Goal Programming (GP) is a method that requires ordinal and cardinal information for multiple objective decision making. In GP, deviation variables (from goals) with assigned priorities and weights are minimized instead of optimizing the objective criterion directly as in LP. The general form of goal programming may be expressed as follows:

$$\text{Minimize:} \quad z = \sum_{i=1}^{m} (P_{oi}d_i^{+} + P_{ui}d_i^{-}) \tag{4.41}$$

$$\text{Subject to:} \quad \sum_{j=1}^{n} (a_{ij}x_j) + d_i^{-} - d_i^{+} = b_i , \quad \text{for } i=1, 2, \ldots, m \tag{4.42}$$

$$x_j, d_i^{-}, d_i^{+} \geq 0 \qquad \qquad \text{for } i=1,2,\ldots,m \atop j=1,2,\ldots,n \tag{4.43}$$

where x_i are the variables in the goal equations, b_i are the targets or goals, a_{ij} are the coefficients of basic variables, d_i^{-} represent the underachievement of goal i, d_i^{+} represent the overachievement of goal i, P_{ui} is the priority associated with d_i^{-}, and P_{oi} is the priority associated with d_i^{+}. If over chievement is acceptable, d_i^{+} can be eliminated from the objective function; if underachievement is satisfactory, d_i^- should be left out of the objective function and if the goal must be achieved exactly as defined, both d_i^+ and d_i^- must be in the objective function. The deviational variables must be ranked according to their priorities, from the most important to the least important. If goals are classified in R ranks, the priority factor P_r (r=1,...,R) should be assigned to the deviational variables. The priority factors have the following relationships: $P_r > > > NP_{r+1}$ (r=1,...,R-1), which implies that the multiplication of N, however large it may be, cannot make P_{r+1} greater than or equal to P_r. The algorithm procedure is carried out by a modified simplex method.

4.4.2 GP VERSUS LP

Assumptions in LP, such as additivity, homogeneity, and linearity must also be met in GP, except unidimensionality. The nature of the LP model requires that goal(s) of management be included in the objective function can be expressed in terms of single measurable criterion, i.e., it is one dimensional optimization problem. Actually, this assumption is seldom satisfied. GP provides the opportunity to handle problems with multiple goals which may be incommensurable. Very often, goals are not only multidimensional but also conflicting. GP allows conflicting goals to be specified and still yield an acceptable solution.

In LP, all constraints are given equal importance and must be satisfied simultaneously, while GP treats both the managerial objectives and the constraints as goals with associated priorities. Since priorities imply that low-order goals are considered only after high-order goals are satisfied or have reached points beyond which they cannot be improved under the given conditions, all the goals are not necessarily to be satisfied.

In LP, one optimizes a function subject to given constraints. Each constraint will have a 'slack variable' associated with it in the solution. These slacks are only dummy variables which are merely slacks between two sides of inequality. In GP, such slacks take on a different meaning - deviational variables. Deviational variables may be represented in two parts, both negative and positive deviations from each specified goal. The deviational variables are the only variables entering into the objective function. It is always the case with GP that there is a minimization type objective function in order to reduce deviations from the goal. Each goal being formulated as a constraint is always expressed in equality form.

In LP, the objective, such as profit maximization or cost minimization, has no target value specified. However, in GP, a reasonable value of goals is required. Alternatively, one could use a right-hand side value that determines either an upper bound in maximization or a lower bound in minimization.

Simplex method is employed in obtaining the solution of both the LP and GP problems. GP may perhaps be taken as a sequential LP because goals incorporated in GP problems are satisfied sequentially from the first priority, second priority, ..., and so on. However, the one selected as the entering variable in GP not only have the largest improvement rate as LP does, but also should not degrade the solution at the higher priority.

The solution of LP model is limited by quantification and, at best, is as good as the cardinal numbers used to quantify the relationships of the variables. The GP model considers both the ordinal and cardinal relationships, and a best solution is simply provided under the given priority structure and set of goals. There are three major differences in solution obtained from LP and GP models. Firstly, the GP technique has multiple objectives to achieve as close as possible, while LP has a single objective to fully optimize. In other words, the GP model simply provides an acceptable or good solution which is cardinal. Secondly, a LP problem can be unbounded while GP problem can not be unbounded. This is because the overall objective of GP is to minimize the summation of nonnegative deviations. Thirdly, an infeasible solution may be obtained in LP problem. Since the priority structure is introduced, an infeasible solution does not occur in GP.

Once the management's objective is specified in LP there is no further demand on management's involvement. The management can only say yes or no to the final outcome, no further decision making effort is required. In GP, however, both the cardinal and ordinal relationships are subjective, and the solution mainly depends on the given priority structure and goals. Hence, management is not only mandatorily involved but also taking a major role in formulation, solution and evaluation processes. Obviously, the decision maker's capability in applying GP technique is greatly enhanced.

Example 4.7

A factory produces two kinds of machines. The production capacity is eight hours a day. Overtime is possible but would require higher expenditure. Production of either of the machines require one hour of production facilities. Due to the limitation of sales force, the factory can sell only four of machine A and six of machine B. The profit of machine A is twice as much of machine B. The manager of the factory considers that the first important goal is to avoid underutilization of production capacity. A second goal is to sell both machines as many as possible. He specifies that machine A is twice as important as machine B. In addition, in view of the high overtime operating cost of

production facilities, the manager wishes to reduce overtime production.   The
manager asks the analyst to devise a strategy to achieve his objective as
nearly as possible.

GP formulation:

$$x_1 + x_2 + d_1^- - d_1^+ = 8 \ ,$$

where, x_1 is the number of units of machine A to be produced,
            x_2 is the number of units of machine B to be produced,
            d_1^- is idle time of production capacity, and
            d_1^+ is overtime operation.

$$x_1 + d_2^- = 4 \ ,$$
$$x_2 + d_3^- = 6 \ ,$$

where, d_2^- represents underachievement of sales goals for Machine A, and
            d_3^- is underachievement of sales goal for machine B.

Three priorities are assigned to the deviation of the goals based on the
consideration of the manager:

P_1 represents the highest priority and is assigned to the underutilization
of production capacity d_1^-.

P_2 is the next priority and is assigned to the underachievement of sales
goals, d_2^- and d_3^-.   Since the profit of machine A is twice as machine B, the
weight for d_2^- is assigned twice as that for d_3^-.

P_3 is the third priority factor assigned to the overtime operation in d_1^+.

Now the goal programming model can be formulated.   The objective is the
minimization of deviations from goals.   Hence, the objective function is
expressed only in terms of the deviational variables.   The deviational variable
associated with the highest preemptive priority must first be minimized to the
fullest possible extent.   When no further improvement is possible in the
highest priority order group, the deviations associated with the next highest
priority are minimized.   Thus, the model can be expressed as shown below:

$$
\begin{aligned}
\text{Minimize:} \quad & z = P_1 d_1^- + 2P_2 d_2^- + P_2 d_3^- + P_3 d_1^+ \\
\text{Subject to:} \quad & x_1 + x_2 + d_1^- - d_1^+ = 8 \\
& x_1 + d_2^- = 4 \\
& x_2 + d_3^- = 6 \\
& x_1, \ x_2, \ d_1^-, \ d_2^-, \ d_3^-, \text{ and } d_1^+ \geq 0.
\end{aligned}
$$

4.4.3   SIMPLEX METHOD OF GOAL PROGRAMMING

The simplex solution procedure for goal programming is very similar to the simplex solution of linear programming; however, there are several distinct differences.   The solution steps to solve a goal programming problem by the modified simplex method can be summarized as follows:

(i)   Set up the initial tableau from the goal programming model

It is assumed that the initial solution is at the origin.   Therefore, all the negative deviational variables in the model constraints should enter the solution base initially.   List the constants (rhs) and the coefficients of all variables in the main body of the table.   Also list the preemptive priority factors and differential weights to the appropriate variables by examining the objective function.   In the simplex criterion (z_j-c_j), list priority levels in the variable column (V) from the lowest at the top to the highest at the bottom. z_j values must be calculated and recorded in the C column.   The last step is to calculate z_j- c_j values for each column starting from the first choice variable to the last positive deviational variable.   For clarification see Table 4.1, using the GP formulation presented earlier.

(ii)   Determine the new entering variable

This step is similar to the identification of the optimum column.   First, find the highest priority level that has not been completely attained by examining the z_j-c_j values in the constant column.   When the priority level is determined, proceed to identify the variable column that has the largest positive z_j-c_j value or the largest negative value if c_j-z_j is used.   The variable in that column will enter the solution base in the next iteration.   If there is a tie between the largest positive values in z_j-c_j at the highest priority level, check the next lower priority levels and select the column that has a greater value at the lower priority level.   If the tie cannot be broken, choose one on an arbitrary basis.   The other column will be chosen in subsequent iterations.

(iii)   Determine the leaving variable from the solution base

This process is identical to finding the key row.   Calculate the value of the constant divided by the coefficients in the optimum column.   Select the row that has the minimum positive or zero value.   The variable in that row will be replaced by the variable in the optimum column in the next iteration.   If there exists a tie when constants are divided by coefficients, find the row that has the variable with the highest priority factor.   This procedure enables the attainment of higher order goals first, and thereby reduces the number of iterations.

(iv)   Determine the new basic feasible solution

First, find the new constant and coefficients of the key row by dividing old values by the intersectional element, i.e., the element at the intersection of the key row and the optimum column.   Second, find the new values for all other rows by using the calculation procedure (of old value - intersectional element of that row x with the new value in the key row in the same column). Third, complete the table by finding z_j and z_j-c_j values for the priority rows.

(v)   Determine whether the solution is optimal

Analyze the level of each goal by checking the z_j value for each priority row.   If the z_j values are all zero, then this is the optimal solution.   If there exists a positive value of z_j, examine the z_j-c_j coefficients for that row.   If there are positive z_j-c_j values in the row, determine whether there are negative z_j-c_j values at a higher priority level in the same column.   If there are negative z_j-c_j values at a higher priority value for the positive z_j-c_j values in the row of interest, then the solution is optimum.   Otherwise, return to step (ii) and continue.   An example simplex tableau for goal programming is shown in Table 4.1.

The simplex solution procedure for goal programming problem can be illustrated in the flowchart as shown in Fig. 4.17.

Table 4.1   Simplex Tableau for Goal Programming of Example 4.7

c_j	V				P_1	P_2	$2P_2$	P_3
		C	x_1	x_2	d_1^-	d_2^-	d_3^-	d_1^+
P_1	d_1^-	8.0	1.0	1.0	1.0	0.0	0.0	-1.0
P_2	d_2^-	4.0	1.0	0.0	0.0	1.0	0.0	0.0
$2P_2$	d_3^-	6.0	0.0	1.0	0.0	0.0	1.0	0.0
	P_3	0.0	0.0	0.0	0.0	0.0	0.0	-1.0
z_j-c_j	P_2	14.0	2.0	1.0	0.0	0.0	0.0	0.0
	P_1	5.0	8.0	1.0	0.0	0.0	0.0	-1.0

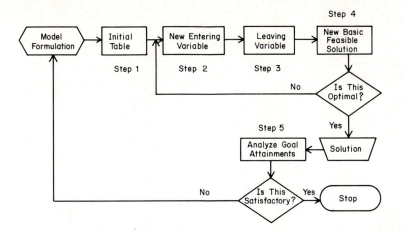

Fig. 4.17 Flowchart of the Simplex Procedure of Goal Programming

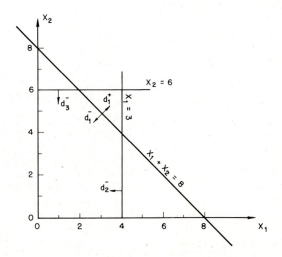

Fig. 4.18 Graphical Representation of Example 4.7

Solution of the Goal Programming Model of Example 4.7.

Minimize $z = P_1 d_1^- + 2P_2 d_2^- + P_2 d_3^- + P_3 d_1^+$

Subject to:

$$x_1 + x_2 + d_1^- \qquad\qquad - d_1^+ = 8$$
$$x_1 \qquad\qquad + d_2^- \qquad\qquad = 4$$
$$x_2 \qquad\qquad + d_3^- \qquad = 6$$
$$x_1 , x_2 , d_1^- , d_2^- , d_3^- , d_1^+ \geq 0$$

(a) Simplex Solution:

COEFFICIENTS IN TABLEAU #   1

```
D 1-      8.00     1.00     1.00     1.00     0.00     0.00    -1.00
D 2-      4.00     1.00     0.00     0.00     1.00     0.00     0.00
D 3-      6.00     0.00     1.00     0.00     0.00     1.00     0.00
```

VALUES IN ZJ-CJ:

```
P 3       0.00     0.00     0.00     0.00     0.00     0.00    -1.00
P 2      14.00     2.00     1.00     0.00     0.00     0.00     0.00
P 1       8.00     1.00     1.00     0.00     0.00     0.00    -1.00
```

PIVOT COLUMN =   1   TABLEAU # 1
PIVOT ROW =   2

COEFFICIENTS IN TABLEAU #   2

```
D 1-      4.00     0.00     1.00     1.00    -1.00     0.00    -1.00
X 1       4.00     1.00     0.00     0.00     1.00     0.00     0.00
D 3-      6.00     0.00     1.00     0.00     0.00     1.00     0.00
```

VALUES IN ZJ-CJ:

```
P 3       0.00     0.00     0.00     0.00     0.00     0.00    -1.00
P 2       6.00     0.00     1.00     0.00    -2.00     0.00     0.00
P 1       4.00     0.00     1.00     0.00    -1.00     0.00    -1.00
```

PIVOT COLUMN =   2   TABLEAU # 2
PIVOT ROW =   1

COEFFICIENTS IN TABLEAU #   3

```
X 2       4.00     0.00     1.00     1.00    -1.00     0.00    -1.00
X 1       4.00     1.00     0.00     0.00     1.00     0.00     0.00
D 3-      2.00     0.00     0.00    -1.00     1.00     1.00     1.00
```

VALUES IN ZJ-CJ:

```
P 3       0.00     0.00     0.00     0.00     0.00     0.00    -1.00
P 2       2.00     0.00     0.00    -1.00    -1.00     0.00     1.00
P 1       0.00     0.00     0.00    -1.00     0.00     0.00     0.00
```

PIVOT COLUMN =   6   TABLEAU # 3
PIVOT ROW =   3

```
COEFFICIENTS IN TABLEAU #   4

X 2      6.00      0.00      1.00      0.00      0.00      1.00      0.00
X 1      4.00      1.00      0.00      0.00      1.00      0.00      0.00
D 1+     2.00      0.00      0.00     -1.00      1.00      1.00      1.00


VALUES IN ZJ-CJ:

P 3      2.00      0.00      0.00     -1.00      1.00      1.00      0.00
P 2      0.00      0.00      0.00      0.00     -2.00     -1.00      0.00
P 1      0.00      0.00      0.00     -1.00      0.00      0.00      0.00
```

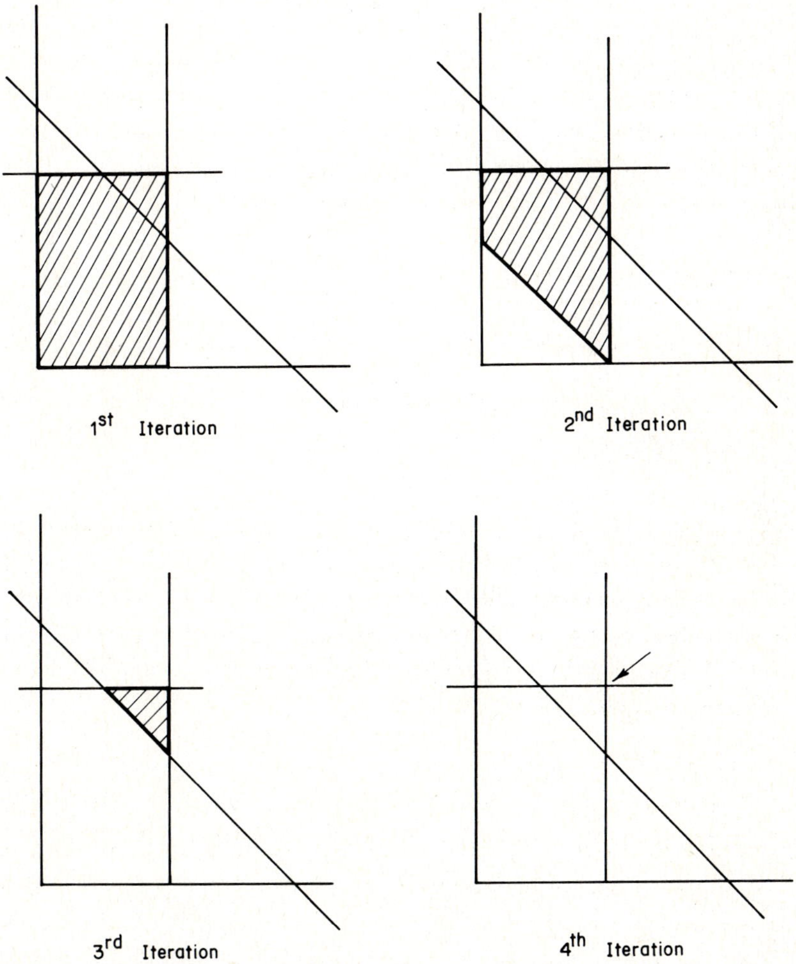

Fig. 4.19 Graphical Solution of Example 4.7

(b) Graphical Solution (Fig.4.19):

Iteration No.	x_1	x_2	d_1^-	d_2^-	d_3^-	d_1^+
1	0	0	8	4	6	0
2	0	0	4	0	6	0
3	4	4	0	0	2	0
4	4	6	0	0	0	2

4.4.4   SOME COMPLICATIONS AND THEIR RESOLUTIONS

The basic approach of goal programming enables one to avoid several complications encountered in linear programming.   For example, problems encountered in linear programming due to inequality in the wrong direction, equality, variables unconstrained in sign, etc., in the original model do not present any difficulty in goal programming.   This is because goals are evalua-ted in terms of both underachievement and overachievement.   However, there are several complications that often emerge in goal programming problems, which are discussed below:

(i) Nonpositive Constant

To explain the nonpositive constant problem, consider the goal constraint shown below.

$$-5x_1 - x_2 + d_1^- - d_1^+ = -25 \tag{4.43}$$

In the initial tableau of simplex goal programming, it is assumed that the solution is at the origin.   Therefore, the deviational variable d_1^- will take on the value -25.   However, the simplex method requires condition of non-negative variables (x_i, d_i^-, $d_i^+ \geq 0$); thus, $d_1^- = -25$ is not permissible.   In order to facilitate the initial solution, both sides are multiplied by -1.   The goal constraint becomes:

$$5x_1 + x_2 + \delta_1^- - \delta_1^+ = 25 \tag{4.44}$$

If the goal is to achieve exactly -25 from the original constraint, it can easily be achieved by minimizing both d_1^- and d_1^+ in (4.43) at the same priority level or minimizing both δ_1^- and δ_1^+ in (4.44) at the same priority level.   However, if the goal is to make the constraint produce -25 or greater, d_1^- must be minimized in (4.43) but in the revised goal constraint (4.44), δ_1^+

should be minimized to derive the same effect. Similarly, to assume the value of -25 or less from the constraint, d_1^+ must be minimized in (4.43) and δ_1^- must be minimized in the revised equation (4.44).

(ii) Tie for Entering Variable

In any goal programming problem, it can easily happen during the iteration that two or more columns have exactly the same positive z_j-c_j value at the highest unattained goal level. When there is such a case, determination of the optimum column and consequently the entering basic variable is based on the z_j-c_j values at the lower priority levels. If the tie cannot be broken, selection between the contending variables may be made arbitrarily. The other variable will generally be introduced into the solution base in the subsequent iterations.

(iii) Tie for Leaving Variable

To determine the variable that will leave the solution base, constants must be divided by the coefficients in the optimum column and then determine the row with the minimum positive quotient. If there are two or more rows with identical minimum positive values, this raises the problem of degeneracy. The resolution of degeneracy should be decided by determining which row has the variable with the higher priority factor as the leaving variable. The solution process can be shortened as the higher priority goals will be attained faster.

(iv) Unbounded Solution

It is possible that because of an unrealistic priority structure of the decision maker or lack of constraints, the problem may allow one or more variables to increase without limit. In most real world problems, however, this situation rarely occurs, since goals tend to be set higher than easily attainable levels within the existing decision making environment. The unbounded solution, if it does occur, also provides some insight in analyzing the decision maker's goal structure. It is often the case that important constraints are omitted in the problem when an unbounded solution is obtained.

(v) Alternate Optimal Solutions

It is possible that two or more points provide optimal solutions that attain exactly the same level of goals. Such an occasion never occurs as long as there is only a single deviational variable (single goal) at each preemp-

tive priority level, and differential weights are assigned among subgoals at
the same priority level.

4.5   INTERACTIVE APPROACH

In many multiobjective optimization problems, the decision maker (DM) does
not have a complete or overall idea of his preferences or his desired level of
performances over a set of objective functions.   There are times that required
preferences are unnecessarily too many.   Hence, instead of the decision maker
readily expressing the overall preference function at the very outset, it is
appropriate that he relies on the progressive definition of his preferences
along with the exploration of the criterion space.   Interactive methods usually
consist of a DM-analyst or DM-computer dialogue. At each iteration, the
decision maker is asked about some tradeoff or preference information based on
the current solution in order to determine a new solution.   The method essen-
tially assumes that the decision maker is unable to indicate "a priori"
preference information due to the complexity of the problem, but that he is
able to give preference information on a local level with respect to a particular solution.   This interactive procedure is certainly advantageous since
it is a learning process for the decision maker to understand the behavior of
the system.   The decision maker becomes part of the overall process giving the
solution obtained a better prospect of being implemented.   The approach has
also less restrictive assumptions as compared to other approaches.   Though
interactive methods are, by and large, very useful, there is no guarantee,
however, that the preferred solution can be obtained within a finite number of
interactive cycles.   Also, much more effort is required of the decision maker
than is so with other approaches.   In the next few subsections several interactive methods are described.

4.5.1   STEP METHOD

The Step Method (STEM) developed by Benayoun, de Montgolfier, Tergny and
Laritchev (1971) employs the interactive approach. The method involves sequential exploration of solutions guided to some extent by the decision maker who
responds to questions posed by the algorithm.   Thus, each iteration is made up
of a calculation phase and a decision making phase.   Before the first cycle, a
payoff matrix is constructed (as in Fig. 4.20).   Since the objectives could not
be maximized at one point, the "ideal solution" (at which the objective
functions are all at their individual maximum as given by the diagonal of the
payoff matrix) is nonfeasible.   In the calculation phase, therefore, the

feasible solution which is "nearest" to the ideal solution is searched.   The
problem then becomes the following:

$$\begin{array}{cccccc}
 & x^{1*} & x^{2*} & \cdots & x^{h*} & \cdots & x^{k*} \\
z_1 & f_1(x^{1*}) & f_1(x^{2*}) & \cdots & f_1(x^{h*}) & \cdots & f_1(x^{k*}) \\
z_2 & f_2(x^{1*}) & f_2(x^{2*}) & \cdots & f_2(x^{h*}) & \cdots & f_2(x^{k*}) \\
 & \vdots & \vdots & \vdots & \vdots & \vdots & \vdots \\
z_\ell & f_\ell(x^{1*}) & f_\ell(x^{2*}) & \cdots & f_\ell(x^{h*}) & \cdots & f_\ell(x^{k*}) \\
 & \vdots & \vdots & \vdots & \vdots & \vdots & \vdots \\
z_k & f_k(x^{1*}) & f_k(x^{2*}) & \cdots & f_k(x^{h*}) & \cdots & f_k(x^{k*})
\end{array}$$

Fig. 4.20   Payoff Matrix of the STEM

Minimize $z = y$ (4.45)

Subject to: $y \geq [f_\ell(x^{\ell*}) - f_\ell(x)] \, \pi_\ell \, ,$ $\ell = 1,\ldots,k$ (4.46)

$\quad\quad\quad\quad x \in X^m$

$\quad\quad\quad\quad y \geq 0$

where X^m is the feasible region at cycle m which includes the original constraint set plus any constraints added in the previous (m-1) cycles; the π_ℓ's
give the relative importance of the distances to the optima.   This can be
obtained through the following equations:

$$\pi_\ell = \alpha_\ell \, / \, \left(\sum_{i=1}^{k} \alpha_i \right) \quad\quad\quad\quad \ell = 1, 2, \ldots, k \quad (4.47)$$

$$\alpha_\ell = \frac{M_\ell - m_\ell}{M_\ell} \cdot \frac{1}{\sqrt{\sum_{j=1}^{n} c_{\ell j}^2}} \, , \quad\quad\quad \ell = 1, 2, \ldots, k \quad (4.48)$$

where M_ℓ and m_ℓ are, respectively, the maximum and minimum values of the ℓth
row of the payoff matrix.   The term $c_{\ell j}$ refers to the coefficient of the jth
decision variable in the ℓth objective function (z_ℓ).   From the first factor in
the expression, it is observed that if the value of z_ℓ does not vary much from
the ideal solution for different x^{h*}, the corresponding objective is not
sensitive to a variation in the weighting values, so a small weight π_ℓ can be

assigned to this objective function. As the variation increases, the weight π_ℓ will correspondingly increase. The second factor normalizes the value taken by the objective function.

In the decision making phase, the solution obtained in the calculation phase, x^m, is presented to the decision maker who compares its objective vector f^m (or z^m) with f^* (or z^*), the ideal one. If some of the objectives are satisfactory and others are not, the decision maker must relax a satisfactory objective f_i^m enough to allow an improvement of the unsatisfactory objectives in the next iteration cycle. If the decision maker gives δ_f as the amount of acceptable relaxation, then the feasible region X^{m+1} for the next cycle is defined by

$$
\left.
\begin{aligned}
&x \in X^m \; , \\[4pt]
&f_i(x) \geq f_i(x^m) - \delta_f \; , \\[4pt]
&f_j(x) \geq f_j(x^m) \; , \qquad j \neq i, \; j = 1, \, 2, \, \ldots, k.
\end{aligned}
\right\} \tag{4.49}
$$

The weight π_i is set to zero and the calculation phase of the cycle m+1 begins. The process stops when all the values obtained for the objective functions are acceptable to the decision maker.

Example 4.8 (Adopted from Hwang (1980))

$$
\begin{aligned}
\text{Maximize} \quad & z_1 = 0.4 \, x_1 + 0.3 \, x_2 \\
\text{Maximize} \quad & z_2 = x_1 \\
\text{Subject to:} \quad & \\
& x_1 + x_2 \leq 400 \\
& 2x_1 + x_2 \leq 500 \\
& x_1 \, , \; x_2 \geq 0
\end{aligned}
$$

Payoff Table:

	x^{1*}	x^{2*}
z_1	130	100
z_2	100	250

Calculation phase:

$$
\alpha_1 = \frac{130-100}{130} \left[\frac{1}{\sqrt{(0.4)^2 + (0.3)^2}} \right] = 0.4615
$$

$$\alpha_2 = \frac{250-100}{250} \left[\frac{1}{(1)^2} \right] = 0.6$$

$$\pi_1 = 0.4615 / (0.4615 + 0.6) = 0.4348$$
$$\pi_2 = 0.6 / (0.4615 + 0.6) = 0.5652$$

Solve the following LP problems:

      Minimize y

      Subject to:

$$x_1 + x_2 \le 400 \qquad \text{(original constraints)}$$
$$2x_1 + x_2 \le 500$$
$$y \ge [130 - (0.4x_1 + 0.3x_2)](0.4348) \qquad \text{(Added constraints)}$$
$$y \ge [250 - x_1](0.5652)$$

The solution: $x^1 = (x_1^1, x_2^1) = (230, 40)$

                    $z^1 = (f_1^1, f_2^1) = (104, 230)$

Decision phase:

The compromise solution x^1 is presented to the decision maker, who compares its objective vector $z^1 = (f_1^1, f_2^1) = (104, 230)$ with the ideal one, $z^* = (f_1^*, f_2^*) = (130, 250)$. If f_2^1 is satisfactory, but f_1^1 is not, the decision maker must relax the satisfactory objective f_2^1 enough to allow an improvement of the unsatisfactory f_1^1. If $\delta f_2 = 30$ is the acceptable amount of relaxation, the feasible region is modified as follows in the next cycle.

$$X^2 = \begin{bmatrix} X^1 \\ f_2(x) \ge f_2^1 - \delta f_2 = 230 - 30 = 200 \\ f_1(x) \ge f_1^1 = 104 \end{bmatrix}$$

Iteration No. 2 - Calculation phase:

$$\pi_1 = 1 \qquad , \qquad \pi_2 = 0$$

Solve the following problem

      Minimize: y

      Subject to: $\{ x \in X^2 , \ y \ge 0 , \ y + (0.4x_1 + 0.3x_2) \ge 130 \}$

The solution: $x^2 = (x_1^2, x_2^2) = (200, 100)$,

                    $z^2 = (f_1^2, f_2^2) = (110, 200)$.

Iteration No. 2 - Decision Phase

The compromise solution x^2 is presented to the decision maker, who compares its objective vector $z^2 = (f_1^2, f_2^2) = (110, 200)$ with the ideal one, $z^* = (f_1^*, f_2^*) = (130, 250)$. If both objectives of the vector z^2 are satisfactory, then z^2 is the final solution.

4.5.2 "GAME THEORETIC" TECHNIQUE

The step by step procedure for solving multicriterion problem using the two person zero-sum game technique, as developed by Belenson and Kapur (1973), is described below.

Step 1.   Construct the payoff matrix as shown in Fig. 4.21

	x^{1*}	x^{2*}	. . .	x^{h*}	. . .	x^{k*}
z_1	$f_1(x^{1*})$	$f_1(x^{2*})$	. . .	$f_1(x^{h*})$	. . .	$f_1(x^{k*})$
z_2	$f_2(x^{1*})$	$f_2(x^{2*})$	. . .	$f_2(x^{h*})$	. . .	$f_2(x^{k*})$
.	.	.	.	.	.	.
z_ℓ	$f_\ell(x^{1*})$	$f_\ell(x^{2*})$	. . .	$f_\ell(x^{h*})$	. . .	$f_\ell(x^{k*})$
.	.	.	.	.	.	.
z_k	$f_k(x^{1*})$	$f_k(x^{2*})$	. . .	$f_k(x^{h*})$	. . .	$f_k(x^{k*})$

Fig. 4.21   Payoff Matrix

Does any x^{h*} generate a satisfactory solution from the decision maker's point of view? If yes, the problem is solved. If no, continue to Step 2.

Step 2.   Normalize the payoff matrix.

For most practical multicriterion programs, disparities will exist between the magnitude of the values generated by the various objective functions.   A simple example would be minimizing risk and maximizing profit.   Risk is expressed as a value between 0 and 1 while profit is in monetary terms. If z_1 represents risk and z_2 represents profit, then for the game, row 2 will always dominate row 1 and the probabilities (or weights) will therefore be forced to equal 0 and 1, respectively.   This is not the right result, thus normalization is necessary.

	x^{1*}	x^{2*}	. . .	x^{h*}	. . .	x^{k*}
z_1	$f_1(x^{1*})/M_1$	$f_1(x^{2*})/M_1$	. . .	$f_1(x^{h*})/M_1$	. . .	$f_1(x^{k*})/M_1$
z_2	$f_2(x^{1*})/M_2$	$f_2(x^{2*})/M_2$	. . .	$f_2(x^{h*})/M_2$	. . .	$f_2(x^{k*})/M_2$
.	.	.	.	.	.	.
.	.	.	.	.	.	.
z_ℓ	$f_\ell(x^{1*})/M_\ell$	$f_\ell(x^{2*})/M_\ell$	. . .	$f_\ell(x^{h*})/M_\ell$	. . .	$f_\ell(x^{k*})/M_\ell$
.	.	.	.	.	.	.
.	.	.	.	.	.	.
z_k	$f_k(x^{1*})/M_k$	$f_k(x^{2*})/M_k$	. . .	$f_k(x^{h*})/M_k$	. . .	$f_k(x^{k*})/M_k$

Fig. 4.22 Normalization of Payoff Matrix

In normalizing the matrix, divide the elements of the ℓth row by M_ℓ as shown in Fig. 4.22, where:

$$M_\ell = f_\ell(x^{\ell*}) \ , \quad \ell = 1, \ 2, \ \ldots, \ k$$

Therefore, the diagonal of the normalized payoff matrix is always equal to 1.

The optimal weights are obtained from solving the game for the normalized payoff matrix rather than the original payoff matrix. It is therefore necessary to determine the equivalent weights for the unnormalized matrix. Let w_ℓ' be the optimal weights of the normalized matrix. The optimal weights for the unnormalized matrix are :

$$w_\ell^* = n_\ell \ / \ \sum_{j=1}^{k} n_j \ , \quad \text{for } \ell = 1,2,\ldots,k \qquad (4.50)$$

where $n_\ell = w_\ell' / M_\ell$,   for $\ell = 1,2,\ldots,k$

If at least one row in the payoff matrix has all entries equal or less than zero, then do the following operations:

Let $K = - \text{Min } f_\ell(x^{h*})$,   for all ℓ and h

Add K to all elements in the payoff matrix before normalizing.

Step 3. Form an equivalent linear program

Maximize: $z = \sum_{\ell=1}^{k} w_\ell^* \ f_\ell(x)$

Subject to: $x \in X$

Example 4.9 (To show step 1 up to part of step 3)

$$\text{Maximize} \quad z_1 = 0.1x_1 + 0.2x_2$$
$$\text{Maximize} \quad z_2 = 10x_1 - 5x_2$$

Subject to:

$$x_1 - x_2 \leq 1$$
$$x_1 + x_2 \leq 7$$
$$x_1 \qquad \leq 5$$
$$\qquad x_2 \leq 3$$
$$x_1 , x_2 \geq 0$$

Payoff matrix:

	(4,3) x^{1*}	(5,0) x^{2*}	
z_1	1.0	0.5	$M_1 = 1$
z_2	25	50	$M_2 = 50$

Normalized matrix:

	x^{1*}	x^{2*}	
z_1	1.0	0.5	$w_1' = 1/2$
z_2	0.5	1.0	$w_2' = 1/2$

$$n_1 = 1/2 \quad , \quad n_2 = 1/100 \quad , \quad \sum n = 51/100$$

$$w_1^* = 50/51 \quad , \quad w_2^* = 1/51$$

Thus,   Maximize $z = \dfrac{50}{51} (0.1x_1 + 0.2x_2) + \dfrac{1}{51} (10x_1 - 5x_2)$

$$= \dfrac{15}{51} x_1 + \dfrac{5}{51} x_2$$

Subject to: $x \in X$

The solution: $x_1^* = 5 \quad , \quad x_2^* = 2$

$$z_1^* = 0.9 \quad , \quad z_2^* = 40$$

	x^{1*}	x^{2*}	x^1
z_1	1	0.5	0.9
z_2	25	50	40

Solve the above formulation and determine a solution x^1.

(A) Was x^1 previously considered?

    If yes, the problem does not have a satisfactory solution.

    If no, continue to Step 3-B.

(B) Is x^1 a satisfactory solution?

    If yes, the problem is solved.

    If no, continue to step 4.

Step 4.   Substitute x^1 for x^{h*} where x^{h*} is the optimum point for the least preferred objective z_h thus forming a new game and repeat steps 1 to 3 in order to obtain a new solution x^2.

(A) Was x^1 previously considered?

    If yes, substitute x_1 for $x_i{}^*$ where $x_i{}^*$ is the optimal point for the next least preferred objective z_i and continue to step 4.

    If no, continue to step 4-B.

(B) Is x^2 a satisfactory solution?

    If yes, the problem is solved.

    If no, substitute x^2 for x^{i*} where x^{i*} is the optimum point for the next least preferred objective z_i, and continue to step 5.

Step 5.   Repeat step 4 until k lesser preferred solution have been considered.   Thus, either a satisfactory solution will be obtained or there does not exist a solution which will satisfy the decision maker.

Example 4.10

$$\text{Maximize} \quad z_1 = -2x_1 + x_2$$
$$\text{Maximize} \quad z_2 = 3x_1 - x_2$$
$$\text{Subject to:}$$
$$-x_1 + x_2 \le 1$$
$$x_1 + x_2 \le 7$$
$$x_1 \qquad \le 5$$
$$x_2 \le 3$$
$$x_1 , x_2 \ge 0$$

Payoff matrix is:

	x^{1*}	x^{2*}		
z_1	1	-10	$M_1 = 1$	$K = 0$
z_2	-1	15	$M_2 = 15$	

Hence, the normalized payoff matrix is:

1	-10	$w_1' = 0.0782$
-1/15	1	$w_2' = 0.922$

$$n_1 = w_1' / M_1 \qquad , \qquad n_2 = w_2' / M_2$$
$$w_1^* = 0.56 \qquad , \qquad w_2^* = 0.44$$

New objective function:

$$z = 0.56 \, (-2x_1 + x_2) + 0.44 \, (3x_1 - x_2)$$
$$= 0.2 \, x_1 + 0.12 \, x_2$$

The solution $\quad x^1 = (5, 2) \quad, \quad z_1 = -8 \quad, \quad z_2 = 13 \qquad$ (unsatisfactory)

	x^{1*}	x^1	
z_1	1	-8	$M_1 = 1$
z_2	-1	13	$M_2 = 13$

$K = 0$

Hence,

1	-8	$w_1' = 0.1068, \quad w_1^* = 0.582$
-1/13	1	$w_2' = 0.9932, \quad w_2^* = 0.417$

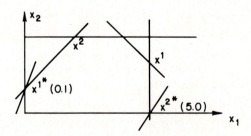

Fig. 4.23 Graphical Illustration of Example 4.10

New objective function

$$z = 0.582 \ (-2x_1 + x_2) + 0.417 \ (3x_1 - x_2)$$
$$= 0.087 \ x_1 + 0.165 \ x_2$$

The solution is $\quad x^2 = (2, \ 3) \quad , \quad z_1 = -1 \quad , \quad z_2 = 3$

If satisfactory, the complete solution is x^2

	x^{1*}	x^{2*}	x^1	x^2
z_1	1	-10	-8	-1
z_2	-1	15	13	3

4.5.3 INTERACTIVE SEQUENTIAL CONVERSION OF OBJECTIVES INTO CONSTRAINTS (ISCOC)

This method was developed by Adulbhan and DeGuia (1977). It is a partial interactive procedure between the decision maker and the algorithm where objectives are assigned goals and treated as constraints in their order of preference.   Thus, each cycle consists of a decision making phase and a calculation phase. The decision making phase involves studying the effects of setting a target to an objective relative to lower priority objectives, after which the desired target is set on it. This objective with the set target is then included in the previous set of constraints and the next preferred objective optimized in the calculation phase. The usefulness of this approach centers on the intermediate sensitivity analysis conducted at each cycle. In contrast to the traditional postoptimality analysis approach, the exploration of a goal for an objective at each cycle is undertaken to sharpen the decision maker's knowledge of its interaction to other objectives. This would enable him to set an acceptable as well as a permissible goal.

The method is a goal attainment type where the objective functions are made to achieve targets $(B_1, B_2, \ldots, B_k)$ in their order of preference $(P_1, P_2, \ldots, P_k)$. The targets are assumed to be unknown at the outset and the search for feasible as well as acceptable targets is carried out in such a way as to advance to the solution of the problem.

Although the iterative use of the regular simplex algorithm could be adopted for the ISCOC method, an algorithm specifically tailored for such purposes would considerably reduce the computational effort required. Hence, the regular simplex algorithm is modified to suit with the requirements of the procedure. The sensitivity analysis mechanism capitalizes on the concepts of choosing the leaving and entering variables.

The regular simplex algorithm as presented by Hillier and Lieberman (1980) is used as basis for ISCOC's Modified Simplex Algorithm. Unless otherwise mentioned explicitly, the procedural steps, rules and considerations of the said algorithm will remain the same.

(a) Maximization Converted into Minimization

It will be recalled that in cases when a minimization problem is encountered, the regular simplex method suggests converting it into an equivalent maximization problem. When maximization objectives are converted to constraints they take the "greater than or equal to" sign. This would require additional computational effort during the iteration process. This can however be simplified by converting instead the maximization objective into its equivalent minimization objective such that the objective-turned constraint takes the "less than or equal to" sign. The resulting Z-values for maximization would then be negative of the true Z-value.

(b) Initial Tableau

Taking into consideration the multiple objectives and their desired optimization processes, the initial tableau of the regular simplex algorithm is modified to the one shown in Fig. 4.24. The following rules apply to the construction of the initial tableau:

STATUS	BASIC VARIABLE	COEFFICIENTS OF														Right Side of Equation	DESIRED OPERA-TION
		X_1	...	X_j	...	X_n	X_{n+i}	...	X_{n+i}	...	X_{n+m}	X_{n+m+1}	...	X_{n+m+l}	... X_{n+m+k}		
P_k	Z_k	$C_{k,1}$	...	$C_{k,j}$	...	$C_{k,n}$	0	...	0	...	0	0	...	0	... 1	0	min. (≤)
⋮	⋮	⋮		⋮		⋮	⋮		⋮		⋮	⋮		⋮	⋮	⋮	
P_l	Z_l	$C_{l,1}$	...	$C_{l,j}$	...	$C_{l,n}$	0	...	0	...	0	0	...	1	... 0	0	or max. (≤)
⋮	⋮	⋮		⋮		⋮	⋮		⋮		⋮	⋮		⋮	⋮	⋮	
P_1	Z_1	$C_{1,1}$	...	$C_{1,j}$	...	$C_{1,n}$	0	...	0	...	0	1	...	0	... 0	0	
C_m	X_{n+m}	$a_{m,1}$	...	$a_{m,j}$	...	$a_{m,n}$	0	...	0	...	1	0	...	0	... 0	b_m	
⋮	⋮	⋮		⋮		⋮	⋮		⋮		⋮	⋮		⋮	⋮	⋮	
C_i	X_{n+i}	$a_{i,1}$	...	$a_{i,j}$	...	$a_{i,n}$	0	...	1	...	0	0	...	0	... 0	b_i	
⋮	⋮	⋮		⋮		⋮	⋮		⋮		⋮	⋮		⋮	⋮	⋮	
C_1	X_{n+1}	$a_{1,1}$	...	$a_{1,j}$	...	$a_{1,n}$	1	...	0	...	0	0	...	0	... 0	b_1	

Fig. 4.24   Initial Tableau

(1) The coefficients of a minimization objective function do not take the opposite signs in the tableau. This is done to facilitate the conversion of

objectives into constraints. The expected values of P_ℓ will then have opposite signs to the real values.

(2)   Slack variables are introduced for both the constraints and the objective functions.

(3)   The desired condition for a maximization process is to achieve at least a certain set target, i.e., equal to or greater than $B_{\ell acc}$; for minimization, less than or equal to $B_{\ell acc}$.

(4)   The objective functions are included in the tableau in their order of preference.

(c)   **Tableau Iterations**

The objective functions are considered one at a time in their order of priorities. The feasibility condition is satisfied first before the optimality condition in finding the optimal set relative to the highest priority objective (thereafter, the feasibility condition is maintained). The number of "working" variables increases as some objectives are converted into constraints. At any time, the variables under consideration would only be x_j, $(j = 1, 2, \ldots, n+m+r)$ where n is the actual number of variables, m is the original number of constraints, and r is the number of objectives already considered. Sensitivity analysis is conducted on the intermediate optimal tableau as shown in Fig. 4.25 where the considered objective is optimal.

STATUS	BASIC VARIABLE	COEFFICIENTS OF											Right Side of Equation	DESIRED OPERA-TION
		x_1	$\cdots$	x_j	$\cdots$	x_n	$\cdots$	x_{n+m}	$\cdots x_{n+m+o-l}$	$\cdots x_{n+m+l}$	$\cdots x_{n+m+2}$	$\cdots x_{n+m+k}$		
P_k	Z_k	$c'_{k,1}$	$\cdots$	$c'_{k,j}$	$\cdots$	$c'_{k,n}$	$\cdots$	$c'_{k,n+m}$	$\cdots$ 0	$\cdots$ 0	$\cdots$ 1		$-B_k$	min. $(\leq)$ or max. $(\leq)$
$\vdots$	$\vdots$	$\vdots$		$\vdots$		$\vdots$		$\vdots$	$\vdots$	$\vdots$	$\vdots$		
P_ℓ	Z_ℓ	$c'_{\ell,1}$	$\cdots$	$c'_{\ell,j}$	$\cdots$	$c'_{\ell,n}$	$\cdots$	$c'_{\ell,n+m}$	$\cdots$ 0	$\cdots$ 1	$\cdots$ 0		$-B_\ell$	
$\vdots$	$\vdots$	$\vdots$		$\vdots$		$\vdots$		$\vdots$	$\vdots$	$\vdots$	$\vdots$		
P_o	Z_o	$c'_{o,1}$	$\cdots$	$c'_{o,j}$	$\cdots$	$c'_{o,n}$	$\cdots$	$c'_{o,n+m}$	$\cdots$ 1	$\cdots$ 0	$\cdots$ 0		$-B_o$	
c_{m+o-1}	$x_{(n+m+o-1)}$	$a'_{m+o-1,1}$	$\cdots$	$a'_{m+o-1,j}$	$\cdots$	$a'_{m+o-1,n}$	$\cdots$	$a'_{m+o-1,n+m}$	$a'_{m+n+o-1,m+n+o-1}$	$\cdots$ 0	$\cdots$ 0		b'_{m+o-1}	
$\vdots$	$\vdots$	$\vdots$		$\vdots$		$\vdots$		$\vdots$	$\vdots$	$\vdots$	$\vdots$		
c_i	$x_{(n+i)}$	$a'_{i,1}$	$\cdots$	$a'_{i,j}$	$\cdots$	$a'_{i,n}$	$\cdots$	$a'_{i,n+m}$	$a'_{i,m+n+o-1}$	$\cdots$ 0	$\cdots$ 0		b'_i	
$\vdots$	$\vdots$	$\vdots$		$\vdots$		$\vdots$		$\vdots$	$\vdots$	$\vdots$	$\vdots$		
c_1	$x_{(n+1)}$	$a'_{1,1}$	$\cdots$	$a'_{1,j}$	$\cdots$	$a'_{1,n}$	$\cdots$	$a'_{1,n+m}$	$a'_{1,m+n+o-1}$	$\cdots$ 0	$\cdots$ 0		b'_1	

Note : B_ℓ represent the value of Z_ℓ when Z_ℓ is minimization. Otherwise, Z_ℓ takes the opposite sign.

Fig. 4.25   Intermediate Optimal Tableau

(d)   Intermediate Sensitivity Analysis (ISA)

An intermediate sensitivity analysis is conducted every cycle, i.e., after each considered objective function achieves optimality to aid the decision maker in the goal setting process.   The information derived from ISA in relation to the objective under consideration are the minimum (or maximum) achievable target and the consequences of setting a target in relation to a lower priority objectives.   The analysis is conducted within the immediate extreme points or the optimal set of the objective under consideration.

The intermediate sensitivity analysis takes into account the effects of assigning a specific goal to an objective relative to lower priority objectives.   Its basic philosophy lies on the idea that by setting a goal to an objective, the initial feasible region will be reduced, limiting the minimum (or maximum) permissible values that the other objective can achieve.

The decision objective refers to the optimized objective function in the intermediate optimal tableau.   It is the objective where a target is to be set and would then be included in the previous set of constraints.   Consequence objectives refer to the lower priority objectives which will be affected when a target is set on the decision objective.   The limits specify the working boundaries of the equations.

DESIRED OPERATION		RELATIONSHIP	LIMITS OF RELATIONSHIP
DECISION OBJECTIVE	CONSEQUENCE OBJECTIVE		
MINIMIZATION $(\leq B'_{0_{acc}})$	MINIMIZATION $(\leq B_{\ell min.})$	$B_{\ell min.} = B'_\ell + R\left[\dfrac{c'_{\ell j}}{c'_{oj}}\right]$ $R = B'_{0_{acc}} - B'_0$	$-B'_0 \leq B'_{0_{acc}} \leq -B'_0 + c'_{oj}\left[\dfrac{b'_i}{a'_{ij}}\right]$
	MAXIMIZATION $(B_{\ell max.})$	$B_{\ell max.} = -B'_\ell + R\left[\dfrac{-c'_{\ell j}}{c'_{oj}}\right]$	
MAXIMIZATION $(\geq B'_{0_{acc}})$	MINIMIZATION $(\leq B_{\ell min.})$	$B_{\ell min.} = B'_\ell + R\left[\dfrac{c'_{\ell j}}{c'_{oj}}\right]$ $R = -B'_{0_{acc}} - B'_0$	$-B'_0 \geq B'_{0_{acc}} \geq -B'_0 + c'_{oj}\left[\dfrac{b'_i}{a'_{ij}}\right]$
	MAXIMIZATION $(\geq B_{\ell max.})$	$B_{\ell max.} = -B'_\ell + R\left[\dfrac{-c'_{\ell j}}{c'_{oj}}\right]$	

NOTATIONS :

0 — decision objective (optimal objective in the intermediate tableau)

ℓ — consequence objective (any lower-priority objective)

R — right-hand side value when the decision objective becomes a constraint

j — column with most negative $C_{\ell j}$, $j = 1, 2, .., n + m + o - 1$

i — row with least $\dfrac{b'_i}{a_{ij}}$

REMARK :

If all C'_{ij}'s are nonnegative, assigning $B_{0_{acc}}$ any value will have no effect on $B_{\ell min.}$ (or $B_{\ell max.}$)

Fig. 4.26   Intermediate Sensitivity Analysis Equations

The equations relating the consequence objective to the decision objective is derived from the concept of leaving variables.   On the other hand, the governing limits to these relationships were obtained from the philosophy of entering variables.

The idea is to choose the most desirable entering variable for each consequence objective and to consider the slack variable associated with the objective-turned-constraint to be the leaving variable.   For this to hold, the right hand side value over the nonzero positive coefficient ratio (i.e. b_j/a_{ij}) of the new constraint must be less than or equal to any other acceptable ratio. Other computations are straightforward as they will only follow the basic iterative rules of the simplex method.   Fig. 4.26 summarizes the resulting relationships.

Example 4.11

A manufacturing firm has discontinued production of a certain unprofitable product type.   In place of this item, the firm plans to produce products 1 and 2.   There are three conflicting goals which enter into consideration namely, revenue maximization, minimization of manpower requirements and minimization of excess capacity in hours.   Raw material availability restricts total production to only 3,000 units per month.   Demand is placed at 4,000 and 6,000 units per month for products 1 and 2, respectively.

The objective functions are stated below in the order of priorities:

$$\text{Minimize} \quad z_1 = 3x_1 + 2x_2 \quad \text{(Thousand manhours/month)}$$
$$\text{Maximize} \quad z_2 = 3x_1 + 5x_2 \quad \text{(Revenue in thousand dollars/month)}$$
$$\text{Minimize} \quad z_3 = 2x_1 - x_2 \quad \text{(Excess capacity in thousand manhours/month)}$$

where x_1 = thousand units of product 1 produced; and
x_2 = thousand units of product 2 produced.

The problem is finding the level of production which will be most satisfactory to the management measured in terms of the above mentioned criteria.

There are only two types of constraints which are to be considered: demand whereby management does not want to produce more than certain limits, and raw material availability:

Demand constraints: $x_1 \leq 4$
$x_2 \leq 6$
Raw material constraint: $x_1 + x_2 \leq 3$
$x_1 , x_2 \geq 0$

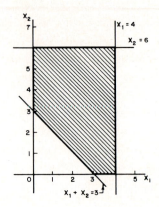

Fig. 4.27a Shaded Area Shows Permissible

Values of (x_1, x_2)

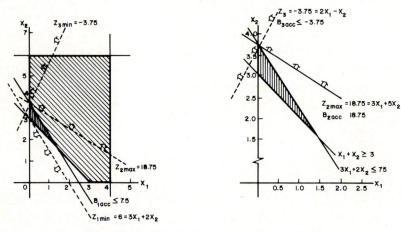

Note : Arrows (⇈) indicate desired movement of objective functions

Fig. 4.27b Cross-hatched Region   Fig. 27c Blow-up of the Cross-hatched

Indicates Remaining Permissible   Section of Fig. 4.27b

Region with $B_{\ell acc} \leq 7.5$

Solution:

It is assumed that each objective aspires to achieve a target $B_{\ell acc}$, $\ell =$ 1, 2, 3, respectively, but which are not known at the outset (Refer to Figs. 4.27a, 4.27b and 4.27c for a graphical representation of the problem).

The initial solution is shown in Table 4.2.

Consider the first objective function (highest priority). The first basic solution in Table 4.11 is infeasible since $x_5 = -3$. The dual simplex algorithm is then applied which seems to be most appropriate, although any feasible seeking procedure may be used. Thus, x_5 leaves and x_2 enters the solution. Applying row operations as usual, the new tableau is shown in Table 4.3.

Table 4.2 Initial Tableau

Status	Basic Var	Coefficients								Equation RHS	Desired Operation
		x_1	x_2	x_3	x_4	x_5	x_6	x_7	x_8		
P_3	z_3	2	-1	0	0	0	0	0	1	0	min.($\leq$)
P_2	z_2	-3	-5	0	0	0	0	1	0	0	max.($\geq$)
P_1	z_1	3	2	0	0	0	1	0	0	0	min.($\leq$)
C_3	x_5	-1	-1	0	0	1	0	0	0	-3	
C_2	x_4	0	1	0	1	0	0	0	0	6	
C_1	x_3	1	0	1	0	0	0	0	0	4	

Table 4.3 Optimal Tableau of the First Objective Function

Status	Basic Var	Coefficients								$-B_\ell/b_i$	Desired Operation
		x_1	x_2	x_3	x_4	x_5	x_6	x_7	x_8		
P_3	z_3	3	0	0	0	-1	0	0	1	3	min.($\leq$)
P_2	z_2	2	0	0	0	-5	0	1	0	15	max.($\geq$)
P_1	z_1	1	0	0	0	2	1	0	0	-6	min.($\leq$)
C_3	x_2	1	1	0	0	-1	0	0	0	3	
C_2	x_4	-1	0	0	1	1	0	0	0	3	
C_1	x_3	1	0	1	0	0	0	0	0	4	

Table 4.3 gives the optimal as well as the feasible solution for the first objective function since all the coefficients of z_1 are nonnegative and the right hand side elements of the constraints are positive. The decision maker learns that the minimum value that could be set for z_1 without violating the constraints is 6, but he should permit some tolerance for the objectives to be

achieved. To aid the decision maker in the goal setting task, an intermediate sensitivity analysis is conducted.

Consider z_1 to be the decision objective. It will be assumed that z_1 will be allowed to take up value equal to or less than that $B_{\ell acc}$ such that B_{1acc} is greater than the minimum value of 6. In so doing, x_6 becomes a basic variable taking a value of $(B_{\ell acc} - 6)$ which is equivalent to the amount of relaxation made.

Table 4.3 shows that x_5 is a potential entering variable and is likely to improve levels of z_2 and z_3. Following the general rule, the leaving variable is selected as the basic variable corresponding to the smallest ratio of the values of the current solution to the positive constraint coefficient of the entering variable. In this case, the leaving variable would be the minimum of $((B_{\ell acc}-6)/2$, $3/1)$ ratios. Since the point of interest is on the effect of the objective turned constraint having a set goal of $B_{\ell acc}$ on the other objective, x_6 will be made the leaving variable. To make this hold true (and prevent an infeasible solution), $(B_{\ell acc}-6)/2 \le 3$ yields $B_{\ell acc} \le 12$. Thus $B_{\ell acc}$ should be equal or less than 12 but greater or equal to 6 ($6 \le B_{\ell acc} \le 12$). Working on the premise that $B_{\ell acc}$ does not take a value exceeding those obtained in the immediate extreme point are the solution sets where the direction of the optimal seeking set is traversing. It could be deduced that the objective turned constraint will be the binding constraint preventing z_2 to achieve a higher maximum. Hence a direct relation exists between $B_{\ell acc}$ and $B_{\ell max}$ and can be derived as

$$-B_{2max} = -15 - (5/2)(B_{\ell acc} - 6)$$
$$B_{2max} = 15 + 2.5\ B_{\ell acc} - 15$$
or $\quad\quad B_{2max} = 2.5\ B_{\ell acc}$
where $\quad 6 \le B_{\ell acc} \le 12$

The effect on z_3 is likewise computed in the same manner. In summary, the following may be obtained (Table 4.4):

Table 4.4   Summary Table

Physical Significance	Basic Var	Desired Operation	Consequence of Setting $z_1 \le B_{\ell acc}$	Limit of Relationship
Add. Manpower Req's	z_1	min ($\le$)	$B_{\ell acc}$	$B_{\ell min} = 6$
Revenue	z_2	max ($\ge$)	$B_{2max} = 2.5\ B_{\ell acc}$	$6 \le B_{\ell acc} \le 12$
Excess capacity	z_3	min ($\le$)	$B_{3min} = -0.5\ B_{\ell acc}$	$6 \le B_{\ell acc} \le 12$

The significance of the above relationship can be better appreciated by the decision maker if presented in a graphical form as shown in Fig. 4.28.

The decision maker studies the consequence of setting a target B_1 in the first objective. He realizes that aspiring for too close to the optimal goal would prejudice the other objectives. Suppose he agrees to set $B_{\ell acc}$ to 7.5. Objective z_1 is included in the set of constraints with a basic variable x_6 and corresponding value of R (right hand side value) equal to 1.5, i.e. 7.5-6. Refer to Fig. 4.27b for the graphical equivalence.

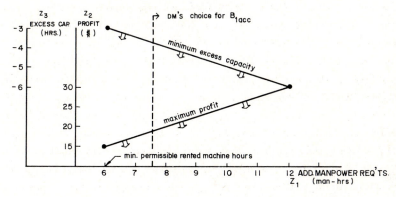

Fig. 4.28   Decision Maker's Guide in Goal Setting for z_1

The next objective function z_2 is considered and the same rules are applied. The variable with the most negative coefficient x_5 is chosen as the entering variable and x_6 is chosen as the leaving variable. After the first iteration, Table 4.5 would be:

Table 4.5 Optimal Tableau

Status	Basic Var	Coefficients								$-B_\ell / b_i$	Desired Operation
		x_1	x_2	x_3	x_4	x_5	x_6	x_7	x_8		
P_3	z_3	3.5	0	0	0	0	0.5	0	1	3.75	min. ($\leq$)
P_2	z_2	4.5	0	0	0	0	2.5	1	0	18.75	max. ($\geq$)
C_4	x_5	0.5	0	0	0	1	0.5	0	0	0.75	
C_3	x_2	1.5	1	0	0	0	0.5	0	0	3.75	
C_2	x_4	-1.5	0	0	1	0	-0.5	0	0	2.25	
C_1	x_3	1.0	0	1	0	0	0.0	0	0	4.00	

It will be observed that all C_{3j}'s are nonnegative. This indicates that assigning B_{2acc} any value would have no effect on B_{3min}. This further indicates that z_3 is already minimum. Hence, B_{2acc} takes the minimum permissible value which is 18.75 while B_{3acc} takes the minimum permissible value of -3.75. The solution set would be: $x_1 = 0$, $x_2 = 3.75$, $x_3 = 4.0$, $x_4 = 2.25$, $x_5 = 0.75$ and $x_6 = 0$. $B_{\ell acc}$ takes a value of $3(0) + 2(3.75) = 7.5$ which the decision maker has actually agreed to set (Fig. 4.27c).

The ISCOC method is not a catch-all technique to all multicriterion optimization problems. It is most useful for goal attainment problem where the decision maker does not have a clear idea of the permissible goals in the "interactions" of these goals.

4.6   COMPROMISE PROGRAMMING

Zeleny's (1973, 1974, 1982) version of compromise programming is similar to other distance-based techniques. It is looking for the best compromise solution that would result in the minimum deviation from the ideal solution.

In compromise programming what is of interest is the comparison of distances of different efficient points (x^{ℓ}, $\ell = 1, 2, \ldots, m$) from the ideal solution which is the point of reference. Given an ideal point x^{*}, the distance of the various points x^k from this ideal, given n attributes measured along n coordinates, can be generalized into the following expression:

$$d_p = \left[\sum_{i=1}^{n} \left[w_i (x_i^{*} - x_i^{\ell}) \right]^p \right]^{1/p} \qquad \ell = 1, 2, \ldots, m \qquad (4.51)$$

The individual deviations $(x_i^{*} - x_i^{\ell})$ can be raised to any power ($p = 1, 2, \ldots, \infty$) before they are summed, and also the weights w_i ($0 < w_i < 1$ and $\sum_i w_i = 1$) can be attached to the different deviations.

For p approaching ∞, the distance measure reduces to the following expression:

$$d_{p \to \infty} = \underset{i}{\text{Max}} \left\{ \left| w_i (x_i^{*} - x_i^{\ell}) \right| \right\} \qquad \begin{array}{l} i = 1, 2, \ldots, n; \\ \ell = 1, 2, \ldots, m. \end{array}$$

This is because the relative contribution of the largest deviation when raised to a large exponent would be extremely larger than all the rest combined, and thus dominates the distance determination. A $p = 1$ implies the "longest" distance between two points in a geometric sense while $p = 2$ measures the shortest distance between any two points in a straight line. For $0 \leq p < 1$, the treatment of the deviations are reduced more while the smaller ones less until for p = 0, all deviations are equal to 1. For negative values of p, the smaller deviations make increasingly larger contributions until for p approaching ∞, the smallest of the deviations completely dominates the distance determination.

When objectives are of different dimensions, the distance measure needs to be corrected to make the individual objectives mutually commensurable. It is therefore necessary to use relative rather than absolute deviations. This can be represented by the following expression:

$$d_p = \left[\sum_{i=1}^{n} \left[w_i \cdot \frac{x_i^* - x_i^\ell}{x_i^*} \right]^p \right]^{1/p} \qquad\qquad \ell = 1, 2, \ldots, m \qquad (4.52)$$

For some choice of weights w_i and p, the compromise solution is the one obtained by minimizing the distance measure d_p subject to the given set of constraints.

For a multiobjective problem, the ideal point is defined by the vector of the individual ideal solutions, $Z^* = [f_1^*, \ldots, f_k^*]$, and therefore the overall multiobjective minimizing objective function can be expressed as follows:

$$d_p = \left[\sum_{\ell=1}^{k} \left[w_\ell \cdot \frac{f_\ell^* - f_\ell(x)}{f_\ell^*} \right]^p \right]^{1/p} \qquad\qquad (4.53)$$

where w_ℓ are weights of the objectives, and f_ℓ^* are the individual optimal solution. It should be noted that when p = 1, the compromise programming technique is equivalent to the global criterion method discussed earlier.

Example 4.12

The following two objective functions are to be maximized:

Maximize: $f_1(x) = 5 x_1 - 2 x_2$
             $f_2(x) = - x_1 + 4 x_2$

Subject to: $- x_1 + x_2 \leq 3$
              $x_1 + x_2 \leq 8$
              $x_1 \qquad \leq 6$
              $x_2 \leq 4$
              $x_1, \quad x_2 \geq 0$

Fig. 4.29 shows the set of efficient solutions which is indicated by the heavily traced boundary of the feasible region X. x^* is the ideal solution at

which the two objective functions would attain their maxima.   The ideal
solutions of the individual objective functions are $Z_1^* = 30$, $x^{1*} = (6, 0)$;
$Z_2^* = 30$, $x^{2*} = (1, 4)$.   The ideal point x^* is at $(8.333, 5.833)$.

At any efficient solution, we determine how close we are to the ideal
solution by using the measure of distance discussed earlier:

$$d_p = \left[\sum_{\ell=1}^{k} \left[w_\ell \cdot \frac{f_\ell^* - f_\ell(x)}{f_\ell^*} \right]^p \right]^{1/p}$$

As a simple illustration, we assume that the two objective functions have
equal weights and $p = 1$.   The compromise programming solution is at $x = (4, 4)$,
where $Z_1 = 12$, $Z_2 = 12$, and the minimum distance d_1 equals to 0.8.

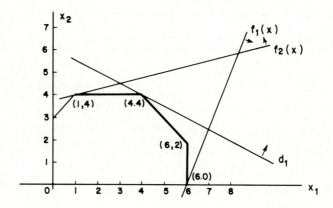

Fig. 4.29 An Example of Compromise Programming

4.7   ELECTRE APPROACH

4.7.1   ELECTRE I

ELECTRE I, Roy (1968), is an interactive multiple criteria decision making
technique designed to handle qualitative and discrete alternatives, to handle
situations where the decision maker can only give a priori preference information on a local level and to give a ranking of the finite number of alternatives.

The basic concept in ELECTRE I is to choose those alternatives which are
preferred for most of the criteria and yet do not cause an unacceptable level

of discontent for any one criterion.   These two aforementioned basic ideas of ELECTRE I necessitate the development of three concepts: one to handle the preference of one alternative to another for any one criterion; a second concept to measure the level of discontent for any one criterion; and a third concept to serve as measure of the decision maker's preference and discontent. These concepts are elaborated as follows:

(i)   Concordance.   For any two alternatives k and ℓ, this concept is a weighted measure of the number of criteria for which alternative k is preferred over   alternative ℓ (denoted k P ℓ)   or for which alternative k is equal to alternative ℓ (denoted k E ℓ).

(ii) Discordance.   This concept handles the set of criteria for which k is not preferred over ℓ and gives a measure of the degree of "discomfort or discontent" as a result of preferring alternative k to alternative ℓ.

(iii) Threshold values.   These are values p and q, between zero and one, defined by the decision maker to quantify the degree of concordance he wants (value of p) and the amount of discordance he can tolerate (value of q).

Aside from the above concepts, the weights of the criteria, w(i) for i = 1, ..., I (where I is the number of criteria) is quantified and given a priori by the decision maker, and these weights do not change during the algorithm.

The steps of the method of this technique are the following:

(i)   Select the weights w(i), for i = 1, ..., I.   The decision makers may be asked or, if not available, a set of weights is chosen and the algorithm is run for each set of weights.

(ii) For each pair (k $\neq$ ℓ) of the alternatives,   the concordance index C(k,ℓ) is computed by the use of the following equation,

$$C(k,\ell) = \frac{\sum\limits_{i \in S} w(i)}{\sum\limits_{i} w(i)} \qquad\qquad S = \{i \,|\, k \text{ P } \ell \text{ or } k \text{ E } \ell\} \qquad (4.54)$$

The set S is the union of the set of criteria for which alternative k is preferred over alternative ℓ and the set of criteria for which k is equal to ℓ. The weights of the criteria in this set are summed up and divided by the sum of the weights of all criteria.

(iii) The discordance index is computed through the following sub-steps: (1) Define an interval scale which will be common to all criteria; (2) Define a range for the interval scale which may be different for each criterion with the "best" rating having the highest value and the "worst" rating having the lowest value of the range; (3) Evaluate for each criterion each of the alternatives and assign the corresponding rating ($f_i(x_j)$) or range value as defined in the interval scale for the criterion; and (4) For each pair ($k \neq \ell$) of alternatives, the discordance index is computed by the use of the following equation,

$$D(k,\ell) = \frac{\max_i \{f_i(x_\ell) - f_i(x_k)\}}{R^*} \tag{4.55}$$

where $f_i(x_k)$ = evaluation of alternative x_k with respect to criterion f_i,

$f_i(x_\ell)$ = evaluation of alternative x_ℓ with respect to criterion f_i,

R^* = largest range of the I criterion scales.

(iv)   The decision maker should specify the values of p and q.

(v)   For each pair ($k \neq \ell$) check the inequalities

$$C(k,\ell) \geq p \quad \text{and} \quad D(d,\ell) \leq q \tag{4.56}$$

If both of the inequalities hold, then in the partial ordering, alternative k is preferred to alternative ℓ.   Otherwise there is no preference order between k and ℓ.

(vi)   Construct the preference graph, where the nodes are the alternatives 1, ..., k and the directed arcs show the preferences among the alternatives.

(vii) Ask the decision maker, whether he/she is satisfied with this partial ordering, i.e., whether a decision can be made with this partial ordering.   If the answer is yes, then the algorithm terminates, and if the answer is no, then go back to (iv) where the decision maker specifies the values of p and q, this time relaxed values of p and q are specified.

The result of ELECTRE I is a preference graph which presents a partial ordering of the alternative systems.   ELECTRE II which is discussed in the next subsection aims at outranking "completely" the different alternatives of the problem.

4.7.2 ELECTRE II

In the ELECTRE I technique, the necessary and sufficient conditions that determine whether one alternative is preferred over another (and thus their ordering) is given by equation (4.56) which may result in just a partial ordering, i.e., there may be cases there the algorithm does not give a preference relationship between two alternatives.   In the ELECTRE II algorithm, Roy and Bertier (1971), complete ordering is accomplished through the introduction of the concepts of strong and weak ranking relationship and the delineation of high, average and low concordance, and high and average discordance.

The concordance condition for the pair of alternatives (k, ℓ) is defined by:

$$C(k,\ell) = \frac{W^+(k,\ell) + W^=(k,\ell)}{W^+(k,\ell) + W^=(k,\ell) + W^-(k,\ell)} \geq p \qquad (4.57)$$

and $$W^+(k,\ell) \geq W^-(k,\ell) \qquad (4.58)$$

where $W^+(k,\ell)$ = sum of weights for which k is "better" than (preferred to) ℓ,

$W^=(k,\ell)$ = sum of weights for which k is "indifferent" to (equal to) ℓ,

$W^-(k,\ell)$ = sum of weights for which k is "worse" than ℓ.

By defining three decreasing levels of concordance threshold values, p^*, p^0 and p^- ($1 \geq p^* \geq p^0 \geq p^-$) which we can call "high", "average" and "low", the following types of concordance can be defined,

1. High concordance given by
$$C(k,\ell) \geq p^* \qquad (4.59)$$
2. Average concordance given by
$$C(k,\ell) \geq p^0 \qquad (4.60)$$
3. Low concordance give by
$$C(k,\ell) \geq p^- \qquad (4.61)$$

In all cases, equation (4.58) should likewise hold.

For any pair of alternatives (k, ℓ), the discordance is given by equation (4.55). By defining two discordance threshold values, q^* and q^0 which we can call a "high" and "average" respectively, the following types of discordance spaces can be defined:

1. Low discordance given by
$$D(k,\ell) \leq q^* \qquad (4.62)$$
2. Average discordance given by
$$q^0 < D(k,\ell) \leq q^* \qquad (4.63)$$
3. High discordance give by
$$q^* < D(k,\ell) \qquad (4.64)$$

In the ranking procedure, two types of ranking relationship concept is introduced and these are the strong relationship S_F and the weak relationship

S_f. The results of these two types of relationship are two preference graphs-
a strong preference graph and a weak preference graph.   The strong and weak
outranking are defined as follows:

(a)   k strongly outranks ℓ if

   (i) the concordance is high and the discordance is average, or

   (ii) the concordance is average and the discordance is low.

(b)   k weakly outranks ℓ if

   (i) both concordance and discordance are low,

   (ii) both concordance and discordance are average.

These two binary relations, (a) and (b), define, respectively, two graphs.
Let all loops or closed paths be eliminated from the graph associated with S_F,
which defines a reduced graph $G_F = (Y, U_F)$, in which the set of nodes Y
corresponds to the set of alternatives X, and the set of arcs U_F to relations
(a).   More precisely, an arc (k,ℓ) is in U_F if and only if k is strongly
preferred to ℓ.   The elimination of closed paths clusters all nodes along a
loop into one class: this operation is called reduction of the graph.   Next, a
graph G_f is defined by the use of the weak outranking relationship S_f.

The ranking procedure consists of a forward ranking, a reverse ranking and
an average ranking.

Forward ranking r'

Define the ranking r' by use of the following iterative scheme:

1.   Start with k=1 and let Y(k=1) = Y (the set of all alternatives) and
      Y(k) be a subgraph of Y, i.e., in the first iteration Y(k) will just
      by Y.

2.   Working from G_F (the graph of strong outranking) select all nodes in
      Y(k) not having a precedent or an incoming arrow (i.e., management
      alternatives which are not strongly outranked by other elements).
      Denote this set of nondominated alternatives by Z(k).

3.   Next, use G_f (the graph of weak outranking) to remove as many ties
      as possible between alternatives in Z(k).   For this purpose, look
      for the set of arcs in U_f with both extremities in Z(k); call this
      set X_f.   Construct the graph (Z(k), X_f).

4.   Select all nodes of (Z(k), X_f) not having a precedent: denote this
      set, which corresponds to the set of nondominated solutions at
      iteration k, by A(k).   The set A(k) consists of all nodes having no
      precedent in either G_F or G_f.

5.   Rank x (the alternative) as: r'(x) = k for every x $\in$ A(k) (i.e.,

every element of the set A(k) will have rank k).

6.   Determine Y(k+1) = Y(k) - A(k) and delete all arcs emanating from A(k).   This removes alternatives that have been ranked in the previous iteration.   If Y(k+1) is an empty set, then all represen- tative elements in the reduced graph of S_F have been ranked.   If Y(k+1) is not empty then set k = k+1 and go to step 2.

Reverse ranking r"

1.   Reverse the direction of the arcs U_F of G_F and U_f of G_f so as to obtain a mirror image of the direct outranking relationship.

2.   Obtain a ranking $\alpha(x)$ on these new graphs by use of the steps in the forward ranking.

3.   Reestablish the correct ranking order by setting:

$$r''(x) = 1 + \max \alpha(x) - \alpha(x) \qquad (4.65)$$

Average ranking r^

In order to define a final ranking r^ use the following relation

$$r^\wedge(x) = [r'(x) + r''(x)]/2 \qquad (4.66)$$

Example 4.13   (Example of Ranking Procedure)

Consider the strong and weak relationship graphs shown in Fig. 30a and 30b, respectively.   Since there are no cycles, then there is no need to reduce the graphs and G_F and G_f will just be S_F and S_f, respectively.   The ranking procedure will be as follows:

Forward ranking
      First Iteration:
1.   k = 1   Y(1) = G_F
2.   Z(1) = {1,2,3}
3. X_f = {(2,3)}
4.   A(1) = {1,2}
5.   Ranking: r'(1) = r'(2) = 1
6.   Y(k+1) = Y(2) = Y(1) - A(1)
             = {3,4,5,6,7,8,9} ≠ φ
      hence continue k = k+1 = 2
         and Y(2) = {3,4,5,6,7,8,9}

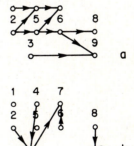

Fig. 4.30 First Iteration

Second Iteration:

2. $Z(2) = \{3,4,5\}$

3. $X_f = \{(4,3)\}$

4. $A(2) = \{4,5\}$

5.   Ranking: $r'(4) = r'(5) = 2$

6. $Y(3) = Y(2) - A(2)$

           $= \{3,6,7,8,9\} \neq \phi$

       hence continue $k = k+1 = 3$.

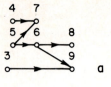

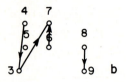

Fig. 4.31   Second Iteration

Third Iteration:

2. $Z(3) = \{3,6,7\}$

3. $U_f = \{(3,7), (6,7)\}$

4. $A(3) = \{3,6\}$

5.   Ranking: $r'(3) = r'(6) = 3$

6. $Y(4) = Y(3) - A(3)$

           $= \{7,8,9\} \neq \phi$

       hence continue $k = k+1 = 4$

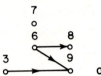

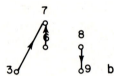

Fig. 4.32   Third Iteration

Fourth Iteration:

2. $Z(4) = \{7,8,9\}$

3. $U_f = \{8,9\}$

4. $A(3) = \{3,6\}$

5.   Ranking: $r'(3) = r'(6) = 3$

6. $Y(4) = Y(3) - A(3) = \{7,8,9\} \neq \phi$ hence continue $k = k+1 = 5$

Fifth Iteration: The fifth iteration yields simply $r'(9) = 5$.

Reverse ranking

1.   Reverse the arcs U_F of G_F and U_f of G_f to obtain, respectively, the
       graphs shown in Fig. 4.33.

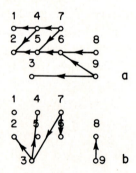

Fig. 4.33   Reverse Ranking

2.   Using the same procedure as in the forward ranking, the following
     ranking $\alpha(x)$ is obtained:

Node	1	2	3	4	5	6	7	8	9
$\alpha(x)$	4	5	2	3	4	3	1	2	1

3.   Reverse the ranking using equation (4.65), with max $\alpha(x)$ = 5, to
     obtain:

Node	1	2	3	4	5	6	7	8	9
$r''(x)$	2	1	4	3	2	3	5	4	5

Average ranking

Using equation (4.66), the average ranking is computed:

Node	1	2	3	4	5	6	7	8	9
$r'(x)$	1	1	3	2	2	3	4	4	5
$r''(x)$	2	1	4	3	2	3	5	4	5
$r^{\wedge}(x)$	1.5	1	3.5	2.5	2	3	4.5	4	5

The final ranking in decreasing order of preference is
                     2,1,5,4,6,3,8,7,9.

In summary, the following advantages may be advanced for the ELECTRE
technique: The technique can handle nonquantifiable criteria; it requires only
an interval scale as compared to cardinal scales required by other techniques;
it is responsive to the preference structure of the decision maker, in that it
considers both his contentment and discontent; and it requires only a priori
articulation of preference at a local level.

Some disadvantages of the technique include the following: It requires a
large set of "a priori" parameters from the decision maker (ELECTRE II),
weights and threshold values; the concepts of concordance and discordance and
the quantification procedure may not be that concrete and appealing to the
decision maker; and for a large number of alternatives the preference graphs
become complicated and difficult to interpret.

4.8 PARAMETRIC APPROACH

There are situations whereby the decision maker's articulation of preference information is not made available a priori or even progressively during the
process. This is true in many real life situations and the analyst has to come

up with some solutions for the decision maker whose involvement will only come
into real play at the end of the process.

There can be a large number of possible solutions, hence the computational
process can be very tedious. It is therefore necessary to reduce this solution
set by only looking at efficient points and, whenever possible, reduce them
further into a smaller subset by introducing some new criteria. The analyst
presents this subset of efficient solutions to the decision maker who would
then choose the must satisfactory solution from this subset after incorporating
his preference on the objectives a posteriori. Hence parametric approach is
also known as the "a posteriori articulation of preference information"
approach.

The fact that the approach does not require any assumption or information
regarding the decision maker's utility function can be considered an advantage.
But its main disadvantage in many cases is that it generates a large number of
efficient solutions and that it becomes very difficult for the decision maker
to choose one which is the most satisfactory. To overcome this main drawback,
the methods are usually linked to some interactive procedures.

For a linear case the algorithms used for generating efficient solutions
are basically variations or extensions of the simplex method; these variations
being mainly cutting the computational effort. For a linear case, for example,
one method usually used is by introducing a parameter into a unified objective
function, say:

$$\text{Maximize:} \qquad \sum_{\ell=1}^{k} w_\ell f_\ell(x) \qquad\qquad (4.67)$$

$$\text{Subject to:} \qquad x \in X$$

In this case w_ℓ do not represent weights of the objectives, they are merely
parameters which are varied between 0 and 1 to generate a set or subset of
efficient solutions. A systematic variation of w_ℓ would result in the generation of a complete efficient solution set if the feasible region is convex.
There are other parametric techniques available which are listed in the
bibliography at the end of this chapter.

4.9   DE NOVO PROGRAMMING

Zeleny (1976, 1982, 1986) suggests a way of looking at a system; instead
of "optimizing a given system" he suggests "designing an optimal system". He
labels the latter as the De Novo Programming approach, which is immensely

desirable in optimal design of high productivity systems with multiple criteria. In this section the presentation of De Novo programming is made using the
product mix problem as an illustrative case.

4.9.1 THEORETICAL FOUNDATIONS

4.9.1.1 Formulation

Traditional single objective linear programming models used for product
mix optimization consist of an objective function and resource constraints.
They are formulated as:

$$\text{Maximize:} \qquad Z = c_1 x_1 + c_2 x_2 + \ldots + c_n x_n \qquad\qquad (4.68)$$

$$\text{Subject to:} \qquad a_{11}x_1 + a_{12}x_2 + \ldots + a_{1n}x_n \leq b_1 \qquad\qquad (4.69)$$
$$a_{21}x_1 + a_{22}x_2 + \ldots + a_{2n}x_n \leq b_2$$
$$\vdots \qquad\qquad \vdots \qquad\qquad\qquad \vdots$$
$$a_{m1}x_1 + a_{m2}x_2 + \ldots + a_{mn}x_n \leq b_m$$
$$x_j \geq 0$$

where x_j = set of decision variables under consideration with each x_j
representing a level of activity;

Z = measure of benefit or objective achievement;

c_j = coefficient of contribution to objective given a level of
activity j;

a_{ij} = level of usage of resource i by activity j;

b_i = given availability of resource i.

This type of formulation involves a decision in level of activities, or in
the context of this section, a product mix. Through the given set of constraints and the availability of resources b_i, the orderly arrangement of
resources and their availability are assumed to have been determined separately.

The De Novo formulation considers the problem of optimization in a total
systems approach. The model comes in the following form:

Maximize: $Z = c_1 x_1 + c_2 x_2 + \ldots + c_n x_n$ (4.70)

Subject to: $a_{11}x_1 + a_{12}x_2 + \ldots + a_{1n}x_n = x_{n+1}$ (4.71)

$a_{21}x_1 + a_{22}x_2 + \ldots + a_{2n}x_n = x_{n+2}$

$$. \qquad . \qquad\qquad . \qquad .$$

$$. \qquad . \qquad\qquad . \qquad .$$

$a_{m1}x_1 + a_{m2}x_2 + \ldots + a_{mn}x_n = x_{n+m}$

$P_1 x_{n+1} + P_2 x_{n+2} + \ldots + P_m x_{n+m} \leq B$ (4.72)

$$x_j, \ x_{n+1} \geq 0$$

where x_{n+i} = set of decision variables representing the level of resource i
to be purchased;

P_i = price of each unit of resource b_i;

B   = total available budget for the system.

The main difference of the two models lie in the treatment of the
resources, these being decision variables x_{n+i} in the De Novo formulation.
The model determines the best mix of not only the output, but also the
combination of inputs still to be acquired.   It is a design of an optimal
system as against the optimization of a given system.   Furthermore, it gives an
integrated and compact idea of utilized resources through the "budget".

Solving the De Novo model can be made simpler by the substitution of x_{n+i}
equations (4.71) into the budget equation (4.72).   Given the market price, P_i
for resource i, let

$P_1 a_{1j} + P_2 a_{2j} + \ldots + P_m a_{mj} = v_j,$ for all j   (4.73)

v_j, therefore, represents the unit variable cost of producing product j.
Using v_j, we can formulate the De Novo model into:

Maximize: $Z = c_1 x_1 + c_2 x_2 + \ldots + c_n x_n$ (4.74)

Subject to: $v_1 x_1 + v_2 x_2 + \ldots + v_n x_n \leq B$ (4.75)

$$x_j \geq 0$$

If there are no other constraints, solving the simplified model is easy
with one objective and one constraint involved.   It clearly resembles that of a
knapsack problem.   The solution procedure would be:

(i) Find $\underset{j}{\text{Max}} \ (c_j/v_j)$.

The ratio (c_j/v_j) represents the profitability of product j (if the objective function is to maximize profit) or the rate of objective achievement per unit cost of the combination of resources used to produce product j. This step searches for the most profitable product.

(ii) For Max (c_j/v_j), say (c_k/v_k) corresponding to x_k, the amount
           j
      of x_k to be produced would be $x_k^* = B/v_j$.

This implies that all our resources will be used to produce the most profitable product x_k, the amount of which will be dictated by the budget in the absence of any other constraints.

If demand limits apply to each product x_j, then De Novo formulation can be solved in the following manner:

(i)   Find Max (c_j/v_j)
            j
(ii)   For Max (c_j/v_j), say (c_k/v_k), produce x_k such that it does not
            j
       exceed the demand limit, or the maximum allowed by the budget.
(iii) If the budget is not used up in producing x_k, select the next
       profitable product Max (c_j/v_j), where $j \neq k$.
                            j
(iv)   Go back to step (ii) until the budget is used up.

The De Novo formulation differs with the traditional product mix models in the following aspects:

(i) Product mix models assume that resources are limited to predetermined amounts. Analysis in availability of additional resources is performed through duality theory and sensitivity analysis. Resources with dual variables greater than zero can be increased at a cost less than the shadow price.

The assumption of "unlimited" resources in De Novo programming does not mean that any amount of resources can be purchased. Rather, it assumes that the supply of resources is more than what the system would require at its maximum. Resources are actually limited because the maximum quantities are governed by the budget which is an important element of De Novo. In effect, as long as the supply of each resource exceeds the ratio of budget over price (B/p_1), this assumption is satisfied.

(ii) De Novo assumes the analysis is made before resources are purchased, still controllable and are not yet fixed. Furthermore, resources are assumed to be divisible, and can be purchased at any desired amount no matter how little they may be. The mix of resources can be controlled; and procured in any combination necessary.   The product mix model does not have any strict assumptions governing the acquisition of resources.   Some resources may have to be purchased at minimum lot sizes as in facility or machine capacities.   Both models, however, assume that usage of these resources are proportional and additive in nature.

(iii)   Product mix models are not sensitive to price factor of the resources.   The concept of pricing of resources only comes in during post optimality and duality analyses.   Resources with surplus are considered "free" goods, with shadow prices equal to zero, because additional acquisition of such resources would not increase profit.   Resources in limited quantities and are fully utilized have shadow prices.   These shadow prices are the additional profit that may be obtained per unit increase in the availability of these resources.

In De Novo, resources are given their corresponding prices based on the actual procurement costs.   Pricing is an input to the model rather than being an output.   The model is factor price sensitive.   Because resources will be purchased at exact quantities, there are no unintentional surplus of resources.

Based on Zeleny (1976), all slack variables (resource surplus) are zero in De Novo programming.   All shadow prices are positive and there are no "free" goods.   Because all resources are properly valued based on their actual costs, the whole concept of duality and its use in the post optimality analysis loses its significance.   There is no need to analyze the marginal impact of marginal changes in individual resources.

(iv)   An important feature of De Novo lies in the budget constraint. This is a single, integrating expression of the portfolio of resources.   It serves as the common denominator or measure of committed or required resources. It acts as the upper limit to the level of activities.

The product mix models do not always have the budget constraint.   At times, it is more difficult to grasp the significance of the portfolio of resources since each resource is expressed in its own unit of measure and there is no single measure of the total value of all resources.

(v)   The De Novo solution comes up with fully utilized resources, no waste or slacks.   Some types of resources may be made available in additional safety or buffer amounts, but, this aspect is handled by adding differentially determined safety percentages to the resources and they normally are not part of the results of the model.   As an optimal design is completed, and levels of desirable resources established, proper levels of spare machine capacities, buffer stocks, safety cash, and other safety additions are then provided.

4.9.1.2 Special Characteristics

Results of the pure De Novo models have the following characteristics:

(1)   In case of unlimited demand for the end products with price constant, De Novo leads to a system designed to produce one single most profitable product.

(2)   The product mix is not sensitive to the budget change; only the amount changes, if there are no demand limits. Increasing the budget simply increases the production of x_k, the most profitable product.

(3)   In case of limited demand for the end products, the variety of production evolves according to the De Novo recommendation - start with the most profitable product, produce as much of it as possible, move to the next profitable product and go on until the budget is used up. Depending on the structure of the demand limits, the product mix builds up as budget is increased.

Numerical Example:

Consider the following linear programming model with three products and three types of resources:

$$\text{Maximize:} \quad z = 25\ x_1 + 10\ x_2 + 18\ x_3 \quad \text{(profit)}$$

$$\begin{aligned}
\text{Subject to:} \quad & 2\ x_1 + 1.5\ x_2 + 1.2\ x_3 \le 400 && \text{(resource 1)} \\
& x_1 + 1.5\ x_2 + 2\ \ \ x_3 \le 500 && \text{(resource 2)} \\
& x_1 + \ \ \ x_2 + \ \ \ x_3 \le 300 && \text{(resource 3)} \\
& x_1,\ x_2,\ x_3 \ge 0
\end{aligned}$$

The above problem can be solved using the simplex method giving the results:

$$x_1{}^* = 71.43, \quad x_2{}^* = 0.0, \quad x_3{}^* = 214.29, \quad z^* = \$5,642.97$$

Suppose the prices of the resources were found out to be $p_1 = \$20$, $p_2 = \$10$ and $p_3 = \$40$, then the total cost of the resources, if predetermined by some other methods and purchased at the indicated amounts, would be:

$$400\ (\$20) + 500\ (\$10) + 300\ (\$40) = \$25,000$$

If purchasing additional resources or altering the mix of resources would be possible, then De Novo takes the amount of raw materials to be purchased as part of the decision variables and formulates the problem as follows:

Maximize: $z = 25\ x_1 + 10\ x_2 + 18\ x_3$ (profit)

Subject to: $2\ \ x_1 + \ \ 1.5\ x_2 + \ \ 1.2\ x_3 \leq x_4$ (resource 1)

$\qquad\qquad\ \ x_1 + \ \ 1.5\ x_2 + \ \ 2\ \ \ \ x_3 \leq x_5$ (resource 2)

$\qquad\qquad\ \ x_1 + \qquad x_2 + \qquad\ x_3 \leq x_6$ (resource 3)

$\qquad\ 20\ x_1 + 10\ \ \ \ x_2 + 40\ \ \ \ x_3 \leq 25000$ (budget)

$\qquad\qquad x_1,\ x_2,\ x_3,\ x_4,\ x_5,\ x_6 \geq 0$

Note that the variable cost of each product can be computed as follows:

$$v_1 = 2\ \ (\$20) + 1\ \ (\$10) + 1(\$40) = \$90$$
$$v_2 = 1.5(\$20) + 1.5(\$10) + 1(\$40) = \$85$$
$$v_3 = 1.2(\$20) + 2\ \ (\$10) + 1(\$40) = \$84$$

Finding the Max (c_j/v_j) to be $(25/90)$ for x_1, the optimal solution is x_1^* = $25000/90 = 277.78$. Thus, the optimal raw material and end product mix would be:

$$x_1^* = 277.78,\ x_4^* = 555.56,\ x_5^* = 277.78,\ x_6^* = 277.78,\ z^* = \$6,944.5$$

The value of the objective function increased from the previous $\$5,642.97$ to $\$6,944.5$ by altering the mix of resources using the same amount of fund, $\$25,000$.

By substituting the resource equations x_4, x_5 and x_6 into the budget equation, we get the equivalent formulation:

Maximize: $z = 25\ x_1 + 10\ x_2 + 18\ x_3$

Subject to: $90\ x_1 + 85\ x_2 + 84\ x_3 \leq 25000$

$\qquad\qquad\qquad x_1,\ x_2,\ x_3 \geq 0$

Suppose the demand for the products are limited to 200 for each product. The result of the product mix model still applies; however, the solution of the De Novo formulation would have to be revised.

Producing 200 units of x_1 would require a budget of $\$18,000$ (i.e. $(\$90)(200))$, leaving a remaining fund of $\$7,000$. The money can be used to produce the next most profitable product x_3 at a quantity of 83.33 (i.e. $\$7,000/\$84)$. The complete solution set would be:

Production   :   200 units of x_1

$\qquad\qquad\qquad\quad$:   83.33 units of x_3

Resource acquisition :   500 units of resource 1 (x_4)

$\qquad\qquad\qquad\quad$:   366.67 units of resource 2 (x_5)

                                    :   283.33 units of resource 3 (x_6)

                                    :   with \$25,000 budget

        Profit   :   \$6,500.00

4.9.2   EFFECTS OF MULTIPLE PRICING

Linear programming models may at times be difficult to apply in actual
business setting because of its assumption of proportionality.   One common
phenomenon encountered is multiple pricing of resources or end products.
Companies may have more than one source of raw materials at different costs, or
quantity discounts being offered for volume purchases, or prices of their goods
going down because of high volume of goods sold.

4.9.2.1   Increasing Cost of Raw Materials

Increasing cost formulation is the simplest form of step function that can
be incorporated into De Novo.   Let us take the simple model

$$\text{Maximize:} \qquad Z = c_1 x_1 + c_2 x_2 \tag{4.76}$$

$$\text{Subject to:} \qquad a_{11} x_1 + a_{12} x_2 = b_1 \tag{4.77}$$

$$a_{21} x_1 + a_{22} x_2 = b_2 \tag{4.78}$$

$$p_1 \; b_1 + p_2 \; b_2 \le B \tag{4.79}$$

$$x_j \, , \; b_1 \ge 0$$

Let p_2 holds only for $b_2 < Q$, where Q is the quantity where the price breaks,
and $p_3 > p_2$ applies for quantities of b_2 over and above Q.   The new model that
can be formulated to take this increasing cost into consideration is as
follows:

Let b_3 = the amount of second type of resource to be purchased from the
              expensive source; and

      p_3 = the price of resource type 2 from the expensive source.

$$\text{Maximize:} \qquad Z = s_1 \; x_1 + s_2 \; x_2 - (p_1 b_1 + p_2 b_2 + p_3 b_3) \tag{4.80}$$

$$\text{Subject to:} \qquad a_{11} x_1 + a_{12} x_2 = b_1 \tag{4.81}$$

$$a_{21} x_1 + a_{22} x_2 = b_2 + b_3 \tag{4.82}$$

$$p_1 b_1 + p_2 b_2 + p_3 b_3 \le B \tag{4.83}$$

$$b_2 \le Q \tag{4.84}$$

$$x_j, \; b_i \ge 0$$

where s_j is the selling price of product j; and other variables having the same
interpretation.

The following notes may be made regarding the new model:

i)   The new model separates the use of the second type of raw material into two variables, b_2 from the cheaper source and b_3 from the more expensive source.   Eqs. (4.78) and (4.79) are revised into Eqs. (4.82) and (4.83) to reflect the different sourcing and costs.

ii)   Since raw materials are of different costs, variable prices of end product are not constant anymore.   Therefore, maximizing the sum of $c_j x_j$, would not be an accurate measure of profit.   Rather, profit equation, Eq. (4.76), should be recalculated by sales less total cost of materials, Eq. (4.80).

iii)   There is no need to specify that b_2 should reach the maximum value of Q first, before allowing $b_3 > 0$.   The optimization model ensures b_2 reaching the maximum value of Q first because of the lower penalty, p_2.

iv)   If the budget is used up, De Novo maximization of revenue and profit are equivalent.   Consider the objective function Eq. (4.80).

$$\text{Maximize:} \qquad Z = s_1 \, x_1 + s_2 \, x_2 - (p_1 b_1 + p_2 b_2 + p_3 b_3)$$

If $(p_1 b_1 + p_2 b_2 + p_3 b_3)$ is constant, then the objective function reduces to:

$$\text{Maximize:} \qquad Z = s_1 \, x_1 + s_2 \, x_2 \qquad\qquad\qquad (4.85)$$

Maximizing revenue and profit are complementary under the De Novo full budget utilization.

4.9.2.2 Quantity Discounts

Quantity discounts offered for volume purchases may be formulated in a simple model as follows.

$$\begin{aligned}
\text{Maximize:} \qquad & Z = s_1 \, x_1 + s_2 \, x_2 & (4.86)\\
\text{Subject to:} \qquad & a_{11} \, x_1 + a_{12} \, x_2 = b_1 & (4.87)\\
& a_{21} \, x_1 + a_{22} \, x_2 = b_2 & (4.88)\\
& p_1 \, b_1 + p_2 \, b_2 \le B & (4.89)\\
& x_j \, , \, b_1 \ge 0 &
\end{aligned}$$

For b_2, p_2 applies for $b_2 < Q$, and p_3 applies to the whole quantity purchased if $b_2 \ge Q$, where $p_3 < p_2$.

The previous formulation is not applicable since the optimization model will prefer using the less expensive material without satisfying the quota.   A different model has to be formulated.

Let b_2 = the amount of type 2 resource if it is purchased at less than the quantity discount volume;

b_3 = the amount of type 2 resource if it is purchased with quantity discount; and

p_3 = the new discount price for the purchase of resource type 2.

$$\text{Maximize:} \quad Z = s_1 x_1 + s_2 x_2 \tag{4.90}$$

$$\text{Subject to:} \quad a_{11} x_1 + a_{12} x_2 = b_1 \tag{4.91}$$

$$a_{21} x_1 + a_{22} x_2 \leq b_2 + M y_1 \tag{4.92}$$

$$a_{21} x_1 + a_{22} x_2 \leq b_3 + M y_2 \tag{4.93}$$

$$P_1 b_1 + P_2 b_2 \leq B + M y_1 \tag{4.94}$$

$$P_1 b_1 + P_3 b_3 \leq B + M y_2 \tag{4.95}$$

$$y_1 + y_2 = 1 \tag{4.96}$$

$$b_2 < Q$$

$$b_3 \geq Q$$

$$y_1, y_2 = 0, 1 \text{ integers}$$

$$x_j, b_1 \geq 0$$

The above model works by establishing optimality condition first. Then, with mixed integer programming, either the pair of Eqs. (4.92) and (4.94), or the pair of (4.93) and (4.95) will hold true. Note that this formulation works only when the proper budget limit has been established.

To generalize, consider the discount price structure in Fig. 4.34.

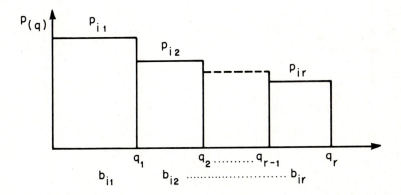

Fig. 4.34 General Discount Price Structure

If resource i is the raw material with discount, the generalized model can be formulated by breaking the raw material variable and constraints into the following:

(i)   The usage equations:

$$\sum a_{ij} x_j \leq b_{i1} + M y_1 \qquad\qquad (4.97)$$

$$\vdots \qquad\qquad \vdots \qquad \vdots$$

$$\sum a_{ij} x_j \leq b_{ir} + M y_r$$

(ii)   Budget equations:

$$\sum p_k b_k + p_{i1} b_{i1} \leq B + M y_1 \qquad\qquad (4.98)$$

$$\vdots \qquad\qquad \vdots \qquad\qquad \vdots$$

$$\sum p_k b_k + p_{ir} b_{ir} \leq B + M y_2$$

where   i   represents the raw material with discount; and

k   all other resources without discounts.

(iii)   Finding the applicable set of equations:

$$y_1 + y_2 + \ldots + y_{r-1} + y_r = 1 \qquad\qquad (4.99)$$
$$y_1 = 0, \quad 1 \text{ integer}$$

(iv)   Establishing limits:

$$b_{i1} < q_1 \qquad\qquad (4.100)$$
$$q_1 < b_{i2} < q_2$$
$$\vdots \qquad \vdots \qquad \vdots$$
$$q_{r-1} < b_{ir} < q_r$$

4.9.2.3   Decreasing Revenues

Consider the following model,

Maximize:	$Z = s_1 \; x_1 + s_2 \; x_2$	(4.101)
Subject to:	$a_{11} \; x_1 + a_{12} \; x_2 = b_1$	(4.102)
	$a_{21} \; x_1 + a_{22} \; x_2 = b_2$	(4.103)
	$p_1 \; b_1 + p_2 \; b_2 \leq B$	(4.104)
	$x_j \; , \; b_i \geq 0$	

If the selling price s_1 would drop if the quantity sold is greater than q_1, with q_2 as the maximum demand, then the model should be revised.

Let x_{11} = the quantity of product 1 sold at price s_{11};

x_{12} = the quantity of product 2 sold if prices drop to s_{12};

q_1 = maximum quantity at which p_1 applies;

q_2 = maximum quantity at which p_2 applies;

s_{11} = higher selling price;

s_{12} = lower selling price as quantity exceeds q_1.

$$\text{Maximize:} \qquad Z = s_{11} \, x_{11} + s_{12} \, x_{12} + s_2 \, x_2 \qquad\qquad (4.105)$$

$$\text{Subject to:} \qquad a_{11} \, (x_{11} + x_{12}) + a_{12} \, x_2 = b_1 \qquad\qquad (4.106)$$

$$a_{21} \, (x_{11} + x_{12}) + a_{22} \, x_2 = b_2 \qquad\qquad (4.107)$$

$$p_1 \, b_1 + p_2 \, b_2 \le B \qquad\qquad (4.108)$$

$$x_j \, , \, b_i \ge 0$$

The problem of mutual exclusiveness of x_{11} and x_{12} can be tackled by

$$x_{11} + M \, x_{12} \le q_1 + N \, y_1 \qquad\qquad (4.109)$$

$$M \, x_{11} + x_{12} \le q_2 + N \, y_2 \qquad\qquad (4.110)$$

$$y_1 + y_2 = 1 \qquad\qquad (4.111)$$

$$x_{11} \le q_1 \qquad\qquad (4.112)$$

$$x_{12} \le q_2 \qquad\qquad (4.113)$$

$$y_1 \, , \, y_2 = 0, \; 1 \; \text{integer}$$

where $N \gg M \, x_{12}$

The model formulated for declining prices has the following characteristics:

(i) If $x_{11} > 0$, then $y_1 = 0$ will make $x_{12} = 0$ by Eq. (4.109). If $x_{11} > 0$, y_1 cannot assume the value of 1, because if $y_1 = 1$, by Eq. (4.111) $y_2 = 0$, and Eq. (4.100) forces $x_{11} = 0$.

(ii) If $x_{12} > 0$, then $y_2 = 0$ will make $x_{11} = 0$ by Eq. (4.100). If $x_{12} > 0$, y_2 will not assume the value of 1, because if $y_2 = 1$, by Eq. (4.111), $y_1 = 0$, and Eq. (4.109) forces $x_{12} = 0$.

(iii) $N \gg M \, x_{12}$ in order for the system of equations to be feasible. Say $N < M \, x_{12}$, $y_2 = 0$ and $x_{11} = 0$ satisfies Eq. (4.110) but Eq. (4.109) will never be satisfied. Therefore, N must be greater than $M \, x_{12}$.

(iv) x_{12} will never take values less than q_1 because if $x_{12} < q_1$, x_{11} will prevail because it has a higher contribution to the objective function.

To generalize the formulation, consider the price structure in Fig. 4.35.

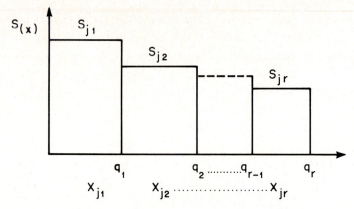

Fig. 4.35   Decreasing Selling Price Structure

The following model revision can be made.

(i)   The objective function has to be revised to

$$\text{Maximize:} \qquad Z = \sum_{r=1}^{R} s_{jr}\, x_{jr} + \sum_{k \neq j} s_k\, x_k \qquad (4.114)$$

where x_k represent products with constant prices, and

x_{jr} represents product with step function price.

(ii)   Resource constraints will be reflected as

$$a_{ij}\left(\sum_{r=1}^{R} x_{jr}\right) + \sum_{k \neq j} a_{ik}\, x_k = b_i \qquad \text{for all i resources} \qquad (4.115)$$

(iii) Equations for mutual exclusiveness of each x_{jr} would be

$$x_{jr} + M\left(\sum_{s \neq r} x_{js}\right) \le q_r + N\, y_r \qquad \text{for all r} \qquad (4.116)$$

$$y_1 + y_2 + \ldots + y_r = 1 \qquad\qquad\qquad\qquad\qquad (4.117)$$

$$x_{jr} < q_r \qquad\qquad\qquad\qquad \text{for all r} \qquad (4.118)$$

$$y_r = 0,\ 1 \qquad\qquad\qquad\qquad \text{for all r}$$

$$N \gg M\, q_r$$

4.9.3 DE NOVO'S APPLICABILITY IN MODM

Multiobjective optimization is premised by the conflict of the objectives. The individual optimum of each objective cannot be achieved if a compromise solution will have to be determined.   This is because the resources in the

traditional product mix model are determined "a priori" and hence the constraint set is fixed. The compromise solution, therefore, is one which gives
the individual objectives lesser values than their individual optimum or ideal
solutions. The so-called "ideal" solution is, in fact, infeasible as shown in
Fig. 4.36.

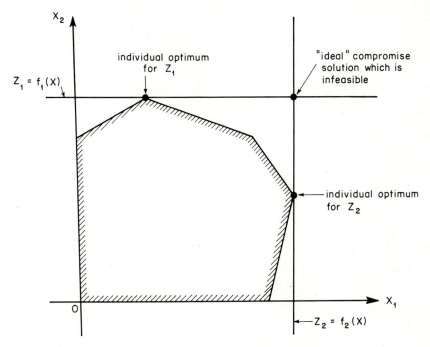

Fig. 4.36 Traditional Biobjective Product Mix Solution Set
Showing Infeasible Ideal Compromise Solution

In the case of De Novo formulation where the resources are not fixed at
the outset, it is possible to readjust the resource constraints in such a way
that the originally infeasible ideal solution becomes feasible as depicted in
Fig. 4.37. If the budget restriction does not allow readjustment of the
resource constraints to cause full achievement of the ideal solution, it is
suffice to aspire for a near-satisfaction of the ideal solution. It is also
possible in some cases that with the same budget, the ideal solution is even
overachieved.

Zeleny (1986) developed the following example to illustrate optimal design
of systems using De Novo. The remaining part of this section features Zeleny's
example in great detail.

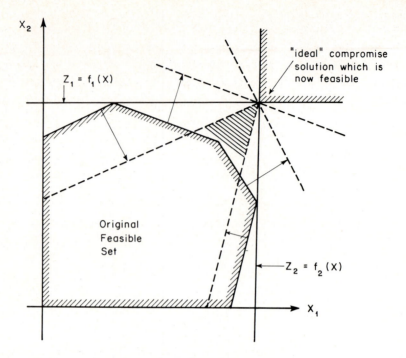

Fig. 4.37 De Novo Biobjective Product Mix Solution Set
Now Feasible Ideal compromise Solution

Let us assume that we have a park of six machine types whose capacities are to be devoted to the production of three products. Current capacity portfolio is available, measured in machine-hours per week for each machine type. Each hour of machine capacity has its unit price according to the machine type. Necessary data are summarized in Table 4.6.

Table 4.6 Current Portfolio of Available Capacities

Machine type	Available	Unit price ($100 per hour)
Milling machine	1400	0.75
Lathe	1000	0.60
Grinder	1750	0.35
Jig saw	1325	0.50
Drill press	900	1.15
Band saw	1075	0.65

In Table 4.6, observe that the total capacity cost of the current system is: $(0.75)1400 + (0.60)1000 + (0.35)1750 + (0.50)1325 + (1.15)900 + (0.65)1075$ = \$4658.75.

The three products have their respective capacity (technological) requirements summarized in Table 4.7.

Table 4.7 Technological Coefficients

Machine type	Product 1	Product 2	Product 3
Milling machine	12	17	0
Lathe	3	9	8
Grinder	10	13	15
Jig saw	6	0	16
Drill press	0	12	7
Band saw	9.5	9.5	4

Obviously, the above situation can be represented by a linear programming model in order to compute the most effective mix of the three products. In order to do so in a more realistic manner, let us postulate at least three objective functions of interest: Profits, Quality and Worker Satisfaction - all to be maximized. The following linear programming problem then applies:

$$
\begin{aligned}
\text{Maximize:} \quad & z_1 = 50\,x_1 + 100\,x_2 + 17.5\,x_3 && \text{(Profits)} \\
& z_2 = 92\,x_1 + 75\,x_2 + 50\,x_3 && \text{(Quality)} \\
& z_3 = 25\,x_1 + 100\,x_2 + 75\,x_3 && \text{(Worker satisfaction)} \\
\text{Subject to:} \quad & 12\,x_1 + 17\,x_2 \leq 1400 \\
& 3\,x_1 + 9\,x_2 + 8\,x_3 \leq 1000 \\
& 10\,x_1 + 13\,x_2 + 15\,x_3 \leq 1750 \\
& 6\,x_1 + 16\,x_3 \leq 1325 \\
& 12\,x_2 + 7\,x_3 \leq 900 \\
& 9.5\,x_1 + 9.5\,x_2 + 4\,x_3 \leq 1075
\end{aligned}
$$

The above linear programming problem can be solved with respect to each objective function separately. We obtain the following results:

$$
\begin{aligned}
z_1: \quad & x_1 = 44.94, & x_2 = 50.63, & \quad x_3 = 41.77 & \text{and } z_1 = 8041.14, \\
z_2: \quad & x_1 = 92.27, & x_2 = 0, & \quad x_3 = 47.95 & \text{and } z_2 = 10950.59, \\
z_3: \quad & x_1 = 45.22, & x_2 = 49.61, & \quad x_3 = 43.52 & \text{and } z_3 = 9355.895.
\end{aligned}
$$

Obviously the three different solutions maximize the three different and separate objective functions. Rarely can we think of a situation when only one single objective would be sufficient in production decision making. Normally, we are interested in all objectives simultaneously: profits, quality, worker satisfaction - and often many more.

Individual maxima of the postulated objectives are not attainable all at the same time. They represent an ideal, unattainable preferential value of conceptual importance: $z^* = (8041.14;\ 10950.59;\ 9355.895)$.

This desirable performance z^* remains unattainable with respect to the current system of available machine capacities. In modern production however, the question is less how to manage a "given" system, and more how to design it optimally. The unit prices of the machine capacities were listed in Table 4.6; we can purchase more or less of the capacities at their current prices.

Using the De Novo programming, the "optimal" portfolio of machine capacities can be computed and is presented in Table 4.8.

Table 4.8 Optimal Design of Capacities,
Making Given "Ideal" feasible

Machine type	Recommended availability (machine-hours/week)	Original availability
Milling machine	1426.52	1400
Lathe	945.37	1000
Grinder	1858.31	1750
Jig saw	1114.58	1325
Drill	853.37	900
Band saw	1150.605	1075

The total cost of the system recommended in Table 4.8 is $4574.0792, which is over $84 less than the one in Table 4.6. Observe also that, in Table 4.8, we compare the original with the recommended capacities in order to show the nature of the changes involved in the transformation from substandard to optimal portfolio of resources.

The recommended portfolio of capacities has properties which can be revealed by solving the following LP problem:

Maximize:
$$z_1 = 50\ x_1 + 100\ x_2 + 17.5\ x_3$$
$$z_2 = 92\ x_1 + 75\ x_2 + 50\quad x_3$$
$$z_3 = 25\ x_1 + 100\ x_2 + 75\quad x_3$$

Subject to:
$$12\ x_1 + 17\ x_2 \qquad\qquad \leq 1426.52$$
$$3\ x_1 + 9\ x_2 + 8\ x_3 \leq 945.37$$
$$10\ x_1 + 13\ x_2 + 15\ x_3 \leq 1858.31$$
$$6\ x_1 + \qquad\quad 16\ x_3 \leq 1114.58$$
$$12\ x_2 + 7\ x_3 \leq 853.37$$
$$9.5\ x_1 + 9.5\ x_2 + 4\ x_3 \leq 1150.605$$

Solving the above problem with respect to any of the three objective functions, we obtain the following optimal solution:

$$x^* = (x_1{}^*,\ x_2{}^*,\ x_3{}^*) = (57.79,\ 43.12,\ 47.99).$$

Substituting x^* into the appropriate objective functions, we obtain:

$$z_1{}^* = 8041.35,\ z_2{}^* = 10950.18,\ z_3{}^* = 9356.00,$$

or, in other words, the previously identified ideal solution z^* has now become feasible; it is attainable, and even at lower costs. We simply have to operate an optimal system, rather than operate a suboptimal system "optimally". Some $86 left from the previously "given" system can therefore be spent on addition-al resources and the "ideal" z^* even exceeded.

Why anybody would wish to operate more costly system, which does not maximize all three objective functions at the same time, is certainly a question worth pondering.

The following observations should be made:

(1) It is obvious that the ideal z^* is only relative to a particular given system: its value is therefore as arbitrary as the system generating it. Each system, including the optimally designed one, will be characterized by its own "ideal".

(2) In the framework of optimal system design, the system ideal must be established as a point of reference for superior, high-productivity performance. Each system ideal is then relative only to the total amount of money allowed to be spent.

What is the system ideal in the example presented here?

As we were able to solve a "given" system with respect to each objective separately, we can also design an optimal system with respect to each objective

separately. Using De Novo programming again, we can optimally design a system
with respect to:

$$z_1: \quad x_1 = 0, \quad x_2 = 109.16813, \quad x_3 = 0 \quad \text{and} \quad z_1 = 10916.813,$$
$$z_2: \quad x_1 = 198.4558, \quad x_2 = 0, \quad x_3 = 0 \quad \text{and} \quad z_2 = 18257.933,$$
$$z_3: \quad x_1 = 0, \quad x_2 = 0, \quad x_3 = 162.32578 \quad \text{and} \quad z_3 = 12174.433.$$

The three alternative optimal designs are summarized in Table 4.9.

Table 4.9   Alternative Optimal Designs
With Respect to three Criteria

Machine type	Recommended		
	relative to z_1	relative to z_2	relative to z_3
Milling machine	1855.8582	2381.4696	0
Lathe	982.51317	595.3674	1298.6062
Grinder	1419.1856	1984.558	2434.8867
Jig saw	0	1190.7348	2597.2124
Drill press	1310.0175	0	1136.2804
Band saw	1037.0972	1885.3301	649.30312

Check that each of the three optimal designs in Table 4.9 costs an equal
amount of money: \$4658.75. This is intentionally make identical with the cost
of the originally "given" system (Table 4.5).

Correspondingly, the system ideal relative to the budget (of \$4658.75) is:

$$z^* = (10916.813; \ 18257.933; \ 12174.433)$$

Each of the above three levels (profits, quality, worker satisfaction) can
be attained separately, but not all of them together: the system ideal is
infeasible and cannot be attained without increasing the total amount of money
spent, *ceteris paribus*.

There are two basic ways of approaching this problem. (1) Keep the budget
fixed and explore the tradeoffs between the three objective functions and their
corresponding optimal designs; the result will be a traditional MCDM solution,
balancing multiple criteria in the best possible (but still suboptimal) way.
(2) Allow budget to increase so as to make the system ideal feasible; the

result would then be metaoptimal: i.e. no tradeoffs necessary, all objectives maximized at the same time, temporary equilibrium reached and the "path" of its maintenance defined.

For example, the feasibility of the above system ideal z^* can be achieved by solving the following system of equations:

$$50\ x_1 + 100\ x_2 + 17.5\ x_3 = 10916.813$$
$$92\ x_1 +\ 75\ x_2 + 50\ \ \ \ x_3 = 18257.933$$
$$25\ x_1 + 100\ x_2 + 75\ \ \ \ x_3 = 12174.433$$

giving $x_1 = 131.341$, $x_2 = 29.683$, and $x_3 = 78.976$.

The corresponding optimal portfolio of capacities is presented in Table 4.10, and would cost $6021.812 at the unit prices introduced in Table 4.5. So far, we have used the initial budget of $4658.75 for the sake of comparison. The difference, $1363.062, represents the additional costs necessary for attaining previously determined maxima of all three criteria (system ideal z^*), all at the same time.

Table 4.10 Metaoptimal design and its costs

Machine type	Recommended (machine-hours/week)	Costs ($)
Milling machine	2080.703	1560.5272
Lathe	1292.978	775.7868
Grinder	1184.64	414.624
Jig saw	2051.662	1025.831
Drill press	909.028	1045.3822
Band saw	1845.632	1199.6608
Total	9364.643	6021.812

Suppose that we do not allow any spending in excess of $4658.75. We then simply distribute this budget according to the optimal design proportions of Table 4.10. This way we can control and maintain the optimality of design for any budget level. The corresponding product mix (x_1, x_2, x_3) will then satisfy the following system of equations:

$$12 \ x_1 + \ 17 \ x_2 \qquad\qquad\qquad \leq 1609.7266$$
$$3 \ x_1 + \ 9 \ x_2 + \ 8 \ x_3 \leq 1000.3066$$
$$10 \ x_1 + \ 13 \ x_2 + 15 \ x_3 \leq \ 916.49057$$
$$6 \ x_1 + \qquad\qquad 16 \ x_3 \leq 1587.2594$$
$$12 \ x_2 + \ 7 \ x_3 \leq \ 703.26545$$
$$9.5 \ x_1 + 9.5 \ x_2 + \ 4 \ x_3 \leq 1427.8652$$

Observe that, because the system is already optimally designed, we no longer need to refer to objective functions; their best possible values (for the money spent) are certain to be automatically obtained.   In fact, the solution to the above system is readily known (using the definition of metaoptimality and the ratio of budgetary change):

$$x_1 = 101.61142, \quad x_2 = 22.964131, \quad x_3 = 61.099459$$

Corresponding levels of the three objective functions are:

$$z_1 = 8446.2246, \quad z_2 = 14125.532, \quad z_3 = 9419.158.$$

System ideal $z_1^* = (8846.2246; 14125.532; 9419.158)$ is attainable with the budget of \$4658.75, and can be compared with the system ideal $z_2^* = (10916.813; 18257.933; 12174.433)$,   attainable with the budget of \$6021.812.   In other words, the additional \$1363.062 bring in the extra performance (2470.589; 4132.401; 2755.275) with respect to the three criteria.

Observe that the variety of production (optimal mix) is here correctly aligned with the number of decision criteria.   Under the conditions of un-limited demand, variety of production emerges directly in response to the number of objective functions, and not as a mathematical reflection of sub-optimality of an arbitrary system.   When there is a single objective function and unlimited demand, only a single, most profitable product should be produced by an optimal system.   A suboptimal, arbitrarily "given" system will recommend multiple products even with respect to a single objective - because of its suboptimality.

Multiple products arise in optimally-designed systems only in response to either demand limitations or multiple criteria (or both).   The purpose of the presented methodology is not to condone the suboptimal functioning of a given system as given, but to suggest ways of design such that optimal functioning would be achieved and maintainable over time.

Once we design a metaoptimal system (with respect to multiple objectives) and determine the level of budget at which it can be implemented, then its metaoptimality can be maintained at negligible or small computational costs. Changes in prices, technological coefficients, objective functions, demand limitations, etc., can be incorporated and new design versions prepared, mostly by inspection. Computational effort remains negligible.

Only when we cannot (all constraints are fixed or mandated), or do not wish to (the "given" system has a nostalgic value), design a new, optimal system, will traditional LP methodology remain useful and unchallenged. Most intermediate cases (partially given systems) can be handled effectively via De Novo Programming.

REVIEW QUESTIONS

1)   In applying the traditional way of handling multiobjective optimization one optimizes the most important objective and converts all other objectives as constraints. Explain the main drawback of this approach.

2)   What are the main advantage(s) and disadvantage(s) of the unified objective method or the utility function method of MODM.

3)   In the global criterion method, interpret the characteristic(s) of the global function when the exponent p equals 1 and when p > 1.

4)   Describe the compromise constraint technique for MCDM. Why is LP's post-optimality analysis useful in the biobjective case?

5)   In goal programming, differentiate between a goal constraint and a resource (structural or system) constraint.

6)   What advantages does goal programming have over linear programming in regard to generating a solution?

7)   Can the standard LP simplex algorithm be applied to any goal programming problem? If no, why not? If yes, explain how this is accomplished.

8)   Explain the optimality test associated with goal programming's modified simplex algorithm.

9)   Comment on the pros and cons of the interactive approach to MCDM.

10) Comment on the pros and cons of the parametric approach to MCDM.

11) What is the relation of postoptimality analysis with the sequential conversion of objectives to constraints as an approach to MODM?

12) Enumerate instances that would justify the use of each of the following MODM approaches:

     i)   Single Objective Approach
     ii)   Unified Objective Approach
     iii) Goal Programming Approach
     iv)   Interactive Approach
     v)   Parametric Approach

13) Show how can MODM be used to solve a single-objective linear fractional programming problem.

14) Given the following LP formulation.

     Maximize: $40x_1 + 45x_2 + 24x_3$ (profit)
     Subject to: $2x_1 + 3x_2 + x_3 \leq 100$ (resource 1)
                     $3x_1 + 3x_2 + 2x_3 \leq 120$ (resource 2)
                     $x_1, x_2, x_3 \geq 0$

     Solve the above problem via the goal programming approach with a target profit of $2,000.

15) Given the following formulation of the problem:

     Minimize $z = P_1d_1^- + P_2d_2^- + P_3d_3^-$
     Subject to: $10 x_1 + 15 x_2 + d_1^- - d_1^+ = 40$
                     $100 x_1 + 100 x_2 + d_2^- - d_2^+ = 1,000$
                     $x_2 + d_3^- - d_3^+ = 7$
                     $x_1, x_2, d_1^-, d_1^+, d_2^-, d_2^+, d_3^-, d_3^+ \geq 0$

     Develop the initial tableau and perform one iteration. Show the second tableau. Interpret the solutions obtainable from the second tableau. Comment on its optimality.

16) Develop the initial simplex tableau:

$$\text{Min.} \quad P_1(3d_1^- + d_1^+) + P_2d_2^- + P_3(d_3^- + 2d_4^-)$$

$$\text{s.t.} \quad 15x + 12y + 15z + d_1^- - d_1^+ = 20,000$$

$$6x + 14y + 8z + d_2^- = 12,000$$

$$5x + 6y + 2z + d_3^- - d_3^+ = 10,000$$

$$x + 5y + z + d_4^- - d_4^+ = 5,000$$

$$\text{All variables} \geq 0$$

17) Consider the goal programming tableau below:

Objective Column	Variable Column	Constant Column	0 x	0 y	0 z	$3P_1$ d_1^-	P_1 d_1^+	P_2 d_2^-	P_3 d_3^-	0 d_3^+	$2P_3$ d_3^-	0 d_3^+
0	z	1333.3	1	0.8	1	0.07	-0.07	0	0	0	0	0
P_2	d_2^-	1333.3	-2	7.6	0	-0.53	0.53	1	0	0	0	0
P_3	d_3^-	7333.3	3	4.4	0	-0.13	1.13	0	1	-1	0	0
$2P_3$	d_4^-	3666.7	0	4.2	0	-0.07	0.07	0	0	0	1	-1
	P_3	14666.7	-3	-12.8	0	0.27	-0.27	0	0	1	0	2
$c_j - z_j$	P_2	1333.3	2	-7.6	0	0.53	-0.53	0	0	0	0	0
	P_1	0	0	0	0	3.00	1.00	0	0	0	0	0

(a) Is this tableau "optimal"? Give reason.

(b) If not "optimal", what are the "key row" and "key column"?

(c) Comment on the achievements of goals.

18) Given the following goal programming problem:

$$\text{Minimize:} \quad z = P_1d_4^+ + P_2d_5^- + P_3d_1^- + P_4(d_2^+ + d_3^+)$$

$$\text{Subject to:} \quad 6x_1 + 4x_2 + d_1^- - d_1^+ = 100$$

$$2x_1 + x_2 + d_2^- - d_2^+ = 10$$

$$x_1 + x_2 + d_3^- - d_3^+ = 8$$

$$3x_1 + 2x_2 + d_4^- - d_4^+ = 34$$

$$x_2 + d_5^- = 7$$

$$x_1, x_2, d_1^-, d_1^+, d_2^-, d_2^+, d_3^-, d_3^+, d_4^-, d_4^+, d_5^- \geq 0$$

(a) Show the initial tableau including the index values.

(b) Identify the incoming and the outgoing variable in part (a)

(c) Given the following tableau resulting from a subsequent iteration of part (a), interpret the results of this tableau: that is, what is the solution at this step? Which goals have been met? What are the values of the decision variables?

Tableau at a Given Iteration

Objective Column	Variable Column	Constant Column	0 x_1	0 x_2	P_3 d_1^-	0 d_1^+	0 d_2^-	P_4 d_2^+	0 d_3^-	P_4 d_3^+	0 d_4^-	P_1 d_4^+	P_2 d_5^-
P_3	d_1^-	66	0	0	1	-1	0	0	-6	6	0	0	2
0	d_2^-	1	0	0	0	0	1	-1	-2	2	0	0	1
0	x_1	1	1	0	0	0	0	0	1	-1	0	0	-1
0	d_4^-	16	0	0	0	0	0	0	0	1	1	-1	0
0	x_2	7	0	1	0	0	0	0	0	0	0	0	1
	P_4	0	0	0	0	0	0	1	0	1	0	0	0
	P_3	-66	0	0	0	1	0	0	6	-6	0	0	-2
$c_j - z_j$	P_2	0	0	0	0	0	0	0	0	0	0	0	1
	P_1	0	0	0	0	0	0	0	0	0	0	1	0

19) A company produces three products, A, B, and C. The schedule of labor time required in departments 1 and 2 and the materials required are given below:

	Product			Available at
	A	B	C	normal levels
Department 1 labor	2	6	5	4,000 hours
Department 2 labor	3	3	8	2,000 hours
Material	4	3	6	3,000 units

Products A, B and C sell at unit prices of $100, $150 and $300, respectively. At normal prices, the variable costs per unit are $70, $80 and $130, respectively. Overtime labor in department 1 would cost $2.00 per hour above normal rates in department 1 and $3.00 per hour above normal rates in department 2. Additional material can be acquired at a premium of $2.00 per unit.

Management has listed the following goals, in order of decreasing priority:

i) Have no idle time in either department. The relative weights on the two idle times are considered to be equal.

ii) Achieve the minimum sales levels of 100 units of each product. Again, equal weights are to be assigned to the three deviations in this category.

iii) Overtime should not exceed 100 hours in department 1 and 300 hours in department 2. Within this goal, the deviations are equally ranked.

iv) Achieve a contribution toward overhead (overhead does not include material and labor) and profits of $20,000.

v) Satisfy all market demands, which are estimated to be 1,000 for product A, 400 for product B, and 150 for product C. Within this goal, the deviations are to be weighted according to the normal unit contributions toward overhead and profits.

Set up the goal programming model to determine the best product mix that would satisfy the management's goals.

20) Given the following resource constraints: $g_1(x) \le b_1$, $g_2(x) \le b_2$ and $g_3(x) \le b^3$ where these resources are three types of capital intensive facilities. If management wishes to achieve a profit, $f(x)$, of M monetary units, construct both the short-term and long-term goal programming models of the problems. Also discuss your formulations.

21) Consider a production planning situation in which a single product is manufactured in a facility. The company is faced with a large demand and fixed capacity in the short run, so that its alternatives include (1) run overtime at a cost of 150 percent of regular production, (2) subcontract, or (3) hire temporary employees. Management is leery of utilizing the last two alternatives because of a reduction in quality as well as increased costs. The basic data are shown in the table.

	Normal Production	Overtime	Subcontract	Temporary employees
Hours required per unit	2.0	2.0	2.5	3.0
Cost per hour, $	10.0	15.0	8.0	8.0
Average quality level, %	99.0	98.0	95.0	90.0
Hours available	= Total of 100			
Required quality level	= 98%			

Management has several goals: Meeting demand, keeping production costs with budget, and maintaining quality levels. After much discussion, it is decided to use the following priorities:

Priority 1: Meeting demand.

Priority 2: Achieve the quality level of 98 percent.

Priority 3: Stay within the production budget of $2200.

Formulate a goal programming model that will determine the number of units produced by normal production, overtime, subcontract, and by temporary employees.

22) The R&D Division of a certain company has develop three new products. The impact of each of the new products (per unit rate of production) on the company's profitability is as follows:

Factor	Unit Contribution product		
	1	2	3
Long-run profit	20	15	25
Employment level	5	3	4
Earnings next year	8	7	5

To decide on which mix of these products should be produced, management wants primary consideration given to the following criteria:

i)   Long-run profit,

ii)   Stability in the work force,

iii) Achieving an increase in the company's earnings next year.

Three production stages are required in manufacturing these new products and the amount of time required for the products to be in each of the production stages are shown in the table below:

	Product			Existing Maximum
	1	2	3	Capacity (year-hours)
Stage 1	10	20	30	S_1
Stage 2	30	20	10	S_2
Stage 3	15	20	5	S_3

(a) Develop a goal programming formulation for the following goals:

P_1: Long-run profit of P.

P_2: Stability in available level of employment at E. Management prefers hiring over firing by a ratio of 2 to 1.

P_3: Short-run earnings target of S.

(b) If management is planning for expansion, show the goal programming model that can generate information on the expansion requirements of the production stages to assure achievement of goals.

23) A company manufactures three lines of men's wear: Types A, B, and C. The company is a family-owned-and-operated business, but the majority of employees of the firm are not members of the family. Because of the competitive nature of the business and the high demand for labor in the industry, it is extremely important that employee satisfaction be maintained. Management feels that a key step toward meeting the needs of its employees is offering full employment, even if this requires excess production and write-off. Fortunately, management expects the demand for its products to remain relatively high. As a matter of fact, to meet some demand it may be necessary to employ overtime operations.

All three lines of wear are fabricated in two departmental operations. The table shown below is a schedule of the weekly labor and material requirements used in the fabrication process. The unit prices of the three lines are $100, $150 and $250, respectively. Management has determined that at the normal production level, the variable costs are $70, $80 and $100 per piece, respectively. Overtime costs are $2 per hour above the normal rate for department 1 and $3 per hour above the normal rate for department 2. Extra material can be acquired at a cost of $2 per yard above the normal cost.

Management has forecast that the market demand for type A is 1000 units per week, while the demand for the other two types is 500 and 200 units, respectively, and 50 units each of the two remaining products.

In analyzing the problem, management has identified, in priority order, the following goals:

i) Utilize all available production capacity, i.e., no idle time should exist in either department.

ii) Meet the breakeven production levels in each of the product lines.

iii) Since labor shortages will likely exist in department 2 and other personnel can be shifted to department 2 on overtime, overtime in this department can be greater than that in department 1. However, overtime in department 2 should be limited to 600 hours. Overtime in department 1 should not exceed 200 hours.

iv) Achieve a weekly profit goal of $20,000.

v) Meet all market demands. Within this goal, differential weights should be used to reflect the normal unit contribution to profits.

Time and Material Requirements and Resources

	Product Requirements (Per Unit)			Resources
	A	B	C	(Labor and Material)
Dept.1	4 hours	12 hours	10 hours	8000 hours
Dept.2	6 hours	6 hours	16 hours	4000 hours
Material	8 sq yd	6 sq yd	12 sq yd	8000 sq yd

(a) Formulate the problem in a goal programming format.

(b) Formulate the problem in an ordinary multiobjective optimization format (ignore the priority order).

24) A company produces television sets. The company has three production lines. The production rate for line 1 is 4 sets per hour, for line 2 is 3 sets per hour, and for line 3 is 2 sets per hour. The regular production capacity is 90 hours a week for all the lines. The gross profit from an average television set is $100. The top management of the firm has the following goals for the next week in the order of decreasing priority:

i) Meet the production goal of 300 sets for the week.

ii) Limit the total overtime operation to 6 hours for line 3.

iii) Avoid the underutilization of regular working hours for all lines. Differential weights should be assigned according to the production rate of each line.

iv) Minimize the sum of overtime operations for lines 1 and 2. Again, differential weights should be assigned according to the relative cost of an overtime hour. It is assumed that the cost of operation is identical for all lines.

Formulate the problem using the Goal Programming model. Also, show the initial "modified" simplex tableau together with all the index values.

25) A company manufactures two types of cameras. The production process for manufacturing the cameras is such that the two departmental operations are required. To produce their standard camera requires 2.5 hours of production time in department 1 and 3.5 hours in department 2. To produce their deluxe model requires 5 hours of production time in department 1 and 3.5 hours in department 2. Currently, 90 hours of labor are available each week in each of the departments. This labor time is a somewhat restrictive factor since the company has a general policy of avoiding overtime, if possible. The manufacturer's profit on each standard camera is $50, while the profit on the deluxe model is $70. Management has set the following goals:

P_1 (priority 1): Avoid overtime operations in each department.

P_2 (priority 2): Prior sales records indicate that, on the average, a minimum of 15 deluxe cameras can be sold weekly. Management would like to meet these sales goals. However, production time limits the production of this number of cameras for each type. Since the deluxe camera has a higher profit margin, the sales goals should be weighted by the profit contribution for the respective cameras.

P_3 (priority 3): Maximize profits.

Solve this MCDM problem using goal programming.

26) Using the game theoretic approach of Belenson and Kapur, solve the following MODM problem:

Maximize: $z_1 = 2x_1 + x_2$
Maximize: $z_2 = -2x_1 + x_2$
Subject to: $-x_1 + x_2 \leq 1$
             $x_1 + x_2 \leq 7$
             $x_1 \qquad \leq 5$
             $\qquad x_2 \leq 3$
             $x1, \quad x2 \geq 0$

Assume that the DM's preference on the objectives is $z_1 > z_2$ and that he/she is not satisfied with the initial payoff table. Only determine the first compromise solution. Also describe when and how the algorithm moves on to the second iteration.

27) Consider the following objective functions and their individual optimal solutions:

$$\text{Maximize:} \qquad Z_1 = 2x_1 + x_2, \quad x_1^{(1)*} = 2, \; x_2^{(1)*} = 1$$
$$\text{Maximize:} \qquad Z_2 = x_1 + 2x_2, \quad x_1^{(2)*} = 1, \; x_2^{(2)*} = 2$$
$$\text{Subject to:} \qquad x_1, x_2 \in X$$

Use the game theoretic approach to determine the weights of the objectives.

28) Suppose that management is aiming at two objectives of a firm in a competitive business environment - maximization of profit and maximization of sales revenue.   The problem is on the production of two types of capital goods which require the use of three types of resources.

The unit selling price for product type 1 is $21,000 while that of product type 2 is $5,000.   The unit profit for product type 1 is $1,000 and for product type 2 is $4,000.   Due to production limitations, only a maximum of 60 units is allowed for product type 2.   The raw materials available for the following month is only good for a total of 70 units for both products.

(a) Formulate the problem and determine the compromise solution using the Step Method (STEM).   Carry the method to the second iteration (or cycle) by assuming that in the decision making phase of the first cycle, the DM decides to relax the profit objective by 10 percent.

(b) Formulate the problem and determine the preferred solution using the global criterion method and the game theoretic method.

29) A manufacturing firm has decided to cease production of a certain obsolete product type.   Instead, the firm plans to produce products 1 and 2.   There are three conflicting goals which enter into consideration namely, revenue maximization (z_1), minimization of manpower requirements (z_2), minimization of excess capacity in hours (z_3).   Raw material availability restricts total production to only 3,500 units per month with each product type requiring the same amount of raw materials.   Demand forecast is placed at 4,500 and 6,500 units per month for products 1 and 2, respectively. Assume that the objectives are expressed in the following form: $z_1 = 4x_1 + 5x_2$ (thousand dollars per month), $z_2 = 3x_1 + x_2$ (thousand manhours per month), and $z_3 = 3x_1 - x_2$ (thousand manhours per month).

a)   Show the first round formulation of the problem using the Step

Method.

b)   Show the compromise constraint method formulation of the problem assuming equal weights for all objectives.

30)   Use the two-person-zero-sum game theoretic approach of Belenson and Kapur in solving the following problem:

$$\text{Minimize} \qquad z_1 = -x_1 - 2x_2$$
$$\text{Minimize} \qquad z_2 = -3x_1 - x_2$$
$$\text{subject to:} \qquad x_1 + x_2 \leq 6$$
$$2x_1 + x_2 \leq 9$$
$$0 \leq x_1 \leq 4$$
$$0 \leq x_2 \leq 5$$

Assume that the DM is not satisfied with the initial solution matrix. Develop only the second solution matrix.

31)   Using the game theoretic approach of Belenson and Kapur solve the following problem: Max. $z_1 = 10x_1 - 8x_2$ and Max. $z_2 = 6x_2 - 15x_1$, s.t. $x_1 \leq 5$, $x_2 \leq 5$, $x_1 + x_2 \leq 8$, x_1 and $x_2 \geq 0$. Assume that z_1 is more preferred over z_2 and the result of the first iteration is not acceptable to the decision maker. The DM is satisfied of the result of the second iteration.

32)   Consider the following problem:

$$\text{Maximize} \qquad z_1 = -x_1 + 3x_2$$
$$\text{Maximize} \qquad z_2 = 2x_1 + x_2$$
$$\text{Maximize} \qquad z_3 = -2x_1 + x_2$$
$$\text{Subject to:} \qquad -x_1 + x_2 \leq 1$$
$$x_1 + x_2 \leq 7$$
$$x_1 \leq 5$$
$$x_2 \leq 3$$
$$x_1, \ x_2 \geq 0$$

(a)   Develop the first cycle formulation of the problem using the Step Method.

(b)   Develop the compromise constraint method formulation considering the weights of z_1, z_2 and z_3 to be $w_1 = 0.1$, $w_2 = 0.3$ and $w_3 = 0.6$.

(c)   Solve the problem using Zeleny's compromise programming.

33) Consider the following MODM problem:

$$\text{Maximize:} \quad z_1 = f_1(x), \quad z_2 = f_2(x), \quad \text{and} \quad z_3 = f_3(x)$$
$$\text{Subject to:} \quad g_i(x) \leq b_i, \quad i = 1, 2, \ldots, m.$$
$$x \geq 0$$

If the problem's payoff table is the following:

	x_1^*	x_2^*	x_3^*
z_1	60	-19	-66
z_2	-12	9	7
z_3	-5	9	13

And allowing that

$$\sum_j (c_{1j})^2 = 36, \quad \sum_j (c_{2j})^2 = 100, \quad \sum_j (c_{3j})^2 = 64$$

develop the first cycle formulation using the Step Method.

34) Consider the following LP product mix model with three products and three types of resources:

$$\text{Maximize:} \quad Z = 25x_1 + 10x_2 + 18x_3$$
$$\text{Subject to:} \quad 2x_1 + 1.5x_2 + 1.2x_3 \leq 400 \quad \text{(resource 1)}$$
$$x_1 + 1.5x_2 + 2x_3 \leq 520 \quad \text{(resource 2)}$$
$$x_1 + x_2 + x_3 \leq 300 \quad \text{(resource 3)}$$
$$x_1, x_2, x_3 \geq 0$$

a)   Suppose the prices of the resources are $p_1 = \$20$, $p_2 = \$10$ and $p_3 = \$40$, reformulate the problem using De Novo formulation with the same amount of money used for purchasing of resources in both formulations.

b)   Solve the problem formulated in a) assuming the demand for each product is limited to 250.

35) The product mix problem of a production system can be modeled as a biobjective LP: Maximize $z_1 = x_1 + x_2$ and Maximize $z_2 = x_1 - x_2$, subject

to $x_1 \leq 5$ (resource 1), $x_2 \leq 5$ (resource 2), and x_1 & $x_2 \geq 0$.

a) Redesign the system such that the ideal solutions of both objectives are achieved.

b) What is the financial advantage of the redesigned system if the price of the resources are $p_1 = p_2$, $p_1 = 2p_2$ and $p_1 = p_2/2$.

c) Solve the original problem using the compromise constraint method. Assume equal weights for both objectives.

36) Consider the following biobjective LP problem:

$$\begin{array}{lll} \text{Maximize} & z_1 = 3x_1 + x_2 \\ \text{Maximize} & z_2 = x_1 + 2x_2 \\ \text{Subject to:} & x_1 + x_2 \leq 7 \\ & x_1 \qquad \leq 5 \\ & \qquad x_2 \leq 5 \\ & x_1, \quad x_2 \geq 0 \end{array}$$

(a) Using the design approach (De Novo) to MODM, what should be the resource constraints such that the original ideal values of the objective functions remain the same.

(b) Solve the problem using the compromise constraint method.

37) Consider the following problem:

$$\begin{array}{lll} \text{Maximize:} & z_1 = 2x_1 + x_2 \\ & z_2 = x_1 - x_2 \\ \text{Subject to:} & x_1 \leq 5 & \text{(resource type 1)} \\ & x_2 \leq 3 & \text{(resource type 2)} \\ & x_1, x_2 \geq 0 \end{array}$$

a) Using the De Novo Programming approach redesign the system such that the ideal solution of the conflicting objectives are fully achieved. If the price of resource type 1 is 1.5 times that of resource type 2, what is the cost implication of the redesigned system.

b) Solve the problem using the compromise constraint technique. What is the compromise solution? What are the values of the two objective functions?

REFERENCES

1. Adulbhan, P. and A. A. DeGuia, 1977. An Interactive Approach to Multi-criterion Optimization. Operations Research, Operations Research Society of America, Vol. 24, No. 4.

2. Adulbhan, P. and P. Sukchareonpong, 1978. Minimum Deviation Approach for Multiple-Objective Optimization. Preceedings of the 8th International Conference of IFORS, Toronto, June 19-23, 1978.

3. Adulbhan, P. and M. T. Tabucanon, 1977. Bicriterion Linear Programming. Computers and Operations Research, 4:147-153.

4. Adulbhan, P. and M. T. Tabucanon, 1980. Multicriterion Optimization in Industrial Systems. Chapter 9, Decision Models for Industrial Systems Engineers and Managers, AIT, Bangkok, Thailand.

5. Arbel, A. and S. S. Oren, 1986. Generating Search Directions in Multi-objective Linear Programming Using the Analytic Hierarchy Process. Socio-Economic Planning Sciences, 20:369-374.

6. Armstrong, R., A. Charnes and C. Haksever, 1988. Implementation of Successive Linear Programming Algorithms for Non-Convex Goal Programming. Computers & Operations Research, 15:37-50.

7. Armstrong, R., A. Charnes and C. Haksever, 1987. Successive Linear Programming for Ratio Goal Problems. European Journal of Operational Research, 32:426-434.

8. Bahmani, N. and H. Blumberg, 1987. Consumer Preference and Reactive Adaptation to a Corporate Solution of the Over-the-Counter Medication Dilemma - An Analytic Hierarchy Process Analysis. Mathematical Modelling, 9:293-298.

9. Balas, E., 1967. Discrete Programming by the Filter Method. Operations Research, 15:915-957.

10. Banai-Kashani, A. R., 1987. Dominance and Dependence in Input-Output Analysis: The Nonlinear (Network) Approach. Mathematical Modelling, 9:377-380.

11. Barbeau, E. J., 1987. Reciprocal Matrices of Order 4. Mathematical Modelling, 9:321-326.

12. Barlow, J. A. and F. Glover, 1987. A Multicriteria Stratification Framework for Uncertainty and Risk Analysis. International Journal on Policy and Information, 11:77-86.

13. Belenson, S. M. and K. C. Kapur, 1973. An Algorithm for Solving Multi-criterion Linear Programming With Examples. Operational Research Quarterly, 24:65-78.

14. Bell, D. E., D. L. Keeney and H. Raiffa, (eds), 1977. Conflicting

Objectives in Decisions. International Institute for Applied Systems Analysis, John Wiley and Sons, Chichester.

15. Benayoun, R., J. De Montgolfier, J. Tergny, and O. Laritchev, 1971. Linear Programming with Multiple Objective Functions: Step Method (STEM). Mathematical Programming, 1:366-375.

16. Benson, H. P., 1986. An Algorithm for Optimizing Over the Weakly-Efficient Set. European Journal of Operational Research, 25:192-199.

17. Bogetoft, P., 1986. General Communication Schemes for Multiobjective Decision Making. European Journal of Operational Research, 26:108-122.

18. Bouyssou, D. and B. Roy, 1987. The Concept of Discrimination Thresholds in Multiple Criteria Analysis. INFOR, 25:302-313 (in French).

19. Briskin, L. E., 1966. A Method of Unifying Multiple Objective Functions. Management Science, 12:B406-B416.

20. Brown, K. S. and J. B. Revelle, 1978. Quantitative Methods for Managerial Decisions. Addison-Wesley Publishing Co.

21. Buchanan, J. T. and H. G. Daellenbach, 1987. A Comparative Evaluation of Interactive Solution Methods for Multiple Objective Decision Models. European Journal of Operational Research, 29:353-359.

22. Chalmet, L. G., L. Lemonidis, and D. J. Elzinga, 1986. An Algorithm for the Bi-Criterion Integer Programming Problem. European Journal of Operational Research, 25:292-300.

23. Chanas, S. and B. Florkiewicz, 1987. A Fuzzy Preference Relation in the Vector Maximum Problem. European Journal of Operational Research, 28:351-357.

24. Changkong, V. and Y. Y. Haimes, 1983. Multiobjective Decision Making - Theory and Methodology, North-Holland.

25. Charnes, A. and W. W. Cooper, 1961. Management Models and Industrial Applications of Linear Programming. Wiley, New York.

26. Charnes, A. and W. W. Cooper, 1977. Goal Programming and Multiple Objective Optimization. European Journal of Operations Research, 1:39-54.

27. Charnes, A., W. W. Cooper, and T. Sueyoshi, 1986. Least Squares/Ridge Regression and Goal Programming/Constrained Regression Alternatives. European Journal of Operational Research, 27:146-157.

28. Churchman, C. W., R. L. Ackoff, and E. L. Arnoff, 1957. Introduction to Operations Research. Wiley, N.Y.

29. Clayton, E. R. and L. J. Moore, 1972. Goal vs. Linear Programming. Journal of System Management, Vol. 23, No. 11, Issue No. 139.

30. Cochrane, J. L. and M. Zeleny, eds., 1973. Multiple Criteria Decision Making. University of South Carolina Press.

31. Contini, B., 1968. A Stochastic Approach to Goal Programming. Operations

Research, 16:576-586.

32. Cooper, M. W., 1987. Modelling Nonlinearities of Multicriteria Locational Decisions. Mathematical Modelling, 8:207-208.

33. Crowder, L. J. and V. A. Sposito, 1987. Comments on "An Algorithm for Solving the Linear Goal-Programming Problem by Solving its Dual". Journal of the Operational Research Society, 38:335-340.

34. Dantzig, G. B., 1963. Linear Programming and Extensions. Princeton University Press, Princeton, New Jersey.

35. Dauer, J. P., 1987. Analysis of the Objective Space in Multiple Objective Linear Programming. Journal of Mathematical Analysis and Applications, 126:579-593.

36. Dauer, J. P. and R. J. Krueger, 1977. An Iterative Approach to Goal Programming. Operations Research Quarterly, 28:671-681.

37. Dauer, J. P. and W. Stadler, 1986. A Survey of Vector Optimization in Infinite-Dimensional Spaces, Part 2. Journal of Optimization Theory and Applications, 51:205-242.

38. Davis, K. R., and P. G. McKeown, 1981. Quantitative Models for Management. Kent Publishing Company, Boston, Massachusetts.

39. Debeljak, C. J., Y. Y. Haimes, and M. Leach, 1986. Integration of the Surrogate Worth Trade-Off Method and the Analytic Hierarchy Process. Socio-Economic Planning Sciences, 20:375-386.

40. DeTurck, D. M., 1987. The Approach to Consistency in the Analytic Hierarchy Process. Mathematical Modelling, 9:345-352.

41. Dorweiler, V. P., 1987. Legal Case Planning Via the Analytic Hierarchy Process: Litigation - or - Conflict Resolution. Mathematical Modelling, 9:251-264.

42. Driankov, D., 1987. An Outline of a Fuzzy Sets Approach to Decision Making with Interdependent Goals. Fuzzy SEts and Systems, 21:275-288.

43. Dror, M. and S. I. Gass, 1987. Interactive Scheme for a MOLP Problem Given Two Partial Orders: One on Variables and One on Objectives. Applied Mathematics and Computation, 24:195-209.

44. Durier, R. and C. Michelot, 1986. Sets of Efficient Points in a Normed Space. Journal of Mathematical Analysis and Applications, 117:506-528.

45. Durinovic, S., M. N. Katehakis, J. A. Filar, and H. M. Lee, 1986. Multiobjective Markov Decision Process with Average Reward Criterion. Large Scale Systems, 10:215-226.

46. Dyer, J. S., 1972. Interactive Goal Programming. Management Science, 19:62-70.

47. Easton, A., 1973. Complex Managerial Decisions Involving Multiple Objectives. Wiley, N. Y.

48. Egudo, R. R. and M. A. Hanson., 1987. Multiobjective Duality with Invexity. Journal of Mathematical Analysis and Applications, 126:469-477.

49. Evren, R., 1987. Interactive Compromise Programming. Journal of the Operational Research society, 38:163-172.

50. Flores, B. E. and D. C. Whybark, 1986. Multiple Criteria ABC Analysis. International Journal of Operations and Production Management, Vol. 6, No. 3, pp. 38-46.

51. Fotr, J., 1986. Value and Utility Functions in Multicriteria Decision Making, Ekonomicko-Matematicky Obzor, 22:283-298 (in Czech).

52. Gal, T. and K. Wolf, 1986. Stability in Vector Maximization - Survey. European Journal of Operational Research, 25:169-182.

53. Geoffrion, A. M., 1967. Solving Bicriterion Mathematical Programs. Operations Research, 15:39-54.

54. Geoffrion, A. M., 1968. Proper Efficiency and the Theory of Vector Maximization. Mathematical Analysis and Applications, 22:618-630.

55. Geoffrion, A. A., J. S. Dyer, and A. Feinberg, 1972. An Interactive Approach for Multicriterion Optimization With an Application to the Operation of an Academic Department. Management Science, 19:357-368.

56. Gibbs, T. E., 1973. Goal Programming. Journal of Systems Management, May pp. 38-41.

57. Gibson, M., J. J. Bernardo, C. Chung, and R. Badinelli, 1987. A Comparison of Interactive Multiple-Objective Decision Making Procedures. Computers & Operations Research, 14:97-106.

58. Guevara, L. D., 1977. Interactive Approaches for Solving Multicriterion Optimization Problems. Master's Thesis, Asian Institute of Technology.

59. Hansen, P., J. F. Thisse, and R. E. Wendell, 1986. Efficient Points on a Network. Networks, 16:357-368.

60. Haimes, Y. Y., W. A. Hall, and H. T. Freedom, 1975. Multiple Objective Optimization in Water Resource Systems. Elsevier.

61. Harker, P. T., 1987. Shortening the Comparison Process in AHP. Mathematical Modelling, 8:139-141.

62. Hartley, R. V., 1976. Operations Research: A Managerial Emphasis. Goodyear Publishing Co. Inc., pp. 11.

63. Henig, M. I and Z. Ritz, 1986. Multiplicative Decision Rules for Multi-objective decision Problems. European Journal of Operational Research, 26:134-141.

64. Hessel, M. and M. Zeleny, 1987. Optimal System Design: Towards New Interpretation of Shadow Prices in Linear Programming. Computers & Operations Research, 14:265-271.

65. Hillier, F. S. and G. J. Lieberman, 1980.   Introduction to Operations Research. Holden-Day, Inc., San Francisco, U.S.A.

66. Hirsch, G., 1976.   Logical Foundations, Analysis and Development of Multicriterion Methods. Ph.D. Dissertation, University of Pennsylvania.

67. Hobbs, B. F., 1986.   What Can We Learn From Experiments in Multiobjective Decision Analysis?   IEEE Transactions on Systems, Man, and Cybernetics, SMC-16:384-394.

68. Horst, R. and H. Tuy, 1987.   On the Convergence of Global Methods in Multiextremal Optimization.   Journal of Optimization Theory and Applications, 54:253-272.

69. Hsia, W. S. and T. Y. Lee, 1987.   Proper D-Solutions of Multiobjective Programming Problems with Set Functions. Journal of Optimization Theory and Applications, 53:247-258.

70. Hughes, W. R., 1986.   Deriving Utilities Using the Analytic Hierarchy Process. Socio-Economic Planning Sciences, 20:393-396.

71. Hwang, C. L. and A. S. M. Masud, 1979. Multiple Objective Decision Making - Methods and Applications: A State-of-the-Art Survey. Springer-Verlag.

72. Hwang, C. L., A. S. M. Masud, S. R. Paidy, and K. Yoon, 1980. Mathematical Programming with Multiple Objectives: A Tutorial.   Computers and Operations Research: A Special Issue on Mathematical Programming with Multiple Objective, Vol. 7, No. 1-2.

73. Ignizio, J. P., 1976. Goal Programming and Extensions. Lexington Books.

74. Ignizio, J. P., 1987.   A Reply to "Comments on an Algorithm for Solving the Linear Goal-Programming Problem by Solving its Dual. Journal of the Operational Research Society, 38:1149-1154.

75. Ignizio, J. P., 1987.   "Goal Aggregation via Shadow Prices - Some counterexamples": A Reply. Large Scale Systems, 12:87-88.

76. Ignizio, J. P. and J. H. Perlis, 1979.   Sequential Linear Goal Programming: Implementation Via MPSX. Computers and Operations Research, 6:141-145.

77. Ijiri, Y., 1965. Management Goals and Accounting for Control. Chicago, RandMcnally.

78. Inuiguchi, M., H. Ichihashi and H. Tanaka. Decision Procedure Based on Model concept and its Application to Fuzzy Multiobjective Linear Programming Problem. Journal of the Operations Society of Japan, 30:4, 1987, pp. 471-492.

79. Jaaskelainen, V. and S. M. Lee. A Goal Programming Model for Financial Planning. Copenhagen Journal of Business Economic, pp. 292-303.

80. Jacquet-Lagrèze E., 1974.   How we can use the notion of Semiorders to Build Outranking Relations in Multicriteria Decision Making. METRA, Vol.

13, No. 1.

81. Jacquet-Lagrèze, E., R. Meziani, and R. Slowinski, 1987. MOLP with an
     Interactive Assessment of a Piecewise Linear Utility Function. European
     Journal of Operational Research, 31:350-357.

82. Jahn, J., 1986. Existence Theorems in Vector Optimization. Journal of
     Optimization Theory and Applications, 50:397-406.

83. Jahn, J., 1987. Parametric Approximation Problems Arising in Vector
     Optimization. Journal of Optimization Theory and Application, 54:503-516.

84. Jain, S. and D. Bhatia, 1986. Generalized Saddle Points in Multi-
     Objective Bilinear Programming. OPSEARCH, Vol. 23, No.3, pp.142-150.

85. Johnsen, E., 1968. Studies in Multi-objective Decision Models, Monograph
     No. 1. Economic Research Center, Lund, Sweden.

86. Kaliszewski, I., 1987. A Modified Weighted Tchebycheff Metric for
     Multiple Objective Programming. Computers & Operations Research, 14:315-
     324.

87. Kapur, K. C., 1970. Mathematical Methods of Optimization for Multi-
     objective Transportation Systems. Socio-economic Planning Science,
     4:451-467.

88. Keeney, R. L. and H. Raiffa, 1976. Decisions with Multiple Objectives:
     Preferences and Value Trade-offs. John Wiley and Sons, New York.

89. Keown, A. J., B. W. Taylor, III, and J. M. Pinkerton, 1981. Multiple
     Objective Capital Budgeting Within the University. Computers & Operations
     Research, 8:59-70.

90. Kirkwood, G. W. and L. C. van der Feltz, 1987. Microcomputer Programs for
     Multi-Objective Decision Analysis. Operations Research Letters, 6:285-
     296.

91. Kok, M., 1986. The Interface with Decision Markers and Some Experimental
     Results in Interactive Multiple Objective Programming Methods. European
     Journal of Operational Research, 26:96-107.

92. Köksalan, M., 1987. Practical Approaches in Multiple criteria Decision
     Making Problems. Makina Tasarim ve Ymalet Dergisi, 1:117-121 (in
     Turkish).

93. Korhonen, P. and J. Laakso, 1986. Solving Generalized Goal Programming
     Problems Using a Visual Interactive Approach. European Journal of
     Operational Research, 26:355-363.

94. Korhonen, P. and J. Wallenius, 1986. Some Theory and an Approach to
     Solving Sequential Multiple-Criteria Decision Problems. Journal of the
     Operational Research Society, 37:501-508.

95. Korhonen, P. J., 1987. VIG - A Visual Interactive Support system for
     Multiple Criteria Decision Making. Belgian Journal of Operations

Research, Statistics and Computer Science, 27:4-15.

96. Korhonen, P., J. Wallenius, and S. Zionts, 1986.   Two Interactive
     Procedures for Multicriterion Optimization With Multiple Decision Makers.
     Sbornik Trudov, 12:4-16 (in Russian).

97. Korhonen, P., 1987.   The Specification of a Reference Direction Using the
     Analytic Hierarchy Process. Mathematical Modelling, 9:361-368.

98. Korhonen, P., H. Moskowitz, and J. Wallenius, 1986.   A Progressive
     Algorithm for Modeling and Solving Multiple-Criteria Decision Problems.
     Operations Research. 34:726-731.

99. Kornbluth, J. S. H., 1986.   Multiple Objective Dynamic Programming with
     Forward Filtering. Computers & Operations Research, 13:517-524.

100. Kunsch, P. L. and J. Teghem, Jr., 1987.   Nuclear Fuel Cycle Optimization
     Using Multi-Objective Stochastic Linear Programming.   European Journal of
     Operational Research, 31:240-249.

101. Lai, H. C. and C. P. Ho, 1986.   Duality Theorem of Nondifferentiable
     Convex Multiobjective Programming.   Journal of Optimization Theory and
     Applications, 50:407-420.

102. Laskey, K. B. and G. W. Fischer, 1987.   Estimating Utility Functions in
     the Presence of Response Error. Management Science, 33:965-980.

103. Lauro, G. L. and A. P. J. Vepsalainen, 1986.   Assessing Technology
     Portfolios for Contract Competition: An Analytic Hierarchy Process
     Approach. Socio-Economic Planning Sciences, 20:407-415.

104. Lawler, E. L., 1976.   Combinatorial Optimization: Networks and Matroids.
     Holt, Rinehart & Winston, USA.

105. Lazimy, R., 1986.   Interactive Relaxation Method for a Broad Class of
     Integer and Continuous Nonlinear Multiple Criteria Problems. Journal of
     Mathematical Analysis and Applications, 116:553-573.

106. Lee, S. M., 1972.   Goal Programming for Decision Analysis.   Auerabach
     Publishers Inc.

107. Lee, S. M., 1972-1973. Goal Programming for Decision Analysis of Multiple
     Objectives. Sloan Management Review, Vol. 14.

108. Lee, S. M. and M. M. Bird, 1970.   A Goal Programming Model for Sales
     Effort Allocation. Business Perspective, 6:17-21.

109. Lee, S. M. and E. R. Clayton, 1972. A Goal Programming Model for Academic
     Resource Allocation. Management Science, Vol. 18, No. 8.

110. Lee, S. M., E. R. Clayton, and B. W. Taylor, III, 1978.   A Goal
     Programming Approach to Multi-Period Production Line Scheduling.
     Computers & Operations Research, 5:205-211.

111. Lee, S. M. and R. L. Luebbe, 1987. A Zero-One Goal-Programming Algorithm
     Using Partitioning and constraint Aggregation. Journal of the Operational

Research Society, 38:633-642.

112. Lee, S. M. and L. J. Moore, 1977. Multi-Criteria School Busing Models. Management Science, 23:703-716.

113. Leitmann, G. and A. Marzollo, eds., 1975. Multicriteria Decision Making. Springer-Verlag.

114. Levine, P. and J. C. Pomerol, 1986. PRIAM, an Interactive Program for Choosing Among Multiple Attribute Alternatives. European Journal of Operational Research, 25:272-280.

115. Li, D. and Y. Y. Haimes, 1987. Hierarchical Generating Method for Large-Scale Multiobjective Systems. Journal of Optimization Theory and Applications, 54:303-334.

116. Li, H. L., 1987. Solving Discrete Multicriteria Decision Problems Based on Logic-Based Decision Support Systems. Decision Support Systems, 3:101-120.

117. Liu, B. and S. Xu,, 1987. Development of the Theory and Methodology of the Analytic Hierarchy Process and Its Applications in China. Mathematical Modelling, 9:179-148.

118. Loganathan, G. V. and H. D. Sherali, 1987. A Convergent Interactive Cutting-Plane Algorithm for Multiobjective Optimization. Operations Research, 35:365-377.

119. Luc, D. T., 1987. About Duality and Alternative in Multiobjective Optimization. Journal of Optimization Theory and Applications, 53:303-308.

120. Luc, D. T., 1987. Scalarization of Vector Optimization Problems. Journal of Optimization Theory and Applications, 55:85-192.

121. Luc, D. T., 1987. Connectedness of the Efficient Point Sets in Quasi-concave Vector Maximization. Journal of mathematical Analysis and Applications, 122:346-354.

122. Luhandjula, M. K., 1987. Multiple Objective Programming Problems with Possibilistic Coefficients. Fuzzy Sets and Systems, 21:135-146.

123. Malakooti, B. and G. I. D'Souza, 1987. Multiple Objective Programming for the Quadratic Assignment Problem. International Journal of Production Research, 25:285-300.

124. Mareschal, B., 1986. Stochastic Multicriteria Decision Making and Uncertainty. European Journal of Operational Research, 26:58-64.

125. Markland, R. E. and s. K. Vickery, 1986. The Efficient computer Implementation of a Large-Scale Integer Goal Programming Model. European Journal of Operational Research, 26:341-354.

126. Martel, J. M., G. R. D'Avignon, and J. Couillard, 1986. A Fuzzy Outranking Relation in Multicriteria Decision Making. European Journal of

Operational Research.   25:258-271.

127. Martins, E. Q. V., 1987.   On a particular Quadratic Network Problem. European Journal of Operational Research, 29:317-327.

128. Michalowski, W., 1987.   Evaluation of a Multiple Criteria Interactive Programming Approach: An Experiment.   INFOR, 25:165-173.

129. Minch, R. P. and G. L. Sanders, 1986.   Computerized Information Systems Supporting Multicriteria Decision Making.   Decision Sciences, 17:395-413.

130. Mojka, A., J. Weinberger, and J. Hampl, 1987.   Multicriterial Optimization of Simulation Model of Blade Root Machining system.   Ekonomicko-Matematicky Obzor, 23:306-313 (in Czech).

131. Ng, K. Y. K., 1987.   Goal Programming Method of Weighted Residuals and Optimal Control Problems.   IEEE Transactions on Systems, Man, and Cybernetics, SMC-17:102-106.

132. Novak, J., 1986.   Stability Analysis of Nondominated solutions in Linear Vector Optimization.   Ekonomicko-Matematicky Obzor, 22:451-461 (in Czech).

133. Nunamaker, T. R. and J. F. Truitt, 1987.   Rationing discretionary Economic Resources: A Multiobjective Approach.   Decision Sciences, 18:524-534.

134. Nykamp, P. and A. Van Delft, 1977.   Multi-criteria Analysis and Regional Decision-Making.   Martinus Nyhoff, Leiden, Netherlands.

135. Nykowski, I., 1986.   Bicriterion Linear Transportation Problem.   Przeglad Statystyczny, 33:9-26 (in Polish).

136. Olson, D. L. and S. R. Swenseth, 1987.   A Linear Approximation for Chance-Constrained Programming.   Journal of the Operational Research Society, 38:261-268.

137. Olson, D. L., M. Venkataramanan, and J. L. Mote, 1986.   A Technique Using Analytical Hierarchy Process in Multiobjective Planning Models.   Socio-Economic Planning Sciences, 20:361-368.

138. Ozernoy, V. M., 1987.   Some Issues in the Mathematical Modelling of Multiple criteria Decision Making Problems.   Mathematical Modelling, 8:212-215.

139. Pais, A. G., 1987.   Cone Extreme Points and Faces.   Journal of Mathematical Analysis and Applications, 126:223-228.

140. Park, Y. B. and C. P. Koelling, 1986.   A Solution of Vehicle Routing Problems in a Multiple Objective Environment.   Engineering Costs and Production Economics, 10:121-132.

141. Pasternak, H. and U. Passy.   Bicriterion Function in Annual Activity Planning.   Education and Research, 325-341.

142. Patrone, F. and S. H. Tijs, 1987.   Unified Approach to Approximate Solutions in Games and Multi-Objective Programming.   Journal of Optimization Theory and Applications, 52:273-278.

143. Pavlik, J. 1987. One-Dimensional Optimization with Two Hierarchically Ordered Criteria and its Application in Structural Balancing. Ekonomicko-Matematicky Obzor, 23:314-330 (in Czech).

144. Penot, J. and A. Sterna-Karwat, 1986. Parameterized Multicriteria Optimization: Continuity and Closedness of Optimal Multi-functions. Journal of Mathematical Analysis and Applications, 120:150-168.

145. Plastria, F. A., 1981. The Electre I and II Methods for Multicriteria Decision Making. Working Seminar Paper, Division of Industrial Engineering and Management, Asian Institute of Technology, June.

146. Pomerol, J. C. and T. Trabelsi, 1987. An Adaptation of PRIAM to Multi-objective Linear Programming. European Journal of Operational Research, 31:335-341.

147. Preckel, P. V., A. M. Featherstone, and T. G. Baker, 1987. Interpreting Dual Variables for Optimization with Nonmonetary Objectives. American Journal of Agricultural economics, 69:849-851.

148. Prévôt, M., 1986. Fuzzy Goals Under Fuzzy constraints. Journal of Mathematical Analysis and Applications, 118:180-193.

149. Proll, L. G., 1987. Goal Aggregation Via Shadow Prices - Some Counter-examples. Large Scale Systems, 12:83-85.

150. Radcliff, B., 1986. Computer-Assisted Approaches to Multiattribute Decision Making, Evaluation Review, 10:578-593.

151. Rakshit, A., 1987. Discrete Time Dynamic Multiobjective Programming Progress Report. Systems and Industrial Engineering Department, The University of Arizona, Tucson, Arizona.

152. Ramesh, R., M. H. Karwan, and S. Zionts, 1986. A Class of Practical Interactive Branch and Bound Algorithms for Multicriteria Integer Programming. European Journal of Operational Research, 26:161-172.

153. Rao, J. R., R. N. Tiwari, and B. K. Mohanty, 1988. A Method for Finding Numerical Compensation for fuzzy Multicriteria Decision Problem. Fuzzy Sets and Systems, 25:33-42.

154. Rao, S. S., 1987. Multiobjective Optimization of Fuzzy Structural Systems. International Journal for Numerical Methods in Engineering, 24:1157-1172.

155. Rasmussen, L. M., 1986. Zero-one Programming with Multiple criteria. European Journal of Operational Research, 26:83-95.

156. Romero, C., 1986. A Survey of Generalized Goal Programming (1970 - 1982). European Journal of Operational Research, 25:183-191.

157. Roy, B., 1968. Classement Et Choix En Prèsence De Points De Une Multiples (La Mèthode Electre). Reune Francaise d'Informatique et Recherche Opèrationelle, nr 8-VI.

158. Roy, B. and P. Bertier, 1971. La Mèthode Electre II (Une Mèthode de Classement En Prèsence De Critères Multiples). SEMA, Working paper nr 142.

159. Roy, B., 1971. Problems and Methods with Multiple Objective Functons. Mathematical Programming, 1:239-266.

160. Roy, B., 1987. Meaning and Validity of Interactive Procedures as Tools for Decision Making. European Journal of Operational Research, 31:361-366.

161. Ruefli, T. W., 1971. A Generalized Goal Decomposition Model. Management Science, 17:B505-B518.

162. Saatcioglu, Ö., 1987. A Multi-Attribute Assignment Goal-Programming Model with Incentives. Journal of the Operational Research Society, 38:361-366.

163. Saaty, T. L., 1987. The analytic Hierarchy Process - What It Is and How It Is Used. Mathematical Modelling, 9:161-178.

164. Saaty, T. L., 1987. How to Handle Dependence with the Analytic Hierarchy Process. Mathematical Modelling, 9:369-376.

165. Sadagopan, S. and A. Ravindran, 1986. Interactive Algorithms for Multiple Criteria Nonlinear Programming Problems. European Journal of Operational Research, 25:247-257.

166. Sakawa, M. and H. Yano, 1986. Interactive Fuzzy Decision Making for Multiobjective Nonlinear Programming Using Minimax Problems. Fuzzy Sets and Systems, 20:31-34.

167. Sakawa, M., H. Yano, and T. Yumine, 1987. An Interactive Fuzzy Satisficing Method for Multiobjective Linear Programming Problems and Its Application. IEEE Transactions on Systems, Man, and Cybernetics, SMC-17:654-661.

168. Schagen, I. P., 1986. Internal Modelling of Objective Functions for Global Optimization. Journal of Optimization Theory and Applications, 51:345-354.

169. Schneeweiss, C., 1987. On a Formalization of the Process of Quantitative Model Building. European Journal of Operational Research, 29:24-41.

170. Schniederjans, M. J., 1986. A Statistical Screening Procedure for Goal Programming Algorithm Selection. Socio-Economic Planning Sciences, 20:155-160.

171. Selbirak, T., 1986. Computer Program for the Zionts-Wallenius Interactive Multiple Objective Programming Procedure. Przeglad Statystyczny, 33:27-40 (in Polish).

172. Sharp, J. A., 1987. Haulier Selection - An Application of the Analytic Hierarchy Process. Journal of the Operational Research Society, 38:319-328.

173. Srinivasan, V. and Y. H. Kim, 1987. Credit Granting: A comparative Analysis of Classification Procedures. Journal of Finance, 42:665-680.

174. Starr, M. K. and M. Zeleny, eds, 1977. Multiple Criteria Decision Making. North-Holland.

175. Sterna-Karwat, A., 1986. A Note on the Solution Set in Optimization with Respect to Cones. Optimization, 17:297-303.

176. Sterna-Karwat, A., 1987. Continuous Dependence of Solutions on a Parameter in a Scalarization Method. Journal of Optimization Theory and Applications, 55:417-434.

177. Steuer, R. E., 1976. Linear Multiple Objective Programming With Interval Criterion Weights. Management Science, 23:305-316.

178. Steuer, R. E. An Interactive Multiple Objective Linear Programming Procedure. Multiple Criteria Decision Making, North-Holland, Amsterdam.

179. Stewart, T. J. 1987. An Interactive Multiple Objective Linear Programming Method Based on Piecewise Linear Additive Value Functions. IEEE Transactions on Systems, Man, and Cybernetics, SMC-17:799-805.

180. Stewart, T., 1987. Pruning of Decision Alternatives in Multiple Criteria Decision Making, Based on the UTA Method for Estimating Utilities. European Journal of Operational Research, 28:79-88.

181. Sunaga, T., M. A. Mazeed, E. Kondo, and T. Kiyota, 1987. A Practical Approach to Multiobjective Programming Problems. Transactions of the Japan Society of Mechanical Engineers, 53:2172-2176.

182. Swartz, C., 1987. Pshenichnyi's Theorem for Vector Minimization. Journal of Optimization Theory and Applications, 53:309-318.

183. Szidarovszky, F., M. E. Gershon and L. Duckstein, 1986. Techniques for Multiobjective Decision Making in Systems Management. Elsevier Science Publishers B. V., Amsterdam, The Netherlands.

184. Tabucanon, M. T., 1977. Multiobjective Linear Programming for Decision Making in Industrial Systems. Doctoral Dissertation, Asian Institute of Technology.

185. Tabucanon, M. T. and P. Adulbhan, 1979. A Technique for Solving Linear Programming Problems With Multiple Objectives. Procedings of the Pacific Conference on Operations Research, April 23-28, 1979, Seoul, Korea.

186. Tegham, J., Jr., D. Dufrane, M. Thauvoye, and P. Kunsch, 1986. STRANGE: An Interactive Method for Multi-objective Linear Programming under Uncertainty. European Journal of Operational Research, 26:65-82.

187. Thanassoulis, E., 1987. Two Optimality Tests for Differentiable Concave Value Functions in Linear Multi-Objective Programming Problems. Operations Research Letters, 6:53-60.

188. Ünlü, G., 1987. A Linear Bilevel Programming Algorithm Based on

Bicriteria Programming. Computers & Operations Research, 14:173-180.

189. Uy, E. T., 1986.   De Novo Formulation: Resource and Product Mix Optimization. M. Eng. Research Study, RSPR No. IE 86-2, Asian Institute of Technology.

190. Vályi, I., 1987.   Approximate Saddle Point Theorems in Vector Optimization. Journal of Optimization Theory and Applications, 55:435-448.

191. Verma, R. K., 1986. Multiobjective Optimization of a Queueing system. Optimization, 17:103-115.

192. Vetschera, R., 1986. Sensitivity Analysis for the ELECTRE Multicriteria Method. Zeitschrift für Operations Research, 30:99-117.

193. Warburton, A., 1987.   Approximation of Pareto Optima in Multiple Objective, Shortest-Path Problems. Operations Research, 35:70-79.

194. Weir, T., 1987.   A Converse Duality Theorem in Multiple Objective Programming. Operations Research Letters, 6:129-130.

195. Weir, T., B. Mond, and B. D. Craven, 1986.   On Duality for Weakly Minimized Vector Valued Optimization Problems. Optimization 17:711-721.

196. Werners, B., 1987. Interactive Multiple Objective Programming Subject to Flexible constraints. European Journal of Operational Research, 31:342-349.

197. Wheelwright, S. C. (advisory ed.), 1976. Decision Making: A Short Course for Professionals. John Wiley and Sons.

198. White, D. J., 1986. Epsilon Efficiency. Journal of Optimization Theory and Applications, 49:319-338.

199. Wiecek, M., 1987.   Multiobjective Models in Identification of Random Fields. European Journal of Operational Research, 32:267-275.

200. Wierzbicki, A. P., 1986.   On the Completeness and Constructiveness of Parametric Characterizations to Vector Optimization Problems.   OR Spektrum, Vol. 8, No. 2, pp.73-88.

201. Wu, N. L., 1987.   A Note on an Application of the Analytic Hierarchy Process. Decision Sciences, 18:687-688.

202. Yoon, K., 1987.   A Reconciliation Among Discrete compromise Solutions. Journal of the Operational Research Society, 38:277-286.

203. Yu, P. L. and E. Takeda, 1987.   A Verification Theorem of Preference Separability for Additive Value Functions.   Journal of Mathematical analysis and applications, 126:382-396.

204. Zahedi, F., 1986.   A Simulation Study of Estimation Methods in the Analytic Hierarchy Process.   Socio-Economic Planning Sciences, 20:347-354.

205. Zahedi, F., 1987. A Utility Approach to the Analytic Hierarchy Process.

Mathematical Modelling, 9:387-395.

206. Zeleny, M., 1973. Compromise Programming. In "Multiple Criteria Decision-Making", J. L. Cochrane and M. Zeleney (eds.), University of South Carolina Press, pp. 262-301.

207. Zeleny, M., 1974. Linear Multiobjective Programming. Springer-Verlag, New York.

208. Zeleny, M., 1976. Multiobjective Design of High Productivity Systems. Procedings of Joint Automatic Control Conference, Paper APPL9-4, New York.

209. Zeleny, M., 1982. Multiple Criteria Decision Making, McGraw-Hill, New York.

210. Zeleny, M., 1986. Optimal System Design with Multiple Criteria: De Novo Programming Approach. Engineering Cost and Production Economics. Special Issue on Multiple Criteria Decision Making, 10:89-94.

211. Zeleny, M., 1986. An External Reconstruction Approach (ERA) to Linear Programming. Computers & Operations Research, 13:95-100.

212. Zhukovin, V. E., F. V. Burshtein, and E. S. Korelov, 1987. A Decision Making Model with Vector Fuzzy Preference Relation. Fuzzy Sets and Systems, 22:71-80.

213. Zionts, S. and S. Wallenius, 1980. Identifying Efficient Vectors: Some Theory and Computational Results. Operations Research, 24:785-793.

214. Zlobec, S., 1986. Input Optimization: III. Optimal Realization of Multi-Objective Models. Optimization, 17:429-445.

215. Zopounidis, C., 1987. Multicriteria Decision Making Methodology for the Evaluation of the Risk of Failure and an Application. Foundations of Control Engineering, 12:45-46.

CHAPTER V

MCDM APPLICATIONS IN PRODUCTION MANAGEMENT

5.1 INTRODUCTION

A "production system" is a unified assemblage of hardwares which include workers, production facilities (including tools, jigs and fixtures), materials handling equipment, and other supplementary devices. This is supported by the software, which is production information, namely, production method and technology. This system performs on production objects (raw materials or other parts) to generate useful products, thereby creating utility. The structural aspect of a production system is a static spatial structure of a plant layout. It influences the effectiveness of the transformation process in production. The transformational aspect of production systems is to convert factors of production, especially, raw materials, into finished products, aiming maximum productivity. This is the "flow of materials", which constitutes the "production process system" or "production logistic system". The procedural aspect of production systems constitutes the so-called "management cycle", which consists of planning, implementation, and control. This aspect of production system has two phases: "strategic production planning" and "operational production management".

Strategic production planning deals with long term production problems existing between the system and its surrounding environment. It includes, among others, establishing production objectives, product planning or deciding what commodities the firm should produce, timely acquisition of production resources, and optimal allocation of these resources to the various subsystems in the organization for effective use.

Operational production management is concerned with solving short term problems involved in the system, subject to the policies established in strategic production planning. Its aim is to ensure smooth flow of production information and continuous operation of production processes. It consists of five stages, namely:

(i) Aggregate production planning - determining kinds of products and their quantities to be produced in specified time periods.

(ii) Production process planning - determining the production process or route which effectively converts inputs (factors of production) into outputs (finished products).

(iii) Production scheduling - establishing an actual implementation time schedule for every job concerned with production; that is, when, with what machine, and who does the operation?

(iv) Production implementation - executing actual production operations.

(v) Production control - modifying the deviation between the actual production performance and the production standard which has been set at the planning stages.

Production activities are efficiently and economically executed in a plant (the structural aspect of manufacturing system) by completely unifying the flow of materials (production process system) and the flow of information (production management system), which are treated based on the transformational and procedural aspects of production systems. This unified and integrated production study may be called "Production/Manufacturing Systems Engineering".

The value of produced goods is determined by the following three criteria: quality, cost/price, and volume/delivery. Hence, it is the overall objective of production management to make products with the desired function at a fast rate and the lowest possible cost according to a specified production plan.

Structures and functions of production systems differ, depending on the types of products and the nature of production processes of the firm. The production function in manufacturing firms is based on the flow of materials; that is, factors of production, especially raw materials, are acquired from the external environment, and converted into finished products that are brought to market as commodities. This is the logistic system, which is a serial flow of procurement, manufacture, sales and inventory. The procurement (or purchasing) subsystem acquires required quantities of production resources for manufacturing in predetermined dates. The manufacturing subsystem makes products (commodities) required by the sales division, in relation to finished product inventory. The sales subsystem delivers commodities of required quantities at reasonable prices and at appropriate periods according to consumers' orders or market demands. It is the inventory subsystem that provides the buffer for raw materials, goods-in-process, and finished products.

Effective production is executed in the logistic system through the operation planning system. The major functions in this system which include production planning, sales planning and product planning, are undertaken based on the forecast of future demands for the finished products. In order to produce the quantities of specified products established as sales goals, detailed feasible plans for operating the logistic system are established in the production planning subsystem by materials planning, facilities planning, manpower planning, process planning and scheduling, and inventory planning. Thus, procurement of factors of production, especially raw materials, plant layout, man-job assignment, conversion process of raw materials into the products, etc. are designed.

If the logistic system is not executed as designed because of occurrence of unforseen situations, such as the breakdown of production facilities, absence of workers, delivery delay of raw materials, etc., follow-up is performed by the operation control system.   Controlling the flow of raw materials to finished products (purchasing control, production control, quality control, sales control, and inventory control) and controlling of resources of man, machine, and money (personnel control, facilities control, and cost control) are undertaken.

Top management supervises the logistic system and the operation planning and control systems, giving appropriate directions and orders to lower level systems.   This is the function of the administrative planning system.   This system establishes proper management objectives.

The set of criteria for decision making may vary from firm to firm. A manufacturer facing a steady and reliable demand is likely to be concerned with low cost and rapid delivery.   A market creating firm, in contrast, would typically emphasize reliable delivery and product flexibility.   Innovative firms are most likely concerned with high quality, reliable delivery, and the learning capacity of the employees. Additional criteria are taken into account by different firms at different times: consistent quality, low investment, volume flexibility, good working conditions, low pollution, product classification, and some others.   Using some combination of criteria could affect the success or failure of a firm. Using no criteria or too many criteria are both undesirable extremes and usually signal bad management.

5.2 AGGREGATE PRODUCTION PLANNING

Aggregate production planning is, hitherto, the area in production management wherein multiple criteria decision making techniques have been extensively applied.   The problem is concerned with specifying the optimal quantities to produce, the labor force to be maintained, and the inventory levels in order to meet demand for a prespecified planning horizon under multiple criteria. A typical aggregate production planning problem may have the following multiple objectives: minimize total cost, minimize amount of

inventory, maintain balanced labor force and workload, minimize use of overtime, etc.

5.2.1 GENERALIZED MODEL

This model capitalizes on the strength of goal programming in incorporating multiple goals and other policy considerations and to make an analysis that
allow the firm to efficiently view the effects of change in its goal structure
and target levels.

This model is formulated for multiple products, plants and periods. The
decision variables are purchase amounts of raw materials, emergency
(unexpected/rush delivery) purchases, regular time production, overtime
production, sales workers hired and fired in each period, and amount to be
transported. The state variables are inventory of each raw material, inventory
of each product in the plant, inventory of each product in the warehouse, and
workforce level in each period. Initial values of inventory levels and
workforce levels are assumed to be known.

Definition of subscripts:

$i = 1, \ldots, I$ denote the types of products

$j = 1, \ldots, J$ denote the plant locations

$k = 1, \ldots, K$ denote the raw material purchase locations

$r = 1, \ldots, R$ denote the types of raw materials

$t = 1, \ldots, T$ denote the time periods

$w = 1, \ldots, W$ denote the warehouse locations

Definition of variables:

$RN(r,k,j,t)$ = amount of raw material r purchased from location k in
period t at normal prices in plant j.

$RE(r,k,j,t)$ = amount of raw material r purchased from location k in
period t at emergency prices in plant j.

$XN(i,j,t)$ = amount of product i produced by plant j in period t in
normal time.

$XO(i,j,t)$ = amount of product i produced by plant j in period t in
overtime.

$X(i,j,t)$ = total amount of product i produced by plant j in period t.

$T(i,j,w,t)$ = quantity transshipped from plant j to warehouse w of
product i in period t.

$IRM(r,j,t)$ = inventory level of raw material r, in plant j at the end of period t.

W (j,t)   = workforce level in plant j during period t.

FG (i,j,t)   = finished goods inventory level of item i in plant j at the end of period t.

WI (i,w,t)   = inventory level at warehouse w for item i at the end of period t.

D (i,w,t)   = demand for item i at warehouse w in period t.

H (j,t)   = no. of workers hired in plant j during period t.

L (j,t)   = no. of workers fired in plant j during period t.

b (r,j,t)   = requirement of raw material r by plant j for production of finished goods during period t.

Constraints:

(i) Raw Materials (Input System)

The decision variable RN (i,j,t) must have an upper and lower bound. These bounds indicate the minimum and the maximum batch size restricted by transportation, investment and other considerations that could exist in practical situations.

$$RNMIN(r,j) \leq RN(r,j,k,t) \leq RNMAX(r,j)$$

There is no need for bounds on RE (i,j,t) since they are purchased at random and in small quantities. Hence, capacity or transportation restrictions do not affect them.

Balance equation for each item of raw material to ensure that the level of present stock equals the level in previous period plus purchased quantity in present period minus quantity used in production is expressed as

$$IRM(r,j,t) = IRM(r,j,t-1) + RN(r,j,k,t) + RE(r,j,k,t) - b(r,j,t)$$

Constraint to represent total availability of raw materials in different periods is

$$RN(r,k,i,j,t) + RE(r,k,j,t) \leq A(r,t)$$

where A (r,t) is the maximum quantity available from all sources for raw material r in period t.

The inventory level (IRM) must have an upper and lower bound constraints restricted by investment policy and space considerations.

$$IRMIN(r,j,t) \leq IRM(r,j,t) \leq IRMAX(r,j,t)$$

(ii) Processing (Production) System

Constraints to represent normal and maximum capacity of plant are

$$\sum_i m(i,j)\, XN(i,j,t) \leq CMAX(j)$$

$$\sum_i m(i,j)\, XO(i,j,t) \leq a(j,t)\, CMAX(j)$$

where, $m(i,j)$ = machine time per unit of item i in plant j (machine hr/unit);

   $a(j,t)$ = fraction of machine capacity available for overtime;

   $CMAX(j)$ = maximum machine capacity in plant j.

Constraints to indicate raw material requirement of each item are obtained from the bill of materials or the product specifications of each item in each plant. This requirement is the demand faced by the raw material inventory system. Thus

$$\sum_i a1(r,i,j)\, X(i,j,t) = b(r,j,t)$$

$$X(i,j,t) = XN(i,j,t) + XO(i,j,t)$$

where $a1(r,i,j)$ is the amount of raw material r required to make one unit of i in plant j.

Machines will have set up costs and hence uneconomical if used below a certain level. It might require some special purpose tools which need not be purchased for very low degree of utilization. If some machines are rented, then the factory has to rent it for a minimum of hours. Thus, the constraint to ensure minimum level of utilization of machine capacity is expressed as

$$\sum_i m(i,j)\, XN(i,j,t) \geq CMIN(j)$$

where $CMIN(j)$ is the minimum level of utilization in plant j.

Unit cost of production are calculated for an average level of activity, hence, one needs to ensure that the solution does not provide extreme values for which the cost parameters are not valid. Thus, the upper and lower bounds on the quantity of products made are incorporated into the model as

$$LX(i,j) \leq X(i,j,t) \leq UX(i,j)$$

where,

$LX(i,j)$ = the minimum quantity of item i that must be produced in plant j;

$UX(i,j)$ = the maximum quantity of item i that can be produced in plant j.

Sub-contracting can be included in this model by considering it as a separate plant with production cost parameter equal to the price charged by the contractor. There is no inventory and workforce level for this plant.

(iii) Labor Force

Total labor force level equals labor level in the previous period plus worker hired minus worker fired during the period. Labor force balance is expressed as

$$W(j,t) = W(j,t-1) + H(j,t) - L(j,t)$$

A minimum number of laborers is essential for the system to continue running, while the maximum level is determined by management policy. The constraint to indicate the minimum and maximum workers' level is expressed as

$$WMIN(j) \leq W(j,t) \leq WMAX(j)$$

where $WMIN(j)$ and $WMAX(j)$ are the minimum and maximum worker level allowed in plant j.

Since productivity is not the same in normal and overtime production, coefficients are introduced. Constraints to represent availability of labor for normal and overtime hours are

$$\sum_i \ell(i,j) \; XN(i,j,t) \leq r \; W(j,t)$$

$$\sum_i \ell(i,j) \; XO(i,j,t) \; p \leq a(j,t) \; r \; W(j,t)$$

where,

$\ell(i,j)$ = Labor time for one unit of item i in plant j (man-hr/unit);

r = Regular time per worker (man-hr/day);

$a(j,t)$ = Fraction of regular workforce available for overtime in plant j in period t;

P = Production coefficient in overtime as fraction of normal time.

(iv)   Finished Goods Inventory

Present stock equals inventory level in previous period plus produced quantity in present period minus quantity distributed to warehouse in present period.   Hence, the finished goods inventory balance equation is

$$FG(i,j,t) = FG(i,j,t-1) + X(i,j,t) - T(i,j,w,t)$$

Upper and lower bounds on inventory level are introduced as

$$FGMIN(i,j) \leq FG(i,j,t) \leq FGMAX(i,j)$$

where FGMIN and FGMAX are the lower and upper limits allowed for item i in plant j.

(v)   Transshipment - Plant to Warehouse

Upper and lower bounds on the decision variable $T(i,j,k,t)$ are set to ensure that the average unit transportation cost calculations remain valid. Thus,

$$TMIN(j,w) \leq \sum_i T(i,j,w,t) \leq TMAX(j,w)$$

where TMIN and TMAX are the minimum and maximum levels of shipment allowed from plant j to warehouse w.

(vi)   Warehouse

Stock level at the end of the present period equals the stock level at the end of the previous period plus the quantity shipped into the warehouse during the present period minus the sales in the present period.   This warehouse stock level balance equation is expressed as

$$WI(i,w,t) = WI(i.w.t-1) + T(i,j,w,t) - D(i,w,m,t)$$

Upper and lower bounds on warehouse inventory level are introduced via the following relationship:

$$WMIN(i,w) < WI(i,w,t) < WMAX(i,w)$$

(vii)   Total Budget Constraint

$$
\begin{aligned}
&\sum_i \sum_j \sum_k \sum_t c(1,i,k,t)\ RN(i,j,k,t) \\
&+ \sum_i \sum_j \sum_k \sum_t c(1,i,k,t)\ RE(i,j,k,t) \qquad\qquad (I)\\
&+ \sum_i \sum_j \sum_t c(2,i,j,t)\ IRM(i,j,t) \\[4pt]
&+ \sum_i \sum_j \sum_t c(3,i,j,t)\ X(i,j,t) \qquad\qquad\quad (II)\\[4pt]
&+ \sum_j \sum_t c(4,t)\ w(j,t) \\
&+ \sum_i \sum_j \sum_t co(4,t)\ \ell(i,j)\ XO(i,j,t) \qquad\quad (III)\\[4pt]
&+ \sum_i \sum_j \sum_t c(5,i,j,t)\ FG(i,j,t) \qquad\qquad\quad (IV)\\[4pt]
&+ \sum_i \sum_j \sum_w \sum_t c(6,i,j,w,t)\ T(i,j,w,t) \qquad (V)\\[4pt]
&+ \sum_i \sum_w \sum_t c(7,i,w,t)\ WI(i,w,t) \quad \le\ BT \qquad (VI)
\end{aligned}
$$

where,

$c(1,i,k,t)$ = normal cost or raw material i from location k in period t;

$ce(1,i,k,t)$ = emergency cost of raw material i from location k in period t;

$c(2,i,j)$ = cost of storing raw material i in plant j;

$c(3,i,j)$ = unit cost of production (excluding labor and raw material) for item i in plant j;

$c(4,t)$ = normal labor cost during period t;

$o(4,t)$ = overtime labor cost during period t;

$c(5,i,j)$ = cost of storing one unit of finished product in plant j;

$c(6,i,j,w,t)$ = cost of transportation for one unit of i from j to w in period t

$c(7,i,w)$ = cost of storing one unit of product i in warehouse w;

BT   = total budget for the planning horizon;

(I)   = total (purchase + storage) raw material cost for the planning horizon;

(II)   = total production cost;

(III)   = total labor cost (normal + overtime);

(IV)   = total storage cost of finished goods;

(V)   = total transshipment cost;

(VI)   = total storage cost at warehouse.

(viii)   Cash flow

It is assumed that credit is given for all external expenses, purchase and transportation for one period and that all storage space is owned by the company. Labor expenditure will have to be paid in the same period when it is incurred.

$$
\left.
\begin{aligned}
& \sum_i \sum_j \sum_k c(1,i,k,t\text{-}1)\ RN(i,j,k,t\text{-}1) \\
& + \sum_i \sum_j ce(1,i,k,t\text{-}1)\ RE(i,j,k,t\text{-}1)
\end{aligned}
\right\} \quad (I)
$$

$$
+ \sum_i \sum_j f(1,t\text{-}1)\ c(3,i,j,t)\ X(i,j,t\text{-}1) \qquad (II)
$$

$$
\left.
\begin{aligned}
& + \sum_j c(4,t)\ w(j,t) \\
& + \sum_i \sum_j co(4,t)\ \ell(i,j)\ XO(i,j,t)
\end{aligned}
\right\} \quad (III)
$$

$$
+ \sum_j \sum_w c(6,i,j,w,t\text{-}1)\ T(i,j,w,t\text{-}1)\ \leq\ c(t) \qquad (IV)
$$

where

$f(1,t)$ = represents fraction of production cost that is incurred as cash in period t paid in t+1;

$c(t)$ = maximum cash outflow allowed in period t;

(I) = raw material purchase payment;

(II) = production purpose payment;

(III) = labor wages;

(IV) = transportation payment.

(ix)   Demand

$$
DMIN(i,w,t) \leq D(i,w,t) \leq DMAX(i,w,t)
$$

where $DMIN(i,w,t)$ and $DMAX(i,w,t)$ are minimum and maximum forecasted sales.

(x)   Cost Control Goals

Goals to maintain each cost component (production, labor, raw material, inventory, and transportation) within the target amount for each period are included for each period since cost control is done almost monthly.

a) Raw Material

$$\sum_i \sum_j \sum_k c(1,i,k,t) \, RN(i,j,k,t) + \sum_i \sum_j \sum_k ce(1,i,k,t) \, RE(i,j,k,t)$$

$$+ d^-(R,t) - d^+(R,t) = TCR(t)$$

where, $TCT(t)$ = target of cost for raw material in period t;

$d^-(R,t)$, $d^+(R,t)$ = deviational variables in period t.

b) Storage

$$\sum_i \sum_j c(2,i,j) \, IRM(i,j,t) + \sum_i \sum_j c(5,i,j) \, FG(i,j,t)$$

$$+ \sum_i \sum_w c(7,i,w) \, WI(i,w,t) + d^-(s,t) - d^+(s,t) = TCS(t)$$

where,

$TCS(t)$ = target storage cost of raw materials, finished goods at plant and warehouse in period t.

c) Labor

$$\sum_j c(4,t) \, W(j,t) + \sum_i \sum_j co(4,t) \, \ell(i,j) \, XO(i,j,t)$$

$$+ d^-(L,t) - d^+(L,t) = TCL(t)$$

where, $TCL(t)$ = the target labor cost in period t.

d) Production

$$\sum_i \sum_j c(3,i,j,t) \, X(i,j,t) + d^-(P,t) - d^+(P,t) = TCP(t)$$

where $TCP(t)$ = target production cost in period t.

e) Transportation

$$\sum_i \sum_j \sum_w c(6,i,j,w,t) \, T(i,j,w,t) + d^-(T,t) - d^+(T,t) = TCT(t)$$

where $TCT(t)$ = target cost incurred on transportation.

(xi)   Goal to maximize profit

Profit target is fixed for the whole planning horizon and hence need not be included for each period.

$$\sum_i \sum_w \sum_t r(i) \, D(i,w,t) - (\text{Total cost for all periods})$$

$$+ \, d^-(p) - d^+(p) = TCP$$

where TCP = represents target profit.

(xii)   Goal to produce   certain items at specified places to the maximum amount
        possible

Since the quality of certain items produced at some plants is more superior, therefore, a goal is established to send as much as possible in certain routes and avoid sending in other routes.

$$X(i,j,t) + dx^-(i,j,t) - dx^+(i,j,t) = TCX(i,j,t)$$

$$\text{for specified } i \text{ and } j$$

where $TCX(i,j,t)$ = Target for producing ith item in jth plant during period t.

$$T(i,j,w,t) + dT^-(i,j,w,t) + dT^+(i,j,w,t) = TRT(i,j,w,t)$$

$$\text{for specified } i, \ j, \text{ and } w$$

where $TRT(i,j,w,t)$ =   Target for transporting ith item from jth plant to wth warehouse.

(xiii) Goals to ensure that each plant is supplied with raw materials only from
        certain locations

$$RN(r,k,j,t) + dR^-(r,k,j,t) - dR^+(r,k,j,t) = TRR(r,k,j,t)$$

$$\text{for specified } r, \ k \text{ and } j$$

where $TRR(r,j,k,t)$ =   Target for purchasing raw material r from kth supplier to jth plant.

When the targets are set to zero, the goal of not producing certain items at some locations is imposed.

(xiv) Goal to maintain workforce stability

The workers will perceive greater job security if the firm does not make frequent and significant changes in the overall workforce.   Hence, it is desirable to reduce fluctuations in the workforce.

$$Dw(t) + d^-(w,t) - d^+(w,t) = WFC(t)$$

$$Dw(t) = | \sum_j H(j,t) - \sum_j L(j,t) |$$

where,

$Dw(t)$ — the net change in workforce level at the end of period t;

$WFC(t)$ — desired workforce level change in period t.

(xv) Goal to smoothen cost in each period during the planning period

This is aimed at avoiding large fluctuations in cost for each period. High peaks and low valleys in the cost distribution is undesirable.

$$\sum_i \sum_j \sum_k c(1,i,k,t) \; RN(i,j,k,t)$$

$$+ \sum_i \sum_j \sum_k ce(1,i,k,t) \; RE(i,j,k,t)$$

$$+ \sum_i \sum_j c(2,i,j,t) \; IRM(i,j,t)$$

$$+ \sum_i \sum_j c(3,i,j,t) \; X(i,j,t)$$

$$+ \sum_j c(4,t) \; w(j,t)$$

$$+ \sum_i \sum_j co(4,t) \; \ell(i,j) \; XO(i,j,t)$$

$$+ \sum_i \sum_j c(5,i,j,t) \; FG(i,j,t)$$

$$+ \sum_i \sum_j \sum_w c(6,i,j,w,t) \; T(i,j,w,t)$$

$$+ \sum_i \sum_w c(7,i,w,t) \; WI(i,w,t)$$

$$+ d^-(c,t) - d^+(c,t) \qquad = AC$$

where AC = Average budgeted cost for each period = BT/T.

The priorities and weights for different goals are not explicitly stated because these depend on the decision maker and the particular environment in which the model is applied.

The goal programming model of the aggregate planning problem involving purchase, production and logistics provides the decision maker with a model which is general enough to include many of the conflicting objectives facing the firm.   The major advantage of using GP is the facility to perform sensitivity analysis which gives the decision maker a better insight of the tradeoffs that exist among the conflicting goals.

One of the major drawbacks of the generalized model is its size and hence the computational difficulty.   The solution technique suggested for such a large scale model is the GP decomposition technique.   The constraints interlinking the various subsystems (called the A matrix) consist of the balanced equations for the input system, finished goods inventory and warehouse inventory.   The independent constraints in the subsystem (called the B matrix) will be constraints involving only the variables of the subsystem (e.g. production capacity, labor capacity, etc.).   Having segregated the problem, the GP decomposition technique becomes applicable.

Actual implementation of the model is dependent on the particular firm and its production characteristics.   It may be necessary to alter the complexity of the model to make it applicable to a specific production setting.   Data collection for a model of this type should be of little difficulty since most of the parameters are those normally measured in production operations.

One can see the important features that need to be considered while developing an aggregate production planning model.   The workforce and inventory levels are critical state variables that must be included.   One can also appreciate the different types of constraints encountered in the problem.   Use of GP aids in conducting sensitivity analysis which sharpens the decision maker's perception of the tradeoffs available.   One can also observe the importance of including parameters that can be conveniently and accurately estimated.   In developing a comprehensive model one also appreciates the importance of linking the various subsystems of the aggregate system.   This phenomenon is apparent in the models developed recently.   In the generalized model, a few additional subsystems have been linked in the aggregate planning system.

However, there exists wide scope for further improvement in aggregate production planning models.   One could include the multistage with interdependence between the products, stochastic demands and range estimates (instead of point estimates) for parameters.   The introduction of piecewise linear cost functions would make the models closer to reality.   The above suggestions for improvements along with computational testing provides opportunities for further research in this direction.

5.2.2 OTHER MODELS

Hindelang and Hill's model (1978) is formulated for a single plant with several departments each having the capability to produce one or more products. The decision variables incorporated in the model are the aggregate production rate, the workforce level, the amount of overtime work and the total amount of subcontracting.

This model is one of the few models which segregates the overall cost function into three major components, namely, workforce size, production rate and inventory costs. With this, management has flexibility in penalizing deviations from the various types of costs depending on the goals set by the firm.

The major economic constraints incorporated in the model are:

(i)   A budget constraint quantifying a strict limitation on cash over-flows on a departmental or plant wide basis.

(ii) A constraint which shows other limited resources required to produce various products.

(iii) An inventory balance equation for work-in-process units.

(iv) An inventory balance equation for all finished products.

(v)   Constraints showing upper and/or lower limits on any decision variable in the model.

This model is unique in the sense that factors like job relation, labor force stability, and segregation of costs have been explicitly considered.

Masud and Hwang's Model (1980) is an aggregate planning model for multiple product, single facility case. The decision variables are regular time production, overtime production, and sales of each product per period. The state variables are inventory and workforce levels. Initial values of inventory and workforce levels are assumed to be known.

This can be considered to be one of the most comprehensive models developed. Most of the pertinent factors are incorporated and designed in a realistic fashion. However, inventory carrying cost is not included and the other cost parameters are valid only for a range of production quantities, hence, upper and lower bounds need to be specified. It also suggests that production operations do not work under a pre-specified budget constraint.

Arthur and Lawrence's Model (1982) is a management planning model for developing production and shipping patterns for a firm with several products from its multiple processing locations through its multiple transshipment points to its customers. The production and shipping model involves the production of I items at J processing centers which are shipped to K transshipment points before meeting the demands of M customers over L periods of the planning horizon.

This is one of the few models that includes the transportation sector in aggregate planning. Consequently, the design of decision variables are slightly different from other models and the objectives appear very practical.

The following objectives are included:

(i)   Minimize the amount by which total costs exceed their target level.

(ii) Minimize the amount by which the final inventory of each item exceeds its desired level.

(iii) Minimize the amount of each item produced at a location and shipped to a transshipment point beyond its maximum desired levels.

(iv) Maximize the total amount of an item produced at a location above the minimum desired level.

(v)   Maximize the amount supplied by a transshipment point of an item delivered to a customer in the planning horizon.

In this model, the workforce level is neglected. However, it is justified for some companies where the workforce level is not essential in determining the production rate. Constraints on inventory level are very important but many models do not include them explicitly.

5.3   MULTISTAGE PRODUCTION PLANNING AND SCHEDULING

5.3.1   INTRODUCTION

A basic production stage consists of production line or production facilities and inventory bank (store) for a product. For instance, a manufacturing unit capable of handling only fabrication and welding or melting and casting or machining and assembling would be a basic production stage. It receives inputs from raw materials and/or from one or more other stages (Fig. 5.1).

Fig. 5.1 Basic Production Stage

The various production stages linked together by in-process inventories form a multistage production system.   The characteristic of such a system is that in-process inventories at different stages form a finished product.   The output of a given production stage will be fed into an inventory bank (i.e. store) from which the units can be used either as inputs to downstream produc- tion stages or to supply market requirements for the stage's products.   The products at each stage can be different and more than one (Fig. 5.2).

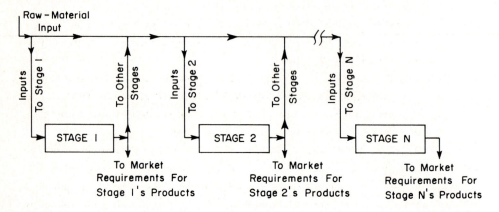

Fig. 5.2 Multistage Production System

5.3.2 MODEL FORMULATION

The model involves production of items $i = 1,\ldots,I$ at stage $j = 1,\ldots J$ in time period $t = 1,\ldots,T$ of the planning horizon unless otherwise specified.

B_{jit} = Backlog of stage j's product i, at the end of period t (units)

HNT_{jt} = Workers hired at non-transferable stage j, in period t (man-day)

HT_t = Total (cumulative) workers hired for transferable stage in period t

I_{jit} = Inventory of stage j's product i, at the end of period t (units)

LNT_{jt} = Workers laid off at nontransferable stage j in period t

LT_t = Total (cumulative) workers laidoff for transferable stage in period t

R_{jit} = Number of units of stage j's product i, subcontracted in period t (units)

S_{jit} = Market requirements (demand) of stage j's product i, in period t (units)

WNT_{jt} = Workforce at nontransferable stage j in period t ($j=1,\ldots,K$)

WT_t = Total workforce of transferable stages in period t

X_{Rjit} = Regular time production of stage j's product i, in period t (units)

X_{Ojit} = Overtime production of stage j's product i, in period t

The objective function of the model is to minimize the deviations from the goals, either positive or negative, having certain preemptive priorities and weights.

$$\text{Min.} \quad Z = [P_1 h_1(d^-, d^+), \ P_2 h_2(d^-, d^+), \ \ldots, \ P_5 h_5(d^-, d^+)]$$

Workforce Constraint:

Workforce of all the stages cannot be combined together in order to find out optimal production and workforce levels. Accordingly, stages have been classified into two types: stages whose workforce can be transferred to other stages; stages whose nature of work dictates specialized skill and knowledge, hence workforce is not transferable amongst these stages.

Suppose there are "K" stages whose workforce is not transferable amongst stages, then

$$W_t = WNT_t + WT_t \qquad \text{and} \qquad WNT_t = \sum_{j=1}^{K} WNT_{jt}$$

where W_t is the total workforce of all stages in period t and WNT_t the total workforce of nontransferable stages in period t.

Constraints for Stages whose Workers are not Transferable:

Regular time and overtime production cannot be more than the available labor.

$$\sum_{i=1}^{I} a_{ji} X_{Rjit} \leq \delta_R \ WNT_{jt}$$

where, a_{ji} = labor time required to produce one unit of production stage j's product i (man-hour/unit); and

δ_R = regular time per worker (man-hour/man-day).

$$\sum_{i=1}^{I} a_{ji} X_{Ojit} \leq \delta_{ot} \ \beta_{jt} \ WNT_{jt}$$

where δ_{ot} and β_{jt} are overtime per worker (man-hour/man-day) and fraction of regular workforce available for overtime at nontransferable stage j, respectively, in period t.

Workforce in each period equals workforce in the previous period plus the change in workforce in the current period:

$$WNT_{jt} = WNT_{jt-1} + HNT_{jt} - LNT_{jt}$$

Workforce in each period cannot be more than the maximum employable workforce in that period:

$$WNT_{jt} \leq WNT_{jtmax}.$$

Constraints for Stages whose Workers are Transferable:

$$\sum_{j=J-K}^{J} \sum_{i=1}^{I} a_{ji} X_{Rjit} \leq \delta_R WT_t$$

$$\sum_{j=J-K}^{J} \sum_{i=1}^{I} a_{ji} X_{Ojit} \leq \delta_{ot} \beta_t WT_t$$

$$WT_t = WT_{t-1} + HT_t - LT_t$$

$$WT_t \leq WT_{tmax}.$$

where β_t is the fraction of regular workforce available at all other trans-ferable stages (cumulative) on overtime in period t.

Production Capacity Constraints:

Regular time and overtime production in any period can not be more than the available machine capacity in that period.

$$\sum_{i=1}^{I} b_{ji} X_{Rjit} \leq M_{jt}$$

where,

b_{ji} = machine time required to produce one unit of production stage j's product i (man-hour/unit); and

M_{jt} = regular time machine capacity available at stage j in period t (machine hour).

$$\sum_{i=1}^{I} b_{ji} X_{Ojit} \leq O_{jt}$$

where O_{jt} = overtime machine capacity available at stage j in period t.

The machine utilization in each period cannot be less than a certain minimum capacity:

$$\sum_{i=1}^{I} b_{ji} \, X_{Rjit} \geq M_{jtmin}.$$

Inventory Constraints:

The demand over and above the available production capacity must either be backlogged into the next period or has to go unsatisfied. The backlogs can be only for the market requirements. The requirements for the subsequent production stages cannot be backlogged and has to be fulfilled during that period, since production levels are variable themselves. However, backlog for the market must be fulfilled within the next period.

Usually it does not happen that all of the stages produce marketable products. Often the lower numbered stages provide component parts to higher numbered stages which in turn are further processed and assembled at the final stage(s) to a marketable product form. In periods of heavy demand, when the firm can not fulfill the market requirements, it can subcontract the component parts or even the products of different stages to other firms.

Inventory of any product at the end of any period is equal to the inventory of that product at the end of the previous period plus regular and overtime production and quantity subcontracted in that period minus the quantity sold in that period and backlogged of the previous period plus the quantity to be backlogged in the current period minus the quantity required for the next stages.

$$I_{jit} = I_{jit-1} + X_{Rjit} + X_{Ojit} + R_{jit} - (S_{jit} + B_{jit-1}) + B_{jit}$$

$$- \sum_{k=j+1}^{J} \sum_{n=1}^{I} \alpha_{jikn} \, (X_{Rknt} + X_{Oknt})$$

where $\alpha_{jikn} \geq 0$ is the number of units of production stage j's product i required to produce one unit of stage k's ($k = j+1,\ldots,J$) product n ($n = 1,\ldots,I$) and would be zero if stage j's product i is not being used for the production of stage k's product n. Note that Inventory I_{jit} and Backlog B_{jit} cannot take place simultaneously in any time period.

Inventory of the previous period plus regular and overtime production and quantity subcontracted in any period must be greater than the minimum sales of that period plus the quantity backlogged of the previous period and quantity required for the subsequent stages.

$$I_{jit-1} + X_{Rjit} + X_{Ojit} + R_{jit} \geq (S_{jitmin} + B_{jit-1})$$

$$+ \sum_{k=j+1}^{J} \sum_{n=1}^{I} \alpha_{jikn} (X_{Rknt} + X_{Oknt})$$

Sales should be within certain lower and upper limits:

$$S_{jitmin} \leq S_{jit} \leq S_{jitmax}$$

where S_{jitmin} is minimum sales of stage j's product i and S_{jitmax} is maximum forecasted sales of stage j's product i, in period t (units).

The inventory equations for the last production stage J are:

$$I_{Jit} = I_{Jit-1} + X_{RJit} + X_{OJit} + R_{Jit} - (S_{Jit} + B_{Jit-1}) + B_{Jit}$$
$$I_{Jit-1} + X_{RJit} + X_{OJit} + R_{Jit} \geq (S_{Jitmin} + B_{Jit-1})$$
$$S_{Jitmin} \leq S_{Jit} \leq S_{Jitmax}$$

Goal Constraints:

Profit is the main objective of most organizations. This goal constraint is concerned with maximizing the contribution to profit over the planning horizon.

$$\underbrace{\sum_{t=1}^{T} \sum_{j=1}^{J} \sum_{i=1}^{I} r_{jit} S_{jit}}_{\text{(revenue)}} - \underbrace{\sum_{t=1}^{T} C_{RT} W_t}_{\text{(labor cost)}} - \underbrace{\sum_{t=1}^{T} \sum_{j=1}^{J} \sum_{i=1}^{I} C_{Ot} (a_{ji} X_{Ojit})}_{\text{(overtime cost)}}$$

$$- \underbrace{\sum_{t=1}^{T} \sum_{j=1}^{J} \sum_{i=1}^{I} C_{Mjit} (X_{Rjit} + X_{Ojit})}_{\text{(material cost)}} - \underbrace{\sum_{t=1}^{T} \sum_{j=1}^{J} \sum_{i=1}^{I} C_{Cjit} R_{jit}}_{\text{(subcontracting cost)}}$$

$$+ d_i^- - d_i^+ = DCP$$

where,

r_{jit} = selling price per unit of production stage j's product i in period t ($/unit);

C_{Rt}/C_{Ot} = regular time/overtime pay rate in period t ($/man-day) ($/man-hour);

c_{Mjit} = raw material cost to produce one unit of stage j's product i in period t ($/unit);

c_{Cjit} = subcontracting cost of stage j's product i in period t ($/unit);

d_i^-/d_i^+ = underachievement/overachievement of the ith goal; and

DCP = desired contribution to profit ($).

Subcontracting, usually, involves a higher cost (due to subcontractors' overhead and profits, etc.) per unit of output. Hence this goal constraint is to minimize the amount of expenditure in subcontracting:

$$\sum_{t=1}^{T} \sum_{j=1}^{J} \sum_{i=1}^{I} c_{Cjit} R_{jit} + d_2^- - d_2^+ = TSC$$

where TSC = total subcontracting cost over all the periods ($).

Stabilization of workforce is necessary for economic and efficient running of a firm. Each trained worker is an asset of the firm and the firm losses this asset if the worker finds work elsewhere. At the same time employment ups and downs affect the reputation of the firm and the quality of labor available. Thus this goal constraint is concerned with maintaining a balanced workforce.

$$\sum_{t=1}^{T} \sum_{j=1}^{J} (HNT_{jt} + LNT_{jt}) + \sum_{t=1}^{T} (HT_t + LT_t) + d_3^- - d_3^+ = TCW$$

where TCW = total change in workforce over all the periods (man-day).

A heavy amount of capital is tied up in inventories but at the same time these are necessities for effective utilization of the facilities and staff in the face of demand fluctuations. So this goal constraint considers the minimization of inventory expenditure.

$$(1/T) [\sum_{t=1}^{T} \sum_{j=1}^{J} \sum_{i=1}^{I} c_{Sjit} I_{jit}] + d_4^- - d_4^+ = ACI$$

where,

c_{Sjit} = standard cost of stage j's product i in period t, ($/unit); and

ACI = average capital investment in inventory ($/period).

Postponing an order often causes loss of customer goodwill which in turn would almost certainly lead to lost orders and therefore lost profit in the future. Hence this goal constraint deals with the minimization of backorders.

$$(1/T) \; [\; \sum_{t=1}^{T} \; \sum_{j=1}^{J} \; \sum_{i=1}^{I} \; r_{jit} \; B_{jit} \;] + d_5^- - d_5^+ = ASB$$

where ASB = average loss of sales due to backorders ($/period).

5.3.3 MODEL APPLICATION

An example is formulated to illustrate the model application. A simple case of a manufacturing firm producing products A (Diesel engines) and B (Pumps) with four stages and three time periods.   Products A and B are being manufactured in two independent production shops comprising of machining and assembling sections.   The two other shops, i.e. foundry and fabrication, manufacture component parts which are then machined and assembled in the respective shops.   There are four stages, namely, stage 1 (foundry), stage 2 (fabrication), stage 3 (machining and assembling of product A) and stage 4 (machining and assembling of product B).   The skill and knowledge required at foundry (stage 1) and fabrication (stage 2) are quite different from each other and also from the machining and assembling of A and B (stages 3 and 4), hence their workforces are not transferable to other shops.   The nature of work at machining and assembling of product A (stage 3) and machining and assembling of product B (stage 4) is quite similar, hence their workforces are transferable amongst each other but not to foundry (stage 1) and fabrication (stage 2).

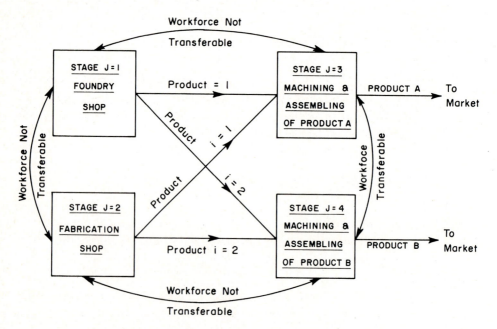

Fig. 5.3 Multistage Production Example

One unit of stage 3's product, i.e. product A, requires one unit of stage 1 and one unit of stage 2's product. One unit of stage 4's product, i.e. product B, requires one unit of stage 1 and one unit of stage 2's product. It is also assumed that the market requirements of stage 1 and 2's products are zero in any time period. The market requirements of these stages can serve as repair or replacement parts of products A and B. Subcontracting is considered for stages 1 and 2 only which manufactures component parts. Fig. 5.3 illustrates the example and the data are given in Table 5.2.

Table 5.2 Data for Model Application

a. Product Sales Data

j	i	sales (units)	Period t 1	2	3
3	1	min	100	150	80
		max	200	400	250
4	1	min	400	500	450
		max	700	1000	800

b. Labor and Machine Time Data

j	i	a_{ji}	b_{ji}
1	1	4	3
	2	5	4.5
2	1	2	1.5
	2	3	2
3	1	5	4
4	1	4	2.5

c. Workforce & Machine Capacity Data

j		Period t 1	2	3
1	W_{max}	400	450	400
	M_{jt}	2500	2600	2500
2	W_{max}	350	250	300
	M_{jt}	1100	1000	1050
3	W_{max}	70	68	80
	M_{jt}	430	400	550
4	W_{max}	210	242	220
	M_{jt}	1200	1600	1400

d. Cost Data

j	i	c_{Mjit}	c_{Cjit}	c_{Sjit}	r_{jit}
1	1	15	80	63	-
	2	50	100	75	-
2	1	25	65	51	-
	2	20	70	54	-
3	1	20	-	186	270
4	1	15	-	210	300

e. Miscellaneous Data

	Period t			
	1	2	3	
β_{1t}	0.3	0.3	0.3	
β_{2t}	0.4	0.4	0.4	
β_t	0.4	0.4	0.4	
δ_{ot}	4	4	3	
	(man-hour/man-day)			
Fraction of capacity for overtime use	0.5	0.6	0.6	

C_{Rt} = 68 \$/man-day (Assumed to be constant over the planning horizon).

C_{Ot} = 17 \$/man-hour (Assumed to be constant over the planning horizon).

δ_R = 8 man-hour/man-day.

At least 80% of the capacity of each stage must be used in each period. Machine capacity for overtime use O_{jt} must be fraction of the regular machine capacity M_{jt} as given below. (Assumed to be the same for each stage).

Other data are given below:

Initial Values:

W_{10} = 380 W_{20} = 300 W_0 = 290

I_{110}= 30 I_{120}= 100 I_{210}= 0 I_{220} = 50

I_{310}= 10 B_{310}= 0 I_{410}= 0 B_{410} = 50

Goals:

(1) Desired contribution to profit, DCP = \$ 350,000

(2) Total subcontracting cost, TSC = \$ 10,000

(3) Total change in workforce, TCW = 125 man-day

(4) Average capital investment in inventory, ACI = \$ 12,000/period

(5) Average loss of sales due to backorders, ASB = \$ 25,000/period

The model consists of 105 decision variables, 120 structural constraints and 5 goal constraints. The following priority structure is considered.

P_1 : Highest Priority : Maximize contribution to profit.

P_2 : Second Priority : Minimize changes in workforce.

P_3 : Third Priority : Minimize amount of subcontracting.

P_4 : Fourth Priority : Minimize amount of backorders.

P_5 : Fifth Priority : Minimize amount of inventory.

The GP objective function resulting from the priority assignment is:

$$\text{Min.} \quad Z = P_1 d_1^- + P_2 d_3^+ + P_3 d_2^+ + P_4 d_5^+ + P_5 d_4^+$$

Table 5.3 compares the actual solution obtained with the goal levels. The goals assigned to priorities P_1, P_2, P_3 and P_5 were achieved. However P_4 goal could not be achieved.

In order to see if the unachieved backorders goal at priority P_4 can be achieved by rearranging priorities and what would be its effect on other goals, the model was solved for another two different sets of priority structures. The solutions to each set of priority structure along with the priorities assigned to each of the goals are given in Table 5.4.

Table 5.3   Goal Achievements in First Case

Priority	Goal Type	Goal Level	Actual Solution	Achieved/ Not Achieved
P_1	Contribution to Profit ($)	350,000	350,000	Achieved
P_2	Changes in workforce (man-day)	125	125	Achieved
P_3	Subcontracting ($)	10,000	10,000	Achieved
P_4	Backorders/period ($)	25,000	34,429	Not Achieved
P_5	Inventory/period ($)	12,000	4,926	Achieved

Table 5.4   Summary of Solution

Goal Type	Goal Level	Priority 1st Case / Actual Solution 2nd Case	Achieved or Not Achieved 3rd Case	
Contribution to Profit ($)	350,000	(1) 350,000 Achieved	(1) 350,000 Achieved	(5) 246,713 N/Achieved
Changes in workforce (man-day)	125	(2) 125 Achieved	(3) 195 N/Achieved	(4) 125 Achieved
Subcontracting ($)	10,000	(3) 10,000 Achieved	(4) 12,339 N/Achieved	(3) 10,000 Achieved
Backorders/period ($)	25,000	(4) 34,429 N/Achieved	(2) 31,507 N/Achieved	(1) 0 Achieved
Inventory/period ($)	12,000	(5) 4,926 Achieved	(5) 8,848 Achieved	(2) 12,000 Achieved

In the second case, as we see from the Table, the backorders goal could not be achieved even by giving the second highest priority (while keeping the first priority the same as in the first case).   Rather, this made two more priorities P_3 and P_4 not achieved which were achieved in the first case.   A third case, then, assigning the highest priority to the backorders goal was considered.   The priority structure and results of this case can be seen in Table 5.4.   The results show that it is possible to achieve backorders goal and others but by sacrificing contribution to profit goal by $103,287 ($350,000 - $246,713).

5.4   PRODUCTION PLANNING: THE CASE OF A CEMENT PLANT

The manufacturing process of a cement factory can be generally considered as composed of three major stages, namely: quarrying and raw materials blending; reaction or burning stage in a rotary kiln; and milling of kiln clinker.

For the plant considered by Adulbhan and Tabucanon (1979), the raw materials used consist of marl, clay and 25% red earth.   Because of the softness of the raw materials, the wet process is employed. These raw materials are crushed, milled and blended in two stages - coarse and fine milling operations - to form a homogeneous mix.   The subsequent reaction is influenced by the degree of final milling, which is called the milling of slurry, together with the homogeneity of the blend as well as by its chemical composition.   As the process employed is wet, milling takes place in the presence of large quantity of water making the final raw material, called slurry, to contain about one-third of its weight with water.

The raw material in the form of a slurry is then fed into the kiln by means of a feed control device.   During its passage down the kiln, the slurry undergoes a series of physical and chemical changes.   The chemical reactions are complex, a smaller amount of reaction taking place in the liquid state and a larger amount in the solid state.   Clinker from the kiln falls on to a grate cooler which is fed by air from the secondary air fan.

The last stage of the process involves the reduction of the kiln product to the finely divided final product, now called cement.   In the milling operation, a desired proportion of gypsum is added.   Gypsum is used to act as retarder for cement setting.   Cement output (unpacked) is stored in the cement silos.

Table 5.5 presents the major production facilities with their corresponding maximum capacities.   The layout of these facilities is shown in Fig. 5.4. The major facilities are indicated by alphabetical notations (a,b,c,...).

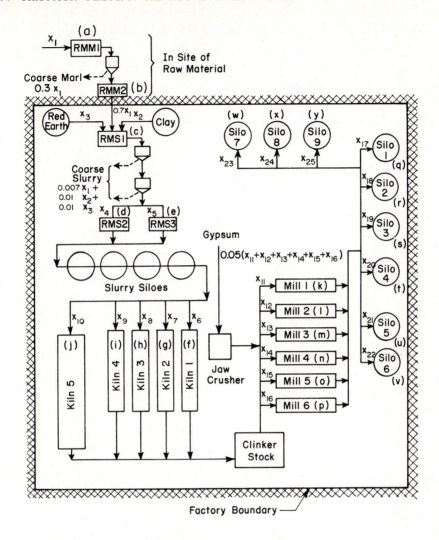

Fig. 5.4   A Cement Factory Facility Layout

The amounts of material input to each major production facility (x_j,
$j=1,\ldots,n$) are chosen as decision variables in this optimization model.   The
model is developed in monthly production planning basis.   Three essential sets
of constraints are considered: balance equations of materials throughout the
process; available capacity of production facilities; and forecasted customer
demand.

Table 5.5 Capacity of Major Production Facilities

Section	Facility name	Max Capacity (tons/month)
Marl quarrying	Raw Mill 1	315,000
	Raw Mill 2	189,000
Slurry preparation	Raw Mill 1	252,000
	Raw Mill 2	94,500
	Raw Mill 3	157,500
Burning	Rotary kiln 1	15,000
	Rotary kiln 2	15,000
	Rotary kiln 3	15,000
	Rotary kiln 4	15,000
	Rotary kiln 5	60,000
Cement Mill	Mill 1	13,860
	Mill 2	22,050
	Mill 3	22,050
	Mill 4	22,050
	Mill 5	22,050
	Mill 6	22,050
Inventory	Silo 1	38,000
	Silo 2	38,000
	Silo 3	87,000
	Silo 4	87,000
	Silo 5	70,000
	Silo 6	70,000
	Silo 7	4,000
	Silo 8	4,000
	Silo 9	4,000

Material Balance Constraints:

Material balance constraints represent balance equations due to the loss and addition of materials in the process. The balance equations, which consist of marl loss, slurry loss, maximum marl output (160,000 tons/month, established by management as caused by raw material constraint), maximum slurry output (200,000 tons/month,...), loss due to the evolution of carbon dioxide in converting slurry to clinker, and the addition of gypsum in the milling stage, are briefly summarized as follows: at marl quarrying section, about 30% of marl is lost due to the coarse milling operation of Raw mill 1; about 1% loss of slurry is found in the coarse slurry milling operation of slurry Raw mill 1; in converting slurry to clinker, 37.5% decrease in its weight is usually found due to the evolution of carbon dioxide from limestone; at milling section, 5% weight of material is increased due to the addition of gypsum.

Fig. 5.5 gives the process flow diagram showing the amounts of material (by weight) input to each facility as well as the incurred losses. Junctions are introduced for convenience and to help clarify the process flow diagram. With the aid of Fig. 5.5, the material balance constraints can be formulated.

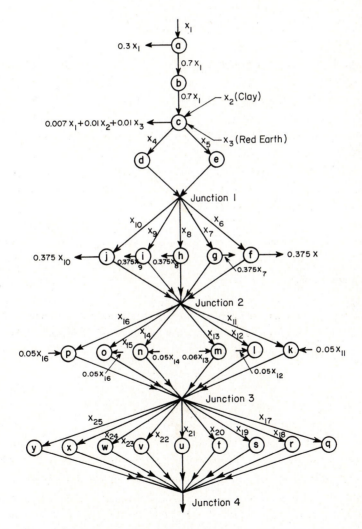

Fig. 5.5 Process Flow Diagram of Cement Manufacturing

Maximum Marl and slurry output,

$$0.7x_1 = 160,000,$$
$$x_4 + x_5 = 200,000.$$

Raw material proportions,

$$0.175x_1 + 0.25x_2 - 0.75x_3 = 0.$$

Material balance at node c,

$$0.693x_1 + 0.99x_2 + 0.99x_3 + x_4 - x_5 = 0.$$

Material balance at junction 1,

$$x_4 + x_5 - x_6 - x_7 - x_8 - x_9 - x_{10} = 0.$$

Material balance at junction 2,

$$0.625x_6 + 0.625x_7 + \ldots + 0.625x_{10} - x_{11} - x_{12} - \ldots - x_{16} = 0.$$

Material balance at junction 3,

$$1.05x_{11} + 1.05x_{12} + \ldots + 1.05x_{16} - x_{17} - x_{18} - \ldots - x_{25} = 0.$$

Capacity Constraints:

Capacity constraints are based on the total amount of input materials as losses are not incurred at the beginning of the process.   The following constraints are developed with reference to Fig. 5.5 and Table 5.5.

$$x_1 \leq 315,000$$
$$0.7x_1 \leq 189,000$$
$$0.7x_1 + x_2 + x_3 \leq 252,000$$
$$x_4 \leq 94,000$$
$$x_5 \leq 157,500$$
$$x_6 \leq 15,000$$
$$x_7 \leq 15,000$$
$$x_8 \leq 15,000$$
$$x_9 \leq 15,000$$

$$x_{10} \qquad\qquad\qquad \leq \quad 60,000$$
$$1.05x_{11} \qquad\qquad\qquad \leq \quad 13,860$$
$$1.05x_{12} \qquad\qquad\qquad \leq \quad 22,050$$
$$1.05x_{13} \qquad\qquad\qquad \leq \quad 22,050$$
$$1.05x_{14} \qquad\qquad\qquad \leq \quad 22,050$$
$$1.05x_{15} \qquad\qquad\qquad \leq \quad 22,050$$
$$1.05x_{16} \qquad\qquad\qquad \leq \quad 22,050$$
$$x_{17} \qquad\qquad\qquad \leq \quad 38,000$$
$$x_{18} \qquad\qquad\qquad \leq \quad 38,000$$
$$x_{19} \qquad\qquad\qquad \leq \quad 87,000$$
$$x_{20} \qquad\qquad\qquad \leq \quad 87,000$$
$$x_{21} \qquad\qquad\qquad \leq \quad 70,000$$
$$x_{22} \qquad\qquad\qquad \leq \quad 70,000$$
$$x_{23} \qquad\qquad\qquad \leq \quad 4,000$$
$$x_{24} \qquad\qquad\qquad \leq \quad 4,000$$
$$x_{25} \leq \quad 4,000.$$

Each node of Fig. 5.5 corresponds to a constraint in the above set.

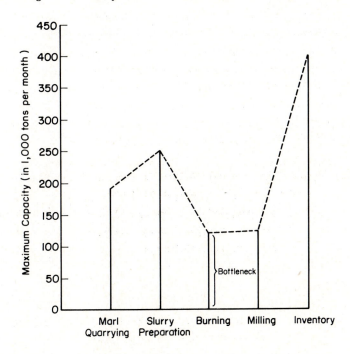

Fig. 5.6 Maximum Capacities of Major Operations of
Cement Plant

The management decision is to utilize the full capacity of the plant. Fig. 5.6 shows that in the existing design, the bottleneck is in the burning section. The full capacity of this section also dictates the maximum capacity of the factory; thus production is only constrained at most, to this amount at the burning stage:

$$x_6 + x_7 + x_8 + x_9 + x_{10} = 120,000.$$

The firm's management wants to optimize certain objectives in their response to numerous factors that shape the firm. Three cases of decision making are distinguished below:

Case 1: Minimization of manufacturing cost, Z_1

The cost of raw materials and other incurred costs are not included in the objective function since it is treated as an exogenous variable in this context. Table 5.6 provides the manufacturing cost coefficients of the major production facilities. This is done by setting the unit variable cost of Rotary kiln 1 equal to 1.0. Based on this, the other coefficients are then determined by normalizing them with respect to this coefficient. The reason behind the indexing system adopted here is two-fold: one is for convenience in the mathematical and overcomputational manipulations, and the other is to maintain the confidentiality of the real costs incurred by the plant under study.

The objective function can be derived as follows.

Minimize: $Z_1 = 0.2x_1 + 0.1(1.7x_1) + 0.22(0.7x_1 + x_2 + x_3) + 0.1x_4 + 0.1x_5 + x_6$
$+ 0.9x_7 + 1.2x_8 + 1.1x_9 + x_{10} + 0.171(1.05x_{11}) + 0.13(1.05x_{12})$
$+ 0.19(1.05x_{13}) + 0.15(1.05x_{14}) + 0.13(1.05x_{15}) + 0.12(1.05x_{16})$
$+ 0.121x_{17} + 0.121x_{18} + 0.123x_{19} + 0.122x_{20} + 0.122x_{21} + 0.120x_{22}$
$+ 0.120x_{23} + 0.120x_{24} + 0.120x_{25}$

or simplified as

Minimize: $Z_1 = 0.424x_1 + 0.22x_2 + 0.22x_3 + 0.1x_4 + 0.1x_5 + x_6 + 0.9x_7 + 1.2x_8$
$+ 1.1x_9 + x_{10} + 0.179x_{11} + 0.137x_{12} + 0.2x_{13} + 0.168x_{14} + 0.137x_{15}$
$+ 0.126x_{16} + 0.121x_{17} + 0.121x_{18} + 0.123x_{19} + 0.122x_{20} + 0.122x_{21}$
$+ 0.120x_{22} + 0.120x_{23} + 0.120x_{24} + 0.120x_{25}.$

Case 2: Maximization of capacity utilization, Z_2

For the sake of viability and stability of the firm, underutilization of the existing facilities has to be overcome. Capacity utilization can be formulated as follows.

Table 5.6 Manufacturing Cost Coefficients

Section	Facility name	Normalized cost Coefficients per unit ton of material
Marl quarrying	Raw mill 1	0.200
	Raw mill 2	0.100
Slurry preparation	Raw mill 1	0.220
	Raw mill 2	0.100
	Raw mill 3	0.100
Burning	Rotary kiln 1	1.000
	Rotary kiln 2	0.900
	Rotary kiln 3	1.200
	Rotary kiln 4	1.100
	Rotary kiln 5	1.000
Cement milling	Mill 1	0.171
	Mill 2	0.130
	Mill 3	0.190
	Mill 4	0.150
	Mill 5	0.130
	Mill 6	0.120
Inventory	Silo 1	0.121
	Silo 2	0.121
	Silo 3	0.123
	Silo 4	0.122
	Silo 5	0.122
	Silo 6	0.120
	Silo 7	0.120
	Silo 8	0.120
	Silo 9	0.120

$$\text{Maximize:} \quad Z_2 = \frac{x_1}{315} + \frac{0.7x_1}{189} + \frac{0.7x_1+x_2+x_3}{252} + \frac{x_4}{945} + \frac{x_5}{157.5} + \frac{x_6}{15} + \frac{x_7}{15} + \frac{x_8}{15}$$

$$+ \frac{x_9}{15} + \frac{x_{10}}{60} + \frac{1.05x_{11}}{13.86} + \frac{1.05x_{12}}{22.05} + \frac{1.05x_{13}}{22.05} + \frac{1.05x_{14}}{22.05}$$

$$+ \frac{1.05x_{15}}{22.05} + \frac{1.05x_{16}}{22.05} + \frac{x_{17}}{38} + \frac{x_{18}}{38} + \frac{x_{19}}{87} + \frac{x_{20}}{87} + \frac{x_{21}}{70} + \frac{x_{22}}{70}$$

$$+ \frac{x_{23}}{4} + \frac{x_{24}}{4} + \frac{x_{25}}{4}$$

The above function, called capacity utilization, is the summation of the individual utilization factor (i.e. load divided by maximum capacity) of all major production facilities (or nodes in Fig. 5.5). A simplified version (by 100,000 in x_i's) of the above function is:

$$\begin{aligned}\text{Maximize:} \quad Z_2 = {} & 0.965x_1+0.397x_2+0.397x_3+1.058x_4+0.636x_5+6.667x_6 \\ & +6.667x_7+6.667x_8+6.667x_9+1.667x_{10}+7.575x_{11}+4.762x_{12} \\ & +4.762x_{13}+4.762x_{14}+4.762x_{15}+4.762x_{16}+2.632x_{17}+2.632x_{18} \\ & +1.150x_{19}+1.150x_{20}+1.429x_{21}+1.429x_{22}+25x_{23}+25x_{24}+25x_{25}.\end{aligned}$$

Case 3:   Minimization of manufacturing cost and maximization of capacity utilization

When management decides to optimize the two objective functions simultaneously, the decision making situation becomes a bicriterion case:

$$\text{Minimize:} \quad Z_1 = f_1(x_1,x_2,\dots,x_{25}),$$
$$\text{Maximize:} \quad Z_2 = 10^{-5}f_2(x_1,x_2,\dots,x_{25}).$$

Suppose that management decided to have equal relaxation on these objectives until a feasible compromise is reached. Using the compromise constraint technique as discussed in Section 6, Chapter IV, the compromise constraint is derived as follows:

$$\frac{w_1}{2.458} \, [-f_1(x_1,x_2,\ldots,x_{25}) + 216,987.54]$$

$$- \frac{w_2}{47.431} \, [f_2(x_1,x_2,\ldots,x_{25}) - 1,623,350.44] = 0$$

Or,

$9.147x_1+4.642x_2+4.642x_3+2.988x_4+2.566x_5+25.964x_6+24.034x_7$
$+29.823x_9+20.964x_{10}+11.029x_{11}+7.406x_{12}+8.621x_{13}+8.004x_{14}$
$+8.621x_{15}+7.193x_{16}+4.967x_{17}+4.967x_{18}+3.524x_{19}+3.504x_{20}$
$+3.783x_{21}+3.754x_{22}+27.316x_{23}+27.316x_{24}+27.316x_{25} = 5,696,020.83.$

Discussion and interpretation of results:

Results of the optimization models are presented in Table 5.7.   A corollary summary is given in Table 5.8.

Allocation of the materials in the first three major operations - marl, quarrying, slurry preparation, and burning - are all the same for the three cases.   Data (Tables 5.5 and 5.6) show that smaller capacity facilities for the first three major operations bear smaller manufacturing cost; thus model results for all cases are in unison.

The burning stage serves as the bottleneck of the whole process, substantiated by the 100% utilization of all rotary kilns.   That the design of the production system is far below optimal, since full utilization of the burning power corresponds to a considerably less utilization of the other facilities. The inventory section lies on the extreme - it tolerates five silos to be idle, indefinitely, for cases 1 and 3, and four silos unused for case 2.   This problem - uneven utilization of facilities - deserves management's primal concern.

The factory under study is evidently typical of a system with a far-from-optimal design.   Allocations of process materials in the light of optimization are mostly falling outside the desirable range of a facility.   This is not only technically unhealthy; it also reduces productivity of the concerned facility and the plant as a whole.

Table 5.7 Monthly Material Allocation to Major Production Facilities
when Factory is Operating at Full Capacity

		Material Allocations		
Variable	Description	Case 1	Case 2	Case 3
x_1	Marl input to RMS 1	129,870	129,870	129,870
x_2	Clay input to RMS 1	0	0	0
x_3	Slurry input to RMS 1	30,303	30,303	30,303
x_4	Slurry input to RMS 2	94,500	94,500	94,500
x_5	Slurry input to RMS 3	25,500	25,500	25,500
x_6	Slurry input to kiln 1	15,000	15,000	15,000
x_7	Slurry input to kiln 2	15,000	15,000	15,000
x_8	Slurry input to kiln 3	15,000	15,000	15,000
x_9	Slurry input to kiln 4	15,000	15,000	15,000
x_{10}	Slurry input to kiln 5	60,000	60,000	60,000
x_{11}	Clinker input to mill 1	0	13,200	0
x_{12}	Clinker input to mill 2	21,000	21,000	21,000
x_{13}	Clinker input to mill 3	0	21,000	0
x_{14}	Clinker input to mill 4	12,000	19,800	12,000
x_{15}	Clinker input to mill 5	21,000	0	21,000
x_{16}	Clinker input to mill 6	21,000	0	21,000
x_{17}	Cement input to Silo 1	0	38,000	0
x_{18}	Cement input to Silo 2	0	28,750	0
x_{19}	Cement input to Silo 3	0	0	0
x_{20}	Cement input to Silo 4	0	0	0
x_{21}	Cement input to Silo 5	0	0	0
x_{22}	Cement input to Silo 6	70,000	0	67,393
x_{23}	Cement input to Silo 7	4,000	4,000	4,000
x_{24}	Cement input to Silo 8	4,000	4,000	3,357
x_{25}	Cement input to Silo 9	750	4,000	4,000

Table 5.8 Utilization of Major Production Facilities when
Factory is Operating at its Full Capacity

| | | Percent utilization | | |
Section	Facility name	Case 1	Case 2	Case 3
Marl quarrying	Raw mill 1	41.25	41.25	41.25
	Raw mill 2	48.15	48.15	48.15
Slurry preparation	Raw mill 1	48.10	48.10	49.10
	Raw mill 2	100	100	100
	Raw mill 3	16.19	16.19	16.19
Burning	Rotary kiln 1	100	100	100
	Rotary kiln 2	100	100	100
	Rotary kiln 3	100	100	100
	Rotary kiln 4	100	100	100
	Rotary kiln 5	100	100	100
Cement milling	Mill 1	0	100	0
	Mill 2	100	100	100
	Mill 3	0	100	0
	Mill 4	57.20	94.30	57.20
	Mill 5	100	0	100
	Mill 6	100	0	100
Inventory	Silo 1	0	100	0
	Silo 2	0	75.65	0
	Silo 3	0	0	0
	Silo 4	0	0	0
	Silo 5	0	0	0
	Silo 6	100	0	96.28
	Silo 7	100	100	100
	Silo 8	100	100	83.93
	Silo 9	18.75	100	100 100

5.5   PRODUCTION PLANNING: SHORT VERSUS LONG TERM

Rifai and Pecenka (1978) suggested goal programming as an effective technique in production planning wherein short-term and long-term goal achievements are distinguished. An illustrative example is presented below.

A certain company manufactures and markets two types of color television sets.   Type X contributes \$100 to profit, while type Y contributes \$120 to profit.   The delivery of these television sets to distributors is limited by storage and packaging capacities of 120,000 square inches and 64,000 seconds, respectively.   Televisison type X requires 60 square inches for storage while type Y requires 120 square inches.   In the packaging center, television type X requires 80 seconds while type Y requires 40 seconds.

If the marketing manager has only one objective, such as the maximization of profit, the problem may be formulated in an LP form as follows:

$$\text{Maximize:} \qquad Z = 100 \ x + 120 \ Y$$
$$\text{Subject to:} \qquad 60 \ X + 120 \ Y \le 120,000 \qquad \text{(Storage capacity)}$$
$$80 \ X + \ 40 \ Y \le \ 64,000 \qquad \text{(Packaging capacity)}$$
$$X, \ Y \ge 0$$

As can be noticed in using LP, one objective was singled out, i.e. the maximization of profit.   Now assume that the marketing manager has two objectives to achieve:

(1)   Realize a 12% rate of return on investment, equivalent to \$700,000 contribution to profit.   This strategy is considered to be the primary goal (i.e. P_1).

(2)   Maximize the utilization of the storage and packaging capacities. This strategy is considered to be a secondary goal (i.e. P_2).

Here, the marketing manager would like to see whether the available resources are sufficient to achieve his goals (this is a short-term strategy). If, however, the available resources cannot attain this task, the marketing manager would like to determine what strategy he should adopt to realize these goals (this is a long-term strategy).   Here, GP can play an important role in addressing these issues.

SHORT-TERM PLANNING:

In order for the marketing manager to determine to what extent the goals he has set will be achieved, taking into consideration the available resources, the above problem should be formulated in terms of GP as follows:

$$\text{Minimize:} \qquad P_1 \ (d_1^- + d_1^+) + P_2 \ (d_2^- + d_3^-)$$
$$\text{Subject to:} \qquad 100 \ X + 120 \ Y + d_1^- + d_1^+ = 700,000$$
$$60 \ X + 120 \ Y + d_2^- = 120,000$$
$$80 \ X + \ 40 \ Y + d_3^- = 64,000$$
$$X, \ Y, \ d_1^+, \ d_1^-, \ d_2^-, \ d_3^- \ge 0$$

where: d_1^- = underachievement of the profit goal,

   d_1^+ = overachievement of the profit goal,

   d_2^- = underutilization of the storage capacity,

   d_3^- = underutilization of the packaging capacity,

   P_1 = the first priority goal to be achieved (i.e. the achievement of $700,000 profit),

   P_2 = the second priority goal to be achieved (i.e. the minimization of the underutilized storage and packaging capacities).

Note that the first goal equation has two deviational variables (d_1^+ and d_1^-), which means that the intention is to achieve exactly $700,000 profit, while, for goal 2, the variables d_2^- and d_3^- are only added since we need to minimize the underutilization of the two capacities.   The overachievement variables d_2^+ and d_3^+ are not added because the goal is to minimize the underachievement.

The above problem is solved by the simplex method of GP.   Table 5.9 presents the optimal solution.

Table 5.9   Final Simplex Tableau

Objective column	Variable column	Constant column	0	0	P_1	P_1	P_2	P_2
			X	Y	d_1^-	d_1^+	d_2^-	d_3^-
P_1	d_1^-	564,000	0	0	1	-1	-7/9	-2/3
0	Y	800	0	0	0	0	1/90	-1/120
0	X	400	1	0	0	0	-1/180	1/60
C_j-Z_j	P_2	0	0	0	0	0	1	1
C_j-Z_j	P_1	-564,000	0	0	0	2	7/9	2/3

Solution stub

In the solution stub of Table 5.9 one can see two sections labeled C_j-Z_j P_1 and C_j-Z_j P_2.   Commencing with section C_j-Z_j P_1: it reads C_j-Z_j P_1 -564,000. This means that the first priority goal (P_1) is underachieved by $564,000. From the solution stub, it can be seen that variable d_1^-, which represents the underachievement of the first priority goal (P_1), has a value of $564,000. However, the C_j-Z_j P_2 section shows a zero value under the constant column, this means that the second priority goal (P_2) is totally achieved.   Another way to verify this point is by taking a glance at the variables in the solution stub. It can be seen that the deviational variables d_2^- and d_3^- are not there, which means that their values are zero. According to the simplex method, any variable which does not appear in the solution stub has a value of zero.

Moreover, the solution stub shows that the best product mix in the short term is to sell 400 units of television type X and 800 units of television type Y.

The questions, which the marketing manager faces now, are: what re- source(s) he should increase, by how much, and also what product mix he should sell in order to realize all the predetermined goals mentioned above. Obvious- ly, answers to such questions entail long-term planning.

LONG-TERM PLANNING:

The above solution (Table 5.9) demonstrates a very important fact that GP is a satisficing technique which attempts to achieve predetermined goals according to their rank of importance given the available resources. One may ask, "Can the GP model be manipulated in such a way as to optimize all goals in consideration?" The answer is yes.

It is now time to determine how the GP model can be used to achieve the previously mentioned long-term strategy of the marketing manager.

Having this objective in mind, one can rearrange the equations of the short range planning and make them suitable for the long term, as follows:

$$\text{Minimize:} \quad P_1 (d_1^- + d_1^+) + P_2 d_2^- + 0 d_2^+ + P_2 d_3^- + 0 d_3^+$$

$$
\begin{aligned}
\text{Subject to:} \quad & 100\ X + 120\ Y + d_1^- - d_1^+ = 700{,}000 \\
& 60\ X + 120\ Y + d_2^- - d_2^+ = 120{,}000 \\
& 80\ X + 40\ Y + d_3^- - d_3^+ = 64{,}000 \\
& X,\ Y,\ d_1^+,\ d_1^-,\ d_2^+,\ d_2^-,\ d_3^+,\ d_3^- \geq 0
\end{aligned}
$$

Comparing the above equations with those for the short term, the following differences can be noted:

(1) In the long-term mode, an overachievement variable (d^+) has been inserted in each capacity constraint equation, while the short-term capacity constraint equations do not have such a variable.

(2) The insertion of the d_2^+ and d_3^+ variable in the long-term model requires assigning to them zero coefficients in the objective function. This means that there is no restriction on their increase as long as this increase will satisfy the predetermined objectives.

The answer to the above formulation is shown in Table 5.10.

Table 5.10   Final Simplex Tableau

Objective column	Variable column	Constant column	0	0	P_1	P_1	P_2	0	P_2	0
			X	Y	d_1^-	d_1^+	d_2^-	d_2^+	d_3^-	d_3^+
0	d_3^+	169,333 1/3	-140/3	0	1/3	-1/3	0	0	-1	1
0	Y	5,833 1/3	5/3	1	1/120	-1/120	0	0	0	0
0	d_2^+	58,000	40	0	1	-1	-1	1	0	0
$C_j - Z_j$	P_2	0	0	0	0	0	1	0	0	0
$C_j - Z_j$	P_1	0	0	0	1	1	0	0	0	0

Solution stub

The solution stub of Table 5.10 shows that, in order to optimize fully all the predetermined goals, the following strategy should be adopted:

(1)   Increase the storage as well as the packaging capacities by 58,000 square inches and 169,333.3 seconds, respectively. This can be observed from the values of d_3^+ and d_2^+ in the solution stub.

(2)   Sell only product Y and eliminate product X. Product X should be eliminated since variable X did not appear in the solution stub.

Table 5.11   Comparison of the Short- and Long-term Results

	Short-term result	Long-term result
Goal(s) optimized	Goal two	Goal one and two
Product mix solution	Produce 400 units of X	Produce zero units of X
	Produce 800 units of Y	Produce 5833.3 units of Y

If the marketing manager follows this strategy, his predetermined goals will be fully optimized. A glance at the solution stub of Table 5.10 shows that the $C_j - Z_j$ values of P_1 and P_2 in the constant column are zero. This means that goal number 1 and goal number 2 are fully optimized. In other words, the above strategy will allow the marketing manager to realize a 12% rate of return on investment and, in the meantime, he will optimize the utilization of the scarce resources. To give a better picture of the results of the short-term vs. long-term solution, Table 5.11 shows a summary of these results.

It should be noted again that the above explanation is based on the assumption that goals can be rank ordered. This is a subjective operation and is likely to vary from one decision maker to another, posing a preliminary problem of another dimension. There are other quantitative techniques which can be used to minimize the subjectivity involved in rank ordering. Thus, the focus of the above discussion has been on goals, goals which can be strictly defined and quantified. Goal programming is a powerful analytical method for dealing with numerous and multidimensional goals to yield optimal outcomes in the long term.

5.6 MACHINE SEQUENCING WITH FORBIDDEN EARLY SHIPMENTS

Most bicriterion machine sequencing problems deal with the following criteria: minimizing both weighted flow time and maximum tardiness, minimizing both total flow time and maximum penalty cost, minimizing both total flow time and number of tardy jobs, minimizing both maximum tardiness and the crashing costs. The machine sequencing problem discussed in this section concerns one with forbidden early shipment with two criteria.

Fry and Leong (1986) looked at machine scheduling in a bicriterion context wherein tardiness is not the only criterion but also earliness as a measure of inventory. If a job which is finished early cannot be shipped (forbidden early shipments), then that job must be held in inventory until its due date where it incurs an inventory carrying cost. Since a penalty is recognized for jobs completed early, an optimal schedule may have inserted machine idle time. This is contrary to the American bias of keeping workers busy and not allowing downstream workstations to become idle. This concept of inserted idle time has been recognized by the Japanese with promising results. The production concepts of Just-in-Time (JIT), Zero Inventories, Kanban and Stockless Production recognize the advantages of having workstations sit idle. In order to implement a true pull production system, management must recognize the instances where the cost of allowing workstations to sit idle is offset by the savings of reduced inventory.

By recognizing earliness as an explicit penalty in an optimizing procedure, the transition to such pull systems as JIT could be enhanced. Unfortunately, the incorporation of earliness as a penalty greatly complicates the problem. Earliness is not a regular measure of performance; thus, the optimal solution may not be a permutation schedule. There is a finite number of permutations, although N! can be quite large. The number of nonpermutation

schedules is infinite because of the continuous variable representing the
inserted machine idle time.

The problem illustrated is a single-machine job shop.   All jobs are
simultaneously available for processing.   N represents the number of jobs, and
job processing times p_i and due dates d_i are known in advance.   The single
machine can process only one job at a time and will do so until completion.

Assume the following notations:

C_i	=	completion time of the job in the ith position;
Y_i	=	amount of machine idle time directly preceding the job in the ith position;
P_i	=	processing time of the job in the ith position;
X_{ji}	=	1 if job j is assigned to position i in sequence, 0 otherwise;
S_i	=	the identification (ID) of the job occurring in position i in sequence;
d_i	=	due date of the job in the ith position.

Consider the Gantt chart in Fig. 5.7 illustrating the model variables.

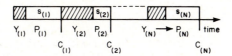

Fig. 5.7   Gantt Chart

Since a job can be assigned to only one position in sequence, the following sets of equations are introduced:

$$\sum_{j=1}^{N} X_{ji} = 1, \qquad i = 1, 2, \ldots, N;$$

$$\sum_{i=1}^{N} X_{ji} = 1, \qquad j = 1, 2, \ldots, N.$$

The due date goal constraints reflecting an earliness and tardiness
variable are presented as:

$$C_i + \ell_i^- - \ell_i^+ = d_i, \qquad i = 1, 2, \ldots, N,$$

where: ℓ_i^- = earliness of the job in position i, and ℓ_i^+ = tardiness of the job
in position i.   These will be referred to as deviational variables.   Since

$$C_i = \sum_{k=1}^{i} Y_k + \sum_{k=1}^{i} P_k,$$

$$P_i = \sum_{j=1}^{N} X_{ji} P_j, \quad \text{and}$$

$$d_i = \sum_{j=1}^{N} X_{ji} d_j,$$

the goal constraints can be rewritten as:

$$\sum_{k=1}^{i} Y_k + \sum_{j=1}^{N} \sum_{k=1}^{i} X_{jk} P_j + \ell_i^- - \ell_i^+ = \sum_{j=1}^{N} X_{ji} d_j, \qquad i=1,2,\ldots,N$$

The objective function is a result of a weighted sum of earliness and tardiness penalties. Thus,

$$\text{Min } Z = w_h \sum_{j=1}^{N} \ell_j^- + w_t \sum_{j=1}^{N} \ell_j^+$$

where: w_h = per unit of time penalty associated with holding an item in inventory; and w_t = per unit of time penalty associated with finishing a job tardy.

The model is illustrated using a sample problem given in Table 5.12.

Table 5.12 Sample Problem

Job	1	2	3	4	5	6	7	8
P_j	6	5	2	4	2	4	3	4
d_j	29	27	18	10	24	9	34	38

When the cost of holding inventory is greater than the cost of being tardy, more jobs would be expected to be finished after their due dates. In Fig. 5.8, run 1, we see that 4 jobs are tardy and only 1 is early. The make span is 40 and total machine idle time is 10 time units.

In the second run, when $w_h = 2 = w_t$, the make span is decreased to 38 since the total inserted idle time is decreased to eight units. There are now three early jobs and only one tardy job. The sequence has changed from $(6\rightarrow4\rightarrow 3\rightarrow5\rightarrow2\rightarrow1\rightarrow7\rightarrow8)$ to $(6\rightarrow4\rightarrow3\rightarrow2\rightarrow5\rightarrow1\rightarrow7\rightarrow8)$ by switching jobs 2 and 5.

In the third run, where $w_h=1$ and $w_t=3$, the resulting schedule is that there are 0 tardy jobs and 4 early jobs. The make span is 38 and the sequence is still (6->4->3->2->5->1->7->8). The total idle time is still 8 units of time but is inserted differently.

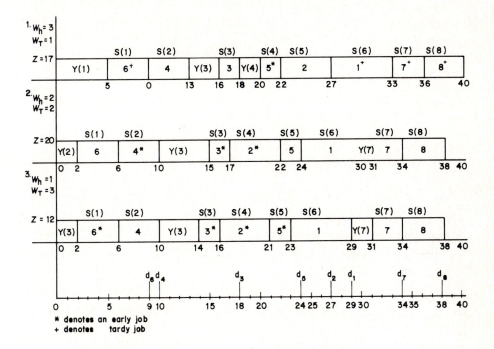

Fig. 5.8 Model Results of Job Scheduling

The total penalty over the three runs is also different, with values of $Z=17$, $Z=20$ and $Z=12$ for the three runs.

In Table 5.13, the average CPU time required to solve each set of problem size is presented. The average for $N=14$ is biased downward, since, after an hour of CPU time, optimal solutions had not been verified for 2 of the 10 problems solved. As can be seen in Fig. 5.9, CPU time grows in an almost exponential manner as problem size increases.

To solve larger problems, some means of curtailing the enumeration becomes necessary. This implies some type of combinatorial technique, such as branch and bound or dynamic programming. Using this type of procedure, curtailment could be accomplished via strong bounding or dominance theorems that could determine the ordering of jobs before the enumeration begins. Implementing these techniques would require some procedure to insert idle time as the enumeration is performed.

Job size	CPU time(s)
8	36.03
10	84.49
12	349.19
14	1744.94

Table 5.13

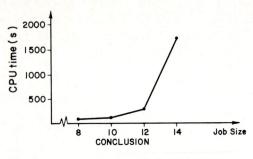

Fig. 5.9   CPU Time

5.7   QUALITY CONTROL MODEL: DESIGNING A SAMPLING PLAN

The quality of a product varies due to a number of causes, such as, differences among machines and processing conditions, differences among workers, differences among raw material qualities, and also due to the variations of each of these factors over time.   These factors naturally require effective control mechanisms.

Sampling plan is one of the most accepted means to check the quality of products.   It does not only control the quality of the products that go to the market, but it also gives information to management if some corrective measures ought to be taken within the process.

In designing a sampling plan, quality control is not the only objective that should be taken into account.   Other objectives like minimization of cost of inspection and testing, among others, also play an important role in determining the sample size.   So, before designing a sampling plan, management should consider all relevant objectives carefully.   In this subsection, a simple indicative model is presented using GP.

Model Formulation:

Objective - 1: Maximization of Reliability of Product Quality.

Once the price and delivery terms are being fixed by management, a product's quality is the important factor that greatly influences a customer's reaction towards the product's marketability.   Management can maintain a high level of customer satisfaction through consistent and acceptable product quality which can be achieved by minimizing the number of defects that goes to the market. This will finally keep the Average Outgoing Quality (AOQ) to the minimum.

The average number of defects passing the inspection equals $[P_a \cdot p \cdot (N-n)]$, where, P_a = Probability of acceptance of a lot, p = Expected fraction defective in a lot, N = Lot size, n = Sample size.   Therefore,

$$AOQ = \frac{P_a \cdot p \cdot (N - n)}{N - p \cdot n - (1 - P_a) \cdot p \cdot (N-n)}$$

This AOQ should approach the desired outgoing quality Q.   Rearranging the equation and introducing deviational variables, the mathematical relationship becomes

$$P_a \cdot p \cdot (N - n) - Q [N - p \cdot n - (1 - P_a) \cdot p \cdot (N - n)] + d_1^- - d_1^+ = 0$$

Objective - 2: Minimization of Cost.

Every production unit tries to minimize its cost so that the net value added is maximized.   In quality control, cost usually includes cost of inspection cost due to defective items going to the market and cost due to good items classified as bad (Type-I error)

Let, C_i = Cost of inspecting an item

   C_d = Damage cost incurred if a defective item slips to the market

   C_g = Damage cost incurred if a good item is classified as bad.

Therefore, the cost functions can be formulated as follows:

   Cost of inspection = $[P_a \cdot n + (1-P_a)N] \cdot C_i$

   Cost due to defective items = $[(1-E_2) \cdot P_a \cdot (N-n) \cdot p + E_2 \cdot N \cdot p] \cdot C_d$

   Cost due to Type-I error = $[P_a \cdot n + (1-P_a) \cdot N] \cdot E_1 \cdot (1-p) \cdot C_g$

In the above expressions, E_1 is the probability that a good item is classified as bad, and E_2 is the probability that a bad item is classified as good.

Since the total cost is to be minimized, the objective is set to zero, and an overachievement is minimized.   Summing the above costs and introducing the appropriate deviational variable, the equation becomes

$$[P_a \cdot n + (1-P_a) \cdot N] \; C_i + [(1-E_2) \cdot P_a \cdot (N-n) \cdot p + E_2 \cdot N \cdot p] \cdot C_d$$
$$+ [P_a \cdot n + (1-P_a) \cdot N] \cdot E_1 \cdot (1-p) \cdot C_g - d_2^+ = 0$$

Objective - 3: Optimal Manpower Utilization in Inspection Testing.

With a view of getting reliable data, the inspectors and sample testing personnel should be given ample time allowance to work arising from the presence of defectives. This is because if too much time is given to handle defectives then it is mere wastage of manpower; also, they might commit mistakes in deciding that a product is defective even if it is not. Also, if inadequate time is allowed for handling defectives, they might also commit mistakes in deciding that a product is good even if it is not. Hence, management should utilize its manpower optimally.

The average inspection load per lot (i.e. average items to be inspected per lot) is given by the following expression $P_a \cdot n + (1 - P_a) \cdot N$.

Let R be the rate of production in units per day and T be the time in hours required to inspect and test a single item by a person. Therefore, the following information can be determined:

No. of lots per day $= R/N$

No. of items to be inspected per day $= (R/N) \cdot [P_a \cdot n + (1 - P_a) \cdot N]$

No of man-hours required to inspect a day's production

$$= (R/N) \cdot [P_a \cdot n + (1 - P_a) \cdot N] \cdot T.$$

If M is the man-hour available, then the above expression should approach the value of M. Adding deviational variables, the equation becomes

$$(R/N) \cdot [P_a \cdot n + (1 - P_a) \cdot N] \cdot T + d_3^- - d_3^+ = M$$

In this model, only one decision variable, the sample size n is considered. However, the number of variables can be increased by considering double or multiple sampling plan, and considering other factors as well. The model presented shows the applicability of goal programming in quality control problems.

5.8 BATCH PRODUCTION PLANNING

This section presents a multiple criteria production planning model for batch production developed by Wang and Duckstein (1983). The model consists of determining the amount of I different products to be manufactured by J possible processes in T planning periods. The demand is given in each period, and no shortages are planned. The nominal capacity of each process may be exceeded by

running overtime.   The labor force may be adjusted at the beginning of each
period and the total workforce may be increased through overtime.   The finished
products are inspected by the Quality Assurance Department and defective units
are rejected.   The average rejection percentage of each product from each
process is given.

Five objectives to be minimized over the planning periods are defined as
follows:

1.   Total production and inventory holding cost ($).
2.   Total sales value of rejected products ($).
3.   Total fluctuation in work force (man-day).
4.   Total overtime labor man-hour (man-hours).
5.   Total unused regular process capacity (hours).

The problem is to determine the amount of each product to be produced by a
given process in each period such that a satisfactory compromise between the
five objectives is achieved.   To facilitate the development of the mathematical
formulation, the following notations for parameters and decision variables are
used throughout this section.

Let indices be defined as follows:

product i = 1, ..., I;
Process j = 1, ..., J;
Time   t = 1, ..., T.

Decision Variables

X_{ijt} = quantity of product i to be produced by process j on regular time
in period t (units).

Y_{ijt} = quantity of product i to be produced by process j on overtime in
period t (units).

I_{it} = on-hand inventory of product i at the end of period t (units).

H_t = work force hired in period t (man-day).

L_t = work force laid off in period t (man-day).

W_t = work force in period t (man-day).

P_{jt} = unused regular process capacity for process j (hours).

Parameters

a_{ij} = labor time for each unit of product i produced by process j (man-
hour/unit).

b_{ij} = process time (including setup time) for each unit of product i produced by process j (hour/unit).

c_{ij} = unit production cost (excluding labor cost) for product i produced by process j ($/unit).

d_{it} = demand for product i in period t (units).

e_t = overtime labor cost in period t ($/man-hour).

f_t = fraction of regular work force available for overtime use in period t $(0 \le f_t \le 1)$.

g_{jt} = fraction of regular process time available for overtime use for process j in period t $(0 \le g_{jt} \le 1)$.

h_i = inventory holding cost per unit of product i in each period ($/unit/period).

k_t = regular labor cost in period t ($/man-day).

m_{jt} = regular process capacity for process j in period t (hours).

q_{ij} = average rejection percentage of product i produced by process j (%/unit).

r_j = overtime process cost of process j ($/hour).

s_i = unit selling price of product i ($/unit).

μ = regular work hours per man-day (man-hours/man-day).

Based on the above notation, the objectives and constraints of the formulation can now be expressed mathematically.

Objectives

1. Minimize total production and inventory holding cost:

$$\text{Minimize } U_1 = \sum_{i=1}^{I} \sum_{j=1}^{J} \sum_{t=1}^{T} c_{ij} (X_{ijt} + Y_{ijt}) + \sum_{t=1}^{T} k_t W_t$$

$$+ \sum_{i=1}^{I} \sum_{j=1}^{J} \sum_{t=1}^{T} e_t (a_{ij} Y_{ijt}) + \sum_{i=1}^{I} \sum_{j=1}^{J} \sum_{t=1}^{T} r_i (b_{ij} Y_{ijt})$$

$$+ \sum_{i=1}^{I} \sum_{t=1}^{T} h_i I_{it}$$

2. Minimize total sales value of rejected products:

$$\text{Minimize } U_2 = \sum_{i=1}^{I} \sum_{j=1}^{J} \sum_{t=1}^{T} s_i q_{ij} (X_{ijt} + Y_{ijt}).$$

3. Minimize total fluctuation in workforce:

$$\text{Minimize} \quad U_3 = \sum_{t=1}^{T} (H_t + L_t)$$

4. Minimize total overtime labor man-hours:

$$\text{Minimize} \quad U_4 = \sum_{i=1}^{I} \sum_{j=1}^{J} \sum_{t=1}^{T} a_{ij} Y_{ijt}$$

5. Minimize total unused regular process capacity:

$$\text{Minimize} \quad U_5 = \sum_{j=1}^{J} \sum_{t=1}^{T} P_{jt}$$

Constraints

1. Production-inventory-demand relationship constraints:

$$I_{it} = I_{i,t-1} + \sum_{j=1}^{J} X_{ijt}(1-q_{ij}) + \sum_{j=1}^{J} Y_{ijt}(1-q_{ij}) - d_{it}$$

$$I_{it} \geq 0, \quad X_{ijt} \geq 0, \quad Y_{ijt} \geq 0.$$

2. Process capacity constraints:

$$\sum_{i=1}^{I} b_{ij} X_{ijt} + P_{jt} = m_{jt}$$

$$\sum_{i=1}^{I} b_{ij} Y_{ijt} \leq g_{jt} m_{jt}$$

$$P_{jt} \geq 0.$$

3. Labor constraints:

$$W_t = W_{t-1} + H_t - L_t$$

$$\sum_{i=1}^{I} \sum_{j=1}^{J} a_{ij} X_{ijy} \leq \mu W_t$$

$$\sum_{i=1}^{I} \sum_{j=1}^{J} a_{ij} Y_{ijy} \leq \mu f_t W_t$$

$$H_t \geq 0, \ L_t \geq 0, \ W_t \geq 0.$$

The formulation specified above has a total of $T(2IJ + I + J + 3)$ decision variables and $T(I + 2J + 3)$ constraints.   A major characteristic of the formulation is that all the objectives and constraints are linear and the decision variables are nonnegative. Another important feature of the model is that the objectives do not have the same unit of measurement.

Note that additional constraints may be included in the formulation for a particular application. For example, there may be a physical limitation on the total amount of storage space available in a given period. This would require the establishment of a constraint on the total inventory holding in each period. In addition, the total number of hirings and lay-offs may be restricted to a certain ceiling due to the limited resources in personnel management. The inclusion of these and other constraints is straight forward and will not have a major effect on the complexity of the model and its solution methods.

A numerical example is presented in this section to illustrate how multiple criteria decision making technique can be applied to develop a production plan. The example consists of three $(I=3)$ different products which are to be produced by two $(J=2)$ possible processes in three $(T=3)$ planning periods.   The relevant values of the parameters specified in the previous section as well as the initial values of some decision variables are given below.

a_{ij}		Process 1	Process 2
	1	2.0	1.5
Product	2	3.0	4.0
	3	1.0	2.0

b_{ij}		Process 1	Process 2
	1	1.2	1.5
Product	2	1.0	1.3
	3	1.8	1.6

c_{ij}		Process 1	Process 2
	1	20.0	25.0
Product	2	15.0	30.0
	3	25.0	18.0

d_{it}		1	2	3
	1	1000	600	900
Product	2	400	500	500
	3	1100	800	700

$e_t = 30.0$, $t = 1, 2, 3$.

$f_t = 20\%$, $t = 1, 2, 3$.

$g_{1t} = 15\%$, $g_{2t} = 20\%$, $t = 1, 2, 3$.

$h_1 = 2.0$, $h_2 = 5.0$, $h_3 = 3.0$.

$k_t = 20.0$, $t = 1, 2, 3$.

m_{jt}	Period 1	2	3
Process 1	1500	1200	1000
2	1400	1500	1700

q_{ij}	Process 1	2
1	0.10	0.08
Product 2	0.12	0.05
3	0.06	0.10

$r_1 = 100$, $r_2 = 200$.

$s_1 = 100.0$, $s_2 = 150.0$, $s_3 = 180.0$.

$\mu = 8.0$.

Initial Values

$I_{10} = 50.0$, $I_{20} = 60.0$, $I_{30} = 80.0$, $W_0 = 400.0$.

Table 5.14   Payoff Matrix of Marginal (Efficient) Solutions
versus Optimal Objective Function Values

Objective to be minimized	Objective 1 ($)	2 ($)	3 (man-days)	4 (man-days)	5 (hours)
U_1	174,142	92,447	323	176	0
U_2	459,516	54,764	171	1,658	308
U_3	414,130	79,753	33	2,079	538
U_4	191,789	76,467	393	59	0
U_5	350,009	61,259	227	1,254	0

If the above example problem is solved with respect to either one of the objectives, the formulation becomes a linear program. The optimal values of the objective functions and the decision variables (rounded to the nearest integers) from each of the five single-objective problems are given in Table 5.14. Note that each of the diagonal element (i,i) in Table 5.14 gives the minimal or marginal value of the corresponding objective U_i when objective U_i is minimized. It is clear from these results that optimizing one objective may cause serious deterioration in the quality of another objectives. The problem that a decision maker now faces is to find a "satisficing" solution based on the consideration of all five objectives.

The compromise programming method is applied to the example problem to illustrate how a compromise solution can be reached by a decision maker. First we normalize objective U_i to [0,1]. To do this, we first find the maximum and minimum values of U_i subject to the original constraints. Let V_i and v_i be the maximum and minimum values of objective U_i, respectively. Objective U_i is then transformed to u_j, through $u_i = (U_i - v_i)/(V_i - v_i)$. This process is applied to all the objectives. Suppose the minimax approach is adopted by the decision maker and all five objectives are given equal weights, then the reduced single objective problem of compromise programming has the following objectives:

$$\text{Minimize   max } (|U_i{}^* - u_i|, \quad i = 1, \ldots, 5)$$

where $U_i{}^*$ denotes the "ideal point" for objective u_i. In this particular example, $U_i{}^* = 0$, for all i, is assumed. The compromise programming solution leads to the following values of the original objectives obtained from the reduced problem are:

$$U_1 = 239,841, \qquad U_2 = 64,304, \qquad U_3 = 270, \qquad U_4 = 242, \qquad U_5 = 0.$$

Thus, compromise programming (minimax distance) leads to a well balanced "satisficing" solution.

5.9   RESOURCE AND PRODUCT MIX PROBLEM: CASE STUDY

5.9.1   PRODUCTION SITUATION

The company, a certain Chocolate Manufacturers, Inc. (Chocoman), is a manufacturer of various types of chocolate bars, candy and waffer. It has both production and marketing capability to produce and sell all or a mixture of the following products:

  (i)   Milk Chocolate Bars, 250 gm weight,
  (ii)   Milk Chocolate Bars, 100 gm weight,
  (iii)   Crunchy Chocolate Bars, 250 gm weight,
  (iv)   Crunchy Chocolate Bars, 100 gm weight,
  (v)   Chocolate with Nuts, 250 gm weight,
  (vi)   Chocolate with Nuts, 100 gm weight,
  (vii)   Chocolate candy, packed in 300 gm weight each,
  (viii) Chocolate waffer, packed in 12 pcs at 10 gm per piece.

For production of these products, the following materials are used:

(i)   Cocoa,

(ii)   Milk,

(iii)   Nuts,

(iv)   Confectionery sugar,

(v)   Flour (for waffers),

(vi)   Aluminum foil for packaging,

(vii)   Paper for packaging,

(viii)   Plastic sheets for packaging.

Usage of these raw materials vary for each product. For cocoa, milk, nuts, sugar and flour, these are measured by weight in kilograms. For packaging the end products, the use of aluminum foil, paper and plastic sheets are measured by area in square feet. Details of raw material usage are presented in Table 5.15.

The following major facilities are used for production:

(i)   Cooking and melting vats,

(ii)   Mixing machines,

(iii)   Forming machines,

(iv)   Grinding machines,

(v)   Waffer making machines,

(vi)   Cutting machines,

(vii)   Packaging type machine for paper and foil wrappings,

(viii)   Packaging type 2 machine for sealing plastic.

Facilities (i) to (vi) are expressed in ton-hours. These machines are limited both by tonnage weight capacity and hours of operations. Cutting and packaging facilities are expressed in hours. Operations of these facilities are independent of the product weight. Details of the facility usage are presented in Table 5.16.

Labor is also an input in production. Indirect labor required such as administrative, supervisory, maintenance, etc. are excluded from consideration since the associated costs are fixed in nature. Direct labor required for manufacturing the products, such as those required in packaging, are considered and details of the requirements are included in Table 5.16.

The company undertakes periodic planning, taking into consideration various alternatives available from the subsystems, and with objectives geared towards maximizing the benefit of the company as a whole.

Table 5.15 Material Requirements for the
Production of Chocoman Products

					Product Types			
Materials required (per 1000 units)	Milk 250	Choco 100	Crunchy 250	Choco 100	Choco 250	W/ Nuts 100	Candy	Waffer
Cocoa (kg)	87.5	35	75	30	50	20	60	12
Milk (kg)	62.5	25	50	20	50	20	30	12
Nuts (kg)	0	0	37.5	15	75	30	0	0
Conf. Sugar	100	40	87.5	35	75	30	210	24
Flour (kg)	0	0	0	0	0	0	0	72
Alum. Foil (ft^2)	500	0	500	0	500	0	0	250
Paper (ft^2)	450	0	450	0	450	0	0	0
Plastic (ft^2)	60	120	60	120	60	120	1600	250

Table 5.16 Facility Usage in the
Production of Chocoman Products

					Product Types			
Facility Usage (per 1000 units)	Milk 250	Choco 100	Crunchy 250	Choco 100	Choco 250	W/ Nuts 100	Candy	Waffer
Cooking (ton-hours)	0.5	0.2	0.425	0.17	0.35	0.14	0.6	0.096
Mixing (ton-hours)	0	0	0.15	0.06	0.25	0.1	0	0
Forming (ton-hours)	0.75	0.3	0.75	0.3	0.75	0.3	0.9	0.36
Grinding(ton-hours)	0	0	0.25	0.1	0	0	0	0
Waffer mkg(ton-hrs)	0	0	0	0	0	0	0	0.3
Cutting (hours)	0.1	0.1	0.1	0.1	0.1	0.1	0.2	0
Packaging 1 (hours)	0.25	0	0.25	0	0.25	0	0	0.1
Packaging 2 (hours)	0.05	0.3	0.05	0.3	0.05	0.3	2.5	0.15
Labor (hours)	0.3	0.3	0.3	0.3	0.3	0.3	2.5	2.5

5.9.2 UNLIMITED DEMAND SITUATION

Chocoman is in the process of preparing a monthly plan for the next manufacturing period. Raw materials and facilities available are presented in Table 5.17.

Prices of the end products are given in Table 5.18.

Table 5.17 Material and Facility Availability

Material/Facility (units)	Availability
Cocoa (kg)	100,000
Milk (kg)	120,000
Nuts (kg)	60,000
Confectionery Sugar (kg)	200,000
Flour (kg)	20,000
Aluminum foil (ft^2)	500,000
Paper (ft^2)	500,000
Plastic (ft^2)	500,000
Cooking (ton-hours)	1,000
Mixing (ton-hours)	200
Forming (ton-hours)	1,500
Grinding (ton-hours)	200
Waffer making (ton-hours)	100
Cutting (hours)	400
Packaging 1 (hours)	400
Packaging 2 (hours)	1,200
Labor (hours)	1,000

Table 5.18 Prices of End Products

Product	Price/100 pcs.
Milk Chocolate, 250 gm	$375
Mild Chocolate, 100 gm	150
Crunchy Chocolate, 250 gm	400
Crunchy Chocolate, 100 gm	160
Chocolate with Nuts, 250 gm	420
Chocolate with Nuts, 100 gm	175
Chocolate Candy	400
Chocolate Waffer	150

(i) What would be the optimal product mix considering the resources as fixed?

(ii) If prices of the raw materials and labor are given in Table 5.19, quantities of materials to be purchased may still be relayed to the supplier and changed, direct labor can still be varied through hiring of contractual workers, using the same amount of money to acquire the existing portfolio of resources worth $400,000, what would be the optimal resource and product mix?

Table 5.19   Prices of Raw Materials

Material (units)	Price ($/unit)
Cocoa (kg)	1.20
Milk (kg)	0.50
Nuts (kg)	2.00
Confectionery Sugar (kg)	0.15
Flour (kg)	0.25
Aluminum Foil (ft^2)	0.06
Paper (ft^2)	0.02
Plastic (ft^2)	0.03
Labor (hours)	10.00

Product Mix Model Formulation:

The linear programming model can be formulated with the following variables:

MB = Milk Chocolate of 250 gm to be produced (in '000),
MS = Milk Chocolate of 100 gm to be produced (in '000),
CB = Crunchy Chocolate of 250 gm to be produced (in '000),
CS = Crunchy Chocolate of 100 gm to be produced (in '000),
NB = Chocolate with Nuts of 250 gm to be produced (in '000),
NS = Chocolate with Nuts of 100 gm to be produced (in '000),
CD = Chocolate Candy to be produced (in '000 packs)
WF = Chocolate Waffer to be produced (in '000 packs).

The objective of the company is to maximize profit which is, alternatively, equivalent to maximizing gross contribution. Since the prices of the end products, usage and cost of raw materials are given, the variable cost can be computed. For example, for milk chocolate of 250 gm size:

For every 100 units of Milk Chocolate, 250 gm,

Price	$375.00

Material usage and costing

Cocoa (kg)	(87.5)($1.20) =	$105.00
Milk (kg)	(62.5)($0.50) =	$31.25
Sugar (kg)	(100.0)($0.06) =	$15.00
Foil (ft^2)	(500.0)($0.06) =	$30.00
Paper (ft^2)	(450.0)($0.02) =	$9.00
Plastic (ft^2)	(60.0)($0.03) =	$1.80
Labor (hour)	(0.3)($10.00) =	$3.00
Total variable cost		= $195.05
Gross contribution ($375.00 - $195.05)		$179.95

The whole objective function can be written as:

Maximize: $Z = 179.95\ MB + 82.9\ MS + 153.08\ CB + 72.15\ CS$
$$+ 129.95\ NB + 69.9\ NS + 208.5\ CD + 83\ WF$$

There are two sets of constraints, raw material availability and facility capacity constraints.   Based on the material consumption of each product as shown in Table 5.15, facility usage shown in Table 5.16 and the resource availability shown in Table 5.17, the constraints can be written down for each material and facility.   These are presented, together with the objective function in Model 1.

De Novo Formulation:

The De Novo formulation has the same end product variables.   Aside from this set of variables, raw material requirements are also decision variables. Let

C = amount of cocoa to be purchase, in kg,

M = amount of milk to be purchased, in kg,

N = amount of nuts to be purchased, in kg,

S = amount of sugar to be purchased, in kg,

F = amount of flour to be purchased, in kg,

A = amount of aluminum foil to be purchased, in ft^2,

PP = amount of paper to be purchased, in ft^2,

PL = amount of plastic to be purchased, in ft^2,

DL = number of hours of direct labor to be available.

Model 1   Unlimited Demand, Product Mix Model

Maximize:

$$Z = 179.95MB + 82.9MS + 153.08CB + 72.15CS + 129.95NB + 69.9NS + 208.5CD + 83WF$$

Subject to:

Material constraints

Cocoa	87.5MB +	35MS +	75CB +	30CS +	50NB +	20NS +	60CD +	12WF ≤100,000
Milk	62.5MB +	25MS +	50CB +	20CS +	50NB +	20NS +	30CD +	12WF ≤120,000
Nuts			37.5CB +	15CS +	75NB +	30NS		≤ 60,000
Sugar	100MB +	40MS +	87.5CB +	35CS +	75NB +	30NS +	210CD +	24WF ≤200,000
Flour								72WF ≤ 20,000
Foil	500MB +		500CB +		500NB +			250WF ≤500,000
Paper	450MB +		450CB +		450NB +			≤500,000
Plastic	60MB +	120MS +	60CB +	120CS +	60NB +	120NS +	1600CD +	250WF ≤500,000

Facility Constraints

Cook	0.5MB +	0.2MS +	0.425CB +	0.17CS +	0.35NB +	0.14NS +	0.6CD +	0.096WF ≤1,000
Mix			0.15CB +	0.06CS +	0.25NB +	0.1NS		≤ 200
Form	0.75MB +	0.3MS +	0.75CB +	0.3CS +	0.75NB +	0.3NS +	0.9CD +	0.36WF ≤1,500
Grind			0.25CB +	0.1CS				≤ 200
Wfrmkg								0.3WF ≤ 100
Cut	0.5MB +	0.1MS +	0.1CB +	0.1CS +	0.1NB +	0.1NS +	0.2CD	≤ 400
Pkg1	0.25MB +		0.25CB +		0.25NB +			0.1WF ≤ 400
Pkg2	0.05MB +	0.3MS +	0.05CB +	0.3CS +	0.05NB +	0.3NS +	2.5CD +	0.15WF ≤1,000

Labor	0.3MB +	0.3MS +	0.3CB +	0.3CS +	0.3NB +	0.3NS +	2.5CD +	0.25WF ≤1,000

All variables ≥ 0

The objective function remains the same, to maximize profit. The material constraints in the product mix model are changed to material requirement equations. Exact quantities of each raw material will be purchased to satisfy the needs of the product mix. The facility constraints remain as is. Labor is treated as one of the variable resources and included in the budget equation. The complete model is shown in Model 2A. By substituting the raw material and labor equations into the budget equation, a simplified model, Model 2B can be used. Solving the two models, the results obtained are presented in Table 5.20.

Model 2A   Unlimited Demand, De Novo Formulation (Complete Model)

Maximize:
Z = 179.95MB + 82.9MS + 153.08CB + 72.15CS + 129.95NB + 69.9NS + 208.5CD + 83WF

Subject to:

Material constraints

Cocoa	87.5MB +	35MS +	75CB +	30CS +	50NB +	20NS +	60CD +	12WF = C
Milk	62.5MB +	25MS +	50CB +	20CS +	50NB +	20NS +	30CD +	12WF = M
Nuts			37.5CB +	15CS +	75NB +	30NS		= N
Sugar	100MB +	40MS +	87.5CB +	35CS +	75NB +	30NS +	210CD +	24WF = S
Flour								72WF = F
Foil	500MB +		500CB +		500NB +			250WF = A
Paper	450MB +		450CB +		450NB +			= PP
Plastic	60MB +	120MS +	60CB +	120CS +	60NB +	120NS +	1600CD +	250WF = PL

Labor   0.3MB +0.3MS + 0.3CB + 0.3CS + 0.3NB + 0.3NS + 2.5CD + 0.25WF = DL

Budget   1.2C +0.5M +2N +0.15S +0.25F +0.06A +0.02PP +0.03PL +10DL ≤ 400,000

Facility Constraints

Cook	0.5MB +	0.2MS +	0.425CB +	0.17CS +	0.35NB +	0.14NS +	0.6CD +	0.096WF	≤1,000
Mix			0.15CB +	0.06CS +	0.25NB +	0.1NS			≤ 200
Form	0.75MB +	0.3MS +	0.75CB +	0.3CS +	0.75NB +	0.3NS +	0.9CD +	0.36WF	≤1,500
Grind			0.25CB +	0.1CS					≤ 200
Wfrmkg								0.3WF	≤ 100
Cut	0.1MB +	0.1MS +	0.1CB +	0.1CS +	0.1NB +	0.1NS +	0.2CD		≤ 400
Pkg1	0.25MB +		0.25CB +		0.25NB +			0.1WF	≤ 400
Pkg2	0.05MB +	0.3MS +	0.05CB +	0.3CS +	0.05NB +	0.3NS +	2.5CD +	0.15WF	≤1,000

All variables ≥ 0

Model 2B   Unlimited Demand, De Novo Formulation (Simplified model)

Maximize:
Z = 179.95MB + 82.9MS + 153.08CB + 72.15CS + 129.95NB + 69.9NS + 208.5CD + 83WF

Subject to:

Budget 195.05MB+67.1MS+246.93CB+87.85CS+290.05NB+105.1NS+191.5CD+67WF ≤ 400,000

Facility Constraints

Cook	0.5MB +	0.2MS +	0.425CB +	0.17CS +	0.35NB +	0.14NS +	0.6CD +	0.096WF	≤1,000
Mix			0.15CB +	0.06CS +	0.25NB +	0.1NS			≤ 200
Form	0.75MB +	0.3MS +	0.75CB +	0.3CS +	0.75NB +	0.3NS +	0.9CD +	0.36WF	≤1,500
Grind			0.25CB +	0.1CS					≤ 200
Wfrmkg								0.3WF	≤ 100
Cut	0.1MB +	0.1MS +	0.1CB +	0.1CS +	0.1NB +	0.1NS +	0.2CD		≤ 400
Pkg1	0.25MB +		0.25CB +		0.25NB +			0.1WF	≤ 400
Pkg2	0.05MB +	0.3MS +	0.05CB +	0.3CS +	0.05NB +	0.3NS +	2.5CD +	0.15WF	≤1,000

All variables ≥ 0

Table 5.20   Results of Unlimited Demand Models

	Product Mix Model	De Novo Formulation
Profit (objective)	287,622	398,087
Revenue	634,524	740,000
Variable Cost	346,862	341,913
Budget	400,000	341,913

Product Mix:

Milk Chocolate, 250 gm	345	400
Milk Chocolate, 100 gm	757	3,600
Crunchy, 250 gm	0	0
Crunchy, 100 gm	0	0
Choco w/ Nuts, 250 gm	2,000	0
Choco w/ Nuts, 100 gm	0	0
Waffer	278	333

Resource utilization:

	Planned	Utilized	Inventory	Required	Inc (Dec)
Cocoa	100,000	100,000	0	165,000	65,000
Milk	120,000	83,810	36,190	119,000	(1,000)
Nut	60,000	60,000	0	0	(60,000)
Sugar	200,000	131,429	68,571	192,000	(8,000)
Flour	20,000	20,000	0	24,000	4,000
Foil	500,000	241,843	258,157	283,333	(216,667)
Paper	500,000	155,159	344,841	180,000	(320,000)
Plastic	500,000	420,979	79,021	539,333	39,333
Labor	1,000	1,000	0	1,283	283

Facility utilization:

	Available	Utilized	% Capacity	Utilized	% Capacity
Cook	1,000	630	63%	952	95%
Mix	200	200	100%	0	0%
Form	1,500	1,186	79%	1,500	100%
Grind	200	0	0%	0	0%
Wfrmkg	100	83	83%	100	100%
Cutting	400	310	78%	400	100%
Pkg 1	400	114	28%	133	33%
Pkg 2	1,200	886	74%	1,150	96%

Problem Statistics:

Variable	8	8
Constraints	17	9
No. of Iterations	5	4
Job CPU time (sec)	1	1

The following observations and comments can be made about the use of De Novo:

(i)   The De Novo model is able to come up with a higher revenue and profit. Product mix from the traditional model is more varied. The De Novo specializes in more profitable products first until some constraints limit the production.

(ii) The De Novo results show that the money actually needed for purchasing raw materials can be reduced from $400,000 to $342,000. This means that the facilities are the limiting factors of the total output of the system.

(iii) A budget of $400,000 in the product mix model produces some slacks in raw materials. This may be considered as raw material inventories and are not wasted. The De Novo comes up with a higher volume and value of products. This implies that inventories are in the form of finished products instead of raw materials.

(iv) Machinery utilization for the product mix model is more balanced. The De Novo mix loads some machineries to the maximum and leaves others idle.

(v)   The De Novo model has less constraints. The optimal solution can be obtained in less iterations and computer time. However, after obtaining the product mix, a separate computation of material requirements has to be made.

5.9.3 LIMITED DEMAND SITUATION

Specializing in the production of a few products may be unrealistic at times. The results of both models can be improved if the marketing department can give some inputs in the model, say, product mix requirements.

The following conditions and requirements were established by the marketing department of Chocoman:

(i)   Product mix requirements. It has been specified that big sized products (250 gm) of each type should not exceed 60% of the small sized product (100 gm), such that

$$MB \leq 60\% \ MS$$
$$CB \leq 60\% \ CS$$
$$NB \leq 60\% \ NS$$

(ii) Main product line requirement. Suppose that Chocoman wants to preserve its image as the leading chocolate bar manufacturer. Marketing and top management have specified that total sales from candy and waffer products should not exceed 15% of the total revenues from the chocolate bar products.

(iii) Demand limits for each product have been established as follows:

Product	Limit ('000 units)
Milk Chocolate, 250 gm	500
Milk Chocolate, 100 gm	800
Crunchy Chocolate, 250 gm	400
Crunchy Chocolate, 100 gm	600
Chocolate with Nuts, 250 gm	300
Chocolate with Nuts, 100 gm	500
Chocolate Candy	200
Waffer	400

Find the optimal product mix under the same technical considerations as the Unlimited Demand Models.

Product Mix Model:

The variables, objective function and material and facility constraints of this model are the same as that of Model 1. Additional constraints have to be added to satisfy the conditions specified by marketing, they are:

Product mix requirements:

$$MB \leq 60\% \ MS$$
$$CB \leq 60\% \ CS$$
$$NB \leq 60\% \ NS$$

Main product line requirement:
$$400 \ CD + 150 \ WF \leq 15\% \ (375 \ MB + 150 \ MS + 400 \ CB$$
$$+ \ 160 \ CS + 420 \ NB + 175 \ NS)$$

Demand limits:

MB $\leq$ 500		NB $\leq$ 300	
MS $\leq$ 800		NS $\leq$ 500	
CB $\leq$ 400		CD $\leq$ 200	
CS $\leq$ 600		WF $\leq$ 400	

The complete set of constraints and the objective function are shown in Model 3.

Model 3 Optimization Under Limited Demand and Product Mix Requirements, Product Mix Model

Maximize:

Z = 179.95MB + 82.9MS + 153.08CB + 72.15CS + 129.95NB + 69.9NS + 208.5CD + 83WF

Subject to:

Material constraints

Cocoa	87.5MB +	35MS +	75CB +	30CS +	50NB +	20NS +	60CD +	12WF	≤100,000
Milk	62.5MB +	25MS +	50CB +	20CS +	50NB +	20NS +	30CD +	12WF	≤120,000
Nuts			37.5CB +	15CS +	75NB +	30NS			≤ 60,000
Sugar	100MB +	40MS +	87.5CB +	35CS +	75NB +	30NS +	210CD +	24WF	≤200,000
Flour								72WF	≤ 20,000
Foil	500MB +		500CB +		500NB +			250WF	≤500,000
Paper	450MB +		450CB +		450NB +				≤500,000
Plastic	60MB +	120MS +	60CB +	120CS +	60NB +	120NS +	1600CD +	250WF	≤500,000

Facility Constraints

Cook	0.5MB +	0.2MS +	0.425CB +	0.17CS +	0.35NB +	0.14NS +	0.6CD +	0.096WF	≤1,000
Mix			0.15CB +	0.06CS +	0.25NB +	0.1NS			≤ 200
Form	0.75MB +	0.3MS +	0.75CB +	0.3CS +	0.75NB +	0.3NS +	0.9CD +	0.36WF	≤1,500
Grind			0.25CB +	0.1CS					≤ 200
Wfrmkg								0.3WF	≤ 100
Cut	0.5MB +	0.1MS +	0.1CB +	0.1CS +	0.1NB +	0.1NS +	0.2CD		≤ 400
Pkg1	0.25MB +		0.25CB +		0.25NB +			0.1WF	≤ 400
Pkg2	0.05MB +	0.3MS +	0.05CB +	0.3CS +	0.05NB +	0.3NS +	2.5CD +	0.15WF	≤1,000

Labor   0.3MB + 0.3MS + 0.3CB + 0.3CS + 0.3NB + 0.3NS + 2.5CD + 0.25WF ≤1,000

Size Mix Constraint

$$MB \leq 60\% \ MS$$
$$CB \leq 60\% \ CS$$
$$NB \leq 60\% \ NS$$

Product Mix Constraint (for company image)

400 CD + 150 WF ≤ 15% (375 MB + 150 MS + 400 CS + 160 CS + 420 NB + 175 NS)

Demand Constraints

MB ≤ 500	NB ≤ 300
MS ≤ 800	NS ≤ 500
CB ≤ 400	CD ≤ 200
CS ≤ 600	WF ≤ 400

All variables ≥ 0

Model 4   Optimization Under Limited Demand and
Product Requirements, De Novo Formulation

Maximize:

$Z = 179.95MB + 82.9MS + 153.08CB + 72.15CS + 129.95NB + 69.9NS + 208.5CD + 83WF$

Subject to:

Budget $195.05MB+67.1MS+246.93CB+87.85CS+290.05NB+105.1NS+191.5CD+67WF \leq 400,000$

Facility Constraints

```
Cook    0.5MB +0.2MS +0.425CB +0.17CS +0.35NB +0.14NS + 0.6CD +0.096WF ≤1,000
Mix                  0.15CB +0.06CS +0.25NB + 0.1NS                     ≤  200
Form    0.75MB +0.3MS + 0.75CB + 0.3CS +0.75NB + 0.3NS + 0.9CD + 0.36WF ≤1,500
Grind                0.25CB + 0.1CS                                     ≤  200
Wfrmkg                                                         0.3WF    ≤  100
Cut     0.1MB +0.1MS + 0.1CB + 0.1CS + 0.1NB + 0.1NS + 0.2CD           ≤  400
Pkg1    0.25MB +        0.25CB +        0.25NB +              0.1WF     ≤  400
Pkg2    0.05MB +0.3MS +0.05CB + 0.3CS +0.05NB + 0.3NS + 2.5CD + 0.15WF ≤1,000
```

Size Mix Constraint

$$MB \leq 60\% \ MS$$
$$CB \leq 60\% \ CS$$
$$NB \leq 60\% \ NS$$

Product Mix Constraint (for company image)

$400 \ CD + 150 \ WF \leq 15\% \ (375 \ MB + 150 \ MS + 400 \ CS + 160 \ CS + 420 \ NB + 175 \ NS)$

Demand Constraints

$MB \leq 500$	$NB \leq 300$
$MS \leq 800$	$NS \leq 500$
$CB \leq 400$	$CD \leq 200$
$CS \leq 600$	$WF \leq 400$

All variables ≥ 0

Table 5.21   Results of Optimization Models
With Limited Demand

	Product Mix Model	De Novo Formulation
Profit (objective)	266,157	344,379
Revenue	592,533	744,375
Variable Cost	326,376	399,998
Budget	400,000	400,000

Product Mix:

	Product Mix Model	De Novo Formulation
Milk Chocolate, 250 gm	239	480
Milk Chocolate, 100 gm	800	800
Crunchy, 250 gm	0	360
Crunchy, 100 gm	600	600
Choco w/ Nuts, 250 gm	300	47
Choco w/ Nuts, 100 gm	500	500
Chocolate Candy	80	118
Waffer	278	333

Resource utilization:

	Planned	Utilized	Inventory	Required	Inc (Dec)
Cocoa	100,000	100,000	0	138,419	38,419
Milk	120,000	77,644	42,356	99,877	(20,113)
Nut	60,000	46,500	13,500	41,033	(18,967)
Sugar	200,000	137,753	62,247	183,756	(16,244)
Flour	20,000	20,000	0	24,000	4,000
Foil	500,000	338,830	161,170	526,855	(26,855)
Paper	500,000	242,447	257,553	399,197	(100,803)
Plastic	500,000	457,082	42,918	552,930	52,930
Labor	1,000	1,000	0	1,214	214

Facility utilization:

	Available	Utilized	% Capacity	Utilized	% Capacity
Cook	1,000	63	63%	844	84%
Mix	200	161	81%	152	76%
Form	1,500	1,146	76%	1,461	97%
Grind	200	60	30%	150	75%
Wfrmkg	100	83	83%	100	100%
Cutting	400	260	65%	302	76%
Pkg 1	400	162	41%	255	64%
Pkg 2	1,200	838	70%	959	80%

Problem Statistics:

	Product Mix Model	De Novo Formulation
Variable	8	8
Constraints	22	13
No. of Iterations	11	10
Job CPU time (sec)	1	1

De Novo Formulation

Using the simplified model, Model 2B, the new marketing constraints are included. Model 4 is the revised model.

The results of the two models are presented in Table 5.21. The following comments can be made:

(i)   By including the requirements of the marketing department, results for both the product mix and De Novo models are more realistic, and distributed evenly.

(ii) The budget in De Novo is fully utilized to purchase raw materials. This indicates a more efficient use of capital.   Funds are channeled to purchase a portfolio of resources that can produce more, without any slacks.

(iii) Machinery utilization are more balanced in both cases compared to the earlier Unlimited Demand Models.

(iv) With less constraints, the De Novo still requires less iterations.

Through the use of De Novo, the following benefits can be obtained:

(i)   Higher system performance.

(ii) Higher returns to capital (budget).

(iii) If there are excess funds, De Novo can point this out as shown in the Unlimited Demand Model, Model 2. The model not only maximizes benefit, but also minimizes cost.

(iv) The concept of end product inventory in place of raw material inventory contributes to faster turnover of resource usage.

(v)   De Novo requires less constraints to model a system, therefore, requiring less computation.

However, the following costs and difficulties may be encountered:

(i)   More time and manpower had to be devoted to data gathering and integration, especially on the prices of raw materials.

(ii) Additional manpower would be required to coordinate with the subsystems in model formulation and decision implementation. This might prove to be very difficult unless top management strongly advocates and requires integrated planning to be adopted as a practice of the company.

5.9.4 MULTIOBJECTIVE DECISION MODELS

Three MCDM methods have been chosen, namely: the global criterion approach, the compromise constraint method, and the step method. The emphasis of this section is to observe the performance characteristics of De Novo formulation.

There are two Chocoman models used, one for the traditional product mix model, while the other with the De Novo formulation. The management of the company aspires for five objectives - simultaneous maximization of revenue, profit, market share of chocolate bar products, units of products produced, and plan machinery utilization.

(i) Maximize revenue.

Revenue is equal to price multiplied by units produced. Therefore,

$$\text{Maximize} \quad Z_1 = 375 \text{ MB} + 150 \text{ MS} + 400 \text{ CB} + 160 \text{ CS} + 420 \text{ NB} + 175 \text{ NS} + 400 \text{ CD} + 150 \text{ WF}$$

(ii) Maximize profit.

Profit is equivalent to gross contribution in these models. The variable cost can be calculated and profit would be selling price less variable cost. Therefore,

$$\text{Maximize} \quad Z_2 = 179.95 \text{ MB} + 82.90 \text{ MS} + 153.08 \text{ CB} + 72.15 \text{ CS} + 129.95 \text{ NB} + 69.90 \text{ NS} + 208.50 \text{ CD} + 83 \text{ WF}$$

(iii) Maximize market share of chocolate bar products.

Maximizing market share is equivalent to maximizing the tonnage of chocolate bars produced. For every 1,000 units of 250 gram chocolate bar, the weight would be 0.25 tons. Therefore,

$$\text{Maximize} \quad Z_3 = 0.25 \text{ MB} + 0.10 \text{ MS} + 0.25 \text{ CB} + 0.10 \text{ CS} + 0.25 \text{ NB} + 0.10 \text{ NS}$$

(iv) Maximize the units of products produced.

The advertising department would like to maximize the exposure of the company's brand name. In order to achieve this, the consumers had to be constantly reminded of the product through the packaging. In order to maximize on the repeated exposure of the brand, the units of products sold must be maximized. This, therefore, would be

$$\text{Maximize} \quad Z_4 = \text{MB} + \text{MS} + \text{CB} + \text{CS} + \text{NB} + \text{NS} + \text{CD} + \text{WF}$$

(v) Maximize plant machinery utilization.

To maximize plant utilization, the machines should be loaded to the maximum tonnage for maximum number of hours. Since coefficients of usage are given in Table 5.16, the total machine capacity utilization can be calculated by adding usage of each machine per product. For the cutting and packaging machines, since there are no restrictions on weight, the loading can be assumed unity, and simply added to the others. The objective function would be

$$\text{Maximize} \quad Z_5 = 1.65 \text{ MB} + 0.9 \text{ MS} + 1.975 \text{ CB} + 1.03 \text{ CS}$$
$$+ 1.75 \text{ NB} + 0.94 \text{ NS} + 4.2 \text{ CD} + 1.006 \text{ WF}$$

Objectives 1 and 2 can be considered as overall company goals. Objectives 3 and 4 are marketing subsystem considerations while objective 5 is of interest to the production subsystem.

For the product mix model, the following are the materials and labor availability:

Cocoa	100,000 kg
Milk	120,000 kg
Nuts	60,000 kg
Sugar	200,000 kg
Flour	20,000 kg
Aluminum Foil	500,000 ft^2
Paper	500,000 ft^2
Plastic	500,000 ft^2
Labor	1,000 hours

The two models, De Novo model and Product Mix model, are presented with the set of objective functions in Model 5 and Model 6.

The payoff matrices for the product mix model and the De Novo formulation are given in Table 5.22.

It can be observed that De Novo achieves a higher optimum for all objectives and the minimum objective satisfaction exceeds the product mix model maximum. However, this is of course highly dependent on the assumed parameters of raw material availability. For this particular exercise, the De Novo also exhibits a smaller range of deviation between the maximum and the minimum.

Model 5   Multiobjective Model, De Novo Formulation

Maximize:

Revenue
$$Z_1 = 375MB + 150MS + 400CB + 160CS + 420NB + 175NS + 400CD + 150WF$$

Profit
$$Z_2 = 179.95MB + 82.9MS + 153.08CB + 72.15CS + 129.95NB + 69.9NS + 208.5CD + 83WF$$

Market share of Chocolate Bars
$$Z_3 = 0.25MB + 0.1MS + 0.25CB + 0.1CS + 0.25NB + 0.1NS$$

Units produced
$$Z_4 = MB + MS + CB + CS + NB + NS + CD + WF$$

Plant utilization
$$Z_5 = 1.65MB + 0.9MS + 1.975CB + 1.03CS + 1.75NB + 0.94NS + 4.2CD + 1.006WF$$

Subject to:

Budget $195.05MB + 67.1MS + 246.93CB + 87.85CS + 290.05NB + 105.1NS + 191.5CD + 67WF \leq 400,000$

Facility Constraints

Cook	$0.5MB$	$+0.2MS$	$+0.425CB$	$+0.17CS$	$+0.35NB$	$+0.14NS$	$+0.6CD$	$+0.096WF \leq 1,000$
Mix			$0.15CB$	$+0.06CS$	$+0.25NB$	$+0.1NS$		≤ 200
Form	$0.75MB$	$+0.3MS$	$+0.75CB$	$+0.3CS$	$+0.75NB$	$+0.3NS$	$+0.9CD$	$+0.36WF \leq 1,500$
Grind			$0.25CB$	$+0.1CS$				≤ 200
Wfrmkg								$0.3WF \leq 100$
Cut	$0.1MB$	$+0.1MS$	$+0.1CB$	$+0.1CS$	$+0.1NB$	$+0.1NS$	$+0.2CD$	≤ 400
Pkg1	$0.25MB$		$+0.25CB$		$+0.25NB$			$0.1WF \leq 400$
Pkg2	$0.05MB$	$+0.3MS$	$+0.05CB$	$+0.3CS$	$+0.05NB$	$+0.3NS$	$+2.5CD$	$+0.15WF \leq 1,000$

Size Mix Constraint

$$MB \leq 60\% \ MS$$
$$CB \leq 60\% \ CS$$
$$NB \leq 60\% \ NS$$

Product Mix Constraint (for company image)

$$400 \ CD + 150 \ WF \leq 15\% \ (375 \ MB + 150 \ MS + 400 \ CS + 160 \ CS + 420 \ NB + 175 \ NS)$$

Demand Constraints

$MB \leq 500$	$NB \leq 300$
$MS \leq 800$	$NS \leq 500$
$CB \leq 400$	$CD \leq 200$
$CS \leq 600$	$WF \leq 400$

All variables ≥ 0

Model 6 Multiobjective Model, Product Mix Formulation

Maximize:

Revenue
$Z_1 =$ 375MB + 150MS +   400CB +   160CS +   420NB + 175NS +   400CD +150WF

Profit
$Z_2 =$179.95MB + 82.9MS + 153.08CB + 72.15CS + 129.95NB + 69.9NS + 208.5CD + 83WF

Market share of Chocolate Bars
$Z_3 =$ 0.25MB + 0.1MS +   0.25CB +   0.1CS +   0.25NB + 0.1NS

Units produced
$Z_4 =$ MB +   MS +   CB +   CS +   NB +   NS +   CD +   WF

Plant utilization
$Z_5 =$ 1.65MB + 0.9MS + 1.975CB + 1.03CS +   1.75NB + 0.94NS + 4.2CD +1.006WF

Subject to:

Facility Constraints

Cook	0.5MB +0.2MS +0.425CB +0.17CS +0.35NB +0.14NS + 0.6CD +0.096WF ≤1,000
Mix	0.15CB +0.06CS +0.25NB + 0.1NS ≤ 200
Form	0.75MB +0.3MS + 0.75CB + 0.3CS +0.75NB + 0.3NS + 0.9CD + 0.36WF ≤1,500
Grind	0.25CB + 0.1CS ≤ 200
Wfrmkg	0.3WF ≤ 100
Cut	0.1MB +0.1MS + 0.1CB + 0.1CS + 0.1NB + 0.1NS + 0.2CD ≤ 400
Pkg1	0.25MB + 0.25CB + 0.25NB + 0.1WF ≤ 400
Pkg2	0.05MB +0.3MS +0.05CB + 0.3CS +0.05NB + 0.3NS + 2.5CD + 0.15WF ≤1,000

Facility Constraints

Cook	0.5MB +0.2MS +0.425CB +0.17CS +0.35NB +0.14NS + 0.6CD +0.096WF ≤1,000
Mix	0.15CB +0.06CS +0.25NB + 0.1NS ≤ 200
Form	0.75MB +0.3MS + 0.75CB + 0.3CS +0.75NB + 0.3NS + 0.9CD + 0.36WF ≤1,500
Grind	0.25CB + 0.1CS ≤ 200
Wfrmkg	0.3WF ≤ 100
Cut	0.1MB +0.1MS + 0.1CB + 0.1CS + 0.1NB + 0.1NS + 0.2CD ≤ 400
Pkg1	0.25MB + 0.25CB + 0.25NB + 0.1WF ≤ 400
Pkg2	0.05MB +0.3MS +0.05CB + 0.3CS +0.05NB + 0.3NS + 2.5CD + 0.15WF ≤1,000

Size Mix Constraint

MB ≤ MS   CB ≤ CS   NB ≤ NS

Product Mix Constraint (for company image)

400 CD + 150 WF ≤ 15% (375 MB + 150 MS + 400 CS + 160 CS + 420 NB + 175 NS)

Demand Constraints

MB ≤ 800	CB ≤ 750	NB ≤ 500	CD ≤ 400
MS ≤ 1000	CS ≤ 800	NS ≤ 800	WF ≤ 1000

All variables ≥ 0

Table 5.22 Payoff Matrices for Product Mix and De Novo Models

Product Mix Model

	z_1	z_2	z_3	z_4	z_5
x^{1*}	641110	273590	343.92	2610.44	3410.72
x^{2*}	636852	275202	349.03	2829.00	3410.44
x^{3*}	598745	247040	371.43	2259.60	2840.99
x^{4*}	614212	273421	349.83	3254.20	3448.94
x^{5*}	603472	261968	323.17	2700.45	3508.33
Optimal	641110	275202	371.43	3254.20	3508.33
Minimum	598745	247040	323.17	2259.60	2840.99
Range	42365	28162	48.26	994.60	667.34
% Deviation	6.6%	10.2%	13.0%	30.6%	19.0%

Total Deviation	79.4%
Average Deviation	15.8%

De Novo Formulation

	z_1	z_2	z_3	z_4	z_5
x^{1*}	778739	378739	436.67	3628.92	4453.53
x^{2*}	778739	378739	436.67	3628.92	4453.53
x^{3*}	750648	350652	487.91	3031.62	3896.45
x^{4*}	772360	372359	429.08	3736.50	4460.05
x^{5*}	769241	369241	427.27	3519.92	4633.51
Optimal	778739	378739	487.91	3736.50	4633.51
Minimum	750648	350652	427.27	3031.62	3896.45
Range	28091	28087	60.64	704.88	737.06
% Deviation	3.6%	7.4%	12.4%	18.9%	15.9%

Total Deviation	58.2%
Average Deviation	11.6%

5.9.4.1 Global Criterion Method

(i)   Product Mix Model.

Referring to Table 5.22 for the individual objective function optimum, the following global criterion objective function can be derived.

Minimize   F = [641110 - (375 MB + 150 MS + ... + 150 WF)] / 641110

+ [275202 - (179.95 MB + 82.9 MS + ... + 83 WF)] / 275202

+ [371.43 - (0.25 MB + 0.10 MS + ... + 0.10 NS)] / 371.43

+ [3254.2 - (MB + MS + ... + WF)] / 3254.2

+ [3508.33 - (1.65 MB + 0.9 MS + ... + 1.006 WF)] / 3508.33

Simplifying the equation,

Minimize $F = 5 - [26.89 \text{ MB} + 13.68 \text{ MS} + 27.22 \text{ CB} + 13.82 \text{ CS}$
$+ 26.06 \text{ NB} + 13.71 \text{ NS} + 18.09 \text{ CD} + 20.4 \text{ WF}](10^{-4})$

Which is equivalent to

Maximize $F' = 26.89 \text{ MB} + 13.68 \text{ MS} + 27.22 \text{ CB} + 13.82 \text{ CS}$
$+ 26.06 \text{ NB} + 13.71 \text{ NS} + 18.09 \text{ CD} + 20.4 \text{ WF}$

(ii)   De Novo Model.

The De Novo multiobjective model can be derived similarly.   The resulting objective function is

Maximize $F' = 20.93 \text{ MB} + 10.79 \text{ MS} + 19.08 \text{ CB} + 10.91 \text{ CS}$
$+ 20.4 \text{ NB} + 10.86 \text{ NS} + 22.39 \text{ CD} + 8.97 \text{ WF}$

Use these two objective functions in their respective model, under their respective sets of constraints.

The results of the global criterion multiobjective models are shown in Table 5.23.

The De novo model is able to achieve higher levels of objective satisfaction.   However, with respect to deviational characteristics, the product mix model has values closer to the maximum achievable results.

Table 5.23   Results of Global Criterion Models

	z_1	z_2	z_3	z_4	z_5
Product Mix					
Maximum	641110	275202	371	3254	3508
Model Result	614212	273421	350	3254	3449
Deviation (%)	4.20	0.65	5.82	0.00	1.69
Total Deviation (%)	12.35				
Average Deviation (%)	2.47				
De Novo					
Maximum	778739	378739	488	3737	4634
Model Result	778739	378739	437	3629	4454
Deviation (%)	0.00	0.00	10.50	2.88	3.88
Total Deviation (%)	17.27				
Average Deviation (%)	3.45				

5.9.4.2 Compromise Constraint Method

For the models in this problem, for each objective, the weight w_i and $\sqrt{\sum c_{ij}^2}$ are given and calculated as follows:

	w_i	$\sqrt{\sum c_{ij}^2}$
z_1	0.3	859.2
z_2	0.3	374.2
z_3	0.2	0.466
z_4	0.1	2.828
z_5	0.1	5.576

Using the weights and $\sqrt{\sum c_{ij}^2}$, the following objective function can be derived for both the product mix and De Novo models,

$$
\begin{aligned}
\text{Maximize} \quad Z = \ & (0.3/859.2) \ (375 \ MB + 150 \ MS + \ldots + 150 \ WF) \\
& + (0.3/374.2) \ (179.95 \ MB + 82.9 \ MS + \ldots + 83 \ WF) \\
& + (0.2/0.466) \ (0.25 \ MB + 0.1 \ MS + \ldots + 0.1 \ NS) \\
& + (0.2/2.828) \ (MB + MS + \ldots + WF) \\
& + (0.1/5.576) \ (1.65 \ MB + 0.9 \ MS + \ldots + 1.006 \ WF) \\
& + (dm_{12} - dp_{12}) + (dm_{13} - dp_{13}) + (dm_{14} - dp_{14}) \\
& + (dm_{15} - dp_{15}) + (dm_{23} - dp_{23}) + (dm_{24} - dp_{24}) \\
& + (dm_{25} - dp_{25}) + (dm_{34} - dp_{34}) + (dm_{35} - dp_{35}) \\
& + (dm_{45} - dp_{45})
\end{aligned}
$$

(i)   Product mix model.

The compromise constraints for the product mix model are formulated for each pair of objectives. The optimal values for each objectives are obtained from Table 5.22. For objectives 1 and 2,

$$
\begin{aligned}
& (0.3/859.2) \ [(375 \ MB + 150 \ MS + \ldots + 150 \ WF) - 641110] \\
& \quad - (0.3/374.2) \ [(179.59 \ MB + 82.9 \ MS + \ldots 83 \ WF) - 275202] \\
& \quad + dm_{12} - dp_{12} \ = 0
\end{aligned}
$$

which may be simplified as

$$
\begin{aligned}
& -0.013 \ MB - 0.0141 \ MS + 0.017 \ CB - 0.002 \ CS + 0.043 \ NB \\
& \quad + 0.0051 \ NS - 0.027 \ CD - 0.0141 \ WF - dm_{12} + dp_{12} = 3.22
\end{aligned}
$$

Other pairs can be calculated similarly. The whole set of compromise constraints is presented in Model 7.

Model 7   Compromise Constraint Product Mix Model

Maximize:

$$Z = 0.4450 \text{ MB} + 0.2120 \text{ MS} + 0.4400 \text{ CB} + 0.2100 \text{ CS} + 0.4260 \text{ NB} + 0.2120 \text{ NS}$$
$$+ 0.4200 \text{ CD} + 0.1720 \text{ WF} - (dm_{12} + dp_{12} + dm_{13} + dp_{13} + dm_{14} + dp_{14}$$
$$+ dm_{15} + dp_{15} + dm_{23} + dp_{23} + dm_{24} + dp_{24} + dm_{25} + dp_{25}$$
$$+ dm_{34} + dp_{34} + dm_{35} + dp_{35} + dm_{45} + dp_{45})$$

Subject to:

Compromise Constraints

Between

Z1 & 2: $-0.0130 \text{ MB} - 0.0141 \text{ MS} + 0.0170 \text{ CB} - 0.0020 \text{ CS} + 0.0430 \text{ NB}$
$+ 0.0051 \text{ NS} - 0.0270 \text{ CD} - 0.0141 \text{ WF} - dm_{12} + dp_{12}$ $=$ 3.22

Z1 & 3: $0.0240 \text{ MB} + 0.0095 \text{ MS} + 0.0330 \text{ CB} + 0.0129 \text{ CS} + 0.0400 \text{ NB}$
$+ 0.0182 \text{ NS} + 0.1400 \text{ CD} + 0.0524 \text{ WF} - dm_{13} + dp_{13}$ $=$ 64.44

Z1 & 4: $0.0956 \text{ MB} + 0.0170 \text{ MS} + 0.1046 \text{ CB} + 0.0204 \text{ CS} + 0.1116 \text{ NB}$
$+ 0.0257 \text{ NS} + 0.1046 \text{ CD} + 0.0170 \text{ WF} - dm_{14} + dp_{14}$ $=$ 108.78

Z1 & 5: $0.1014 \text{ MB} + 0.0363 \text{ MS} + 0.1046 \text{ CB} + 0.0373 \text{ CS} + 0.1156 \text{ NB}$
$+ 0.0442 \text{ NS} + 0.0647 \text{ CD} + 0.0344 \text{ WF} - dm_{15} + dp_{15}$ $=$ 160.93

Z2 & 3: $0.0370 \text{ MB} + 0.0236 \text{ MS} + 0.0330 \text{ CB} + 0.0149 \text{ CS} - 0.0030 \text{ NB}$
$+ 0.0131 \text{ NS} + 0.1670 \text{ CD} + 0.0665 \text{ WF} - dm_{23} + dp_{23}$ $=$ 61.22

Z2 & 4: $0.1086 \text{ MB} + 0.0311 \text{ MS} + 0.0876 \text{ CB} + 0.0224 \text{ CS} + 0.0686 \text{ NB}$
$+ 0.0206 \text{ NS} + 0.1316 \text{ CD} + 0.0311 \text{ WF} - dm_{24} + dp_{24}$ $=$ 105.56

Z2 & 5: $0.1144 \text{ MB} + 0.0504 \text{ MS} + 0.0876 \text{ CB} + 0.0393 \text{ CS} + 0.0726 \text{ NB}$
$+ 0.0391 \text{ NS} + 0.0917 \text{ CD} + 0.0485 \text{ WF} - dm_{25} + dp_{25}$ $=$ 157.71

Z3 & 4: $0.0716 \text{ MB} + 0.0075 \text{ MS} + 0.0716 \text{ CB} + 0.0075 \text{ CS} + 0.0716 \text{ NB}$
$+ 0.0075 \text{ NS} - 0.0354 \text{ CD} - 0.0354 \text{ WF} - dm_{34} + dp_{34}$ $=$ 44.34

Z3 & 5: $0.0774 \text{ MB} + 0.0268 \text{ MS} + 0.0716 \text{ CB} + 0.0244 \text{ CS} + 0.0756 \text{ NB}$
$+ 0.0260 \text{ NS} - 0.0753 \text{ CD} - 0.0180 \text{ WF} - dm_{35} + dp_{35}$ $=$ 96.49

Z4 & 5: $0.0058 \text{ MB} + 0.0193 \text{ MS} +$ $0.0169 \text{ CS} + 0.0040 \text{ NB}$
$+ 0.0185 \text{ NS} - 0.0400 \text{ CD} + 0.0174 \text{ WF} - dm_{13} + dp_{13}$ $=$ 52.15

Other Constraints specified in Model 6.

<u>Model 8   Compromise Constraint De Novo Model</u>

Maximize:

$Z = 0.4450$ MB $+ 0.2120$ MS $+ 0.4400$ CB $+ 0.2100$ CS $+ 0.4260$ NB $+ 0.2120$ NS

$+ 0.4200$ CD $+ 0.1720$ WF $- (dm_{12} + dp_{12} + dm_{13} + dp_{13} + dm_{14} + dp_{14}$

$+ dm_{15} + dp_{15} + dm_{23} + dp_{23} + dm_{24} + dp_{24} + dm_{25} + dp_{25}$

$+ dm_{34} + dp_{34} + dm_{35} + dp_{35} + dm_{45} + dp_{45})$

Subject to:

Compromise Constraints

Between

$Z1$ & 2: -0.0130 MB $- 0.0141$ MS $+ 0.0170$ CB $- 0.0020$ CS $+ 0.0430$ NB

$+ 0.0051$ NS $- 0.0270$ CD $- 0.0141$ WF $- dm_{12} + dp_{12}$ $= \quad 31.33$

$Z1$ & 3: 0.0240 MB $+ 0.0095$ MS $+ 0.0330$ CB $+ 0.0129$ CS $+ 0.0400$ NB

$+ 0.0182$ NS $+ 0.1400$ CD $+ 0.0524$ WF $- dm_{13} + dp_{13}$ $= \quad 62.51$

$Z1$ & 4: 0.0956 MB $+ 0.0170$ MS $+ 0.1046$ CB $+ 0.0204$ CS $+ 0.1116$ NB

$+ 0.0257$ NS $+ 0.1046$ CD $+ 0.0170$ WF $- dm_{14} + dp_{14}$ $= \quad 139.78$

$Z1$ & 5: 0.1014 MB $+ 0.0363$ MS $+ 0.1046$ CB $+ 0.0373$ CS $+ 0.1156$ NB

$+ 0.0442$ NS $+ 0.0647$ CD $+ 0.0344$ WF $- dm_{15} + dp_{15}$ $= \quad 188.81$

$Z2$ & 3: 0.0370 MB $+ 0.0236$ MS $+ 0.0330$ CB $+ 0.0149$ CS $- 0.0030$ NB

$+ 0.0131$ NS $+ 0.1670$ CD $+ 0.0665$ WF $- dm_{23} + dp_{23}$ $= \quad 94.24$

$Z2$ & 4: 0.1086 MB $+ 0.0311$ MS $+ 0.0876$ CB $+ 0.0224$ CS $+ 0.0686$ NB

$+ 0.0206$ NS $+ 0.1316$ CD $+ 0.0311$ WF $- dm_{24} + dp_{24}$ $= \quad 171.51$

$Z2$ & 5: 0.1144 MB $+ 0.0504$ MS $+ 0.0876$ CB $+ 0.0393$ CS $+ 0.0726$ NB

$+ 0.0391$ NS $+ 0.0917$ CD $+ 0.0485$ WF $- dm_{25} + dp_{25}$ $= \quad 220.54$

$Z3$ & 4: 0.0716 MB $+ 0.0075$ MS $+ 0.0716$ CB $+ 0.0075$ CS $+ 0.0716$ NB

$+ 0.0075$ NS $- 0.0354$ CD $- 0.0354$ WF $- dm_{34} + dp_{34}$ $= \quad 77.27$

$Z3$ & 5: 0.0774 MB $+ 0.0268$ MS $+ 0.0716$ CB $+ 0.0244$ CS $+ 0.0756$ NB

$+ 0.0260$ NS $- 0.0753$ CD $- 0.0180$ WF $- dm_{35} + dp_{35}$ $= \quad 126.30$

$Z4$ & 5: 0.0058 MB $+ 0.0193$ MS $+$ 0.0169 CS $+ 0.0040$ NB

$+ 0.0185$ NS $- 0.0400$ CD $+ 0.0174$ WF $- dm_{13} + dp_{13}$ $= \quad 49.03$

Other Constraints specified in Model 5.

Table 5.24   Results of Compromise Constraint Models

	z_1	z_2	z_3	z_4	z_5
Product Mix					
Maximum	641110	275202	371	3254	3508
Model Result	617725	270655	357	3065	3307
Deviation (%)	3.65	1.65	4.00	5.82	5.75
Total Deviation (%)	20.87				
Average Deviation (%)	4.17				
De Novo					
Maximum	778739	378739	488	3737	4634
Model Result	763654	363656	466	3462	4099
Deviation (%)	1.94	3.98	4.43	7.36	11.54
Total Deviation (%)	29.25				
Average Deviation (%)	5.95				

(ii)   De Novo model.

The De Novo compromise constraints are shown in Model 8.   The same formula is used to derive the ten compromise constraints.

The original material, facility, demand and other constraints are combined with the new objective function, and the compromise constraints to solve for the compromise solution.

The results of the compromise constraint model are shown in Table 5.24.

The product mix model still achieves a closer value to the maximum achievable optimum as shown by the deviations.

5.9.4.3   The Step Method (STEM)

For both the product mix and De Novo models, suppose the objective of the decision maker is to be within 5% of each objectives' optimal values, explore the possibility of attaining this objective by the step method.

(i)   Product mix model.

(a)   First iteration.

Using the formula outlined in the theoretical discussion (Chapter IV, Section 4.5) and the values in Table 5.22, the following factors are computed:

	Max	Min	$\sqrt{\sum c_{kj}^2}$	α_k	π_k
z_1	641110	598745	859.2	$7.69 \cdot 10^{-5}$	0
z_2	275202	247040	374.2	$2.73 \cdot 10^{-4}$	0
z_3	371.43	323.17	0.466	0.278	0.66
z_4	3354.2	2259.6	2.828	0.108	0.26
z_5	3508.3	2841.0	5.576	0.034	0.08

The STEM model is formulated as follows:

> Minimize $\quad$ y
> Subject to
> $\quad$ $y \geq [371.43 - (0.25\ MB + 0.1\ MS + \ldots + 0.1\ NS)]\ 0.66$
> $\quad$ $y \geq [3254.2 - (MB + MS + \ldots + WF)]\ 0.26$
> $\quad$ $y \geq [3508.33 - (1.65\ MB + 0.9\ MS + \ldots + 1.006\ WF)]\ 0.08$
> $\quad$ and the original constraints in Model 6.

The solution set obtained is

$$Z_k = (607901,\ 269677,\ 354.11,\ 3214.96,\ 3365.87)$$

which when compared to the ideal solution

$$Z^* = (641110,\ 275202,\ 371.43,\ 3254.20,\ 3508.33)$$

has the following deviation

$$\% \text{ deviation} = (5.18\%,\ 2.01\%,\ 4.66\%,\ 1.21\%,\ 4.06\%)$$

(b)   Second iteration.

Form the deviations, only objective 1 is not yet satisfied while objectives 2 to 5 are satisfied and could be relaxed. The second iteration would, therefore, be

> Minimize $\quad$ y
> Subject to
> $\quad$ $y = [641110 - (375\ MB + 150\ MS + \ldots + 150\ WF)]\ 1$
> $\quad$ $375\ MB + 150\ MS + \ldots + 150\ WF \geq 607901$
> $\quad$ $179.95\ MB + 82.90\ MS + \ldots + 83\ WF \geq 0.95\ Z_2^*$
> $\quad$ $0.25\ MB + 0.1\ MS + \ldots + 0.1\ NS \geq 0.95\ Z_3^*$
> $\quad$ $MB + MS + \ldots + WF \geq 0.95\ Z_4^*$
> $\quad$ $1.65\ MB + 0.9\ MS + \ldots + 1.006\ WF \geq 0.95\ Z_5^*$
> $\quad$ and the original Model 7 constraints

The new solution set is obtained to be

$$Z_k = (619781,\ 272427,\ 352.86,\ 3091.49,\ 3375.26)$$

with $\%$ deviation $= (3.33\%,\ 1.01\%,\ 5\%,\ 5\%,\ 3.79\%)$ from the individual optimum and acceptable.

(ii)   De Novo Step Method.

(a)   First iteration.

The following values are calculated for the De Novo model as inputs to the STEM equations.

	Max	Min	$\sqrt{\sum c_{kj}^2}$	α_k	π_k
z_1	778739	750648	859.2	$4.21 \cdot 10^{-5}$	0
z_2	378739	350652	374.2	$1.98 \cdot 10^{-4}$	0
z_3	487.91	427.27	0.466	0.266	0.73
z_4	3736.5	3031.6	2.828	0.067	0.19
z_5	4633.5	3896.5	5.576	0.029	0.08

The STEM objective function and constraints are:

Minimize y

Subject to

$y \geq [487.91 - (0.25\ MB + 0.1\ MS + \ldots + 0.1\ NS)]\ 0.73$

$y \geq [3736.5 - (MB + MS + \ldots + WF)]\ 0.19$

$y \geq [4633.51 - (1.65\ MB + 0.9\ MS + \ldots + 1.006\ WF)]\ 0.08$

and the original constraints in Model 5.

Incorporating these into the original set of constraints, the solution vector obtained is

$$z_k = (767063,\ 367062, 452.98,\ 3592.64,\ 4310.08)$$

giving the deviations % deviation = (1.5%, 3.08%, 7.16%, 3.85%, 6.98%) from $z^* = (778739,\ 367062,\ 452.98,\ 3592.64,\ 4310.08)$.

(b)   Second iteration.

Objectives 3 and 5 are not satisfied.   For the second iteration,

	α_i	π_i
z_3	0.266	0.9
z_5	0.0285	0.1

gives us the following formulation:

Minimize   y

Subject to

$$y \geq [487.91 - (0.25 \text{ MB} + 0.1 \text{ MS} + \ldots + 0.1 \text{ NS})] \ 0.9$$

$$y \geq [4633.51 - (1.65 \text{ MB} + 0.9 \text{ MS} + \ldots + 1.006 \text{ WF})] \ 0.1$$

$$0.25 \text{ MB} + 0.1 \text{ MS} + \ldots + 0.1 \text{ NS} \geq 452.98$$

$$1.65 \text{ MB} + 0.9 \text{ MS} + \ldots + 150 \text{ WF} \geq 0.95 \ z_1{}^*$$

$$179.95 \text{ MB} + 82.9 \text{ MS} + \ldots + 83 \text{ WF} \geq 0.95 \ z_2{}^*$$

$$\text{MB} + \text{MS} + \ldots + \text{WF} \geq 0.95 \ z_4{}^*$$

and the original constraints in Model 5.

The solution is still unacceptable:

$$z_k = (766255, \ 366254, \ 454.10, \ 3549.68, \ 4328.90)$$

with % deviation = (1.6%, 3.3%, 6.93%, 5%, 6.57%).

Still objectives 3 and 5 are unacceptable. There had been no improvement, say at least one of objectives 3 and 5 being acceptable, despite full relaxation of objectives 1, 2, and 4. This is an indication of absence of feasible solution, since the third iteration will just be a repetition of the second.

(c)   Check for feasibility.

A check for feasibility by maximizing objective 1, subject to satisfying within 5% of other objectives shows that the situation is not possible. However, if budget is to be increased to $407,325.55, the decision maker's goal would be achieved.

5.9.4.4 Goal Setting and Achievement under De Novo

As noted from the previous section, the reason for infeasibility is the budget. Unlike in the traditional product mix model, when a similar case of infeasibility is tested, it is one of the objective targets that is infeasible.

This special characteristic of De Novo is explored further. As maximum values for each objective function are already established, these values are used for setting the goals for each individual objective.

Given the optimal values, z^*, we would like to explore the feasibility of achieving a certain percentage of these optima.

Models are made for targets of "superoptimality" (every objective would achieve its optimality) and up to 7% range. To achieve within certain ranges of optimality, the causes of infeasibility is always the budget.

To achieve the goals, the required financial resources are found to be:

	Required budget
Superoptimality	$436,000
Within 1% range	430,000
2%	425,100
3%	419,000
4%	413,000
5%	408,000
6%	403,000
7%	400,000

The De Novo allows us to adjust the budget to be able to achieve certain targets of objective satisfaction.

5.9.4.5   General Observations

In cases of fixed budgets, the De Novo models are able to achieve higher optima for all objectives. There is a strong indication that even if only one objective is maximized, the performance of all other objectives would still be very high because of control over a bigger set of variables.

De Novo is a powerful tool for multiobjective goal setting and achievement. Given levels of multiple objective satisfaction, the De Novo expresses its resource infeasibility in terms of one single measure, money. Because of this property, the model can be used to determine the amount of budget to be allocated to a project to be able to achieve some minimum levels of objective satisfaction.

A simple De Novo "heuristic" algorithm is presented in the Appendix.

REFERENCES

1.   Adam, E.E. Jr. and R. J. Ebert, 1982. Production and Operations Management, Concepts, Models and Behavior.   2nd   Edition, Prentice-Hall, Englewood Cliffs, N. J.

2.   Adulbhan, P. and S. Klinpikul, 1975. The Utilization of Linear Programming in Optimizing the Production of a Cement Plant.   Procedings of the International Symposium of the 26th Annual Institute Conference and Convention of the American Institute of Industrial Engineers, Washington, D.C.

3.   Adulbhan, P. and M. T. Tabucanon, 1977. Bicriterion Linear Programming, International Journal of Computers and Operations Research. pp.141-153.

4.   Adulbhan, P. and M. T. Tabucanon, 1979.   A Biobjective Model for
      Production Planning in a Cement Factory.   International Journal of
      Computers and Industrial Engineering, 3:41-51.

5.   Adulbhan, P., and M. T. Tabucanon, 1980.   Multicriterion Optimization in
      Industrial Systems, Decision Models for Industrial Systems Engineers and
      Managers, edited by P. Adulbhan and M. T. Tabucanon, (Bangkok: Asian
      Institute of Technology, distributed by Pergamon Press), Chap. 9.

6.   Arthur, J. L., and K. D. Lawrence, 1980.   Multiple Goal Blending Problem.
      Computers and Operations Research, 7:215-224.

7.   Arthur, J. L., and K. D. Lawrence, 1982.   Multiple Goal Production and
      Logistic Planning in a Chemical and Pharmaceutical Company.   Computers and
      Operations Research, 9:127-137.

8.   Baker, K. R., 1974.   Introduction to Sequencing and Scheduling.   John
      Wiley & Sons Inc.

9.   Bansal, S. D., 1980.   Single Machine Scheduling to Minimize Weighted Sum
      of Completion Times with Secondary Criteria - A Branch and Bound Approach.
      European Journal of Operational Research, 5:177-181.

10.   Belenson, S. M. and K. C. Kapur, 1972.   An Algorithm for Solving
      Multicriterion Linear Programming Problems With Examples. Operational
      Research Quarterly, 24:65-67.

11.   Benayoun, R. J. De Montgolfier, J. Tergny, and O. Laritchev, 1971.   Linear
      Programming with Multiple Objective Functions: Step Method (STEM),
      Mathematical Programing, 1:366-375.

12.   Benson, H. P. and T. L. Morin, 1987.   A Bicriteria Mathematical
      Programming Model for Nutrition Planning in Developing Nations.
      Management Science, 33:1593-1601.

13.   Burns, R. N., 1976.   Scheduling to Minimize the Weighted Sum of Completion
      Times with Secondary Criteria.   Naval Research Logistics Quarterly, Vol.
      23.

14.   Charnes, A. and W. W. Cooper, 1961.   Management Models and Industrial
      Applications of Linear Programming, Vols. 1 & 2. John Wiley & Sons.

15.   Clayton, E. R. and L. J. Moore, 1972.   Goal Versus Linear Programming.
      Journal of Systems Management.

16.   Contini, B., 1968.   A Stochastic Approach to Goal Programming.   Operations
      Research, 16:576-586.

17.   Davis, K. R., and P. G. McKeown, 1981.   Quantitative Models for
      Management.   Kent Publishing Company, Boston, Massachusetts.

18.   Deckro, R. F., 1982.   Multiple Criteria Job Shop Scheduling.   Computers &
      Operations Research, 9:279-286.

19.   DeKluyver, C. A., 1979.   An Exploration of Various Goal Programming

Formulations with Application to Advertising Media Scheduling. Journal of Operations Research Society, 30:167-172.

20. Dileepan, P. and T. Sen, 1988. Bicriterion Static Scheduling Research for a Single Machine. Omega, 16:53-60.

21. Duncan, A. J., 1959. Quality Control and Industrial Statistics. Richard D. Irwin, Inc.

22. Dyer, J. S., 1972. Interactive Goal Programming. Management Science, 19:62-70.

23. Easton, A., 1973. Complex Managerial Decisions Involving Multiple Objectives. Wiley, N. Y.

24. Eilon, S., 1975. Five Approaches to Aggregate Production Planning. AIIE Transactions, 7:118-131.

25. Emmons, H., 1975. One Machine Sequencing To Minimize Mean Flow Time With Minimum Number Tardy. Naval Research Logistics Quarterly, 22:585-592.

26. Emmons, H., 1975. A Note on a Scheduling Problem with Dual Criteria. Naval Research Logistics Quarterly, 22:615-616.

27. Evans, G. W. and S. M. Alexander, 1987. Multiple Objective Decision Analysis for Acceptance Sampling Plans. IIE Transactions, 19:308-316.

28. Fernandez, E., 1986. Bicriterion Design Centering of Electronic Circuits Using Fuzzy Sets and Differential Sensitivity. Foundations of control Engineering, 11:69-80.

29. Fisk, J., 1980. An Interactive Game for Production and Financial Planning. Computers and Operations Research, 7:157.

30. French, S., 1982. Sequencing and Scheduling: An Introduction to the Mathematics of the Job Shop. John Wiley & Sons.

31. Friedrich, O., 1983. The Computer Moves In. Time, January, pp. 6-14.

32. Fry, T. D. and G. K. Leong, 1986. Bi-Criterion Single Machine Scheduling with Forbidden Early Shipments. Engineering Costs and Production Economics, 10:133-137.

33. Fry, T. D. and G. K. Leong, 1987. A Bi-Criterion Approach to Minimizing Inventory Costs on a Single Machine When Early Shipments Are Forbidden. Computers & Operations Research, 14:363-368.

34. Geoffrion, A. M., 1967. Solving Bicriterion Mathematical Programs. Operations Research, 15,39-54.

35. Gibbs, T. E., 1973. Goal Programming. Journal of Systems Management, May 38-41.

36. Glover, F. and F. Martinson, 1987. Multiple-Use Land Planning and Conflict Resolution by Multiple Objective Linear Programming. European Journal of Operational Research, 28:343-350.

37. Gonzalez, J. J., and G. R. Reeves, 1983. Master Production Scheduling: A

Multiobjective Linear Programming Approach. International Journal of Production Research, 21:553-562.

38. Goodman, D. A., 1978. A Goal Programming Approach to Aggregate Planning of Production and Work Force. Management Science, 20:1569-1575.

39. Harvey, C. M., 1986. Value Functions for Infinite-Period Planning. Management Science, 32:1123-1139.

40. Heck. H. and S. Roberts, 1972. A Note on the Extension of a Secondary Criteria. Naval Research Logistics Quarterly, 19:403.

41. Hillier F. S. and G. J. Lieberman, 1967. Introduction to Operations Research. Holden-Day, London.

42. Hindelang, T. J., and J. L. Hill, 1978. A New Model to Aggregate Output Planning. Omega, 6:267-272.

43. Hwang, C. L., A. S. M. Masud, S. R. Paidy and K. Yoon, 1979. Multiple Objective Decision Making - Methods and Applications. Springer-Verlag.

44. Ignizio, J. P., 1976. Goal Programming and Extensions. Lexington Books, Mass., U.S.A.

45. Jaasekelainensa, V., 1969. A Goal Programming Model of Aggregate Production Planning. Swedish Journal of Economics, Vol. 71.

46. Jenkins P. M. and Robson A., 1974. An Application of Linear Programming Methodology for Regional Strategy Making. Regional Studies, 8:267-279.

47. Johnson, L. A. and D. C. Montgomery, 1968. Operations Research in Production Planning Scheduling and Inventory Control. John-Wiley Publishing House.

48. Juran J. M., 1970. Quality Planning and Analysis. McGraw Hill Publishing Co., Ltd.

49. Kao, E. P. C., 1980. A Multiple Objective Decision Theoretic Approach to One-Machine Scheduling Problems. Computers & Operations Research, 7:251-260.

50. Kathawala, Y. and H. Gholamnezhad, 1987. New Approach to Facility Location Decisions. International Journal of Systems Science, 18:389-402.

51. Kikki, P., J. Lappi, and M. Siitonen, 1986. Long-Term Timber Production Planning Via Utility Maximization. TIMS Studies in the Management Sciences, 21:285-296.

52. Kockett A. G. and Muhlemann, 1978. A Problem of Aggregate Scheduling: An Application of Goal Programming. International Journal of Production Research, 16:127.

53. Kornbluth, J., 1973. A Survey of Goal Programming. Omega, 1:193-206.

54. Kornbluth, J. S. H., 1986. Engineering Design: Applications of Goal Programming and Multiple Objective Linear and Geometric Programming. International Journal of Production Research, 24:945-953.

55. Kortanek, K. and A. L. Soyster, 1971. On the Status of Some Multi-Product, Multi-Period Production Scheduling Model. Management Science, Vol. 17.

56. Lawler, E. L., 1973. Optimal Sequencing of A Single Machine Subject to Precedence Constraints. Management Science, 19:544.

57. Lawrence, K. D. and J. J. Burbridge, 1976. A Multiple Goal Linear Programming Model for Coordinated Production and Logistic Planning. International Journal of Production Research. 14:215.

58. Lee, S. M., 1972. Goal Programming for Decision Analysis. Auerbach Publishers Inc., Philadelphia.

59. Lee, S. M., 1971. Goal Programming: Management's Math Model. Industrial Engineering, Vol. 3.

60. Lee, S. M., 1973. Goal Programming for Decision Analysis of Multiple Objectives. Sloan Management Review, 14.

61. Lee, S. M., 1979. Goal Programming Methods for Multiple Objective Integer Programs. OR Monograph Series No. 2, American Institute of Industrial Engineers Inc., Norcross.

62. Lee, S. M. and Clayton E. R., 1972. A Goal Programming Model for Academic Resource Allocation. Management Science, Vol. 18.

63. Lee, S. M., E. R. Clayton, and B. W. Taylor, III, 1978. A Goal Programming Approach to Multi-Period Production Line Scheduling. Computers & Operations Research, 5:205-212.

64. Lee, S. M. and L. J. Moore, 1974. A Practical Approach to Production Scheduling. Production & Inventory Management, 15:79.

65. Lee, S. M. and J. P. Shim, 1987. Multiple Objective Decision Making on the Micro-Computer for Production/Operations Management: An Overview. Socio-Economic Planning Sciences, 21:33-36.

66. Lee, S. M., C. Snyder, and M. Gen, 1982. The Microcomputer: Experience and Implication for the Future of Multiple Criteria Decision Making, in Essays and Surveys on Multiple Criteria Decision Making (Springer-Verlag).

67. Lee, W. B. and B. M. Khumawala, 1974. Simulation Testing of Aggregate Production Planning Models in an Implementation Methodology. Management Science, 20:903-911.

68. Lin, W. T., 1980. A Survey of Goal Programming Applications. Omega, 8:115-117.

69. Lockett, A. G. and A. P. Muhlemann, 1978. A Problem of Aggregate Scheduling and Application of Goal Programming. International Journal of Production Research. 16:127-136.

70. McClure, R. H. and C. E. Wells, 1987. Incorporating Sales force Preferences in a Goal Programming Model for the Sales Resource Allocation

Problem. Decision Sciences, 18:677-681.

71. Magee, J. F. and D. M. Boodman, 1967. Production Planning and Inventory Control. 2nd. Edition, McGraw-Hill.

72. Malakooti, B. and W. H. Balhorn, 1987. Selection of Acceptance Sampling Plans with Multi-Attribute Defects in Computer-Aided Quality Control. International Journal of Production Research, 25:869-888.

73. Masud, A. S. M. and C. L. Hwang, 1980. An Aggregate Production Planning Model and Application of Three Multiple Objective Decision Methods. International Journal of Production Research. 18:741-752.

74. Mellichamp, J. M. and R. M. Love, 1978. Production Switching Heuristics for the Aggregate Planning Problem. Management Science, 24:1242-1252.

75. Moore, J. M., 1968. An N-Job One-Machine Sequencing Algorithm for Minimizing the Number of Late Jobs. Management Science, Vol. 15.

76. Mukyangkoon, S., 1983. Microcomputer-Based Interactive Goal Programming for Production Planning in a Small Diesel Engine Assembly Factory. Master of Engineering Research Study, No. IE83-12, Asian Institute of Technology, Bangkok, Thailand.

77. Panwalkar, S. S., R. A. Dudek, and M. L. Smith, 1973. Sequencing Research and the Industrial Scheduling Problem. Symposium on the Theory of Scheduling and its Applications, Springler, New York.

78. Pasternak, H. and U. Passy, 1973. Bicriterion Function in Annual Activity Planning. Education and Research, 325-341.

79. Ravindran, A., W. S. Shin, J. L. Arthur, and H. Moskowitz, 1986. Nonlinear Integer Goal Programming Models for Acceptance Sampling. Computers & Operations Research, 13:611-622.

80. Rifai, A. K. and J. O. Pecenka, 1986. Goal Achievement Through Goal Programming: Short Versus Long Term. Engineering costs and Production Economics, 10:155-160.

81. Rinks, D. B., J. L. Ringuest, and M. H. Peters, 1987. A Multivariate Utility Function Approach to Stochastic Capacity Planning. Engineering costs and Production Economics, 12:3-13.

82. Saad, G. H., 1982. An Overview of Production Planning Models. Structural Classification and Empirical Assessment. International Journal of Production Research, 20:105-114.

83. Sardana, G. D. and P. Vrat, 1987. Productivity Measurement in a Large Organization with Multi-Performance Objectives: A Case Study. Engineering Management International, 4:157-177.

84. Selen, W. J. and D. D. Hott, 1986. A Mixed-Integer Goal-Programming Formulation of the Standard Flow-Shop Scheduling Problem. Journal of the Operational Research Society, 37:1121-1128.

85. Sen, T. and S. K. Gupta, 1983. A Branch and Bound Procedure to Solve a Bicriteria Scheduling Problem. IIE Transaction, Vol. 15.

86. Silver, E. A., 1967. A Tutorial on Production Scheduling and Workforce Balancing. Operations Research. 15:985-1010.

87. Sinha, S. B. and S. V. C. Sastry, 1987. A Goal Programming Model for Facility Location Planning. Socio-Economic Planning Sciences, 21:251-256.

88. Slowinski, R., 1981. Multiobjective Network Scheduling with Efficient Use of Renewable and Non-renewable Resources. European Journal of Operations Research, 7:265-273.

89. Spronk, J., 1981. Interactive Multiple Goal Programming, Applications to Financial Planning. Boston, USA, Nijhoff Martinus Publishing.

90. Steenge, A. E., 1987. Consistency and Composite Numeraires in Joint Production Input-Output Analysis: An Application of Ideas of T. L. Saaty. Mathematical Modelling, 9:233-244.

91. Su, C. H., 1981. A Goal Programming Model for Solving Product-Mix Problem of an Electrolytic Tinning Line. Master of Engineering Thesis, No. IE-81-15, Asian Institute of Technology, Bangkok.

92. Suksupha, K., 1975. Analysis of Sugar Industry in Thailand with Emphasis on the Maekong River System. Master of Engineering Thesis, No. 1126, Asian Institute of Technology, Bangkok, Thailand.

93. Svetasreni, S., M. T. Tabucanon and P. Adulbhan, 1980. Energy Utilization in a Sugar Mill: A Goal Programming Application. Journal of Industrial Engineering, 13:93-101, Taiwan.

94. Szidarovszky, F., M. E. Gershon and L. Duckstein, 1986. Techniques for Multiobjective Decision Making in Systems Management. Elsevier Science Publishers B. V., Amsterdam, The Netherlands.

95. Tabucanon, M. T., 1977. Multiobjective Linear Programming for Decision Making in Industrial Systems. Doctoral Dissertation, Asian Institute of Technology, Bangkok.

96. Tabucanon, M. T., 1982. Multiobjective Optimization for National Development Planning. H. Paul, T. N. Goh and K. L. Chew (eds.), Operational Research for National Development, 25-58, Operations Research Society of Singapore.

97. Tabucanon, M. T. and Su, C. H., 1982. Modeling the Product-Mix Problem of an Electrolytic Tinning Line. Policy and Information, 6:102-106.

98. Tabucanon, M. T. and S. Mukyangkoon, 1985. Multiobjective Micro-computer-based Interactive Production Planning. International Journal of Production Research, 23:1001-1023.

99. Tabucanon, M. T. and N. Islam, 1983. A Goal Programming Model for Designing Sampling Plan for Quality Control. Journal of Industrial

Engineering.

100. Tabucanon, M. T. and Ghafoor, A., 1986. A Goal Programming Approach to Production Planning and Scheduling in a Multistage Production System, Modelling, Simulation and Control, 4:47-64.

101. Tavares, L. V., 1986. Multicriteria Scheduling of a Railway Renewal Program. European Journal of Operational Research, 25:395-405.

102. Uy, E. T., 1986. De Novo Formulation: Resource and Product Mix Optimization. M. Eng. Research Study, RSPR No. IE 86-2, Asian Institute of Technology.

103. Vickery, S. K. and R. E. Markland, 1986. Multi-Stage Lot Sizing in a Serial Production System. International Journal of Production Research, 24:517-534.

104. Vickson, R. G., 1980. Choosing the Job Sequence and Processing Times to Minimize Total Processing Plus Flow Cost on a Single Machine. Operations Research, Vol. 28.

105. Waghodekar, P. H. and S. Sahu, 1986. Facilities Layout with Multiple Objectives: MFLAP. Engineering Costs and Production Economics, 10:105-112.

106. Wang, C., and L. Duckstein, 1983. Multiple Criteria Decision Making in Batch Production Planning. Department of Systems and Industrial Engineering, University of Arizona, Tucson, Arizona.

107. Wassenhove, L. N. and K. R. Baker, 1982. A Bicriterion Approach to Time/Cost Trade-offs in Sequencing. European Journal of Operations Research, 11:48-54.

108. Wassenhove, L. N. and F. Gelders, 1980. Solving a Bicriterion Scheduling Problem. European Journal of Operational Research, 4:42.

109. Wuwongse, V., 1982. Multiobjective Optimization by Interactive Pairwise Comparison. D. Eng. Thesis, Department of System Science, Tokyo Institute of Technology.

110. Zangwill, W. I., 1966. A Deterministic Multiproduct Multifacility Production and Inventory Model. Operations Research, 14:486-507.

CHAPTER VI

MCDM APPLICATIONS IN BUSINESS MANAGEMENT

MCDM applications cover a wide range of subjects in industrial management including those in manpower, financial and marketing related management functions. In this chapter, four applications are presented in the areas of manpower selection, job assignments, investment decision, and sales force planning.

6.1 MANPOWER PLANNING

Manpower planning is an important activity in an industrial system especially when the organization expands, and in the process new organizational units are established, existing ones are reorganized, merged or amalgamated, and a large number of jobs are to be redesigned. It is an activity of management which is aimed at coordinating the requirements for, and the availability of, the different types of employee. It involves ensuring that the firm has enough of the right kind of employees when needed. Manpower planning needs information from all sorts of people in the organization; foremost of all are the managers of individual departments.

Manpower planning starts with objectives of the firm as inputs. This means that long-range strategic and short-range operational objectives must be worked out linking human resource and business function activities - production, finance and marketing - into a unified sense of direction. Unless such objectives are made known to all people in the firm, different people and different organizational units will probably be striving for conflicting goals.

Strategic manpower planning deals with long-range perspective covering, among others, business needs, externalities, internalities, and other management implications thereof. Answers to questions, such as the following, are within the domain of this long-range planning exercise: What are the implications of the proposed business strategies and their possible constraints and requirements? What can be done in the short-term to prepare for longer-term needs?

Various mathematical models have been applied in manpower planning: Forecasting, organizational change, optimization, and simulation models. Optimization models are used to define future needs under certain constraints and objectives as well as matching individuals with anticipated vacancies, among others.

Illustrative examples related to manpower planning are presented in this chapter to exhibit the fact that multiobjective optimization methods are useful for a variety of manpower management-related problems.

6.1.1 MANPOWER SELECTION AND ALLOCATION DECISIONS

Steuer and Wallace (1978) formulated a goal programming model, as introduced in this subsection, to incorporate a differential and individualized selection and placement strategy for making selection and placement decisions. They attempted to expand the ability of goal programming to be adapted to selection and allocation decisions. The model allows the decision maker to consider applicants from sources for different jobs at the same time. This yields a number of advantages.

(i)   Job applications are considered for several jobs rather than for only one. In a very real sense, the vocational interests of the individual are taken into account by attempting to find the job opening that best fits the individual's profile characteristics.

(ii) The institution realizes economics in recruitment cost because many applications who might have been rejected if considered for only one job, are instead placed on other jobs in the organization.

(iii) By utilizing a classification strategy that attempts to optimize person-job fit across several job categories simultaneously, the firm is assured that the average net outcome resulting from person-job assignments will be most greatly accomplished.

(iv) The differential selection and placement strategy is one that enhances the efficiency and utility of a given battery of information in making selection and placement decisions. It was demonstrated that the lower selection ratio (i.e., number of jobs to be filled/total number of job applicants), the greater the utility of selection battery of any given validity and base rate. The differential selection and placement strategy in the model developed allows the decision maker to maintain advantageous selection ratios by considering several sources of job applicants for each job vacancy.

Once each applicant's individuality has been determined, the objective of the decision maker should be to seek a job assignment for which an individual's

pattern or profile of predicted performance is appropriate both to his own
goals and those of the employing organization. Differential or individualized
selection and placement has been offered as a strategy to assist the decision
maker in this position. According to the strategy, staffing decisions are made
to seek the optimal matching of people and jobs within constraints dictated by
budget, the available labor supply fitting given profiles on relevant decision
criteria (base rates), and the number and types of jobs to be filled (selection
ratio).

A differential selection and placement strategy, is one which combines
selection and placement decisions. At any one point in time, the decision
maker considers all job openings simultaneously as possible assignments for the
entire pool of applicants available. The decision maker does not consider one
job at a time nor does he consider only one applicant at a time. A differential selection and placement strategy is characterized as a special case of
classification problem that also use a "reject" category along with other
decision categories established by the organization's job quotas.

Consider the case of a large firm engaging in a differential individualized selection and placement strategy to staff six positions. All sources of
job applicants will be pooled and considered simultaneously as sources of labor
for at least several of the six positions. Differential validity studies have
been carried out on each job to determine the most desirable set and use of
predictor information in determining subsequent job performance.

In this case, the firm has determined that grade point average (GPA),
previous work experience (in years), and percentile score on a work-related
aptitude test are each predictive of subsequent job performance and sufficiently independent to be used in multiple hurdles in making selection and placement
decisions. In other words, optimal levels on each measure have been determined
and the information will be used in a conjunctive fashion.

Table 6.1 Desired Attribute Levels

Attributes	Job					
	1	2	3	4	5	6
1. GPA	2.5	1.5	2.0	1.5	1.5	1.2
2. Years of experience	10	4	8	0	2	5
3. Aptitude percentile test score	80	70	90	60	30	60

The desired attribute levels for each job (r_{tj}), where t refers to attribute and j refers to job, is displayed in Table 6.1. Grade Point Average
(GPA) values represent minimal values or "floor levels" below which is not
desired to descend unless unavoidable. Years of experience are considered as
most preferred target values for the different jobs. The decision maker wishes
to avoid either going above or below these values. Finally, the Aptitude
Percentile Test Scores are treated as minimal percentile scores below which the
decision maker does not wish to accept unless necessary.

Table 6.2   Average Attribute Levels by Applicant Category

Applicant's category	Attribute		
	GPA	Experience	Aptitude
Indus. engineer (M.S.)	2.5	2	60
Mech. engineer (M.S.)	1.5	10	50
Indus. engineer (B.S.)	2.2	5	65
Mech. engineer (B.S.)	1.2	8	30
Manager (M.B.A.)	2.6	4	40
Manager (B.B.A.)	2.0	2	85
Draftsman (A.A.)	1.5	0	70

The recruitment process has been carried out and pools of available
applicants have been generated in each of seven applicant categories: industrial engineer (M.S. degree), mechanical engineer (M.S. degree) (B.S.
degree), manager (M.B.A. degree), manager (B.B.A. degree) and draftsman (A.A.
degree).

The personnel decision maker has gathered information from each applicant
on the three decision criteria: GPA, Years of Experience, and Aptitude Percentile Test Score. Averages (α_{it}) for each of these criteria have been calculated for the seven categories and are presented in Table 6.2.

The values in Table 6.2, therefore, represent the levels of each decision
criterion available to the company from each category.

One obvious constraint operating is that applicants from any given
category may not qualify for every job. The feasible applicant category-job
combinations are indicated in Table 6.3 by the presence of x's.

Table 6.3   Feasible Applicant Category Job Combinations

Applicant	Job 1	2	3	4	5	6	b_i
Indus. engineer (M.S.)	x_{11}	x_{12}					$\leq$ 5
Mech. engineer (M.S.)	x_{21}		x_{23}				$\leq$ 7
Indus. engineer (B.S.)	x_{31}	x_{32}	x_{33}				$\leq$ 10
Mech. engineer (B.S.)	x_{41}		x_{43}			x_{46}	$\leq$ 20
Manager (M.B.A.)			x_{53}	x_{54}	x_{55}		$\leq$ 25
Manager (B.B.A.)		x_{63}	x_{64}	x_{65}			$\leq$ 50
Draftsman (A.A.)						x_{76}	$\leq$ 5
n_j	5	10	20	30	16	10	

In Table 6.3 the n_j's are the number of applicants available from different categories. The b_i's are the number of job openings in each category.

A goal programming formulation of the above problem is given in the following equations.

$$\min \quad \{ \sum_j v_{1j}^- \qquad - \; w_1 \}$$

$$\min \quad \{ \sum_j (v_{2j}^+ + v_{2j}^-) \quad - \; w_2 \}$$

$$\min \quad \{ \sum_j v_{3j}^- \qquad - \; w_3 \}$$

$$\text{s.t} \quad \sum_i a_{i1}x_{ij} + v_{1j}^- \qquad = \; n_j r_{1j} \quad (1 \leq j \leq 6)$$

$$\sum_i a_{i2}x_{ij} - \qquad v_{2j}^+ + v_{2j}^- \qquad = \; n_j r_{2j} \quad (1 \leq j \leq 6)$$

$$\sum_i a_{i3}x_{ij} + \qquad\qquad v_{3j}^- \; = \; n_j r_{3j} \quad (1 \leq j \leq 6)$$

$$\sum_j x_{ij} \qquad\qquad \leq \; b_i \quad (1 \leq i \leq 7)$$

$$\sum_i x_{ij} \qquad\qquad = \; n_j \quad (1 \leq j \leq 6)$$

all x's are integer and ≥ 0

all v's ≥ 0

Note that the deviational variables are the attributes for each job type. The problem could have been modeled with deviational variables by attribute for each feasible applicant category-job combination, but has not been done so here for simplicity of exposition.

Since the values of Table 6.1 are of different magnitudes by attribute, the criterion values of the equations have been normalized. The scale chosen has a range 0 to 10. This standardization process produces formulation from

$$\min \quad \{\; \alpha_1\beta_2 \sum_j \gamma_j v_{1j}^- / n_j \qquad = \quad z_1 \;\}$$

$$\min \quad \{\; \alpha_2\beta_2 \sum_j \gamma_j (v_{2j}^+ + v_{2j}^-) / n_j \quad = \quad z_2 \;\}$$

$$\min \quad \{\; \alpha_3\beta_3 \sum_j \gamma_j v_{3j}^- / n_j \qquad = \quad z_3 \;\}$$

s.t.   Same constraints as above.

Table 6.4   Objective Function Factors α_t and β_t

Attribute	Factors	
t	α_t	β_t
1	5	1/6
2	2	1/6
3	1/5	1/6

A criterion value Z_t of 0 would indicate that on the average a perfect fit was attained over all jobs for the attribute. That is, each successful applicant would have been perfectly matched with regard to attribute t. A Z-value of 10 would indicate the worst imaginable fit over all job openings for the respective attribute. Values between 0 to 10 would represent average conditions of the two extremes.

The attribute normalization factors α_t along with the deviation averaging factors β_t are given in Table 6.4.

An additional feature of the model is that the six jobs can be ordered in terms of their importance to the firm. In this illustration, for example, job 1 is most important and should be filled first, job 2 is second most important, and so on.   The job filling weights γ_j in Table 6.5 enter the problem as the decision maker feels that it is 50% more important that job 1 be filled properly with respect to either jobs 2 or 3, and jobs 2 and 3 are individually twice as important as jobs 4, 5 and 6.

The n_j in the objective functions ensure that the criterion indices are averages only over those people involved in the different parts of the alloca- tion schedule.

Lastly, the decision maker attempts to express the relative importance placed on the different attribute criterion indices for the most suitable job fit.   Point estimate criterion weights w_t are stipulated in Table 6.6. According to the point estimate weights, the decision maker feels that Aptitude Percentile Test Score is the best single predictor of subsequent job perfor- mance followed by Years of Experience and GPA.

Table 6.5   Job Filling Weights γ_j

Job j	Importance weight γ_j
1	1.8
2	1.2
3	1.2
4	0.6
5	0.6
6	0.6

Table 6.6   Point Estimate Attribute Criterion Weights w_t

Attribute t	Point estimate weights w_t
1	0.2
2	0.2
3	0.6

6.1.2 ASSIGNMENT OF PERSONS TO JOBS

Zanakis (1983) developed a 0-1 goal programming (GP) model based on an actual case example, for assigning projects to engineers in order to prevent project splitting and excessive manpower requirements, complete as many preferred projects as possible and maximize profits while keeping a balanced workload.   For assigning 15 projects to 6 engineers, the GP model contains 90 0-1 decision variables and 28 goals grouped into 5 priorities.   Moreover, because of some computational difficulty, heuristic 0-1 GP is needed.

The following priorities are given by the manager:

P1: Assign no more than one engineer to a particular project, however many projects may be assigned to each engineer.

P2: Make assignments so as to demand no more than the manpower determined to be available for facility plan project.

P3: Assign engineers for completion of as many projects with a higher preference index number.

P4: Maximize the profit to be realized by completion of facility plan projects.

P5: Balance the percentage of each engineer's available time utilized by equitable facility plan workload assignments.

Model formulation:

Priority 1: Only one engineer per project.

$$\sum_{i=1}^{M} X_{ij} + d_j^- - d_j^+ = 1 \qquad\qquad j = 1, \ldots, N$$

where i = subscript for engineer, $i = 1, \ldots, M$.

j = subscript for project, $j = 1, \ldots, N$.

X_{ij} = 1, if the ith engineer is assigned to the jth project, 0, otherwise.

d_k^- = the amount of underachievement of the kth goal.

d_k^+ = the amount of overachievement of the kth goal.

Priority 2: Manpower availability.

$$\sum_{j=1}^{N} t_{ij} X_{ij} + d_{N+i}^- - d_{N+i}^+ = S_i \qquad i = 1, \ldots, M$$

where t_{ij} = the time in hours for the ith engineer to complete the jth project.

S_i = the available time the ith engineer has to spend on facility plan project(considering his other commitments).

Priority 3: Assign as many projects as possible (preference weighted).

No additional equation is needed because (see objective function)

$$\text{Max} \sum_{j=1}^{N} \sum_{i=1}^{M} w_j X_{ij} \quad \text{implies} \quad \text{Min} \sum_{j=1}^{N} w_j n_j$$

where w_j = the preference (weight) given to the jth project.

Priority 4: Profit Maximization.

$$\sum_{i=1}^{M} \sum_{j=1}^{N} (r_j - c_j \, t_{ij}) \, X_{ij} + d_{M+N+1}^- - d_{M+N+1}^+ = U$$

where   U =   any large number.

r_j =   the revenue anticipated from assignment and completion of the jth project.

c_i =   the hourly cost for the ith engineer.

Priority 5: Balanced workload.

$$\frac{\sum_{j=1}^{N} t_{ij} X_{ij}}{S_i} - \frac{\sum_{i=1}^{M} \sum_{j=1}^{N} t_{ij} X_{ij}}{\sum_{i=1}^{M} S_i} + d_{M+N+1+i}^- - d_{M+N+1+i}^+ = 0$$

$i = 1, \ldots M, \quad x_{ij} = 0, 1 \quad \text{and } d_i^-, d_i^+ \geq 0.$

Objective function:

$$\text{Min } a = \{ \sum_{j=1}^{N} d_j^+, \sum_{i=1}^{M} L_{N+i}, \sum_{j=1}^{N} w_j d_j^-, d_{M+N+1}^-,$$

$$\sum_{i=1}^{n} d_{M+N+N+1+i}^- + d_{M+N+N+1+i}^+ \}$$

All model goals are self explanatory. However, for further clarification, note that in the last priority, the first term represents the percent of the ith engineer's time utilized, while the second term represents the average utilization of all engineers.

Zanakis also presented a case example data and solved the model for two cases, with priorities 3 and 4 reversed and compared the result of both cases. Zanakis failed to solve the case example, with N = 15 projects to be assigned to M=6 engineers, directly, with a goal programming model of 90 0-1 decision variables and 28 goals grouped into 5 priorities. Hence, he combined and extended previously successful 0-1 LP heuristics into a multiobjective counterpart for solving the general 0-1 GP problem.

The results obtained are of course heuristic, and no claim of optimality are made.

6.2 FINANCIAL PLANNING

A significant contribution of operations research to the subject of financial planning has been the development of integrated financing and investment modeling in the organization - the formulation of investment and financing opportunities into a mathematical programming model. It is natural in financial planning to speak in terms of targets or goals of company performance indicators such as dividend, liquidity, return on capital, among others. Hence an obvious choice of methodology is MCDM and more specifically goal programming. Following is an example of goal programming application in financial investment.

A certain XYZ investment company is in the process of formulating a five-year plan for its five million capital on hand. The company can choose any combination of the following five types of investment: real estate, stock, bonds, loan, and passbook saving. Real estate investment can be made at the beginning of the first year and will result in a profit of 200% five years later. Stock investment can be made every year and will yield a return of 20% profit at the end of the second year. The dollars invested in bond will yield a 40% profit three years later. Loan investment can be made at the second year which will result in a 80% profit for each dollar at the end of the fifth year. Another loan can be made at the beginning of the fourth year which will return a 30% profit for each dollar two years later. All money not invested is placed in a passbook saving account. The annual interest rate is 8%. In addition, the company will receive an amount of $500,000 at the end of the second year and has to pay an obligation of $700,000 at the end of the third year.

The management of the company has established the following goals:

First goal (priority 1): The allocation of the capital should be placed in a way to minimize risk. Thus the company should diversify its investment. No more than 2 million dollars should be invested in any category during any year.

Second goal (priority 2): The company needs to have at least $500,000 on hand to meet operational and other unexpected expenditures. This money is placed in the passbook account saving at all times.

Third goal (priority 3): The company should pay the $700,000 financial obligation at the end of the third year.

Fourth goal (priority 4): At least 1 million dollars should be invested in real estate since such kind of investment is highly profitable and less risky.

Fifth goal (priority 5): XYZ company would like to maximize total return on investment at the end of the fifth year.

To simplify the situation it is assumed that all investment activities are made at the beginning of a year and all returns are received at year end.

A goal programming model for this case is formulated as follows. Let x_{ij} be the amount of dollars invested in year i in category j, where i = 1, 2, ..., 5, and j = 1 (real estate), 2 (stocks), 3 (bonds), 4 (loan), and 5 (passbook saving). Table 6.7 shows all the possible investment choices in each year of the planning horizon. Both goal constraints and structural constraints are required to formulate the goal priorities. Constraints are required to express the dollars for investment in each of the years.

i) Goal constraints 1-14. Diversification of investments. No investment category should be greater than $2,000,000 in any year. There are fourteen different investment category combinations, each of which requires a goal constraint. These goal constraints are as follows:

$$x_{11} \qquad\qquad\qquad\qquad + d_1^- - d_1^+ = 2,000,000$$
$$\quad x_{12} \qquad\qquad\qquad\quad + d_2^- - d_2^+ = 2,000,000$$
$$\qquad x_{13} \qquad\qquad\qquad + d_3^- - d_3^+ = 2,000,000$$
$$\qquad\quad x_{15} \qquad\qquad\quad + d_4^- - d_4^+ = 2,000,000$$
$$\quad x_{12} + \qquad x_{22} \qquad + d_5^- - d_5^+ = 2,000,000$$

Table 6.7 Investment Structure

Investment	Year (i)				
category (j)	| 1 |	2 |	3 |	4 |	5 |
1) real estate	200%, x_{11} ├──────────────────────────────────────┤
2) stock	20%, x_{12} ├──────────┤
3) bond	40%, x_{13} ├──────────────────┤
5) passbook	8%, x_{15} ├────┤
2) stock	20%, x_{22} ├──────────┤
3) bond	40%, x_{23} ├──────────────────┤
4) loan	80%, x_{24} ├──────────────────────────┤
5) passbook	8%, x_{25} ├────┤
2) stock	20%, x_{32} ├──────────┤
3) bond	40%, x_{33} ├──────────────────┤
5) passbook	8%, x_{35} ├────┤
2) stock	20%, x_{42} ├──────────┤
4) loan	30%, x_{44} ├──────────┤
5) passbook	8%, x_{45} ├────┤

$$x_{13} + \qquad x_{23} \qquad\qquad\qquad + d_6^- - d_6^+ = 2,000,000$$

$$x_{24} \qquad\qquad\qquad + d_7^- - d_7^+ = 2,000,000$$

$$x_{25} \qquad\qquad\qquad + d_8^- - d_8^+ = 2,000,000$$

$$x_{22} + \qquad x_{32} \qquad\qquad\qquad + d_9^- - d_9^+ = 2,000,000$$

$$x_{13} + \qquad x_{23} + \qquad x_{33} \qquad\qquad + d_{10}^- - d_{10}^+ = 2,000,000$$

$$x_{35} \qquad\qquad\qquad + d_{11}^- - d_{11}^+ = 2,000,000$$

$$x_{32} + \qquad x_{42} \qquad\qquad + d_{12}^- - d_{12}^+ = 2,000,000$$

$$x_{24} + \qquad\qquad x_{44} \qquad\qquad + d_{13}^- - d_{13}^+ = 2,000,000$$

$$x_{45} \qquad\qquad\qquad + d_{14}^- - d_{14}^+ = 2,000,000$$

where d_1^-, (d_1^+) = amount ($) by which investment in real estate in year 1 falls short of (exceeds) 2,000,000;

d_2^-, (d_2^+) = amount ($) by which investment in stocks in year 1 falls short of (exceeds) 2,000,000;

d_3^-, (d_3^+) = amount ($) by which investment in bonds in year 1 falls short of (exceeds) 2,000,000;

d_4^-, (d_4^+) = amount ($) by which investment in passbook saving in year 1 falls short of (exceeds) 2,000,000;

d_5^-, (d_5^+) = amount ($) by which total investment in stocks in year 2 falls short of (exceeds) 2,000,000;

d_6^-, (d_6^+) = amount ($) by which total investment in bonds in year 2 falls short of (exceeds) 2,000,000;

d_7^-, (d_7^+) = amount ($) by which total investment in loans in year 2 falls short of (exceeds) 2,000,000;

d_8^-, (d_8^+) = amount ($) by which investment in passbook saving in year 2 falls short of (exceeds) 2,000,000;

d_9^-, (d_9^+) = amount ($) by which total investment in stocks in year 3 falls short of (exceeds) 2,000,000;

d_{10}^-, (d_{10}^+) = amount ($) by which total investment in bonds in year 3 falls short of (exceeds) 2,000,000;

d_{11}^-, (d_{11}^+) = amount ($) by which investment in passbook saving in year 3 falls short of (exceeds) 2,000,000;

d_{12}^-, (d_{12}^+) = amount ($) by which total investment in stocks in year 4 falls short of (exceeds) 2,000,000;

d_{13}^-, (d_{13}^+) = amount ($) by which total investment in loans in year 4 falls short of (exceeds) 2,000,000;

d_{14}^-, (d_{14}^+) = amount ($) by which investment in passbook saving in year 4 falls short of (exceeds) 2,000,000;

Goal constraints are not required in year 5 since prior year goal constraints assure that no more than 2,000,000 dollars will be invested in a given
category in the fifth year.

ii) Goal constraint 15-19.   There should be $500,000 on hand at each year.
A reserve account of $500,000 must be provided during each of the 5 years.   The
reserve accounts are placed in the passbook saving.   Therefore, for passbook
saving investment of each year, there is a goal constraint required.   Thus,

$$x_{i5} + d_{14+i}^- - d_{14+i}^+ = 500,000 \qquad\qquad i = 1, 2, \ldots, 5.$$

where d_{14+i}^-, (d_{14+i}^+) is the amount ($) by which investment in passbook
savings in year i falls short of (exceeds) $500,000.

iii) Goal constraint 20.   Pay for the $700,000 financial obligation.   To
meet this goal, investments made in the first three years that mature at the
end of the third year must be able to cover the amount of $700,000.   This goal
constraints is expressed as follows:

$$1.4\ x_{13} + 1.2\ x_{22} + 1.08\ x_{35} + d_{20}^- - d_{20}^+ = 700,000$$

where d_{20}^-, (d_{20}^+) is the amount ($) by which the value of total investments
that mature the at end of the third year falls short of (exceeds) 700,000.

iv) Goal constraint 21.   At least 1 million dollars should be invested in
real estate.   This goal constraint is expressed as follows:

$$x_{11} + d_{21}^- - d_{21}^+ = 1,000,000$$

where d_{21}^-, (d_{21}^+) is the amount ($) by which investment in real estate in the
first year falls short of (exceeds) 1,000,000.

v) Goal constraint 22:   Maximize total profits.   To maximize total return
on investment it is simply to maximize the return of investments which mature
at the end of the fifth year.   The goal constraint is:

$$3\ x_{11} + 1.8\ x_{24} + 1.4\ x_{33} + 1.2\ x_{42} + 1.3\ x_{44} + 1.08\ x_{55}$$
$$+ d_{22}^- - d_{22}^+ = 100,000,000$$

where 100,000,000 = an arbitrarily large investment return goal.

d_{22}^{-}, (d_{22}^{+}) = amount (\$) by which investments plus accrued profits at the end of year 5 fall short of (exceed) 100,000,000.

vi)   Structural constraints 1-5:   Balance constraints.   Total investments in each year must equal the amount of capital available for investment.   These constraints are:

year 1: $x_{11} + x_{12} + x_{13} + x_{15} = 5,000,000$

2:   $x_{22} + x_{23} + x_{24} + x_{25} = 1.08\ x_{15}$

3:   $x_{32} + x_{33} + x_{35} = 1.2\ x_{12} + 1.08\ x_{25} + 500,000$

4:   $x_{42} + x_{44} + x_{45} = 1.4\ x_{13} + 1.2\ x_{22} + 1.08\ x_{35} - 700,000$

5:   $x_{55} = 1.4\ x_{23} + 1.2\ x_{32} + 1.08\ x_{45}$

The coefficients used with the variables on the right hand side reflect the rate of return on investment in the given investment category.   The amount of \$500,000 in the equation of year 3 is the money received at the end of year 2. The amount of \$700,000 in the equation of year 4 is the amount of obligation that should be paid.

vii)   Objective function.   The objective function for the case is expressed as follows:

$$\text{Minimize}\ \ Z = P_1 \left(\sum_{i=1}^{14} d_i^+ \right) + P_2 \left(\sum_{i=15}^{19} d_i^- \right) + P_3\ d_{20}^- + P_4\ d_{21}^- + P_5\ d_{22}^-$$

The P_1 priority level associated with d_i^+ (i = 1, 2, ..., 14) is the company's main goal which is to diversify the investment.   If this goal is fully achieved, all the d_i^+ will obtain the value of zero.   The P_2 priority level is associated with the second goal of maintaining operational money.   If d_i^- (i = 15, 16, ..., 19) is driven to zero, this goal is achieved. P_3 is associated with the third goal of paying the financial obligation.   This obligation will be fully paid if d_{20}^- receives the value of zero.   At P_4 priority level, if d_{21}^- is zero, then there will be at least \$1,000,000 invested in real estate.   Finally at P_5 priority level, d_{22}^- variable will never be zero in the solution because of the arbitrarily large profit goal of \$100,000,000.   By minimizing d_{22}^- the company can move to its fifth goal of maximizing total return.

The complete mathematical formulation is as follows:

$$\text{Minimize} \quad Z = P_1 \left(\sum_{i=1}^{14} d_i^+ \right) + P_2 \left(\sum_{i=15}^{19} d_i^- \right) + P_3 \, d_{20}^- + P_4 \, d_{21}^- + P_5 \, d_{22}^-$$

Subject to:

$$x_{11} \qquad\qquad\qquad\qquad\qquad\qquad\qquad + d_1^- - d_1^+ = 2{,}000{,}000$$
$$x_{12} \qquad\qquad\qquad\qquad\qquad\qquad\qquad + d_2^- - d_2^+ = 2{,}000{,}000$$
$$x_{13} \qquad\qquad\qquad\qquad\qquad\qquad\qquad + d_3^- - d_3^+ = 2{,}000{,}000$$
$$x_{15} \qquad\qquad\qquad\qquad\qquad\qquad\qquad + d_4^- - d_4^+ = 2{,}000{,}000$$
$$x_{12} + \quad x_{22} \qquad\qquad\qquad\qquad\qquad + d_5^- - d_5^+ = 2{,}000{,}000$$
$$x_{13} + \quad x_{23} \qquad\qquad\qquad\qquad\qquad + d_6^- - d_6^+ = 2{,}000{,}000$$
$$x_{24} \qquad\qquad\qquad\qquad\qquad\qquad + d_7^- - d_7^+ = 2{,}000{,}000$$
$$x_{25} \qquad\qquad\qquad\qquad\qquad + d_8^- - d_8^+ = 2{,}000{,}000$$
$$x_{22} + \quad x_{32} \qquad\qquad\qquad\qquad + d_9^- - d_9^+ = 2{,}000{,}000$$
$$x_{13} + \quad x_{23} + \quad x_{33} \qquad\qquad\qquad + d_{10}^- - d_{10}^+ = 2{,}000{,}000$$
$$x_{35} \qquad\qquad\qquad\qquad + d_{11}^- - d_{11}^+ = 2{,}000{,}000$$
$$x_{32} + \quad x_{42} \qquad\qquad\qquad + d_{12}^- - d_{12}^+ = 2{,}000{,}000$$
$$x_{24} + \qquad\qquad x_{44} \qquad\qquad + d_{13}^- - d_{13}^+ = 2{,}000{,}000$$
$$x_{45} \qquad\qquad + d_{14}^- - d_{14}^+ = 2{,}000{,}000$$

$$x_{i5} + d_{14+i}^- - d_{14+i}^+ = 500{,}000 \qquad i = 1, 2, \ldots, 5.$$
$$1.4 \, x_{13} + 1.2 \, x_{22} + 1.08 \, x_{35} + d_{20}^- - d_{20}^+ = 700{,}000$$
$$x_{11} + d_{21}^- - d_{21}^+ = 1{,}000{,}000$$
$$3 \, x_{11} + 1.8 \, x_{24} + 1.4 \, x_{33} + 1.2 \, x_{42} + 1.3 \, x_{44} + 1.08 \, x_{55}$$
$$+ d_{22}^- - d_{22}^+ = 100{,}000{,}000$$
$$x_{11} + x_{12} + x_{13} + x_{15} = 5{,}000{,}000$$
$$x_{22} + x_{23} + x_{24} + x_{25} = 1.08 \, x_{15}$$
$$x_{32} + x_{33} + x_{35} = 1.2 \, x_{12} + 1.08 \, x_{25} + 500{,}000$$
$$x_{42} + x_{44} + x_{45} = 1.4 \, x_{13} + 1.2 \, x_{22} + 1.08 \, x_{35} - 700{,}000$$
$$x_{55} = 1.4 \, x_{23} + 1.2 \, x_{32} + 1.08 \, x_{45}$$
$$\text{All variables} \geq 0$$

The solution of this model is as follows:

$$x_{11} = 2{,}000{,}000 \qquad x_{12} = 648{,}148 \qquad x_{13} = 500{,}000 \qquad x_{15} = 1{,}851{,}852$$
$$x_{22} = 0 \qquad x_{23} = 0 \qquad x_{24} = 2{,}000{,}000 \qquad x_{15} = 1{,}851{,}852$$
$$x_{32} = 0 \qquad x_{33} = 1{,}277{,}778 \qquad x_{35} = 0$$
$$x_{42} = 0 \qquad x_{44} = 0 \qquad x_{45} = 0$$
$$x_{55} = 0$$
$$d_1^- = 0 \qquad d_1^+ = 0 \qquad d_2^- = 1{,}351{,}852 \qquad d_2^+ = 0$$

$$
\begin{array}{llll}
d_3^- = 1{,}500{,}000 & d_3^+ = 0 & d_4^- = 148{,}148 & d_4^+ = 0 \\
d_5^- = 1{,}351{,}852 & d_5^+ = 0 & d_6^- = 1{,}500{,}000 & d_6^+ = 0 \\
d_7^- = 0 & d_7^+ = 0 & d_8^- = 2{,}000{,}000 & d_8^+ = 0 \\
d_9^- = 2{,}000{,}000 & d_9^+ = 0 & d_{10}^- = 222{,}222 & d_{10}^+ = 0 \\
d_{11}^- = 2{,}000{,}000 & d_{11}^+ = 0 & d_{12}^- = 2{,}000{,}000 & d_{12}^+ = 0 \\
d_{13}^- = 0 & d_{13}^+ = 0 & d_{14}^- = 2{,}000{,}000 & d_{14}^+ = 0 \\
d_{15}^- = 0 & d_{15}^+ = 1{,}351{,}851 & d_{16}^- = 500{,}000 & d_{16}^+ = 0 \\
d_{17}^- = 500{,}000 & d_{17}^+ = 0 & d_{18}^- = 500{,}000 & d_{18}^+ = 0 \\
d_{19}^- = 500{,}000 & d_{19}^+ = 0 & d_{20}^- = 0 & d_{20}^+ = 0 \\
d_{21}^- = 0 & d_{21}^+ = 1{,}000{,}000 & d_{22}^- = -88{,}611{,}111 & d_{22}^+ = 0
\end{array}
$$

6.3   MARKETING MANAGEMENT

Marketing management begins from the point where the products are stored to the point where they are distributed among the consumers. Marketing decisions usually involve pricing, advertising, distribution, among others, and oftentimes management is faced with conflicting objectives. Many applications of MCDM are in the area of advertising to promote sales. On what media to advertise and how to schedule such advertising, known as advertising media planning and scheduling is an application of MCDM. The aim is to produce a list of candidate media and their schedules whenever applicable from which the manager can qualitatively make a final choice.

Advertising media selection can be modeled in a MCDM format. This can be focussed upon development of a goal programming formulation because of its capability of handling such problems by defining targets to be attained.

Another appealing area for applying MCDM in marketing is in salesforce planning. An example is discussed in the remaining part of this section.

The ABC Garment Store sales staff consists of a sales manager and 6 sales persons. In addition, it hires 4 part time sales persons. The manager is paid by a fixed salary plus a bonus, which is 4% on the sales the store achieves above the sales quota for the month. The manager sets the sales quota for the salespersons. The full time sales persons are paid at a fixed salary plus a bonus, which is 10% on the sales he/she achieves above the quota for him/her for the month. The part time sales person is paid on hourly wage, with a 12% bonus on the sales he/she achieves above the sales quota set for him/her.

The regular working schedules for the sales manager and full time sales persons are 168 hours per month. The part time sales persons are required to 50 hours per month.

The sales quota is set by the top management. For the current time it is $25,000. The sales manager sets a quota of $18,000 for the group of full time sales persons and a quota of $3,600 for the group of part time sales persons.

Past experiences show that the full time sales person sells $17 per hour on the average, while the part time sales person sells an average $15 per hour. The sales manager sells an average of $19 per hour.

The following goals are listed to be achieved by the store:

1)   Achieve the $25,000 sales quota for the month;

2)   The sales manager desires to achieve a sales amount of $3,400 for the month;

3)   The group of full time sales persons should meet the sales quota of $18,000 for the month;

4)   The group of part time sales persons should meet the sales quota of $3,600 for the month;

5)   The overtime work for the manager and the full time sales persons should be limited to 32 hours, if possible;

6)   Each part time sales person should work at least 50 hours for the month;

7)   The manager desires to earn a bonus of $150 for the month. It is also desired that each full time and part time staff earns $50 bonus.

The goals from 1 to 7 are associated with first priority to seventh priority, respectively. It is desired to achieve the goals as fully as possible.

For simplicity, assume that the sales persons in either full time or part time groups have the same efficiency within the group. Furthermore, assume that the sales persons in the same group work the same hour during the month.

Using goal programming technique, the number of hours each person should work can be determined. Also, the solution will indicate the achievement of the goals. The mathematical formulation of the problem is discussed as follows. Let:

x_1 = number of hours the manager works during the month;

x_2 = number of hours each full time sales person works during the month;

x_3 = number of hours each part time sales person works during the month.

i)   Goal constraint 1: To achieve the sales quota of $25,000. Since on average the sales manager sells $19 per hour, each full time sales person sells $17 and each part time sales person sells $15, the goal constraint is:

$$19 \; x_1 + (17)\,(6)\, x_2 + (15)\,(4)\, x_3 + d_1^- - d_1^+ = 25,000$$

where d_1^-, (d_1^+) = the amount by which total sales falls short of (exceeds) $25,000;

    ii) Goal constraint 2: The manager desires to achieve his own quota. The constraint is:

$$19 \; x_1 + d_2^- - d_2^+ = 3,400$$

where d_2^-, (d_2^+) = the amount by which the sales manager's achievement falls short of (exceed) $3,400.

    iii) Goal constraint 3: The full time staff should achieve their quota. The constraint is:

$$(17)\,(6)\, x_2 + d_3^- - d_3^+ = 18,000$$

where d_3^-, (d_3^+) = the amount by which the sales the group of full time sales persons' achievement fall short of (exceed) $18,000.

    iv) Goal constraint 4: The part time staff should achieve their quota. The constraint is:

$$(15)\,(4)\, x_3 + d_4^- - d_4^+ = 3,600$$

where d_4^-, (d_4^+) = the amount by which the sales of the group of part time sales persons falls short of (exceed) $3,600.

    v) Goal constraint 5: Overtime hours for the manager and each full time staff limited to 32 hours. Two goal constraints are needed for the overtime limits: one for the regular time and the other for the overtime. For regular time constraint, they are:

$$x_1 \qquad + d_5^- - d_5^+ = 168$$
$$x_2 + d_6^- - d_6^+ = 168$$

where d_5^-, (d_5^+) = the number of hours by which the manager works falls short of (exceeds) 168 hours for the month.

d_5^-, (d_5^+) = the number of hours by which each full time staff works
falls short of (exceeds) 168 hours for the month.

For overtime constraint, they are:

$$d_5^+ \qquad + d_7^- - d_7^+ = 32$$
$$d_6^+ + d_8^- - d_8^+ = 32$$

where d_7^-, (d_7^+) = the number of overtime hours by which the manager works
falls short of (exceeds) 32 hours for the month.

d_8^-, (d_8^+) = the number of overtime hours by which each full time staff
works falls short of (exceeds) 32 hours for the month.

vi)   Goal constraint 6: It is required that each part time staff work 50
hours for the month. The constraint is:

$$x_3 + d_9^- - d_9^+ = 50$$

where d_9^-, (d_9^+) = the number of hours by which each part time staff works
falls short of (exceeds) 50 hours for the month.

vii) Goal constraint 7: $150 bonus earning for the manager and $50 for
the others.

Three goal constraints are needed: one for the manager, the other two for
the full time and part time staff. For the manager, he receives a bonus of 4%
on all sales above $25,000, therefore the constraint is:

$$0.04 \ [19 \ x_1 + (17) \ (6) \ x_2 + (15) \ (4) \ x_3 - 25000] + d_{10}^- - d_{10}^+ = 150$$

where d_{10}^-, (d_{10}^+) = the amount of which the manager's bonus earning falls
short of (exceeds) $150.

The full time staff receives 10% on all sales above the quota set for
their group, thus:

$$0.10 \ [(17)(6) \ x_2 - 18000] + d_{11}^- - d_{11}^+ = (6)(50)$$

where d_{11}^-, (d_{11}^+) = the amount of which the bonus earning of the group of full
time staff falls short of (exceeds) $300.

The part time staff receive 12% on all sales above the quota set for their group, thus:

$$0.12 \ [(15)(4) \ x_3 - 3600] + d_{12}^- - d_{12}^+ = (4)(50)$$

where d_{12}^-, (d_{12}^+) = the amount of which the bonus earning of the group of part time staff falls short of (exceeds) $200.

viii) The objective function is expressed as follows:

$$\text{Minimize} \ \ Z = P_1 \ d_1^- + P_2 \ d_2^- + P_3 \ d_3^- + P_4 \ d_4^- + P_5 \ (d_7^+ + d_8^+)$$
$$+ P_6 \ d_9^- + P_7 \ (d_{10}^- + d_{11}^- + d_{12}^-)$$

The highest priority is given to minimize d_1^-, which is to ensure the realization of the first goal - the achievement of $25,000 sales quota for the grocery. The d_1^+ is not considered in the objective function since management will be happy with the exceeded sales. Same consideration is given to d_2^-, d_3^- and d_4^-. d_7^+ and d_8^+ reflect the number of overtime work exceeding the overtime limit, thus they are included in the objective function with the priority P_5. The next goal is opposite. Since it is required each part time staff to work at least 50 hour per month, the d_9^-, which indicates the hours the part time sales person works less than 50 hours, is minimized at the sixth priority. The last goal is to achieve the bonus. d_{10}^-, d_{11}^- and d_{12}^-, indicating the underachievement of desired bonus, are given the seventh priority. The d_{10}^+, d_{11}^+ and d_{12}^+ are not included in the objective function since the staff would like to have more bonus. By minimizing the above objective function, the management goals are achieved at the highest extent.

The complete mathematical formulation of the problem is:

$$\text{Minimize} \ \ Z = P_1 \ d_1^- + P_2 \ d_2^- + P_3 \ d_3^- + P_4 \ d_4^- + P_5 \ (d_7^+ + d_8^+)$$
$$+ P_6 \ d_9^- + P_7 \ (d_{10}^- + d_{11}^- + d_{12}^-)$$

Subject to:

$$19 \ x_1 + (17) \ (6) \ x_2 + (15) \ (4) \ x_3 + d_1^- - d_1^+ = 25,000$$
$$19 \ x_1 + d_2^- - d_2^+ = 3,400$$
$$(17) \ (6) \ x_2 + d_3^- - d_3^+ = 18,000$$
$$(15) \ (4) \ x_3 + d_4^- - d_4^+ = 3,600$$
$$x_1 + d_5^- - d_5^+ = 168$$
$$x_2 + d_6^- - d_6^+ = 168$$
$$d_5^+ + d_7^- - d_7^+ = 32$$

$$d_6^+ + d_8^- - d_8^+ = 32$$
$$x_3 + d_9^- - d_9^+ = 50$$
$$0.04 \, [19 \, x_1 + (17)(6) \, x_2 + (15)(4) \, x_3 - 25000] + d_{10}^- - d_{10}^+ = 150$$
$$0.10 \, [(17)(6) \, x_2 - 18000] + d_{11}^- - d_{11}^+ = (6)(50)$$
$$0.12 \, [(15)(4) \, x_3 - 3600] + d_{12}^- - d_{12}^+ = (4)(50)$$
$$\text{all variables} \geq 0$$

The solution of this model is as follows:

$x_1 = 178.9$		$x_2 = 200.0$		$x_3 = 87.8$			
$d_1^- =$	0	$d_1^+ =$	4,066.7	$d_2^- =$	0	$d_2^+ =$	0
$d_3^- =$	0	$d_3^+ =$	2,400.0	$d_4^- =$	0	$d_4^+ =$	1,666.7
$d_5^- =$	21.1	$d_5^+ =$	32.0	$d_6^- =$	0	$d_6^+ =$	32.0
$d_7^- =$	0	$d_7^+ =$	0	$d_8^- =$	0	$d_8^+ =$	0
$d_9^- =$	0	$d_9^+ =$	160.7	$d_{10}^- =$	0	$d_{10}^+ =$	12.7
$d_{11}^- =$	60.0	$d_{11}^+ =$	0	$d_{12}^- =$	0	$d_{12}^+ =$	0

REFERENCES

1. Adulbhan P., 1978. Multicriterion Optimization Models. System Models for Decision Making. Asian Institute of Technology, pp. 387-433.

2. Aneja, Y. P. and K. Nair, 1979. Bicriterion Transportation Problem. Management Science, Vol. 25, No. 1.

3. Arbel, A., 1987. Venturing into New Technological Markets. Mathematical Modelling, 9:299-310.

4. Ashton, D.J. and Atkins, 1979. Multicriteria Programming for Financial Planning. Pergamon Press Ltd.

5. Badran, Y., 1984. Departmental Full Costing via Goal Programming Models. European Journal of Operations Research, 17:331-337.

6. Bahmani, N., D. Yamoah, P. Basseer, and F. Rezvani, 1987. Using the Analytic Hierarchy Process to Select Investment in a Heterogeneous Environment. Mathematical Modelling, 8:157-162.

7. Beatty, R. W., and C. E. Schneier, 1977. Personnel Administration: Experimental/Skill-Building Approach. Addison Wesley Publishing Co., Inc.

8. Blair, A. R., R. Nachtmann, J. E. Olson, and T. L. Saaty, 1987. Forecasting Foreign Exchange Rates: An Expert Judgment Approach. Socio-Economic Planning Sciences, 21:363-370.

9.   Bowey, A., 1974. A Guide to Manpower Planning. The Macmillan Press Ltd.

10. Chandrasekaran, G. and R. Ramesh, 1987. Microcomputer Based Multiple Criteria Decision Support System for Strategic Planning. Information & Management, 12:163-172.

11. Charnes A., W. W. Cooper, J. K. Devoe, et. al., 1968. A Goal Programming Model for Media Planning. Management Science, 14:B423-B430.

12. Charnes, A., W. W. Cooper, R. J. Niehaus, and A. Stedry, 1968. Static and Dynamic Assignment Models with Multiple Objectives, and Some Remarks on Organization Design. Management Science, 15:B365-B375.

13. Crum, R. P. and M. Namazi, 1987. Multi-Objective Linear Programming Techniques in Manpower Staff Assignment. Akron Business and Economic Review, 18:95-109.

14. Cumming P. D., K. E. Kendall, C. C. Pegels, J. P. Seagle, and J. F. Shubsda, 1980. A Collection of Planning Model for Regional Blood Suppliers; Description and Validation. Management Science, Vol. 20, No 11.

15. Davis, K. R., and P. G. McKeown, 1981. Quantitative Models for Management. Kent Publishing Company, Boston, Massachusetts.

16. De Kluyuer, C. A., 1979. An Exploration of Various Goal Programming Formulations - With Application to Advertising Media Scheduling. Journal of Operations Research Society, Vol 30.

17. Dijk, D. and M. Kok, 1987. A Comparison of different Modelling Approaches to Strategic Energy Planning. European Journal of Operational Research, 29:42-50.

18. Eckstein, O., 1979. Public Finance. Fourth ed., Prentice-Hall, Inc.

19. Enrick, N. L., 1974. Building up Managerial Manpower Resources. Industrial Management, 16:7-10.

20. Eom, H. B. and S. M. Lee., 1987. A Large-Scale Goal Programming Model-Based Decision Support for Formulating Global Financing Strategy. Information & Management, 12:33-44.

21. Eom, H. B., S. M. Lee, C. A. Snyder, and F. N. Ford, 1987-1988. A Multiple Criteria Decision Support System for Global Financial Planning. Journal of Management Information Systems, 4:94-113.

22. Fraser, J. M., 1971. Introduction to Personnel Management. Nelson.

23. Galbis, V., 1982. Inflation: The Latin American Experience, 1970-79. Finance & Development.

24. Gareth, S., 1971. Manpower Planning: The Management of Human Resources. London, Heinemann.

25. Gower, 1972. Financial Management Handbook, London.

26. Greenwood, A. G. and L. J. Moore, 1987. An Inter-Temporal Multi-Goal Linear Programming Model for Optimizing University Tuition and Fee

Structures. Journal of the Operational Research Society, 38:599-614.

27. Hachadorian, G. E., 1987. Hierarchial Determination of the Risk of Forced Divestment to Foreign Owned Enterprises in LDC's. Mathematical Modelling, 8:163-166.

28. Haire, M., 1976. Approach to an Integrated Personnel Policy. Industrial Relation, 7:107-117.

29. Hämäläinen, R. P. and T. O. Seppäläinen, 1986. The Analytic Network Process in Energy Policy Planning. Socio-Economic Planning Sciences, 20:399-406.

30. Horne, J. C. Van, 1983. Financial Management & Policy, Sixth edition, Prentice-Hall International, Inc.

31. Ignizio, J. P., 1978. An Approach to the Capital Budgeting Problem with Multiple Objectives. The Engineering Economist, 21:259-272.

32. Jensen, R. E., 1987. International Investment Risk Analysis: Extensions for Multinational Corporation Capital Budgeting Models. Mathematical Modelling, 9:265-284.

33. Jose, V. D. and M. T. Tabucanon, 1986. Multiobjective Models for Selection of Priority Areas and Industrial Projects for Investment Promotion. Engineering costs and Production Economics, 10:173-184.

34. Kahalas, H. and D. A. Gray, 1976. A Quantitative Model for Manpower Decision Making. Omega, 685-697.

35. Katz, R., 1982. Career Issues In Human Resource Management. Prentice-Hall, Inc., Englewood Cliffs.

36. Kendall K. E. and S. M. Lee, 1980. Formulating Blood Rotation Policies With Multiple Objectives. Management Science, Vol 20, No 11.

37. Keown, A. J. and J. D. Martin, 1979. A Chance Constrained Goal Programming Model for Working Capital Management. The Engineering Economist, 22:153-174.

38. Khan, M. R., 1979. A capacitated Network Formulation for Manpower Scheduling. Industrial Management, 21(6):24-28.

39. Khorramshahgol, R. and Y. Gousty, 1986. Delphic Goal Programming (DGP): A Multi-Objective Cost/Benefit Approach to R&D Portfolio Analysis. IEEE Transactions on Engineering Management, EM-33:172-175.

40. Klatt, M. and Schuster, 1978. Human Resources Management: A Behavioral Systems Approach. Richard D. Irwin, Inc.

41. Korhonen, A., 1987. A Dynamic Bank Portfolio Planning Model with Multiple Scenarios, Multiple Goals and Changing Priorities. European Journal of Operational Research, 30:13-23.

42. Kornbluth, J. S. H., 1986. Accounting Control in Multiple Objective Linear Programming. OMEGA, 14:245-250.

43. Kotler, Philip, 1976. Marketing Management, Prentice Hall International, Inc.

44. Kwak, N. K. and C. B. Diminnie, 1987. A Goal Programming Model for Allocating Operating Budgets of Academic Units. Socio-Economic Planning Sciences, 21:333-339.

45. Lee, S. M., 1972. Goal Programming for Decision of Multiple Objectives. Sloan Management Review, Winter 1972, pp.11-24.

46. Lee, S. M. and E. R. Clayton, 1972. A Goal Programming Model for Academic Resource Allocation. Management Science. 18:B395-B407.

47. Liang, T. T. and T. J. Thompson, 1987. A Large-Scale Personnel Assignment Model for the Navy. Decision Sciences, 18:234-249.

48. Lilien, G. L. and A. G. Rao, 1984. A Model for Manpower Management. Management Science, 21:1447-1457.

49. Lipson, H. and J. Darling, 1971. Introduction to Marketing: An Administrative Approach. John Wiley & Sons, Inc.

50. Lockett, A. G. and A. E. Gear, 1975. Multistage Capital Budgeting Under Uncertainty. Journal of Financial & Quantitative Analysis.

51. Lockett, G., M. Stratford, B. Cox, B. Hetherington, and P. Yallup, 1987. Modelling a Research Portfolio Using AHP - A Group Decision Process, Mathematical Modelling, 8:142-148.

52. Lootsma, F. A., J. Meisner, and F. Schellemans, 1986. Multi-Criteria Decision Analysis as an Aid to the Strategic Planning of energy R&D. European Journal of Operational Research, 25:216-234.

53. Manbridge, R. L., 1972. Forecasting Financial Requirement. IMS International Inc.

54. McClure, R. H. and C. E. Wells, 1987. Incorporating Sales Force Preferences in a Goal Programming Model for the Sales Resource Allocation Problem. Decision Sciences, 18:677-681.

55. McClure, R. H. and C. E. Wells, 1987. Modeling Multiple Criteria in the Faculty Assignment Problem. Socio-Economic Planning Sciences, 21:389-394.

56. Miller, R. L., 1972. Personal Finance Today. West Publishing Company.

57. Mills, H., 1961. Notes on Game Theory in Marketing Competition, Marketing as a Science. Harvard Business Review, September-October.

58. Min, H., 1987. A Disaggregate Zero-One Goal Programming Model for the Flexible Staff Scheduling Problem. Socio-Economic Planning Sciences, 21:271-282.

59. Mirur, J. B. and M. G. Miner, 1977. Personnel and Industrial Relations. Macmillan Publishing Co., Inc.

60. Mitchell, K. H. and M. G. Bingham, 1986. Maximizing the Benefits of Canadian forces Equipment Overhaul Programs Using Multi-Objective

Optimization. INFOR, 24:251-264.

61. Miyaji, I., K. Ohno, and H. Mine, 1988. Solution Method for Partitioning students into Groups. European Journal of Operational Research, 33:82-90.

62. Miyajima, M. and M. Nakai, 1986. The Municipal Financial Planning Model: A Simultaneous Regression Equations and Goal Programming Approach. European Journal of Operational Research, 27:158-167.

63. Patten, T. H., Jr., 1971. Manpower Planning and the Development of Human Resources. New York, John Wiley & Sons.

64. Pegels, C. C., 1981. A Manpower Training Decision and Evaluation Model. International Journal of Production Research, 19:341-348.

65. Price, W. L., 1978. Solving Goal-Programming Manpower Models Using Advanced Network Codes. Journal of Operations Research Society, 29:1231-1239.

66. ReVelle, C., 1988. Equalizing superpower force Disparities with Optimized Arms Control Choices: A Multiobjective Approach. European Journal of Operational Research, 33:46-53.

67. Rifai, A. K. and J. O. Pecenka, 1986. Goal Achievement Through Goal Programming: Short Versus Long Term. Engineering costs and Production Economics, 10:155-160.

68. Romero, C., F. Amador, and A. Barco, 1987. Multiple Objectives in Agricultural Planning: A Compromise Programming Application. American Journal of Agricultural Economics, 69:78-86.

69. Romero, C. and T. Rehman, 1987. Natural Resources management and the Use of Multiple Criteria Decision-Making Techniques: A Review. European Review of Agricultural Economics, 69:78-86.

70. Schneider, D. P. and K. E. Kilpatrick, 1975. An optimum Manpower Utilization Model for Health Maintenance Organizations. Operations Research, 23:869-889.

71. Schniederjans, M. J. and G. C. Kim, 1987. A Goal Programming Model to Optimize Departmental Preference in Course Assignments. Computers & Operations Research. 14:87-96.

72. Sharda, R. and K. D. Musser, 1986. Financial Futures Hedging via Goal Programming. Management Science, 32:933-947.

73. Sinha, S. B. and S. V. C. Sastry, 1987. General Mathematical Modelling of a Multi-Objective Community Storage Facility System. Socio-Economic Planning Sciences, 21:1-8.

74. Siskos, J. and C. Zopounidis, 1987. The Evaluation Criteria of the Venture Capital Investment Activity: An Interactivity Assessment. European Journal of Operational Research, 31:304-313.

75. Soyibo, A. and S. M. Lee, 1986. A Multiobjective Planning Model for

University Resource Allocation. European Journal of Operational Research, 27:168-178.

76. Srinivasan, V. and G. L. Thompson, 1977. Determining Cost vs. Time Pareto-Optimal Frontiers in Multi-Model Transportation Problems. Transportation Scinece, Vol. 11, No. 1.

77. Steuer, R. E. and R. L. Oliver, 1976. An Applications of Multiple Objective Linear Programming to Media Selection. Omega, 4:455-462.

78. Steuer, R. E. and M. J. Wallace, Jr., 1978. A Linear Multiple Objective Programming Model for Manpower Selection and Allocation Decisions. Management Science, 8:193-208.

79. Tarranza, N. C. and D. G. Carmichael, 1986. A Multicriteria Approach to the Marking-Up of a Bid. Engineering Costs and Production Economics, 10:139-154.

80. Vincke, P., 1986. Analysis of Multicriteria Decision Aid in Europe. European Journal of Operational Research, 25:160-168.

81. Weiss, E. N., 1987. Using the Analytic Hierarchy Process in a Dynamic Environment. Mathematical Modelling, 9:211-218.

82. Welsch, G. A., 1971. Budgeting: Profit Planning and Control, third edition. Prentice-Hall, Inc.

83. Wijngaard, J., 1983. Aggregation in Manpower Planning. Management Science, 29:1427-1435.

84. Wind, Y., 1987. An Analytic Hierarchy Process Based Approach to the Design and Evaluation of a Marketing Driven Business and corporate Strategy. Mathematical Modelling, 9:285-293.

85. Zanakis, S. H., 1983. A Staff to Job Assignment Problem with Multiple Objectives. Computer & Operations Research, 10:357-363.

CHAPTER VII

MCDM APPLICATIONS IN OTHER RELATED AREAS

As discussed in Chapter I, MCDM applications go beyond the limits of an individual firm. The approach is equally applicable to larger industrial systems such as a particular industry of a country or even to a wider scope of regional cooperation among countries. In this chapter, several applications are presented in a macroscopic perspective of industrial systems. These are MCDM application in problems related to project management, diffusion of small industries, industrial promotion and project selection in the national level, tariff determination of traded commodities in a bloc of countries, and sea transportation of cargo among countries.

7.1 PROJECT CRASHING: TIME-COST TRADEOFF

Project crashing problem is primarily concerned with the tradeoff between compressed activity duration and the consequent increase in the direct cost due to crashing. In real life, a project has a number of incommensurate and often conflicting objectives. For instance, meeting a certain contracted date, confining expenses to a fixed budget, minimizing the total project cost, ensuring that certain activities are not crashed for quality reasons, etc., can all be objectives relevant to a project.

Estimates of activity times for projects usually are made for some given level of resources. In many situations, it is possible to reduce the length of a project by injecting additional resources. The impetus to shorten projects may reflect efforts to avoid late penalties or to take advantage of monetary incentives for timely completion of a project, or to free resources for use on other projects. In many cases, however, the desire to shorten the length of a project merely reflects an attempt to reduce the indirect costs associated with running the project, such as facilities and equipment costs, supervision, and labor and personnel costs. Managers often have certain options at their disposal which will allow them to shorten, or crash, certain activities. Among the most obvious options are the use of additional funds to support additional

personnel or more efficient equipment, and the relaxing of some work specifications.   Hence, a project manager may be able to shorten a project, thereby
realizing a saving in indirect project costs, by increasing direct expenses to
speed up the project.   The goal in evaluating time-cost tradeoffs is to
identify a plan which will minimize the sum of the indirect and direct project
costs.

In order to make a rational decision on which activities (if any) to
crash, and on the extent of crashing desirable, a manager needs certain
information on regular time and crash time estimates for each activity, regular
cost and crash cost estimates for each activity, and a list of activities which
are on the critical path.

Activities on the critical path are potential candidates for crashing,
since shortening noncritical activities would not have an impact on total
project duration.   From an economic standpoint, activities should be crashed
according to crashing costs: Crash those with the lowest costs first.
Moreover, crashing should continue as long as the cost to crash is less than
the benefits received from crashing.   These benefits might take the form of
incentive payments for early project completion, or they might reflect savings
in the indirect project costs, or both.   Figure 7.1 illustrates the basic
relationships between indirect, direct, and total project costs due to crashing.   Crashing activities reduces indirect project costs while increasing
direct costs.   The optimum amount of crashing results in minimizing the sum of
these two types of costs.

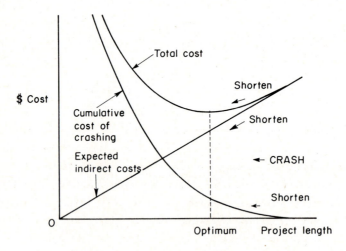

Figure 7.1   Time-Cost Relationship in Projects

The general procedure for crashing is described as follows:

1.   Obtain estimates of regular and crash times, and costs for each
     activity.
2.   Determine the lengths of all paths and path slack times.
3.   Determine which activities are on the critical path.
4.   Crash critical activities, in order of increasing costs, as long as
     crashing costs do not exceed benefits.   Note that two or more paths
     may become critical as the original critical path becomes shorter, so
     that subsequent improvements will require simultaneous shortening of
     two or more paths.   In some cases, it will be most economical to
     shorten an activity which is on two (or more) of the critical paths.
     This is true whenever the crashing cost for a joint activity is less
     than the sum of crashing one activity on each separate path.

A goal programming model was developed by Vrat and Kriengkrairut (1986)
for four types of project goals with a prescribed priority structure on these
goals and a piecewise linear time-cost tradeoff with two segments, as shown in
Fig. 7.2.

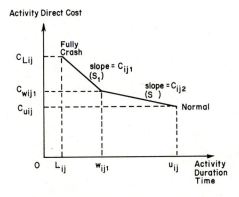

Fig. 7.2   Cost Function with Two Piecewise Linear Segments

The preemptive priorities and weights to be assigned in the goal programming model will depend upon the contingencies of a specific situation and upon
management policy.   For the situation being modeled, the following priority
structure of goals was provided for the project:

P_1:   The first priority is to meet a new specified project completion
       period by minimization of the positive deviation from the actual

project completion period; Minimize d_t^+; d_t^- is acceptable and hence excluded from the objective function.

P$_2$: The second priority is to ensure that certain activities are not crashed for quality (safety) reasons by minimizing the negative deviation of the sum of the durations of those crucial activities. Minimize d_q^-; d_q^+ is acceptable.

P$_3$: The third priority is to confine the project expenses to a specified budget by minimizing the negative deviation of the direct activity costs. Thus, minimize d_b^-, whereas d_b^+ is considered satisfactory.

P$_4$: The fourth priority is to attempt to minimize the total direct cost of crashing by minimizing the negative deviation of activity cost d_c^-. The overachievement deviational variable d_c^+ is considered satisfactory and hence excluded from the objective function. It may be noted that the third and fourth objectives are not mutually exclusive.

The complete goal programming model is as follows:

Minimize:

$$Z = P_1 d_t^+ + P_2 d_q^- + P_3 d_b^- + P_4 d_c^- \qquad (7.1)$$

Subject to:

System constraints:

$$t_i - t_j + \sum_{k=1}^{2} Y_{ijk} \leq 0 \qquad \text{for all } (i,j) \in A \qquad (7.2)$$

$$L_{ij} \leq Y_{ij1} \leq W_{ij1} \qquad \text{for all } (i,j) \in A \qquad (7.3)$$

$$0 \leq Y_{ij2} \leq U_{ij} - W_{ij1} \qquad \text{for all } (i,j) \in A \qquad (7.4)$$

Goal constraints:

$$t_n + d_t^- - d_t^+ = T \qquad (7.5)$$

$$\sum_{(i,j) \in A'} (Y_{ij1} + Y_{ij2}) + d_q^- - d_q^+ = \beta \qquad (7.6)$$

$$\sum_{(i,j) \in A} (C_{ij1} Y_{ij1} + C_{ij2} Y_{ij2}) + d_b^- - d_b^+ = \sum_{(i,j) \in A} K_{ij} - B \qquad (7.7)$$

$$\sum_{(i,j) \in A} (C_{ij1} Y_{ij1} + C_{ij2} Y_{ij2}) + d_c^- - d_c^+ = Q \qquad (7.8)$$

Nonnegativity constraints:

$$Y_{ij1}, Y_{ij2} \geq 0 \qquad \text{for all } (i,j) \in A \qquad (7.9)$$

$$t_i \geq 0 \qquad \text{for all } i \ (i=1, \ldots n) \qquad (7.10)$$

$$d_t^-, d_t^+, d_b^-, d_b^+, d_q^-, d_q^+, d_c^-, d_c^+ \geq 0 \qquad (7.11)$$

Where:

t_i = event occurrence time for event i (i=1,2, ... n);

T = specified project completion period;

U_{ij} = normal time for activity (i,j) (upper bound);

L_{ij} = crash time for activity (i,j) (lower bound);

Y_{ijk} = duration time for kth subactivity of activity (i,j) for k = 1, 2;

W_{ij1} = the intermediate time when the change of cost slope takes place (see Fig. 7.2);

C_{ij1} = cost slope between L_{ij} and W_{ij1} ($C_{ij1} > C_{ij2}$);

C_{ij2} = cost slope between W_{ij1} and U_{ij};

B = the specified budget limit;

β = the specified lower bound to the total activity durations of crucial activities in set A' which should not be crashed beyond this value due to reasons of quality and safety considerations;

Q = goal for total project incremental cost (an arbitrarily chosen large value);

K_{ij} = intercept of the cost function with the cost axis for activity (i,j);

n = number of nodes in the project network;

d^-, d^+ = the deviational variables as defined earlier corresponding to underachievement and overachievement of various priority goals identified by the subscripts to these deviational variables;

A = set of all activities;

A' = set of activities which should not be crashed.

The goal programming model was applied to a construction project. A broader grouping of activities was attempted for ease of analysis. Thus, an activity in the network itself may mean a network of subactivities, and so on. On an aggregate level the project was divided into 48 activities, 35 events and 4 dummy activities. Fig. 7.3. shows the project network with normal activity durations. Table 7.1 gives the list of activities together with normal and fully crash time and normal costs estimated for the situation.

The project time is normally 1034 days. It was desired to compress this to 871 days, i.e. a compression of 163 days is aimed at. The project organiza-

tion was willing to pay an additional amount of approximately 57 million
monetary units (MU) of local currency to obtain this degree of project compression.   The model is partly intended to answer the query as to whether the
promised return on the additional cost involved in project crashing is worthwhile, bearing in mind the other priority goals.   The priority structure was
articulated a priori by the organization and was incorporated in the model.

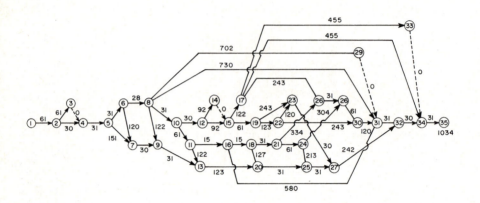

Fig. 7.3   Project Network with Normal Activity Durations

Table 7.1 shows the list of 52 project activities, including 4 dummies.
As the cost data were not readily available, a procedure was evolved to prepare
cost data for crashing with two segments.   This procedure apportioned the
manpower and equipment costs, and the material and other costs in terms of
percentages for each activity to be crashed.   Material and other costs were
treated as fixed, whereas only manpower and equipment costs were influenced by
crashing the activity duration.   Table 7.2 only shows the input data for the
goal programming model for those activities which are potential candidates for
crashing.

Table 7.3 shows the extent of goal achievements for the four goals
according to the priority structure assumed.   It shows that the first two
priority goals are fully achieved and that the last two priority goals were not
fully met.   Thus, it is possible to have the project the quality of the
structure.   However, the contractor will have to operate within a budget of
623.365 million monetary units, and the total incremental direct cost of
crashing is 134.918 million MU.   It was observed that only 27 of the 52
activities are crashable, and that the normal direct cost of crashable activities is 591.467 million MU. Thus, 600 million MU as a goal for budget (B)
is probably inadequate by about 23.365 million MU.

Table 7.1 List of the Project activities and Related Data

Activity	Description	Predecessor(s)	Times (days) normal	Times (days) fully crash	Normal cost (MU)[a]
A1	Demolition 1	–	61	31	659,548
A2	Demolition 2	A1	30	30	335,180
A3	Piling work 1	A1	61	30	9,280,530
A4	Piling work 2	A2, A3	31	15	4,716,335
A5	Piling work 3	A4	151	76	22,973,116
A6	Excavation 1	A4	31	31	145,168
A7	Excavation 2	A6	120	60	561,942
A8	Excavation 3	A5, A7	30	30	140,485
A9	Foundation 1	A6	28	28	3,573,332
A10	Foundation 2	A9	122	92	15,569,518
A11	Foundation 3	A8, A10	31	31	3,956,189
A12	Basement, drainage, trench, wall 1	A9	31	31	8,424,356
A13	Basement, drainage, trench, wall 2	A12	30	30	8,152,603
A14	Basement, drainage, trench, wall 3	A13	92	92	25,001,315
A15	Ground floor 1	A12	61	61	5,525,653
A16	Ground floor 2	A15	122	92	11,051,306
A17	Ground floor 3	A11, A16	123	92	11,141,890
A18	Second floor 1	A15	15	15	2,211,610
A19	Second floor 2	A18	15	15	2,211,610
A20	Second floor 3	A19	127	87	18,724,966
A21	Second floor 4	A17, A20	31	15	4,570,661
A22	Third floor 1	A19	31	31	2,813,133
A23	Third floor 2	A22	61	39	5,535,520
A24	Third floor 3	A23	213	152	19,328,948
A25	Third floor 4	A21, A24	31	31	2,813,133
A26	Fourth floor 1	A14	61	31	5,562,006
A27	Fourth floor 2	A26	243	182	22,156,843
A28	Roof slab, Hanger truss, APF 1	A26	123	92	9,726,583
A29	Roof slab, Hanger truss, APF 2	A28	120	90	9,489,349
A30	Roof slab, Hanger truss, APF 3	A27, A29	30	30	2,372,337
A31	Roof slab, Hanger truss, APF 4	A25, A30	242	180	19,136,854
A32	Air conditioning and ventilation system	A18	580	427	71,898,500
A33	Plumbing	A9	702	550	10,279,087
A34	Electrical works	A9	730	578	169,723,140
A35	Architectural work 1	A13	92	92	19,696,608
A36	Architectural work 2	A14, A15	122	92	26,119,415
A37	Architectural work 3	A36	243	212	52,024,736
A38	Architectural work 4	A37, A45	31	31	6,636,900
A39	Architectural work 5	A38, A46	61	61	13,059,707
A40	Architectural work 6	A39, A44	120	90	25,691,228
A41	Architectural work 7	A32, A33, A34, A40	31	31	6,636,900
A42	Architectural work 8	A31, A41	30	30	6,422,807
A43	Architectural work 9	A42, A47, A48	31	31	6,636,900
A44	Lifts	A28	273	212	20,612,200
A45	Escalators	A22	334	243	19,614,696
A46	Moving sidewalks	A23	304	304	14,034,644
A47	X-ray equipment	A36	455	243	5,811,320
A48	Walk through detector	A36	455	243	166,360
A49	Dummy 1	A3	0	0	0
A50	Dummy 2	A35	0	0	0
A51	Dummy 3	A33	0	0	0
A52	Dummy 4	A48	0	0	0

Source: Contractor of the project under study.
[a]MU: Monetary Units.

(Tables 7.1-7.4 are taken from Engineering Costs and Production Economics, Vol. 10, No. 2, June 1986, pp. 161-172.)

Table 7.2   Input Data for Project Crashing Purpose

Activity	Description	Duration time (days)			Direct cost (MU)			Unit crashing cost (MU/day)		Intercept with cost axis
		T_N	T_I	T_C	C_N	C_I	C_C	S_2	S_1	(K_{ij})
A1	Demolition 1	61	38.5	31	659,548	890,660	979,253	10,271.7	11,812.4	1,345,438
A3	Piling work 1	61	38	30	9,280,530	11,380,060	12,219,872	91,248	104,976.4	15,369,166
A4	Piling work 2	31	19	15	4,716,335	5,811,742	6,231,648	91,284	104,976.4	7,806,295
A5	Piling work 3	151	95	76	22,973,116	28,085,015	30,079,568	91,284	104,976.4	38,057,781
A7	Excavation 2	120	75	60	561,942	751,598	824,299	4,214.6	4,846.8	1,115,103
A10	Foundation 2	122	99.5	92	15,569,518	16,430,946	16,761,160	38,285.7	44,028.6	20,811,787
A16	Ground floor 2	122	99.5	92	11,051,306	11,662,751	11,897,138	27,175.3	31,251.6	14,772,290
A17	Ground floor 3	123	99.75	92	11,141,890	11,773,716	12,015,916	27,175.4	31,251.6	14,891,068
A20	Second floor 3	127	97	87	18,724,966	20,051,932	20,560,602	44,232.2	50,867.0	24,986,034
A21	Second floor 4	31	19	15	4,570,661	5,101,447	5,304,915	44,232.2	50,867.0	6,067,920
A23	Third floor 2	61	38	30	5,535,520	6,161,668	6,412,128	27,223.9	31,307.4	7,351,352
A24	Third floor 3	213	167.25	152	19,328,948	20,574,439	21,051,878	27,233.9	31,307.4	25,810,610
A26	Fourth floor 1	61	38.5	31	5,562,006	6,177,473	6,413,403	27,354.1	31,457.3	7,388,578
A27	Fourth floor 2	243	197.25	182	22,156,843	23,408,294	23,888,017	27,354.1	31,457.3	29,613,236
A28	Roof slab, .. 1	123	99.75	92	9,726,583	10,462,007	10,743,920	31,631.2	36,357.8	14,090,497
A29	Roof slab, .. 2	120	97.5	90	9,489,349	10,201,050	10,473,869	31,631.2	36,375.8	13,747,694
A31	Roof slab, .. 4	242	195.5	180	19,136,854	20,607,703	21,171,528	31,631.2	36,375.8	27,719,179
A32	Air condition	580	465.25	427	71,898,500	73,320,974	73,866,256	12,396.3	14,255.7	79,953,456
A33	Plumbing	702	588	550	10,279,087	10,946,788	11,202,740	5,857	6,735.6	14,907,312
A34	Elect. works	730	616	578	169,723,140	175,024,081	177,056,109	46,499.5	53,474.4	207,964,318
A36	Architectural 2	122	99.5	92	26,119,415	27,323,691	27,785,330	53,523.4	61,551.9	33,448,105
A37	Architectural 3	243	219.75	212	52,024,736	53,269,154	53,746,182	53,523.4	61,551.9	66,795,184
A40	Architectural 6	120	97.5	90	25,691,228	26,895,504	27,357,143	53,523.4	61,551.9	32,896,814
A44	Lifts	273	227.25	212	20,612,200	20,957,624	21,090,036	7,550.3	8,682.8	22,930,789
A45	Escalators	334	265.75	243	19,614,696	20,015,505	20,169,148	5,872.7	6,753.6	21,810,265
A47	X-Ray equip.	455	296	243	5,811,320	6,014,396	6,092,243	1,277.2	1,468.8	6,449,160
A48	Walk through	455	296	243	166,360	171,930	174,209	36.6	43.0	184,656

Sum of K_{ij} 758,284,087

Source: Contractor of project under study.
Note: Only activities to be crashed are mentioned.

Table 7.3   Goal Achievements for Each Priority Level

Priority	Goal type	Goal level	Actual solution	Goals achieved/ not achieved
P_1	Meet completion period (days)	871	871	Achieved
P_2	To ensure the quality of piling works (days)	180	196	Achieved
P_3	Confining the expenses to a fixed budget (MU)	600,000,000	623,365,316.8	Not achieved
P_4	Maximizing the total incremental direct cost (minimizing total direct cost) (MU)	1,000,000,000	134,918,770.2	Not achieved

It is also observed that the additional direct cost of crashing all activities is 31.898 million MU of local currency. Since the client organization is willing to pay 57.855 million MU for project crashing, the model shows adequate return to the contractor in accepting the proposal. Thus, the crashing proposition is worthwhile to both interest groups in the project under consideration.

Sensitivity analysis was carried out to examine the effect of changing the priority structure of goals and of changing the lower unit cost of crashing. In the case of goal priority structure, 8 variants of the basic run were examined.   It was observed that, in all the nine cases examined, the budget goal could not be achieved even if accorded the second highest ranking.   Thus, while the time objective could generally be achieved in all cases, the cost objective could not be achieved, illustrating the typical conflicting nature of these goals.

Table 7.4   Results of Sensitivity Analysis

Sr. No.	Percentage change in the lower unit crashing cost	Value of goals achieved at priority level				Percentage increase in the budget from the linear case
		P_1	P_2	P_3	P_4	
1	Linear case ($S_1 = S_2$)	871	196	609432534	136854552	0
2	+1	871	196	619566620	135496437	1.663
3	0 (basic run)	871	196	623365316	134918770	2.286
4	−1	871	196	626942505	134507485	2.873
5	−2	871	196	630630180	134012969	3.478
6	−3	871	196	634317767	133518392	4.083
7	−4	871	196	638005561	133023965	4.688
8	−5	871	196	641693838	132529469	5.294

Sensitivity analysis was also carried out with respect to changes in the lower unit crashing cost.   It was decreased by 1%, 2%, 3%, 4%, and 5%, and increased by 1%.   The results are shown in Table 7.4, indicating the level of goal achievements at various levels of changes in unit cost.   It may be seen that such a change had absolutely no impact on the attainment of the two topmost priority goals, but it did have an effect on the attainments of cost targets at priority levels 3 and 4.   Such a system behavior is intuitively obvious.   Table 7.4 also shows the percentage increase in the budget compared to the linear approximation case.   An interesting observation that can be made is that the cost function is convex, and, if it is approximated to be linear, the required budget is underestimated.   Thus, for the case under consideration, the sensitivity analysis reveals that time and quality goals are relatively insensitive to changes in system parameters compared to the cost objectives.

7.2 DIFFUSION PATTERNS OF SMALL INDUSTRIES

The problem facing many developing countries is how to establish a small industrial sector which would be sufficiently modern to be viable. Some of the

reasons for the promotion of small industries are: Small industrial enter-
prices provide an effective means of stimulating indigenous entrepreneurship;
the skills of traditional craftsmen can be channeled into new ventures suited
to modern economy; unemployment problem can be alleviated by using labor-
intensive methods; scarce capital is required; the growth of industry becomes
more dispersed geographically; diversification of the industrial structure is
facilitated.

Owing to the basic weakness and handicaps of the small industrial sector
and to the shortage of institutional agencies to provide the services and
facilities needed, governments in developing countries assume certain special
responsibilities for its development. The abundant literature available on
small industries all point out that in order to facilitate the healthy growth
of enterprises in the small industrial sector, governments must render assistance in the financial, technical, and promotional areas. Financial assistance
would include providing credit facilities at reasonable or nominal rates of
interest, providing incentives in the form of wage subsidies, and providing
subsidies and giving tax relief on the purchase of machinery and construction
of buildings.   Among others, technical assistance includes providing the
necessary infrastructure, such as maintenance of roads, water supply, power,
gas, drainage, etc., providing skilled personnel for engineering and management
consultancy, and training the workers in the small industrial sector at
government expense.   Other promotional assistance includes maintaining distribution channels, show rooms, transport facilities to be used by the small
scale industries and providing promotional advice, subsidies for packaging
export goods.

Let m(t) be the number of small scale industrial units at time t. It is
assumed that all these units produce the same type of goods and these are of
similar capacity.

Let n be the total number of units that the government permits to be set
up. It is assumed that the government has made a deliberate decision to promote
this type of industry and that it has complete knowledge of the performance
characteristics of this type of industry.

$$y = \frac{m(t+1) - m(t)}{n - m(t)} \tag{7.12}$$

where y is the proportion of "hold-outs" at time t that decide to establish a
plant by time t+1. It is hypothesized that y is a function of:
   (i)   the proportion of industries that have already been set up by time
          t, i.e., m(t)/n;

(ii)   the financial assistance given Z_1;

(iii) the technical assistance given Z_2;

(iv)   the promotional assistance given Z_3.

Thus

$$y = f \ (m(t)/n, \ Z_1, \ Z_2, \ Z_3) \tag{7.13}$$

Assuming that $m(t)$ can be treated as a continuous variable and y is approximated adequately within the relevant range by a Taylor's expansion that drops
third and higher order terms, then

$$y = g_0 + g_1 \ m(t)/n + g_2 Z_1 + g_3 Z_2 + g_4 Z_3 + (g_5 Z_1 + g_6 Z_2 + g_7 Z_3) \ m(t)/n$$
$$+ g_8 Z_1^2 + g_9 Z_2^2 + g_{10} Z_3^2 + g_{11} Z_1 Z_2 + g_{12} Z_1 Z_3 + g_{13} Z_2 Z_3 \tag{7.14}$$

Simplifying:

$$y = \alpha \ m(t)/n + \theta \tag{7.15}$$

where $\alpha = g_1 + g_5 Z_1 + g_6 Z_2 + g_7 Z_3$, and
$\theta = $ the sum of all terms in the equation not containing $m(t)/n$.

Rewriting (7.15) yields

$$m(t + 1) - m(t) = [n - m(t)][\theta + \alpha m(t)/n] \tag{7.16}$$

If time is measured in fairly small quantities, equation (7.16) can be approximated by the differential equation

$$dm(t)/dt = [n - m(t)][\theta + \alpha m(t)/n], \tag{7.17}$$

the solution of which is

$$m(t) = \frac{n \ [e^{\ell + (\theta + \alpha)t} - \theta/\alpha \ ]}{1 + e^{\ell + (\theta + \alpha)t}} \tag{7.18}$$

where ℓ is the constant of integration. If the boundary condition is imposed,

$$\lim_{t \to -\infty} m(t) = 0$$

this equation becomes

$$m(t) = \frac{n}{1 + e^{-(\ell + \alpha t)}} \tag{7.19}$$

where ℓ is a constant of integration and

$$\alpha = b_0 + b_1 Z_1 + b_2 Z_2 + b_3 Z_3$$

where $b_0 = g_1$, $b_1 = g_5$, $b_2 = g_6$, $b_3 = g_7$, and
             Z_1 = measure of financial assistance,
             Z_2 = measure of technical assistance,
             Z_3 = measure of promotional assistance.

Equation (7.19) is an S-curve reaching n asymptotically as $t \to \infty$. It can be seen that as α increases $m(t)$ increases. Thus, the objective of the planner should be to increase α. The expression for Z_1 to Z_3 are as follows:

$$Z_1 = a_1 x_1 + a_2 x_2 \tag{7.20}$$

where x_1 = level of assistance in the form of credit facilities and wage-subsidies,
      x_2 = level of assistance given in the form of subsidies and tax relief.

$$Z_2 = a_3 x_3 + a_4 x_4 \tag{7.21}$$

where x_3 = level of assistance given by providing and maintaining the infrastructure,
      x_4 = level of assistance given by providing consultancy and training.

$$Z_3 = a_5 x_5 + a_6 x_6 \tag{7.22}$$

where x_5 = level of assistance given by providing promotional advice and giving subsidies for packaging export goods,
      x_6 = level of assistance given by maintaining distribution channels, show rooms, etc.

x_1, x_2, x_3, x_4, x_5, x_6 can vary from 0 to 1. The values a_1, a_2, a_3, a_4, a_5, a_6 are normalized weighting factors obtained after conducting a survey among potential industrialists, i.e.

$$a_1 + a_2 = 1 \quad , \quad a_3 + a_4 = 1 \quad , \quad \text{and} \quad a_5 + a_6 = 1 \ .$$

With this, it is to be expected that the values of Z_1, Z_2, Z_3 can vary from 0 to 1.

In order for the government to convert the above expression into money terms, the terms c_1, c_2, c_3, c_4, c_5, c_6 are introduced. If the maximum expenditure possible is B, then

$$\sum_{i=1}^{6} c_i x_i \leq B \tag{7.23}$$

In addition, the government may wish to specify that each x_i must exceed some value k_2, i.e., to provide some assistance to all 3 areas. Thus we have:

Maximize $Z_1 = a_1 x_1 + a_2 x_2$

Maximize $Z_2 = a_3 x_3 + a_4 x_4$

Maximize $Z_3 = a_5 x_5 + a_6 x_6$

Subject to

$$\sum_{i=1}^{6} c_i x_i \leq B$$

$$x_i \geq k_2 \qquad\qquad i = 1, 2, \ldots, 6$$

$$x_i \leq 1 \qquad\qquad i = 1, 2, \ldots, 6$$

The multicriterion problem can be readily solved by any method discussed in Chapter IV. The values of Z_1, Z_2, Z_3 can be fed into the equation to obtain α. If this value does not give the desired rate of industrialization, the behavior of the multicriterion problem is investigated for another B until the desired α is obtained. The values of b_0, b_1, b_2, b_3 are obtainable by a multiple regression method.

Consider the diffusion of a particular small industry given by

$$\alpha = 0.10 + 0.40 Z_1 + 0.10 Z_2 + 0.20 Z_3$$

Let the multicriterion problem be

Maximize $Z_1 = 0.60 x_1 + 0.40 x_2$

$Z_2 = 0.75 x_3 + 0.25 x_4$

$Z_3 = 0.25 x_5 + 0.75 x_6$

Subject to

$$400,000 x_1 + 400,000 x_2 + 200,000 x_3 + 200,000 x_4 + 150,000 x_5$$
$$+ \ 300,000 x_6 \leq 750,000$$
$$1.00 \geq x_1 \geq 0$$

$$1.00 \geq x_2 \geq 0.10$$
$$1.00 \geq x_3 \geq 0.50$$
$$1.00 \geq x_4 \geq 0.25$$
$$1.00 \geq x_5 \geq 0.25$$
$$1.00 \geq x_6 \geq 0.50$$

At time $t = 0$ let $m = 1$ and $n = 100$, thus $1 = 4.5951$,

$$m(t) = \frac{100}{1 + e^{4.5951 - \alpha t}}$$

The compromise constraint method was used to solve the multicriterion problem and the weights given to Z_1, Z_2, Z_3 were 0.58, 0.14, 0.28, respectively, and were obtained from the expression for α.

The compromise constraint method gives the following formulation.

Maximize $Z = 0.4826x_1 + 0.3217x_2 + 0.1328 x_3 + 0.0443x_4 + 0.0886x_5$
$$+ 0.2656x_6 - (\sigma_{12}^- + \sigma_{12}^+ + \sigma_{23}^- + \sigma_{23}^+ + \sigma_{13}^- + \sigma_{13}^+)$$

subject to:

$$0.4826x_1 + 0.3217x_2 - 0.1328x_3 - 0.0443x_4 - \sigma_{12}^- + \sigma_{12}^+ = 0.5871$$
$$-0.1328x_3 - 0.0443x_4 + 0.0886x_5 + 0.2656x_6 + \sigma_{23}^- - \sigma_{23}^+ = 0.1771$$
$$0.4826x_1 + 0.3217x_2 - 0.0886x_5 - 0.2656x_6 - \sigma_{13}^- + \sigma_{13}^+ = 0.4099$$
$$4x_1 + 4x_2 + 2x_3 + 2x_4 + 1.5x_5 + 3x_6 \leq 7.5000$$
$$x_1 \leq 1.0$$
$$x_2 \leq 1.0$$
$$x_3 \leq 1.0$$
$$x_4 \leq 1.0$$
$$x_5 \leq 1.0$$
$$x_6 \leq 1.0$$
$$x_1 \geq 0.0$$
$$x_2 \geq 0.10$$
$$x_3 \geq 0.5$$
$$x_4 \geq 0.25$$
$$x_5 \geq 0.25$$
$$x_6 \geq 0.50$$

The solution of this problem formulation is as follows:

$$x_1 = 0.391 \qquad x_2 = 0.100 \qquad x_3 = 0.500$$
$$x_4 = 0.250 \qquad x_5 = 0.250 \qquad x_6 = 0.500$$

$$\sigma_{12}^- = 0.000 \qquad \sigma_{23}^- = 0.219 \qquad \sigma_{13}^- = 0.000$$
$$\sigma_{12}^+ = 0.183 \qquad \sigma_{23}^+ = 0.000 \qquad \sigma_{13}^+ = 0.083$$
$$Z = 0.029$$

Table 7.5 gives the value of α for various value of B, i.e., budgets. Fig. 7.4 shows how the number of plants installed varies with time for different budgets.

Table 7.5 Values of α
for Different B

B	α
550,000	0.3508
650,000	0.4108
750,000	0.4708
850,000	0.5167
950,000	0.5615
1,050,000	0.6063
1,150,000	0.6489
1,250,000	0.6885
1,350,000	0.7251
1,450,000	0.7473

Fig. 7.4 Relationship between
Plants Installed and Budgets

7.3 PROJECT SELECTION

Oftentimes it seems that there are more people with different objectives deciding on the worthiness of investments for promotion than there are investments. These people can be classified as project formulators, project evaluators and policy makers. The primary interest lies in helping one group of decision makers, that is policy makers, formulate and select the optimal investment priorities plan for the economy.

Project evaluators receive projects from project proponents and select projects based on "factual information" and investment evaluation criteria. The conventional approach is commonly characterized by project-by-project evaluation. Once projects have been appraised, they go to the policy makers who either accept the investment strategy proposed by the evaluators or reject them.

Policy makers work at different levels of aggregation which implies different perspectives for selecting projects. They are interested in appraising projects for promotion based on chosen characteristics which are quantifiable but which refer directly to the country's developmental objec-tives; these are such factors as employment, income distribution, foreign exchange and the like. In real life situations, these factors have varying degrees of importance. Oftentimes these factors are conflicting.

Policy makers recognize the importance of evaluating projects based upon "efficiency" criteria, and on a project-by-project basis. However, in spite of this fact, there is a demand for models which reveals the full range of impact of selected projects or their contribution to the accomplishment of prespecif-ied national development goals. Moreover, the need arises due to the multi-plicity of objectives to be accomplished in setting the framework for formula-ting investment priorities plan and thereby in the selection of projects eligible for promotion.

In this section, a goal programming model developed by Tabucanon and Jose (1986) is discussed to show the usefulness of MCDM in project selection. The model is presented in two phases, where the first phase deals with the iden-tification of priority areas for investment promotion, and the second phase deals with the selection of projects to be accorded promoted status.

Subscripts used in the models are summarized as follows:

$i = 1, 2, \ldots, e$ for product-types $1, 2, \ldots, e$.

$j = 1, 2, \ldots, m$ for regions $1, 2, \ldots, m$.

$p = 1, 2, \ldots, r$ for r projects applying for promotion.

$k = 1, 2, \ldots, n$ for n identified goals.

The decision variable used in the first phase is X_{ij} which refers to the allowable total production capacity of industrial activities producing product type i in region j.

The spatial distribution of such industrial activities is illustrated in Fig. 7.5. The results obtainable from the model are the "satisficing" values for the cells of the matrix (X_{ij}^{**}, $i = 1, 2, \ldots, e$; $j = 1, 2, \ldots, m$). The deviational variables associated with goal k are denoted d_k^- and d_k^+ for negative deviation and positive deviation, respectively, from the specified targets.

The decision variable used in the second phase is X_p which is a zero-one variable, where X_p equals zero if project p is rejected and X_p equals one if

project p is selected. The results obtainable from the model are the "satisficing" portfolio of projects $(X_p^{**}, p = 1,2, \ldots, r)$. Similarly the deviational variables d_k^- and d_k^+ are used to refer to the negative deviation and
positive deviation, respectively, from the specified targets.

PRODUCT TYPE	REGION					
	1	2	....	j	....	m
1	X_{11}	X_{12}	....	X_{1j}	....	X_{1m}
2	X_{21}	X_{22}	....	X_{2j}	....	X_{2m}
.	.	.		.		.
.	.	.		.		.
i	X_{i1}	X_{i2}	....	X_{ij}	....	X_{im}
.	.	.		.		.
.	.	.		.		.
e	X_{e1}	X_{e2}	....	X_{ej}	....	X_{em}

Fig. 7.5 Spatial Distribution of Industrial Activity

Model Formulation for Phase 1: Identification of Priority Areas for Investment Promotion.

Three national planning objectives are considered in this phase, namely:
improvement of foreign exchange earnings; lessening of unemployment; and
improvement of income distribution.   These objectives can be expressed in
optimization parlance,respectively, as the maximization of exports; the
maximization of total employment; the maximization of employment generated in
the major areas.   These objectives are then converted into goals having
specified targets and with the inclusion of permissible deviations (d_k^-, d_k^+)
from the said targets.

(i)   Export Goal.
The full utilization of production capacity which exceeds the level of
local demand is attained through the export of the manufactured goods.   The
export of manufactures leads to reduced costs and earnings in foreign exchange.   There are a number of factors that govern exports but the most
influential one is local production. Thus maximizing export is tantamount to
maximizing local production.   As far as foreign exchange earnings are concerned, value rather than quantity is strove for.   It is also sensible to

assume that only a portion of total production is exported. Thus, the export goal can be expressed as follows:

$$\sum_{i=1}^{e} f_i \left(\sum_{j=1}^{m} X_{ij} \right) + d_1^- - d_1^+ = F \qquad (7.24)$$

where f_i = unit price of export of product type i multiplied by the portion (in percentage) of local production of product type i to be exported.

  F = target value of export.

The objective is to minimize the underachievement of the export goal, d_1^-.

  (ii) Employment Goal.

  Increasing the level of employment, or reducing the unemployment level, is considered most desirable especially in developing countries where there are large surplus of labor. Manpower is viewed as an important economic resource and as such, the existence of unemployment is regarded as a wastage of important economic resources. Thus, employment generation goal can be expressed as:

$$\sum_{i=1}^{e} \sum_{j=1}^{m} w_{ij} X_{ij} + d_2^- - d_2^+ = W \qquad (7.25)$$

where w_{ij} = average labor requirement to produce product i in region j per unit production.

  W = minimum desirable number of workers employed in production activities.

The objective is to minimize the underachievement of the employment goal, d_2^-.

  (iii) Income Distribution Goal.

  Income distribution may be realized by distributing employment oppor-tunities more evenly among the regions. In most developing countries, regional classification, as far as employment distribution is concerned, can be defined into two main areas: urban areas (regions 1, 2, ..., m-1) and the "rest of the country" (region m). It is thus necessary to cooperatively achieve the following goals:

$$\sum_{i=1}^{e} b_{im} X_{ij} + d_3^- - d_3^+ = I_1 \qquad (7.26)$$

where b_{im} = average labor requirement to produce product i in region j, per unit production, multiplied by the wage index for region m.

I_1 = target value of income generated from various production activities in the "rest of the country".

$$\sum_{i=1}^{e} \sum_{j=1}^{m-1} b_{ij} X_{ij} + d_4^- - d_4^+ = I_2 \qquad (7.27)$$

where b_{ij} = average labor requirement to produce product i in region j, per unit production, multiplied by the wage index for region j (j = 1, 2, ..., m-1).

I_2 = desired value of income generated from various production activities in the urban areas.

The objective is to minimize the underachievement of the income distribution goals, d_3- and d_4^-.

(iv) Investment Planning Constraints.

As mentioned earlier, the government aims to attain self-sufficiency and therefore, total production must at least meet local consumption. This also provides for a measure to reduce imports, thereby improving foreign exchange savings. Thus, the following absolute constraints are necessary:

$$\sum_{j=1}^{m} X_{ij} \geq C_i \qquad \text{for } i = 1, 2, ..., e. \qquad (7.28)$$

where C_i = local consumption for product type i.

Likewise, the government aims to block off fast-growing congestion problem in certain areas. To ensure this, the government sets maximum tolerable production capacities for the regions. This can be represented by the following absolute constraints:

$$\sum_{i=1}^{e} X_{ij} \leq Q_j \qquad \text{for } j = 1, 2, ..., m. \qquad (7.29)$$

where Q_j = maximum tolerable production capacity for region j.

Negative values of the decision and deviational variables are meaningless. Therefore, nonnegativity of all variables are ensured by the following constraints:

X_{ij}, d_k^-, $d_k^+ \geq 0$ for all i, j, k.

(v)   Priority Structure.

The formulation of the goals and constraints is now complete. The goal programming model seeks to minimize certain selected absolute deviations from the set of stated goals. Each of the selected deviations in the GP objective carry priorities such that goals are attained or approached as nearly as possible, in strict order of priority.

The priorities for the problem under consideration are assumed to be the following:

(a) Priority Level 1: Export Goal. The first priority is to minimize the underachievement of the target value of export, thus: $P_1 \cdot d_1^-$.

(b) Priority Level 2:   Employment Goal.   The second priority is to minimize the underachievement of the desired level of employment, thus: $P_2 \cdot d_2^-$.

(c) Priority Level 3:   Income Distributed to the "rest of the country". The third priority is to minimize the underachievement of the desired income generated in the "rest of the country", thus: $P_3 \cdot d_3^-$.

(d) Priority Level 4: Income Distributed to the urban areas. The fourth priority is aimed at minimizing the underachievement of the desired level of income generated in the urban areas, thus: $P_4 \cdot d_4^-$.

Model Formulation for Phase 2: Project Selection for Promotion.

As mentioned earlier, policy makers work at a different level of aggrega-tion implying a different perspective for selecting projects for promotion. They are more interested in selecting that mix of projects for promotion which typically ensures maximum contribution to the country's developmental objec-tives such as employment generation, income distribution, foreign exchange generation, and the like. These objectives can be translated into goals with specified targets.

It is assumed that projects considered for promotion have undergone preliminary studies by the project evaluators and as such, these projects are proved to be economically viable; able to stand on their own in the long run; have environmental protection measures; and have adequate size of market demand for their products or services. Furthermore, the project proponents have already preselected the project sites prior to their application and therefore, such factors as transportation, industrial facilities and other amenities are assumed to have been taken into consideration.

(i)   No Multiples of Projects.

No multiples of projects means that projects must be accepted only once during the specific planning period. Mathematically, this can be represented by the following set of goals: if there are r projects,

$$X_p + d_p^- - d_p^+ = 1 \qquad\qquad \text{for } p = 1, 2, \ldots, r. \qquad\qquad (7.30)$$

The objective is to minimize the overachievement of the acceptance goal, $\sum_p d_p^+$.

(ii)   Employment Goal.

With reference to the discussion of this goal in the first phase of the model, the mathematical expression is:

$$\sum_{p=1}^{r} w_p \, X_p + d_{r+1}^- - d_{r+1}^+ = W \qquad\qquad (7.31)$$

where w_p =   total number of workers involved by project.

   W =   minimum desirable employment level generated in the country.

The objective is to minimize the underachievement of the desirable level of employment in the whole country, d_{r+1}^-.

(iii) Income Distribution Goal.

Improvement of income distribution for the country is represented as the maximization of income generated in the "rest of the country" and the maximization of income generated in the urban areas. Thus:

$$\sum_{p=1}^{r} b_p \, X_p + d_{r+2}^- - d_{r+2}^+ = G_1 \qquad\qquad (7.32)$$

where b_p =   total income of workers employed in project p located in the "rest of the country" or region m.

   G =   target value of income generated in the "rest of the country".

$$\sum_{p=1}^{r} b_p \, X_p + d_{r+3}^- - d_{r+3}^+ = G_2 \qquad\qquad (7.33)$$

where b_p =   total income of workers employed in project p located in the urban areas or regions 1, 2, ..., m-1.

   G =   target value of income generated in the urban capital areas.

The objective is to minimize the underachievement of the income distribution target, $d_{r+2}^- + d_{r+3}^-$.

(iv)   Investment Promotion Priority Goal.

The goal is to promote at least M projects considered under the identified priority areas for investment promotion.   Note that the choice of M value is subjective, and depends on the level set by policy makers.   The basis of this goal comes from the result of the first phase where investment promotion priority areas were identified.   Mathematically, this goal is expressed as:

$$\sum_{p=1}^{r} X_p + d_{r+4}^{-} - d_{r+4}^{+} = M \tag{7.34}$$

where   M =   target number of projects which fall under identified priority areas for investment that planners want to promote.

The objective is to minimize the underachievement of this goal, d_{r+4}^{-}.

(v)   Foreign Exchange Earning Goal.

Increasing foreign exchange potential is expressed as the promotion of export-oriented projects.   This can be represented as the promotion of at least E major foreign exchange earning projects.   Note again that the choice of E value is subjective depending on the level set by policy makers.   Thus:

$$\sum_{p=1}^{r} X_p + d_{r+5}^{-} - d_{r+5}^{+} = E \tag{7.35}$$

where   E =   minimum desirable number of export-oriented projects to be promoted.

The objective is to minimize the underachievement of this goal, d_{r+5}^{-}.

(vi)   Promote Indispensable Projects Goal.

Some projects are considered indispensable and supportive of other projects and as such, the following goals are necessary: If out of r projects, the last h projects are indispensable projects, then:

$$X_p + d_{u+g}^{-} - d_{u+g}^{+} = 1 \qquad \text{for } p = r-h, \ldots, r, \tag{7.36}$$
$$g = 1, \ldots, h,$$
$$u = r+5.$$

The objective is to minimize the underachievement of this goal, $\sum_g d_{u+g}^{-}$.

(vii) Self Sufficiency Goal.

Minimizing import is one way of improving foreign exchange savings.   This can be achieved by setting local production to meet at least the local consumption.   Mathematically this is expressed as:

$$\sum_{p=1}^{r} q_{pi} X_p + d_{s+i}^{-} - d_{s+i}^{+} = G_i \qquad \text{for } i = 1, 2, \ldots, e; \qquad (7.37)$$

$$s = u+h.$$

where q_{pi} = production capacity of project p producing product type i.

   C   = local consumption for product type i.

The objective is to minimize the underachievement of the required local production to meet local consumption, $\sum_i d_{s+i}^{-}$.

   (viii) Noncongestion Goal.

   Production capacity in regions is set to a maximum tolerable value to ensure noncongestion of certain areas.   The following goals are therefore necessary:

$$\sum_{p=1}^{r} q_{pj} X_p + d_{t+j}^{-} - d_{t+j}^{+} = G_j \qquad \text{for } j = 1, 2, \ldots, m; \qquad (7.38)$$

$$t = s+e.$$

where   q   = production capacity of project p located in region j.

   Q   = maximum tolerable production in region j.

The objective is to minimize the overachievement of the maximum tolerable capacity for each region, $\sum_j d_{t+j}^{+}$.

   (ix)   Acceptance-Rejection Constraint.

   A project selected must be accepted in its entirety.   Thus, X_p equals one if project p is selected, and X_p equals zero if it is rejected.   In mathematical terms,

$$X_p = 0, 1 \qquad \text{for} \quad p = 1, 2, \ldots, m. \qquad (7.39)$$

   (x)   Nonnegativity Constraints.

$$X_p, d_k^{-}, d_k^{+} > 0 \qquad \text{for} \quad \text{all } p, k.$$

   (xi)   Priority Structure.

   (a)   Priority Level 1.   The first priority is accorded to prohibition of multiples of projects, to achieve self-sufficiency and to prevent congestion of certain areas.   Therefore, the first priority is to minimize the positive deviation from the desirable acceptance of each project; to minimize the overachievement of the desired level of production to meet at least local consumption of produce; and to minimize the overachievement of the maximum tolerable capacities for the regions, thus:

$$P_1 \left[\sum_{p=1}^{r} d_p^+ + \sum_{i=1}^{e} d_{s+i}^- + \sum_{j=1}^{m} d_{t+j}^+ \right] \tag{7.40}$$

(b)   Priority Level 2.   The second priority is to minimize the under-achievement of the desired levels of employment and income distribution for the country, thus:

$$P_2 \left[d_{r+1}^- + d_{r+2}^- + d_{r+3}^- \right] \tag{7.41}$$

(c)   Priority Level 3.   The third priority is to minimize the under-achievement of the desired number of projects which are considered under the identified priority areas for investment promotion and as such, they are preferred over the other projects. Also, of third priority is the minimization of the negative deviation from the preference over indispensable projects, thus:

$$P_3 \left[d_{r+4}^- + \sum_{g=1}^{h} d_{u+g}^- \right] \tag{7.42}$$

(d)   Priority Level 4.   The fourth priority is to minimize the under-achievement of the desired number of export-oriented projects to be promoted, thus: $P_4 \, d_{r+5}^-$.

The pulp and paper industry of Thailand is taken as the case application of the model.   The said industry covers a wide range of activities relating to pulp and paper production that it necessitates the limitation of the scope. The analysis is therefore restricted to only five product types: pulp, printing and writing paper, industrial use paper, sanitary paper, and others.

The following subscripts are used: i = 1, 2, 3, 4, and 5 for pulp, printing and writing paper, industrial use paper, sanitary paper, and others respectively; j = 1, 2, 3, 4, 5, 6, and 7 for the regions of Bangkok, Samut Prakan, Samut Sakorn, Pathumthani, Nakhon Pathom, Nontaburi, and "rest of Thailand", respectively.

Discussion of Results - Phase 1.

A total of eight computer runs were made on the described GP model of four goals, two absolute constraints and thirty-five variables.   Each of the first five runs was based on alternative priority structures.   The first case run employed the priority structure developed for the initial formulation of the model.   The summary of the "satisficing" values of the decision variables appear in Table 7.6.

Based on the initial formulation, the preferred areas for investment promotion for pulp are "rest of Thailand" being the most attractive over

Nakhon Pathom and Pathumthani. Apart from being labor-intensive, causing pulp firms to be located outside the metropolitan area for income distribution reasons, raw materials for pulp production are easily obtainable in the "rest of Thailand" areas.

For printing and writing paper, the most preferred is Pathumthani, with Bangkok also more preferred than Nontaburi. For industrial use paper, the most favored is Samut Sakorn and Samut Prakan being slightly favored over the "rest of Thailand". Only Bangkok is desirable for sanitary paper, while for other types, Samut Prakan is highly favorable.

The export and income distribution to the "rest of Thailand" goals were over-achieved which is desirable for national development. The two other goals of total employment generation and income distribution in the urban areas were also achieved. The identified priority areas for investment promotion also guarantee that local production meets local consumption or demand for pulp and paper products and the prevention or minimization of congestion of certain areas.

The optimum solution obtained is influenced considerably by the priority structure used. By altering the priorities to reflect emphasis on different goals, alternative optimal solutions can be obtained, reflecting the different priority areas preferred for investment promotion. Aside from the base model, seven other cases were run and their results are shown in Table 7.6. These cases vary only in their priority structure or in local consumption from the base run (Case 1):

Case 1 : Initial formulation.

Case 2 : $P_1(d_2^-)$, $P_2(d_1^-)$, $P_3(d_3^- + d_4^-)$.

Case 3 : $P_1(d_2^- + d_3^- + d_4^-)$, $P_2(d_1^-)$.

Case 4 : $P_1(d_3^- + d_4^-)$, $P_2(d_1^- + d_2^-)$.

Case 5 : $P_1(d_3^- + d_4^-)$, $P_2(d_2^-)$, $P_3(d_1^-)$.

Case 6 : 10 percent increase in local consumption and tolerable production in certain areas.

Case 7 : 15 percent increase in local consumption and maximum tolerable production in certain areas.

Case 8 : 20 percent increase in local consumption and tolerable production in certain areas.

Rather than a binding decision, the results of the first phase GP model can be used as a useful aid in the decision making process, that is, identifying priority areas for investment promotion. As it was, the areas identified by the model are those which best satisfy the multiple goals of the planners.

Table 7.6 Results of the GP Model for Identifying
Priority Areas for Investment Promotion

Unit : Tons

Type of Paper	Region	Spatial Distribution of Pulp and Paper Industrial Activities							
		Alternative Priority Structures					Changed Target Values		
		Case 1	Case 2	Case 3	Case 4	Case 5	Case 6	Case 6	Case 7
Pulp	Bangkok								
	Samut Prakan								123,910
	Samut Sakorn								
	Pathumthani	9,567	36,800		9,576	36,800	40,480	20,160	44,160
	Nakhon Pathom	28,800	28,800	7,454	28,800	28,800			34,560
	Nontaburi								5,016
	Rest of Thailand	174,143	163,105	130,225	183,346	72,080	157,906	139,531	
Printing and Writing	Bangkok	23,675	25,555	24,399	25,555		38,720	40,480	32,685
	Samut Prakan		25,344				17,269		
	Samut Sakorn					28,167			
	Pathumthani	27,224		36,800	27,224				
	Nakhon Pathom								
	Nontaburi	10,300	10,300		8,420	10,300	11,330	11,845	3,069
	Rest of Thailand					22,731		18,054	37,685
Industrial	Bangkok								
	Samut Prakan	84,384	62,498	52,050	84,475	50,829	77,020	91,146	7,250
	Samut Sakorn	104,086	120,300	120,300	120,300	92,133	132,330	138,345	144,360
	Pathumthani							22,160	
	Nakhon Pathom						31,680	33,120	
	Nontaburi								
	Rest of Thailand	59,157	64,829	97,349	42,852	132,488	31,360		145,542
Sanitary Paper	Bangkok	11,525		9,645	9,645	9,663			9,555
	Samut Prakan		11,525			1,862	25,941	34,549	
	Samut Sakorn								
	Pathumthani								
	Nakhon Pathom								
	Nontaburi				1,880				4,275
	Rest of Thailand			1,880					
Others	Bangkok								
	Samut Prakan	24,916	21,457	40,524	24,825	56,609			
	Samut Sakorn								
	Pathumthani								
	Nakhon Pathom								
	Nontaburi								
	Rest of Thailand			5,725			11,013	11,514	12,014

Table 7.7   Results of the GP Model for Selection of Project to be Accorded Promoted Status

Project Number	Product Description	Project Acceptance Level							
		Alternative Priority Structure						Changed Target Values	
		Case 1	Case 2	Case 3	Case 4	Case 5	Case 6	Case 7	Case 8
1	Printing & Writing	1	1	1	1	1	1	1	1
2	Printing & Writing	1	1	1	1	1	1	1	1
3	Industrial Use	1	1	1	1	1	1	1	1
4	Industrial Use	1	1	1	1	1	1	1	1
5	Industrial Use	1	1	1	1	1	1	1	1
6	Printing & Writing; Industrial Use	1	1	1	1	1	1	1	1
7	Industrial Use	0	0	0	0	1	1	0	0
8	Sanitary	1	1	1	1	1	1	1	1
9	Sanitary	1	1	1	1	1	1	1	1
10	Industrial Use; Pulp	1	1	1	1	1	1	1	1
11	Industrial Use	1	1	1	1	1	1	1	1
12	Pulp	1	1	1	1	1	1	1	1
13	Pulp	1	1	1	1	1	1	1	1
14	Pulp	1	1	1	1	1	1	1	1
15	Pulp	1	1	1	1	1	1	1	1

In actuality, the planners have difficulty in deciding which areas are to be accorded priority status because of the multiplicity of national objectives to be met, which are often conflicting. They usually make feasibility studies for this decision process, but proves to be a very tedious task. This area-by-area analysis oftentimes fails to assess the full range of impact of selected areas to the accomplishment of national goals. In this regard, the GP model is perceived as a significant guideline in the process of identifying priority areas for investment promotion. These results are used as part of the basis for the development of phase 2, that is, the selection of projects to be promoted.

Discussion of Results - Phase 2.

Examination of the results summarized in Table 7.7 indicates that for the initial formulation of the project selection model, Case 1, 14 out of 15 projects have the attainable acceptance level of unity (1.00). Only project no.7, involved in industrial use paper, is rejected.

Goals with priority levels 2 and 4 were achieved. The over or under-achievement of some goals were favorable. However, for priority level 1, it is undesirable that the self-sufficiency goal, that is, for local production to meet at least the local consumption or demand for pulp and paper products was underachieved by 38,982 tons, and the noncongestion goal was overachieved by 65,034 tons. Priority level 3 dealing with employment and income distribution goals was underachieved by 2,569 workers and US$180,944, respectively, and likewise are undesirable.

Several cases were tried by either varying the priority structure or by changing target values of goals. Although under and overachievements of goals vary, the results were consistently in favor of accepting all the projects except for project no.7.

7.4 A CASE OF ASEAN PREFERENTIAL TRADE TARIFF ARRANGEMENTS

Less developed countries have come to realize that if they were to attain rapid economic growth, they must minimize reliance on more developed countries. Self-reliance on a regional basis, being less expensive, has become an accepted alternative. Furthermore, cooperation among less developed countries, as exemplified by the Central American Common Market (CACM), has led to expansion of exports and increase in gross domestic products among member countries.

Three interrelated techniques for cooperation have recently been applied to countries comprising the Association of Southeast Asian Nations (ASEAN), namely, Indonesia, Malaysia, Philippines, Singapore and Thailand (Note: The sixth country Brunei became a member after the study was made). These techniques are discussed as follows:

(a) Selective trade liberalization - to enable individual countries to reap the advantages associated with the exchange of commodities in which they have comparative advantage, to allow a movement towards specialization within each country and ensure balanced trade among the countries;

(b) Complementarity agreements - to prepare schemes of specialization for the manufacturing of different products and their subsequent exchange; and

(c) Package deal agreements - to establish large scale industrial projects.

The Preferential Tariff Arrangement (PTA) is a tool by which schemes (a) and (b) above are implemented. Presently, the PTA provides for: (i) voluntary giving of tariff preferences to each other within the region, and (ii) negotiations on preferences which member countries may like to have.

The impact of (i) has so far been minimal because ASEAN members normally voluntarily offer a 10 per cent tariff cut on the import of a particular commodity in which they have little competition. The second, (ii), includes an agreement called the 'first refusals principle' for the basic commodities of rice and crude oil. This stipulates that in time of emergencies (including gluts and shortages), the exportable supply of countries with surpluses must first be offered to buyers within the region and, alternatively, the unsatisfied demand of member countries must first be sought from supplier countries in the region. This scheme has so far been satisfactory for everyone and leads to greater security of supply and demand and expansion of trade among the ASEAN countries.

Trade expansion within ASEAN has a great potential and can be achieved by redirecting ASEAN imports from non-ASEAN sources to intra-ASEAN trade. For example, for the commodity sugar (falling under the 3-digit Standard International Trade Classification) in a recent year, minimal intra-Asean trade occurred despite the fact that Philippines and Thailand were fourth and fifth, respectively, of the world's largest exporters while Malaysia and Singapore ranked the world's major importers. This is one of the reasons why this particular commodity was chosen for the model application. Another is that despite various international sugar agreements, sugar prices have remained one of the most unstable among primary commodity prices. Thus, this application can be considered as an attempt to utilize an ASEAN joint approach towards stabilization of sugar prices and, to a certain extent, of export earnings.

7.4.1   MODEL FORMULATION

This model was developed by Tabucanon and Acio (1982) which took off from
the works of Waverman (1972) and Ramanathan (1979).   While Waverman deals with
border flows of natural gas between U.S. and Canada, Ramanathan applies a model
similar to Waverman's to the five ASEAN member countries.   In both models, the
costs involved in transporting a commodity, given a set of routes available for
the product distribution, are minimized.

A basic structural change is effected by considering not only the cost-
minimizing objective of the importing countries, but also the revenue-maximizing objective of the exporting countries.   This is done to render the model
fair to the exporting members.   With this change, the problem ceases to be a
transportation model of the standard form.

This Preferential Tariff Determination Model seeks to arrive at a set of
differential tariffs that must be levied by the ASEAN countries in order that
the inherent advantage of non-ASEAN over ASEAN buyers and suppliers for a
particular commodity will be eliminated.   The notations used in the model are
as follows:

m : number of countries within ASEAN with a surplus of the commodity;

n : number of countries/regions outside of ASEAN with a surplus;

p : number of countries with ASEAN with a deficit of the commodity;

q : number of countries/regions outside of ASEAN with a deficit;

d_j : excess of consumption over production in country/region j, or demand
           for imports in j;

s_i : excess of production over consumption in country/region i, or supply
           available for export in i;

f_{ij} : per unit f.o.b. price charged by country i to country j;

c_{ij} : per unit c.i.f. prices paid by country j for its purchases, includ-
           ing transportation costs;

x_{ij} : units of commodity to be transferred from country i to country j.

Two sets of equations, one representing 'unconstrained trade' and the
other, 'preferential trade', are derived. In unconstrained trade, market forces
are left to operate and to determine (a) from which regions ASEAN members'
deficits are to be obtained and (b) to which regions ASEAN members' surpluses
are to be sold.   In preferential trade, additional restrictions force intra-
ASEAN trade.   Only when intra-regional demand is satisfied or intra-regional
surplus exhausted, extra-ASEAN trade is considered.   In both cases, the
objective function remains the same.

(i)   Objective function

For all cases, the objective function involves the minimization of costs, (a), for the p ASEAN buyer countries, and maximization of revenue, (b) of the m ASEAN supplier countries. Thus,

$$\text{Min.} \quad a_1 = \sum_{i=1}^{m+n} c_{i1}x_{i1}, \tag{7.43}$$

$$a_2 = \sum_{i=1}^{m+n} c_{i2}x_{i2},$$

$$\vdots \qquad \vdots$$

$$a_p = \sum_{i=1}^{m+n} c_{ip}x_{ip}.$$

$$\text{Max.} \quad b_1 = \sum_{j=1}^{p+q} f_{1j}x_{1j}, \tag{7.44}$$

$$b_2 = \sum_{j=1}^{p+q} f_{2j}x_{2j},$$

$$\vdots \qquad \vdots$$

$$b_m = \sum_{j=1}^{p+q} f_{mj}x_{mj}.$$

Weighting and combining these objectives into a single objective function yields the following:

$$\text{Max.} \quad Z = \sum_{i=1}^{m} w_i b_i - \sum_{j=1}^{p} w_j a_j \tag{7.45}$$

where w_i and w_j are both greater than zero. Furthermore

$$\sum_{i=1}^{m} w_i + \sum_{j=1}^{p} w_j = 1$$

Eq. (7.45) can be interpreted as treating proceeds of sales as inflows and purchases as outflows. This becomes more evident as (7.43) and (7.44) are plugged in (7.45) and the following manipulations are carried out:

$$\text{Max.} \quad Z = \sum_{i=1}^{m} w_i \sum_{j=1}^{p+q} f_{ij} x_{ij} - \sum_{j=1}^{p} w_j \sum_{i=1}^{m+n} c_{ij} x_{ij}, \tag{7.46}$$

$$\text{or,} \quad Z = \left[\sum_{i=1}^{m} w_i \left(\sum_{j=1}^{p} f_{ij} x_{ij} + \sum_{j=p+1}^{p+q} f_{ij} x_{ij} \right) \right]$$

$$- \left[\sum_{j=1}^{p} w_j \left(\sum_{j=1}^{m} c_{ij} x_{ij} + \sum_{j=m+1}^{m+n} c_{ij} x_{ij} \right) \right] \tag{7.47}$$

so,

$$Z = \left[\sum_{i=1}^{m} \sum_{j=p+1}^{p+q} w_i f_{ij} x_{ij} \right] + \left[\sum_{i=1}^{m} \sum_{j=1}^{p} (w_i f_{ij} - w_j c_{ij}) x_{ij} \right]$$

$$- \left[\sum_{i=m+1}^{m+n} \sum_{j=1}^{p} w_j c_{ij} x_{ij} \right] \tag{7.48}$$

The terms in the first pair of brackets in (7.48) represent the revenue inflow to the region whenever the m countries of ASEAN with excess supply of the product ship to any of the q deficit countries outside of the region. The second set of terms, similarly, represents revenue inflow involved in intra-ASEAN transfers of the particular commodity. The third set is a negative quantity representing the outflow of purchase money whenever ASEAN deficit countries obtain their supplies from sources outside of the region. Taken as a whole, the objective function maximizes the weighted net revenue inflow to the region resulting from commodity transfers.

In the course of model application, equal weights have been assigned to each of the member countries to render it acceptable to all. However, manipulation of these weights provides a tool by which benefits or losses accruing to a particular member can be adjusted through relative weightings of the cost-minimizing and revenue-maximizing objectives.

(ii)   Constraints: 'Unconstrained' trade.

The objective function (7.48) is subject to the following constraints:

(a)   that the demand in the region must at least be met by the various regional and extra-regional sources;

$$\sum_{i=1}^{m+n} x_{ij} \geq d_j, \qquad\qquad j = 1, 2, \ldots, p; \qquad\qquad (7.49)$$

(b)   that quantities of the product exported by ASEAN does not exceed the demand of the various extra-regional buyers:

$$\sum_{i=1}^{m} x_{ij} \leq d_j, \qquad\qquad j = p + 1, p + 2, \ldots, p+q; \qquad (7.50)$$

(c)   that the total quantity allocated to various destinations does not exceed the available supply in ASEAN

$$\sum_{j=1}^{p+q} x_{ij} \leq s_i, \qquad\qquad i = 1, 2, \ldots, m; \qquad\qquad (7.51)$$

(d)   that the quantity of the product allocated to ASEAN from extra-regional sources does not exceed what is available:

$$\sum_{j=1}^{p} x_{ij} \leq s_i, \qquad\qquad i = m+1, m+2, \ldots, m+n, \qquad (7.52)$$

(e)   that quantity transfers are not allowed to be negative

$$x_{ij} \geq 0, \qquad\qquad i = 1, 2, \ldots, m, m+1, \ldots, m+n,$$
$$j = 1, 2, \ldots, p, p+1, \ldots, p+q.$$

(iii) Constraints: Preferential trade.

Two types of the preferential trade model are included here, one for the case of a surplus, and the other, for shortage.   For the case of a surplus, (7.49) is changed to:

$$\sum_{i=1}^{m} x_{ij} \geq d_j, \qquad\qquad j = 1, 2, \ldots, p \qquad\qquad (7.53)$$

with the other equations remaining the same.   This constraint comes as a result of giving priority for ASEAN suppliers to get rid of their surplus.   Thus, demands within the region are satisfied internally.

In case of shortage, (7.51) is changed to

$$\sum_{j=1}^{p} x_{ij} \leq s_i, \qquad\qquad i = 1, 2, \ldots, m. \qquad\qquad (7.54)$$

(iv) Derivation of the Preferential Tariff.

Let u_j, r_i and t_i be the dual variables corresponding to constraints (a) to (d), respectively, whether for unconstrained or preferential trade. Dual variables u_j and v_j can be interpreted as the shadow price per unit product in market j, r_i and t_i as the shadow value of a unit of supply in supplier i market.

The dual of the Unconstrained Trade Case model (with constraints defined by (7.49) to (7.52) is as follows:

$$\text{Min.} \quad Y = \sum_{i=1}^{m} r_i s_i + \sum_{i=m+1}^{m+n} t_i s_i - \sum_{j=1}^{p} u_j d_j + \sum_{j=p+1}^{p+q} v_j d_j \qquad (7.55)$$

$$\text{S.t.} \quad r_i + v_j \geq w_i f_{ij}, \qquad\qquad \begin{array}{l} i = 1, 2, \ldots, m, \\ j = p+1, p+2, \ldots, p+q, \end{array} \qquad (7.56)$$

$$r_i - u_j \geq w_i f_{ij} - w_j c_{ij}, \qquad i = 1, 2, \ldots, p, \qquad (7.57)$$

$$t_i - u_j \geq - w_j c_{ij}, \qquad\qquad \begin{array}{l} i = m+1, m+2, \ldots, m+n, \\ j = 1, 2, \ldots, p. \end{array} \qquad (7.58)$$

The objective function of the dual formulation above, (7.55) minimizes the outlay involved in extra-regional transactions. Thus, the total imputed value of supply (first and second terms) is deducted by the amount imputed to ASEAN demand (third term) then added to the imputed value of demand by non-member states (fourth term). The significance of the dual constraints is given below.

Rearranging (7.56) yields $v_j \geq w_i f_{ij} - r_i$. The right hand side can be looked upon as the weighted profit of the ith ASEAN supplier wherein the weighted f.o.b. value offered by ASEAN to extra-regional buyer j is deducted by the product shadow value in the supplier i market. This constraint thus prevents such profit from going above the shadow value price in extra-regional market j.

When the signs are reversed, (7.57) appears as $u_j - r_i \leq w_j c_{ij} - w_i f_{ij}$. Since c_{ij} and f_{ij} are the c.i.f. and f.o.b. prices, respectively, the right-hand side stands for the weighted transportation cost involved in commodity transfers among the ASEAN members. The excess of the shadow price offered in ASEAN market j over the shadow value in ASEAN supplier i must not exceed this transportation cost.

Eq. (7.58) is equivalent to $u_j - t_i \leq w_j c_{ij}$ which says that the excess of the shadow price in the jth ASEAN market over the shadow value of the commodity in the ith extra-regional source must not be greater than the amount that the ASEAN buyer pays for the product.

Under preferential trading, a similar set of dual variables is obtained. Since the two cases have identical number of constraints, the dual variables can be compared. It must be remembered that equality prevails whenever trade between i and j actually exist or may be included in the optimal plan.

Under unconstrained trade, an extra-regional supplier may be satisfying intra-regional demand. Thus, from (7.58),

$$t_i - u_j = - w_j c_{ij}, \qquad \begin{array}{l} i = m+1, \ m+2, \ \ldots, \ m+n, \\ j = 1, \ 2, \ \ldots, \ p. \end{array} \qquad (7.59)$$

However, under conditions of preferential trade and assuming a surplus (denoted by a prime symbol below), this particular extra-regional supplier will be replaced by an ASEAN supplier. Thus,

$$r'_i - u'_j = w_i f'_{ij} - w_j c'_{ij}, \qquad \begin{array}{l} i = 1, \ 2, \ \ldots, \ m, \\ j = 1, \ 2, \ \ldots, \ p. \end{array} \qquad (7.60)$$

Subtracting (7.60) from (7.59) gives

$$(t_i - r'_i) + (u'_j - u_j) = - w_i c_{ij} - (w_i f'_{ij} - w_j c'_{ij}).$$

Rearranging:

$$u'_j - u_j = (w_j c'_{ij}) + (r'_i - t_i) - w_i f'_{ij}. \qquad (7.61)$$

Thus, the difference between the shadow prices in ASEAN market j under conditions of unconstrained and preferential trade $(u'_j - u_j)$ is equal to the weighted amount by which c.i.f. prices paid for goods taken from within ASEAN is higher than that taken from the extra-regional supplier (first term), plus the excess of the shadow value of supply in ASEAN over that in the extra-regional market (second term), all deducted by the weighted f.o.b. price (third term), a factor which accounts for earnings of ASEAN suppliers in intra-ASEAN commodity transfers. In more general terms, the difference in the shadow prices of a given commodity when trade patterns are left to operate by themselves from that when certain regional preferential arrangements are made, constitutes the weighted advantage that the non-regional supplier has over the regional supplier. A way by which this advantage could be removed is the imposition of tariff amounting to $(u'_j - u_j)/w_j$ on the extra-regional supplier. Alternatively, a tariff cut of this amount on the regional supplier could be granted by the ASEAN buyer.

Conditions of glut or surplus bring about the situation of sellers competing for the same market. Shortage, on the other hand, finds many competing buyers for a given supply of commodity. A derivation parallel to the one made above is developed for a shortage situation.

When a shortage prevails (denoted by the double prime symbol), ASEAN countries with excess supply ship only to fellow ASEAN members with shortages:

$$r''_i - u''_j = (w_i f''_{ij} - w_j c''_{ij}), \qquad i = 1, 2, \ldots, m, \qquad (7.62)$$
$$j = 1, 2, \ldots, p.$$

Under unconstrained trade, these supplies may have been due to be shipped to non-regional buyers:

$$r_i + v_j = w_i f_{ij}, \qquad i = 1, 2, \ldots, m, \qquad (7.63)$$
$$j = p+1, p+2, \ldots, p+q.$$

Subtracting (7.62) from (7.63) yields

$$(r_i - r''_i) + (v_j + u''_j) = w_i f_{ij} - (w_i f''_{ij} - w_j c''_{ij}).$$

Transposing and regrouping terms give

$$r_i - r''_i = [w_i f_{ij} - v_j] - [u''_j - (w_j c''_{ij} - w_i f''_{ij})]. \qquad (7.64)$$

The terms in the first pair of brackets represents the excess of the f.o.b. price charged by ASEAN over the shadow value of the product in the jth extra-regional buyer's market. The second, set under conditions of constrained trade, deducts from the first whatever part of the shadow price in the jth ASEAN market is unaccounted for the transportation costs involved in the intra-ASEAN transfers. Thus, the right-hand side can be seen as the weighted advantage that the extra-regional buyer enjoys over the regional buyer when shortage prevails.

Therefore, in case of shortage, extra-regional buyers must be imposed a tariff of the amount $(r''_i - r_i)/w_i$ to remove their purchasing advantage and thus allocate all regional supplies available to the regional buyers.

As in the case of surplus, where feasible, a reduction of existing tariffs by this amount on regional buyers presents another course of action.

7.4.2 MODEL APPLICATION: THE CASE OF THE COMMODITY SUGAR

Using the processed data presented in Tables 7.8 to 7.12, the problem is set up for solution, where for every x_{ij},

Table 7.8   Forecast of ASEAN Supply and Demand
for Sugar (thousand metric tons)[*]

Country	Demand	Supply	(Deficit)/Surplus
Indonesia	1632	1471.5	(160.5)
Malaysia	420	80.0	(340.0)
Philippines	1100	3000.0	1900.0
Singapore	117	110.0	(7.0)
Thailand	820	2500.0	1680.0

[*] Forecasts for 1980 validated with regression analysis of data
presented in UN Statistical Yearbook for Asia and the Pacific (1977).
Observe that a regional surplus is forecasted for 1980.

Table 7.9   Projected F.O.B. Prices for Sugar
(U.S. dollars per ton)[*]

Philippines	250.8
Thailand	221.7

[*] From Philippine Foreign Trade Statistics (1978) and Foreign Trade
Statistics of Thailand (1975).
   Prices adjusted for 1980 through the use of price indices presented
in Drysdale (1978).

Table 7.10   Projected C.I.F. Prices for Sugar
(U.S. dollars per ton)[*]

From (i) \ To (j)	Indonesia (1)	Malaysia (2)	Singapore (3)
Philippines (1)	282.6	233.6	310.3
Thailand (2)	359.0	239.6	251.2
Australia (3)	353.7	129.5	340.6
France (4)	312.2	109.8	218.3
Germany (5)	355.9	441.4	128.3
India (6)	156.7	106.4	126.2
Others (7)	297.5	129.5	335.0

[*] From UN Yearbook of International Trade Statistics (1974, 1975,
1976), Philippine Foreign Trade Statistics (1978) and Foreign Trade
Statistics of Thailand (1975).
   Prices adjusted as in Table 7.9.

Table 7.11   Projected demand for ASEAN Sugar,
1980 (in metric tons)[*]

Buyer	Full Amount	Partial	
		% of full amount	Amount
Japan	2741	25	685.25
OPEC	1441	10	144.1
UK	1898	5	94.9
US	5700	20	1140.0
Others	22207	13	2886.91
Total	33987		4951.19

[*] From Council on International Economic Policy (1975) and US Department of Agriculture (1978).

In the second source scenarios for 7, 15 and 23 cents per pound were given. Tables above are for the 15 cents per pound (330 dollars per ton) scenario. Since world supply exceeds world demand, a glut is being forecast for this scenario.

Under full amount, all the world exporters' products are assumed to enter the open market and thus are fully available for ASEAN purchases while the world's importers can get the whole amount of their deficits from ASEAN suppliers.

Under partial amount, only a percentage of the full amount is the maximum that can be bought by ASEAN importers from and sold by ASEAN exporters to various extra-regional markets. Percentages have been based on the average of past years' (1975, 1976) trade of extra-regional markets with ASEAN. Thus assumption rises from the fact that numerous extra-regional exporting and importing countries of the product sugar have preferential trading arrangements with a number of countries, particularly their respective political allies.

Table 7.12   Projected Supply Available for ASEAN
Purchases, 1980 (in metric tons)[*]

Supplier	Full Amount	Partial	
		% of full amount	Amount
Australia	2764	10.0	276.4
France	1544	0.5	7.72
Germany	727	1.0	7.27
India	25	2.5	6.25
Others	35218	5.0	1760.9
Total	40278		2058.54

[*] See footnote (a) under Table 7.11.

$i = 1$ refers to   Philippines, $j = 1$ refers to   Indonesia,

$i = 2$ Thailand, $j = 2$ Malaysia,

$i = 3$ Australia, $j = 3$ Singapore,

$i = 4$ France, $j = 4$ Japan,

$i = 5$ Germany, $j = 5$ OPEC,

$i = 6$ India, $j = 6$ UK,

$i = 7$ Others, $j = 7$ US,

                                     $j = 8$ Others.

The objective function is formulated as follows.   For the exporting ASEAN countries, maximize revenue:

$$\text{Max.} \quad b_1 = 250.8 \, [x_{11} + x_{12} + x_{13} + x_{14} + x_{15}$$
$$+ x_{16} + x_{17} + x_{18}], \qquad \text{(Philippines)}$$

$$b_2 = 221.7 \, [x_{21} + x_{22} + x_{23} + x_{24} + x_{25}$$
$$+ x_{26} + x_{27} + x_{28}], \qquad \text{(Thailand)}$$

Minimize costs for the ASEAN importers:

$$\text{Min.} \quad a_1 = 282.6x_{11} + 359x_{21} + 312.2x_{41}, \qquad \text{(Indonesia)}$$

$$a_2 = 233.6x_{12} + 239.6x_{22} + 129.5x_{32} + 109.8x_{42}$$
$$+ 441.4x_{52} + 106.4x_{62} + 129.5 \, x_{72} \quad \text{(Malaysia)}$$

$$a_3 = 310.3x_{13} + 251.2x_{23} + 340.6x_{33} + 218.3x_{53}$$
$$+ 126.2x_{63} + 335x_{73}. \qquad \text{(Malaysia)}$$

Applying a weighting factor of 0.2 (such that $w_i = w_j$) and simplifying the unified objective function yields the following:

$$\text{Max.} \quad Z = - \, 6.36x_{11} + 3.44x_{12} - 11.9x_{13}$$
$$+ 50.16 \, [x_{14} + x_{15} + x_{16} + x_{17} + x_{18}] - 27.46x_{21}$$
$$- 3.58x_{22} - 5.9x_{23} + 44.34[x_{24} + x_{25} + x_{26} + x_{27}$$
$$+ x_{28}] - 70.74x_{31} - 25.9x_{32} - 68.12x_{33} - 62.44x_{41}$$
$$- 21.96x_{42} - 44.36x_{13} - 71.18x_{51} - 88.28x_{52} - 25.66x_{53}$$
$$- 31.34x_{61} - 21.24x_{62} - 25.24x_{63} - 59.5x_{71} - 25.9x_{72}$$
$$- 67x_{73}$$

This objective function is subject to the following constraints.

Regional demands:

Indonesia	$x_{11} + x_{21} + x_{31} + x_{41} + x_{51} + x_{61} + x_{71} \geq$	160.5,
Malaysia	$x_{12} + x_{22} + x_{32} + x_{42} + x_{52} + x_{62} + x_{72} \geq$	340,
Singapore	$x_{13} + x_{23} + x_{33} + x_{43} + x_{53} + x_{63} + x_{73} \geq$	7.

Demand of non-ASEAN countries:

Japan	$x_{14} + x_{24} \leq$	2741,
OPEC	$x_{15} + x_{25} \leq$	1441,
UK	$x_{16} + x_{26} \leq$	1898,
US	$x_{17} + x_{27} \leq$	5700,
Rest of the world	$x_{18} + x_{28} \leq$	22207.

Regional Supply:

Philippines	$x_{11} + x_{12} + x_{13} + x_{14} + x_{15} + x_{16} + x_{17} + x_{18} \leq$	1900,
Thailand	$x_{21} + x_{22} + x_{23} + x_{24} + x_{25} + x_{26} + x_{27} + x_{28} \leq$	1680.

Supply from non-ASEAN countries:

Australia	$x_{31} + x_{32} + x_{33} \leq$	2764,
France	$x_{41} + x_{42} + x_{43} \leq$	1544,
Germany	$x_{51} + x_{52} + x_{53} \leq$	727,
India	$x_{61} + x_{62} + x_{63} \leq$	25,
Others	$x_{71} + x_{72} + x_{73} \leq$	35218.

Constraints remain the same for preferential and unconstrained trade except that certain variables are set to zero. In this particular case, where a worldwide and regional glut or surplus occurs, ASEAN buyers are limited to sellers within the region, i.e., $i \leq 2$. Thus, x_{ij} is set to zero for all $i > 2$.

Tables 7.13 and 7.14 show the optimal allocation of ASEAN and extra-regional sugar produce. Note that under conditions of unconstrained trade, the ASEAN buyers obtain their supplies from non-ASEAN sources while ASEAN sellers supply the regions with the highest demands first. Under preferential trade, intra-regional trade is intensified at the same time that total ASEAN trade volume is restricted.

Because of the preferential trade restriction that in times of surplus, the regional buyers must first absorb regional supplies before resorting to outside sources, penalty costs are incurred by regional buyers. Regional loss due to the preferential trading arrangement can be seen in Table 7.15. Losses per member country are computed by multiplying the volume of product diverted from the cheaper extra-regional source to the regional supplier by the difference in c.i.f. prices. Results are shown in Table 7.16.

Table 7.13 Optimal Allocation of ASEAN Sugar (in metric tons) under Unconstrained and Preferential Trade, Full Amount Conditions

From	Indonesia U*	Indonesia P*	Malaysia U	Malaysia P	Singapore U	Singapore P	Japan U	Japan P	OPEC U	OPEC P	UK U	UK P	US U	US P	Others U	Others P	Total U	Total P	Total supply available
Philippines	135.5	160.5	0	340									1764.5	1399.5			1900	1900	1900
Thailand						7					1680	1673					1680	1680	1680
Australia			340	0													340	0	2764
France					7	0											7	0	1544
Germany																			727
India	25	0															25	0	25
Others																			35218
Total	160.5	160.5	340	340	7	7	0	0	0	0	1680	1673	1764.5	1399.5	0	0	3952	3580	43858
Total demand to be satisfied	160.5		340		7		2741		1441		1898		5700		22207		34494.5		

* U stands for uncontrained, P for preferential

Table 7.14 Optimal Allocation of ASEAN Sugar (in metric tons) under Unconstrained and Preferential Trade, Partial Amount Conditions

From	Indonesia U	Indonesia P	Malaysia U	Malaysia P	Singapore U	Singapore P	Japan U	Japan P	OPEC U	OPEC P	UK U	UK P	US U	US P	Others U	Others P	Total U	Total P	Total supply available
Philippines	154.25	160.5	0	340	0	7	301	0	144.1	144.1	94.9	94.9	1140	1140	65.75	13.5	1900	1900	1900
Thailand															1680	1680	1680	1680	1680
Australia																	0	0	276.4
France			7.7	0													7.7	0	7.72
Germany					7	0											7	0	7.27
India	6.25	0															6.25	0	6.25
Others			332.3	0													332.3	0	1760.9
Total	160.5	160.5	340	340	7	7	301	0	144.1	144.1	94.9	94.9	1140	1140	1745.75	1693.5	3933.25	3580	5638.54
Total demand to be satisfied	160.5		340		7		685.25		144.1		94.9		1140		2886.91		5458.66		

Table 7.15 Regional Revenue Inflows
(in U.S. dollars)

Type of Trade	Full Amount	Partial amount
Unconstrained	768536.1	759629.165
Preferential	722436.3	722436.3
Difference	46099.8	37192.865

Table 7.16 Penalty Costs of Preferential Trade
per Regional Buyer (in U.S. dollars)

Country	Full amount	Partial amount
Indonesia	3147.5	786.875
Malaysia	42092.0	35545.69
Singapore	860.3	860.3
Total	46099.8	37192.865

Table 7.17 shows the results of the Preferential Tariff Determination Model. The additional tariff to be levied on the extra-regional sellers to remove their advantage is presented under three tariff conditions that are assumed to prevail within the ASEAN region:

(a) tariffs among members are abolished (column 6);

(b) existing tariffs are reduced by 10% for members (column 7);

(c) tariffs are retained at current existing levels (column 8).

Aside from (b), other conditions can be formulated between the extremes of (a) and (c). For the case of (b), Table 7.17, column 7 shows that except for Indonesia, additional tariffs have to mean that a 10% uniform tariff cut for sugar, if offered by Malaysia and Singapore to Philippines and Thailand (say, as a part of the quarterly quinpartite negotiation) would not suffice to keep extra-regional supplies out of the region.

Table 7.17   Schedule of Preferential Tariffs Prescribed for 1980

(in dollars per ton)

Conditions	Country	Dual variables			Tariff	
		Unconstrained (1)	Preferential (2)	Difference (3)=(2)-(1)	Prescribed* (4)=(3)/0.2	Existing+ (5)
Full	Indonesia	56.52	56.52	0	0	150.5
amount	Malaysia	21.96	46.72	24.76	123.8	94.91
	Singapore	25.66	50.24	24.58	122.9	123.42
Partial	Indonesia	56.52	56.52	0	0	150.5
amount	Malaysia	25.9	46.72	20.82	104.1	94.91
	Singapore	25.66	50.24	24.58	122.9	123.42

Conditions	Country	Additional tariff on outside sellers		
		Assume tariffs within ASEAN abolished (6)=(5)-(4)	Tariff within ASEAN reduced by 10% (7)=(4)-0.1X(5)	Tariffs within ASEAN retained (7)=(4)
Full	Indonesia	0	0	0
amount	Malaysia	28.89	114.3	123.8
	Singapore	0.52	110.59	122.9
Partial	Indonesia	0	0	0
amount	Malaysia	9.19	94.6	104.1
	Singapore	0.52	123.39	122.9

* Weighting factor = 0.2.

+ From International Customs Journal (1979).

7.5 BICRITERION TRANSPORTATION MODELS: A CASE STUDY

This section is divided into two parts. The first part contains a general optimization model for sea transportation of nonperishable single bulk commodity.   The model deals with two objectives from the standpoint of the shipping company, namely, minimization of transportation cost and minimization of opportunity cost.   In the second part, the model is applied to the case of coal transportation from Australia to some of the coal-importing countries in the Asia-Pacific basin.   The models were developed by Tabucanon, Fujiwara and Bhuiyan (1986).

7.5.1. THE MODELS
The following conditions are taken into consideration in the formulation of the model:

(i)   Loaded vessel from a supply port unloads the same amount in one demand port only.

(ii)   In the return voyage, the vessel does not necessarily go back to the same port of the country of origin. It may proceed straight to another port of the same source where its service is demanded. This is because the distances of the different ports of the source country are assumed to be relatively very short as compared to the total distance covered in a route.

(iii) In fulfilling a certain demand, the last trip can be partially loaded.

Model A

$$\text{Minimize:} \quad \sum_r \sum_v C_{rv} N_{rv} \qquad\qquad (7.45)$$

$$\text{Minimize:} \quad \sum_r \sum_v K_v T_{rv} N_{rv} \qquad\qquad (7.46)$$

$$\text{Subject to:} \quad \sum_r T_{rv} N_{rv} \leq T_v \qquad\qquad (7.47)$$

$$\sum_{r \in R^j} \sum_v K_v (N_{rv} - \theta_{rv}) - D_j \qquad \text{for each } j \qquad (7.48)$$

$$\sum_{r \in R_i} \sum_v K_v (N_{rv} - \theta_{rv}) \leq S_j \qquad \text{for each } i \qquad (7.49)$$

$$\theta_{rv} \leq M N_{rv} \qquad \text{for any } r \text{ and } v \qquad (7.50)$$

$$0 \leq \theta_{rv} \leq 1 \qquad \text{for any } r \text{ and } v$$

$$N_{rv} \geq 0 \quad \text{and are integers}$$

where N_{rv} = number of round trips of vessel v on route r,

C_{rv} = cost of a round trip by vessel v on route r,

T_{rv} = time (in days) required to perform a round trip by vessel v on route r,

K_v = maximum coal carrying capacity (in tons) of vessel v, when bunker is fully loaded,

R^j = the set of all routes to demand port j,

D_j = demand (in tons) of port j,

R_i = the set of all routes from supply port i,

S_i = maximum supply (in tons) of port i,

T_v = number of days vessel v is available in the planning period,

θ_{rv} = faction of vessel v to be empty in route r,

M   = very big number.

In the above model, (7.45) represents minimization of transportation cost, and (7.46) represents the second objective which is minimization of tonnage-days used in fulfilling a certain demand which is considered to be the opportunity cost. It can be observed, however, that in real-life situation the second objective is only necessary when the opportunity cost or tonnage-days is very large. Opportunity costs will be translated to profit. (7.47) is the constraint on availability of vessel in the planning horizon. Equation (7.48) is a demand constraint, which allows partially filled vessel due to the term $\sum_v \theta_{rv}$. Supply constraint (7.49) also takes into account of the partially filled vessels starting from each supply port. Constraint $\theta_{rv} \leq MN_{rv}$ takes into account the situation of $\theta_{rv} = 0$ when $N_{rv} = 0$. The model yields the optimal number of trips of vessel v on the different routes in a planning period so as to minimize, in a compromise fashion, the transportation cost and the opportunity cost in fulfilling the demands.

Model B

Minimize: $\sum_r \sum_v C_{rv} N_{rv}$

Minimize: $\sum_r \sum_v K_v T_{rv} N_{rv}$

Subject to: $\sum_r T_{rv} N_{rv} \leq T_v$ for each v   (7.51)

$\sum_{r \in R^j} \sum_v K_v N_{rv} - \sum_{r \in R^j} S_r^+ = D_j$ for each j   (7.52)

$\sum_{r \in R^j} \sum_v K_v N_{rv} - \sum_{r \in R^j} S_r^+ \leq S_i$ for each i   (7.53)

$0 \leq S_r^+ \leq \sum K_v N_{rv}$ for each r   (7.54)

$N_{rv} \geq 0$ and are integers

where S_r^+ is the amount of dummy supply in route r.

In the above model, constraint (7.51) is the same as (7.47), which is the availability of vessels in the planing horizon. Constraint (7.52) ensures the total supply by all fully and partially loaded vessels in all routes terminating at demand port j, equals the demand of port j. similarly, constraint (7.53) makes sure that total supply in routes starting at supply port i by different vessels is not more than the supply of port i. And constraint (7.54) gives the limitation on dummy supply in each route.

These two models are equivalent in the sense that there exists a natural one-to-one correspondence between the set of all Pareto optimal solutions to Model A and the set of all Pareto optimal solutions to Model B. From the computational standpoint, Model B is better than Model A because the former is smaller in size as shown below.

	Number of Constraints	Number of Variables
Model A	$\|K\| + \|J\| + \|I\| +$ $\|I\|\|J\|\|K\| + \|I\|\|J\|\|K\|$	$\|I\|\|J\|\|K\| + \|I\|\|J\|\|K\|$
Model B	$\|K\| + \|J\| + \|I\| + \|I\|\|J\|$	$\|I\|\|J\|\|K\| + \|I\|\|J\|$

where $\|I\|$, $\|J\|$ and $\|K\|$ are the total number of supply ports, demand ports and distinct vessels, respectively.

The Step Method (STEM) developed by Benayoun, De Montgolfier, Tergny and Laritchev is a very good interactive tool for this bicriterion problem. In this approach, the role of the decision maker is needed throughout the process. In order to relieve the decision maker from too much direct involvement in the procedure, a parametric approach can be used. In this approach, the analyst derives all or a subset of the efficient solutions. The decision maker then selects one among these efficient solutions. The decision maker's role therefore comes a posteriori. The parametric approach is in fact a result of trying to systematize the decision maker's judgments in the interactive approach.

In the application of the models in this section, due to the in availability of a real-life decision maker, the STEM is adapted and modified from an interactive procedure to that of a parametric one. This is done by merely systematizing the relaxations in the decision making phase. The result is, therefore, an enumeration of a set of efficient solutions for the decision maker to select.

7.5.2. APPLICATION OF THE MODEL

The model developed is applied here to the problem of assigning ten existing bulk carriers of a shipping company to supply coal from six existing coal supply ports in Australia to five demand ports - one each in the countries of Malaysia, Thailand, Japan, Korea and Taiwan. The draft (meaning the depth

at which the bottom of the vessel is submerged when fully loaded) restrictions
of the vessels and the depths of different ports are listed in Table 7.18.

Supply port Bowen is too shallow for the bulk carriers. Also, vessels
Curtis and Carpentaria have drafts more than the depth of all ports under
consideration. Considering the draft restrictions of the vessels and the depth
of different ports, the feasible routes for different vessels available can be
reduced, as shown in Fig. 7.6 and Table 7.19.

Table 7.18   Depth and Draft of Different Ports and Vessels

Port	Name of the port	Depth (m)	Name of the vessels	Draft (m)
Supply	Bowen, Old Gladstone, Old Haypoint, Old Newcastle, NSW Sydney, NSW Kembala, NSW	6.40 11.58 16.76 11.00 16.00 11.00	Sturt Kestrel Capricon Kerry Cumberland Curtis	13.56 14.76 11.15 11.36 10.69 17.02
Demand	Malaysia Thailand Japan Korea Taiwan	14.00 13.00 18.00 16.50 17.00	Carpentaria Hunter Somersby Shortland	17.02 12.59 14.79 15.024

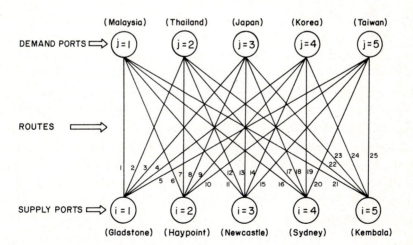

Fig. 7.6   Feasible Route Network of Five
Demand Ports and Five Supply Ports

Table 7.19   Feasible Routes for Different Vessel

Vessel No.	1	2	3	4	5	6	7	8	9	10	11	12	13	14	15	16	17	18	19	20	21	22	23	24	25
1						✓		✓	✓	✓						✓		✓	✓	✓					
2								✓	✓	✓								✓	✓	✓					
3	✓	✓	✓	✓	✓	✓	✓	✓	✓	✓						✓	✓	✓	✓	✓					
4	✓	✓	✓	✓	✓	✓	✓	✓	✓	✓						✓	✓	✓	✓	✓					
5	✓	✓	✓	✓	✓	✓	✓	✓	✓	✓	✓	✓	✓	✓	✓	✓	✓	✓	✓	✓	✓	✓	✓	✓	✓
6						✓	✓	✓	✓	✓						✓	✓	✓	✓	✓					
7								✓	✓	✓								✓	✓	✓					
8								✓	✓	✓								✓	✓	✓					

Legend : $\begin{cases} \boxed{8} \\ \boxed{2}\ \ \boxed{✓} \end{cases}$ Means Route 8 by Vessel 2 or Variable $N_{8,2}$ as Represented in the Model

Vessel No. 1 – Sturt   5 – Cumberland
            2 – Kestrel   6 – Hunter
            3 – Capricorn   7 – Somersby
            4 – Kerry   8 – Shortland

The problem was solved using the MIP package in IBM 3031 and the procedure described as the modified STEM was used to generate five compromise solutions. The detailed results are shown in Table 7.20 and Table 7.21, and transportation cost versus tonnage-days curve showing several efficient solutions are depicted in Fig. 7.7.

The transportation cost versus tonnage-days curve gives five compromise solutions in between two extreme solutions, point 1 (solution 1) and point 7 (solution 7). Point 1 gives solution to minimization of the tonnage-days only, whereas point 7 gives solution to minimization of transportation cost only. Looking at the curve, the decision maker can select any of the seven solutions depending on the importance he gives to the individual objectives. The decision maker's judgement is highly influenced by the behavior of the market in the sense that when competition is high, a shopping company tends to satiate the demand of one customer as soon as possible so as to serve other customers sooner. Whereas when competition is low, a shipping company may just want to maximize profit by merely minimizing transportation cost. The same behavior exists when the demands are high and low, respectively.

Corresponding to each of the points, number of trips to be made by different vessels in different routes, amount (in tons) of empty vessel in different routes and number of days each vessel is to be used are shown in Table 7.20. So, the decision maker should first look at the cost versus tonnage-days curve, select a suitable point (solution) that is best according to him and should assign the vessels according to the corresponding solution in

Table 7.20 Best Compromise Solutions

Solution No.	1	2	3	4	5	6	7
Cost('000 $)	76,615	75,703	69,806	65,255	58,610	57,689	56,228
Tonnage-days ('000)	96,961	97,686	98,454	101,078	102,556	103,011	103,946
Number of trips in different routes by different vessels	N 1,5=6 N 1,4=4 N 2,4=11 N 2,5=2 N 3,3=2 N 3,5=8 N 4,3=7 N 4,5=3 N 6,1=2 N 6,4=2 N 7,4=1 N 7,5=7 N 8,1=3 N 8,4=1 N 8,6=10 N 8,8=5 N 9,1=9 N 9,2=1 N 9,3=1 N10,2=1 N10,4=2 N10,6=8 N10,8=2 N16,1=3 N16,3=1 N17,3=1 N19,7=3 N20,3=1	N 1,4=1 N 2,3=5 N 2,4=14 N 3,5=1 N 4,3=9 N 4,5=5 N 6,1=20 N 7,3=1 N 7,4=1 N 7,5=1 N 8,4=2 N 8,6=3 N 8,8=8 N 9,1=2 N 9,6=1 N10,4=4 N10,6=8 N14,5=1 N18,7=2 N19,7=2 N20,7=2 N21,5=2 N22,5=1	N 1,3=1 N 2,3=11 N 3,3=1 N 3,5=1 N 4,3=15 N 4,4=1 N 4,5=2 N 5,5=1 N 6,4=11 N 6,5=1 N 7,5=9 N 7,6=1 N 8,2=1 N 8,4=1 N 8,6=10 N 8,7=2 N 8,8=6 N 9,1=6 N 9,5=2 N10,6=8 N16,5=1 N19,1=2 N20,1=4 N20,7=3 N21,5=1 N23,6=1	N 1,3=14 N 2,4=10 N 3,3=6 N 3,5=5 N 4,3=2 N 4,5=5 N 6,1=4 N 6,3=1 N 7,5=3 N 7,6=2 N 8,4=1 N 8,6=2 N 8,8=10 N 9,4=2 N10,1=1 N10,6=12 N18,7=1 N19,7=4 N22,5=6	N 1,5=2 N 6,6=7 N 7,6=13 N 8,6=2 N 8,7=6 N 9,8=7 N10,7=3 N10,8=4 N16,3=2 N17,3=1 N18,2=2 N18,7=5 N18,8=3 N19,6=1 N20,7=1	N 1,5=1 N 3,5=1 N 6,6=7 N 7,6=13 N 8,7=7 N 8,8=8 N 9,6=1 N 9,8=7 N10,6=1 N10,7=4 N16,3=1 N16,6=1 N17,3=1 N20,2=2 N20,7=2 N20,8=1	N 1,5=1 N 6,6=8 N 7,6=13 N 8,7=8 N 8,8=6 N 9,6=1 N 9,8=7 N10,7=5 N10,8=3 N16,3=1 N17,3=1 N18,6=1 N18,7=1
Amount of empty vessel in tons in different routes	S 1+= 600 S 2+= 4500 S 4+= 4850 S 9+=20000 S10+= 6400 S19+=20000	S 1+=3100 S 2+= 900 S 3+=7100 S 4+=1500 S10+=8500	S 1+= 6200 S 2+= 1200 S 5+=10600 S 9+= 3700 S10+=20000 S20+=13050	S 2+=14700 S 3+=20000 S 8+=20000 S 9+=20000 S10+= 1000 S18+=12050 S19+= 8100	S 1+=14200 S 7+= 8800 S 8+=11050 S 9+= 3300 S20+=11250	S 1+=10100 S 3+= 1250 S 7+= 8800 S 9+= 3300 S10+=11000	S 1+=10100 S 7+= 8800 S 8+= 8650 S 9+= 3300 S10+= 5950
Number of days different vessel will be used in the planning horizon	V1=567 V2= 95 V3=634 V4=626 V5=696 V6=686 V7=168 V8=289	V1=556 V2=0 V3=520 V4=700 V5=686 V6=483 V7=318 V8=312	V1=478 V2= 40 V3=643 V4=692 V5=670 V6=716 V7=252 V8=234	V1=134 V2=0 V3=652 V4=493 V5=710 V6=718 V7=640 V8=390	V1=0 V2=88 V3=90 V4=0 V5=56 V8=702 V9=610 V10=701	V1=0 V2=104 V3=61 V4=0 V5=64 V6=702 V7=610 V8=693	V1=0 V2=0 V3=61 V4=0 V5=61 V6=695 V7=638 V8=704

KEY: N 8,4=1   means 1 round trip in route 8 by vessel no.4.
    S10+=20000 means 20000 tons in total can be empty in the round trips by different
                     vessel in route number 10. That means 20000 tons empty vessel in route
                     number 10.
    V8=701   means vessel no.8 is used for 701 days.

Table 7.20. From Table 7.20, the decision maker can get a clear idea about the number of days each vessel will be free in the planning horizon. This informa-tion is very important, because knowing this, the decision maker can utilize each vessel such that his earning is maximized for the leftover days in the planning horizon.

Table 7.21   Best Compromise Solutions for 10% Increase in Demand

Solution No.	1	2	3	4	5	6
Cost('000 $)	82,109	72,110	66,155	64,094	58,103	57,109
Tonnage-days ('000)	106,230	124,107	126,055	127,556	128,776	129,313
Number of trips in different routes by different vessels	N 1,4=12 N 2,4=1 N 3,3=1 N 4,3=13 N 4,4=4 N 4,5=2 N 6,1=7 N 7,3=4 N 7,4=6 N 7,5=12 N 8,3=1 N 8,6=7 N 8,8=12 N 9,5=4 N10,1=11 N10,6=11 N19,7=2 N22,5=2	N 1,5=11 N 5,5=1 N 6,6=3 N 7,5=1 N 7,6=13 N 8,7=14 N 8,8=3 N 9,6=5 N 9,8=5 N10,8=7 N17,6=1 N18,2=1 N19,2=2 N20,2=1 N20,7=1	N 2,5=10 N 6,6=9 N 7,6=8 N 8,6=1 N 8,7=7 N 8,8=7 N 9,6=4 N 9,7=5 N10,8=8 N16,3=2 N17,3=1 N18,2=2 N18,7=2 N19,2=1 N19,8=1 N20,2=2	N 1,5=8 N 2,4=1 N 4,5=1 N 6,6=2 N 7,6=14 N 8,6=5 N 8,7=13 N 8,8=1 N 9,7=2 N 9,8=6 N10,8=8 N16,3=2 N16,6=2 N18,2=1 N20,2=2	N 1,5=10 N 2,3=1 N 4,3=2 N 6,6=2 N 7,6=12 N 8,1=1 N 8,7=15 N 8,8=2 N 9,6=3 N 9,8=6 N10,6=1 N10,8=7 N16,3=3 N17,3=5 N20,4=1 N20,6=1	N 1,5=12 N 2,5=1 N 6,6=2 N 7,6=13 N 8,1=1 N 8,7=14 N 8,8=2 N 9,8=8 N10,6=5 N10,8=5 N16,3=1 N17,6=1 N18,7=1 N19,2=1 N20,2=1 N20,4=1
Amount of empty vessel in tons in different routes	S 2+=13900 S 3+= 400 S 9+=20000 S19+= 7700	S 5+=8650 S 6+=6300 S 7+=2300 S 8+=8000 S 9+=8100	S 2+= 6800 S 6+= 9600 S 8+=12050 S 9+= 3950 S10+= 6800	S 1+=10000 S 2+= 1500 S 8+= 950 S 9+= 200 S10+= 6800	S 1+= 1400 S 2+=13800 S 8+= 550 S10+= 1800	S 1+=10400 S 2+= 2300 S 8+= 550 S 9+= 1000 S10+= 800
Number of days different vessel will be used in the planning horizon	V1=586 V2=0 V3=690 V4=685 V5=708 V6=707 V7=112 V7=468	V1=0 V2=204 V3=0 V4=103 V5=450 V6=605 V7=597 V8=585	V1=0 V2=243 V3=90 V4=0 V5=310 V6=695 V7=625 V8=610	V1=0 V2=148 V3=58 V4=29 V5=267 V6=715 V7=648 V8=646	V1=32 V2=0 V3=353 V4=46 V5=280 V6=630 V7=630 V8=689	V1=32 V2=198 V3=0 V4=46 V5=367 V6=690 V7=635 V8=689

Notes: (1)   'Keys' same as in Table 7.21

        (2)   There are only 6 solution points found in this case.

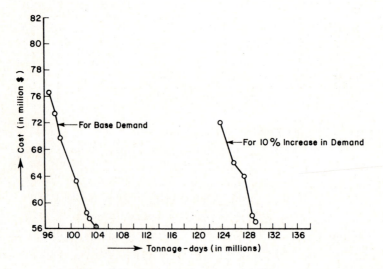

Fig. 7.7 Cost versus Tonnage-days

Looking closely at Table 7.20, some vessels are used in some solution points but are not used in others. This is understandable since using tonnage-days as an objective is given more importance over transportation cost; smaller but higher speed vessels become more preferable. The more importance given to transportation cost the more preferable are the bigger but slower vessels.

Due to computer time limitations, the sensitivity analysis was only done on the demand. And even on this it was only for a 10 percent increase in demand. It can be observed that the tradeoff line (as can be seen in Fig. 7.7) are very similar, i.e., extremely steep in one direction, which is supportive of the fact, as stated earlier, that unless the opportunity cost of tonnage-days is very large, the minimum transportation cost criterion will be suffi-cient. This finding reinforces the notion that the behavior of the tradeoff line is relatively insensitive to changes in demand.

The solutions presented previously are only "near-optimal" solutions as there was no attempt made, due to computer time limitations, to derive exact solutions for illustration purposes. But comparing these solutions with the corresponding continuous optimum solutions (Table 7.22), the integer solutions obtained are really not far off and hence can be described as good.

Table 7.22   Comparison of Near-Optimal and
Continuous Optimal Solutions

	Objective Functions	Integer Solution	Continuous Optimum Solution
	Transportation Cost	56,228,540	54,822,000
	Tonnage-Days	96,961,100	91,418,122
10 % increase in demand	Transportation Cost	57,109.476	56,621,000
	Tonnage-Days	106,230,156	98,567,120

The model gives optimal solution for smaller number of variables due to the fact that the MIP package uses branch-and-bound technique for deriving the integer solution. Using several experimental computer runs in an IBM 3031 system, the best integer solutions were obtained in about 2.5 minutes for problems with about 90 or less variables.

The model does not involve too much complicated data collection. It does not require complex calculations either. It would even be simpler if the two objective functions, at the very outset, are additively combined through the conversion of the tonnage-days into monetary terms. This requires a priori information from the decision maker and the solution procedure does not need an interactive approach thereby cutting the computational time even shorter. However, the main drawback of this is in obtaining the conversion factor from tonnage-days to money. In both cases, however, the model remains the same; the solution procedure is certainly flexible depending upon the real-world situation.

REFERENCES

1.   Adulbhan, P., M. N. Sharif, and M. T. Tabucanon, 1975.   Behavioral Patterns of Textile Industry and Electrical & Electronics Industry of Thailand.   Final Research Report for the General Electric Company (New York), Asian Institute of Technology, Bangkok.

2.   Adulbhan P., J. C. S. Tang, and K. Ramanathan, 1981.   A Multicriterion Approach for Commodity Distribution in a Regional Economic Integration: The Case of ASEAN.   Procedings of the Conference of the Operational Research Society of Singapore, University of Singapore, April, 1981.

3.   Allen, T. W., 1979.   The ASEAN Report, Vol. 2: The Evolution and Programs of ASEAN.   Dow Jones, London.

4.   Anandalingam, G., 1987.   A Multiple Criteria Decision Analytic Approach for Evaluating Acid Rain Policy Choices.   European Journal of Operational Research, 29:336-352.

5.   Aneja, Y. P. and K. Nair, 1979.   Bicriterion Transportation Problem. Management Science, 25:73-78.

6.   Baker, J. R. and K. E. Fitzpatrick, 1986.   Determination of an Optimal Forecast Model for Ambulance Demand Using Goal Programming.   Journal of the Operational Research Society, 37:1047-1060.

7.   Balassa, B., 1973.   Regional Integration in Trade: Policies of Less Developed Countries, in P. Streeten (Ed.), Trade Strategies for Development.   Western Printing Services, Racine, WI, pp. 176-186.

8.   Bana e Costa, C. A., 1988.   A Methodology for Sensitivity Analysis in Three-Criteria Problems: A Case Study in Municipal Management.   European Journal of Operational Research, 33:159-173.

9.   Bard, J. F., 1986.   A Multiobjective Methodology for Selecting Subsystem Automation Options.   Management Science, 32:1628-1641.

10. Bellmore, M., J. C. Liebman and D. H. Marks, 1972.   An Extension of the SZWARC Truck Assignment Problem.   Naval Research Logistics Quarterly, 19:91-100.

11. Benayoun, R., J. De Montgolfier, J. Tergny, and O. Laritchev, 1971. Linear Programming with Multiple Objective Functions: Step Method (STEM). Mathematical Programming, 1:366-375.

12. Current, J. and H. K. Min, 1986. Multiobjective Design of Transportation Networks: Taxonomy and Annotation. European Journal of Operational Research, 26:187-201.

13. Dieperink, H. and P. Nijkamp, 1987. A Multiple Criteria Location Model for Innovative Firms in a Communication Network. Economic Geography, 63:66-73.

14. Dorfman, R., P. Samuelson, and R. Solow, 1958. Linear Programming and Economic Analysis. McGraw-Hill, New York.

15. ECOCEN, 1973. Self-sufficiency Goal Required Export Action. Economic Cooperation, Bulletin No. 10, October.

16. Forman, E. H., 1987. Sensitivity Investigation for a Decision Analysis of the Strategic Defense Initiative (Starwars). Mathematical Modelling, 8:133-138.

17. Garfinkel, R. S. and M. R. Rao, 1971. The Bottleneck Transportation Problem. Naval Research Logistics Quarterly, 18:465-472.

18. Grassin, N., 1986. Constructing Population Criteria for the Comparison of Different Options for a High Voltage Route. European Journal of Operational Research, 26:42-57.

19. Grizzle, G. A., 1987. Pay for Performance: Can the Analytic Hierarchy Process Hasten the Day in the Public Sector? Mathematical Modelling, 9:245-250.

20. Henig, M. I., 1986. The Shortest Path Problem with Two Objective Functions. European Journal of Operational Research, 25:281-291.

21. Jarke, M., M. T. Jelassi, and M. F. Shakun, 1987. MEDIATOR: Toward a Negotiation Support System. European Journal of Operational Research, 31:314-334.

22. Kallio, M., A. Propoi, and R. Seppälä, 1986. A Model for the Forest Sector. TIMS Studies in the Management Sciences, 21:89-112.

23. Klein, G. and P. O. Beck, 1987. A Decision Aid for Selecting Among Information System Alternatives. MIS Quarterly, 11:177-186.

24. Min, H., 1987. A Multiobjective Retail Service Location Model for Fast Food Restaurants. Omega, 15:429-441.

25. Mladineo, N. J. Margeta, J. P. Brans, and B. Mareschal, 1987. Multicriteria Ranking of Alternative Locations for Small Scale Hydro Plants. European Journal of Operational Research, 31:215-222.

26. Norbis, M. I. and J. M. MacGregor Smith, 1988. A Multiobjective, Multi-Level Heuristic for dynamic Resource constrained Scheduling Problems.

European Journal of Operational Research, 33:30-41.

27. Nunamaker, T. R. and J. F. Truitt, 1987. Rationing discretionary Economic Resources: A Multiobjective Approach. Decision Sciences, 18:524-534.

28. Pak, P. S., K. Tsuji, and Y. Suzuki, 1987. Comprehensive Evaluation of New Urban Transportation System by AHP. International Journal of Systems Science, 18:1179-1190.

29. Park, Y. B. and C. P. Koelling, 1986. A Solution of Vehicle Routing Problems in a Multiple Objective Environment. Engineering Costs and Production Economics, 10:121-132.

30. Peniwati, K. and T. Hsiao, 1987. Ranking countries According to economic, Social and Political Indicators. Mathematical Modelling, 9:203-210.

31. Ramanathan, K., 1979. Multicriterion Models for Formulating Preferential Trading Arrangements in the ASEAN Cement Industry. Master of Engineering Thesis, No. IE79-15, Asian Institute of Technology, Bangkok.

32. Ringuest, J. L. and D. B. Rinks, 1987. Interactive Solutions for the Linear Multiobjective Transportation Problem. European Journal of Operational Research, 32:96-106.

33. Romero, C. and T. Rehman., 1987. Natural Resource Management and the Use of Multiple Criteria Decision Making Techniques: A Review. European Review of Agricultural economics, 14:61-90.

34. Roy, B. and D. Bouyssou, 1986. Comparison of Two Decision-Aid Models applied to Nuclear Power Plant Siting Example. European Journal of Operational Research, 25:200-215.

35. Saaty, T. L., 1987. A New Macroeconomic Forecasting and Policy Evaluation Method Using the Analytic Hierarchy Process. Mathematical Modelling, 9:219-232.

36. Schniederjans, M. J. and S. O. Kim, 1987. An Early Settlement of Long-Term Strikes: A Game Theory and Goal Programming Approach. Socio-Economic Planning Sciences, 21:177-188.

37. Schniederjans, M. J. and R. E. Markland, 1986. Estimating Start-up Resource Utilization in a Newly Formed Organization. Interfaces, 16:101-109.

38. Seip, K. L., H. Ibrekk, and F. Wenstop, 1987. Multiattribute Analysis of the Impact on Society of Phosphorus Abatement Measures. Water Resources Research, 23:755-764.

39. Sinuany-Stern, Z. and A. Mehrez, 1987. Discrete Multiattribute Utility Approach to Project Selection. Journal of the Operational Research Society, 38:1133-1140.

40. Srinivasan, V. and G. L. Thompson, 1977. Determining Cost vs. Time Pareto-Optimal Frontiers in Multi-model Transportation Problems.

Transportation Science, 11:1-19.

41. Starr, M. and M. Zeleny, 1977. Multiple Criteria Decision Making. North
     Holland Publishing Company.

42. Tabucanon, M. T., 1978. A Model for Identifying Areas of Industrial
     Investment Priorities for the Board of Investments. Procedings of the
     International Conference on Systems Modeling in Developing Countries, P.
     Adulbhan and N. Sharif eds., Asian Institute of Technology, Bangkok, May
     8-11, 1978.

43. Tabucanon, M. T. and E. Acio, 1982. Multiobjective Optimization Model
     Applied to ASEAN Preferential Trade in Sugar. Large Scale Systems
     3:35-45.

44. Tabucanon, M. T. and R. A. Alivio, 1983. Application of Multiobjective
     Linear Programming in Deriving Preferential Tariff Adjustments. Policy
     and Information, Vol. 7, No. 2.

45. Tabucanon, M. T., O. Fujiwara and M. A. H. Bhuiyan, 1986. Bicriterion
     Optimization Model for Coal Transportation Using Sea Bulk Carriers. Asia-
     Pacific Journal of Operational Research, 3:6-20.

46. Tabucanon, M. T. and V. D. Jose, 1986. Multiobjective Models for Selection
     of Priority Areas and Industrial Projects for Investment Promotion.
     Special Issue on "Multiple Criteria Decision Making", Engineering Costs
     and Production Economics, Vol. 10, No. 2, June, Elsevier.

47. Tayi, G. K., 1986. Bicriteria Transportation Problem: An Alternate
     Approach. Socio-Economic Planning Sciences, 20:127-130.

48. Thore, S. and S. Isser, 1987. A Goaling Format for National Energy
     Security. Mathematical Modelling, 9:51-62.

49. Tomek, I., 1986. Optimum Allocation in Multivariate Stratified Survey as
     a Problem of Multiple Criteria Optimization. Ekonomicko-Matematicky
     Obzor, 22:408-421 (in Czech).

50. Vachnadze, R. G. and N. I. Markozashvili, 1987. Some Applications of the
     Analytic Hierarchy Process. Mathematical Modelling, 9:185-194.

51. van Moeseke, P., 1987. Applied Bi-Objective Programs. Zeitshrift für
     Operations Research, 31:31-54.

52. Vijayalakshmi, B., 1987. An Application of Multi-Objective Modeling: The
     Case of the Indian Sugar Industry. European Journal of Operational
     Research, 28:146-153.

53. Vrat, P. and C. Kriengkrairut, 1986. A Goal Programming Model for Project
     Crashing with Piecewise Linear Time-cost Trade-off. Engineering Costs and
     Production Economics, 10:161-172.

54. Waverman, L., 1972. National Policy and Natural Gas: The Costs of a
     Border. Canadian Journal of Economics, 5:331-348.

55. Waverman, L., 1972.   The Preventive Tariff and the Dual in Linear Programming.   American Economics Review, 62:620-629.

APPENDIX

A HEURISTIC ALGORITHM FOR DE NOVO PROGRAMMING

After several model formulations, testing and detailed study of the results, the De Novo has been observed to have some distinct characteristics making solution by a simpler heuristic algorithm possible. The benefits of linear programming, particularly the product mix applications, may not have been fully utilized by smaller companies not having enough technical capability to apply these tools. Solution search procedures for linear programming, i.e. the simplex and the revised simplex methods, would require some specialized training in linear and matrix algebra, and might be difficult to comprehend for less mathematically oriented persons. Without computer aid, even small models of 10 to 15 variables, and an equal number of constraints would be lengthy and tedious for manual computations.

1. CHARACTERISTICS OF THE DE NOVO HEURISTICS

The following criteria were kept in mind in the design of the heuristic algorithm for De Novo:

i) Computations for the algorithm should be manageable with ordinary hand held calculator.

ii) To apply the algorithm, only a thorough understanding of the product mix system would be necessary. This would include an understanding of the concepts of profitability, product costing, budget or working capital, machine usage, production limits and machine capacity requirements for producing a product. No additional training in linear or matrix algebra would be necessary.

iii) Each step should have a relevant business or technical interpretation. This requirement would make the algorithm more understandable and interesting to use.

iv) The assumptions under which De Novo models using the heuristic algorithm operates must be realistic and relevant.

2. FEATURES OF DE NOVO LEADING TO THE HEURISTICS

The following characteristics of De Novo models were observed which made the heuristic possible:

i)   The De Novo has an integrated expression of resource utilization through the budget constraint.

ii)   The system functions in such a way that not only objective function is maximized, cost represented by budget constraint is likewise minimized. This gives rise to the simultaneous use of two equations, instead of one, to determine the most promising product to be produced.

iii)   The De Novo tends to specialize in more profitable products. The De Novo solution starts with the most profitable product until budget, demand or facilities pose a limit. Then, it chooses the next most profitable product.

iv)   Machines are loaded and used up based on returns (benefit/cost), and not exclusively based on absolute benefit.

3. THE DE NOVO HEURISTICS

3.1 Model Assumptions for the Application of the Heuristics

Assumptions of the standard De Novo models should hold true for the application of the De Novo heuristic. They are:

i)   Products have constant selling prices.

ii)   Variable resources should be "limitless" based on De Novo concept. Facilities or nonconsumable resources maybe fixed or variable.

iii)   Prices of variable resources are available, fixed and without dual pricing schemes. This makes computation of variable cost and gross contribution for each product possible.

iv)   Material and facility usage are proportional. No significant economies of scale exist.

v)   Budget and facility limits are known.

vi)   Demand limits may be considered, but, no product or sales mix requirements can be imposed.

3.2 The Algorithm

The algorithm is divided into two parts, the main program and the machine capacity reallocation subroutine.

i)   The Main Program

The main program of the De Novo heuristics comes up with decisions on which products to produce based on profitability ratios. The most profitable products are produced until some constraints pose a limit. The steps are as follows:

Step 1. Compute profitability ratio of each product

$$P_j = C_j / a_{ij}$$

where C_j = the contribution of product j to the objective function; and
a_{ij} = the coefficient of product j in the budget equation (budget equation is considered as constraint eq. 1)

Step 2. From among the products under consideration, choose the product with the highest P_j.

Step 3. Determine the constraint i limiting the production of product j. Compute for the maximum production possible x_{ij} under each constraint.

$$x_{ij(n)} = f_{i(n)} / a_{ij}$$

where n = the iteration number; and
i = the constraint equation no., the constraints include the budget, facility and demand limits.

Step 4. Production of x_j is chosen from

$$x_{j(n)} = Min \{ x_{ij(n)} \}$$

If $x_{j(n)} = 0$ due to $f_{i(n)} = 0$, go to Machine Capacity Reallocation Subroutine.

If not, proceed to step 5.

Step 5. Update cumulative profit or objective function:

$$Z_{n+1} = Z_n + C_j x_{j(n)}$$

Update facility availability by the equation:

$$f_{i(n+1)} = f_{i(n)} - a_{ij} x_{j(n)}$$

Update budget availability:

$$B_{n+1} = B_n - a_{ij} x_{j(n)}$$

where Z_{n+1}, B_{n+1} and $f_{i(n+1)}$ are the current profit, budget and facility availability after producing $x_{j(n)}$, respectively;

Z_n, B_n, and $f_{i(n)}$ are the profit, budget and facility availability from the previous iteration, respectively; and

a_{ij} are the consumption coefficients of product j of resource i.

Step 6.   a)   Check the budget availability. If $B_{n+1} = 0$, go to step 8, otherwise, go to step 6b.

b)   Are there any new used up facility, $f_{i(n+1)} = 0$? If yes, go to Machine Reallocation Subroutine. Otherwise, go to step 6c.

c)   For $f_{i(n+1)} = 0$, check if all $a_{ij} > 0$ for all products not yet considered. This in effect checks if all unallocated products have to pass any fully utilized machine.

If all $a_{ij} > 0$ for all products not yet considered, this means no further allocation is possible. All unallocated products have to pass a fully utilized machine. Go to Step 7. Otherwise, go to step 2.

Step 7.   Do you want to try to improve solution? If yes, go to step 2. If no, go to step 8.

Step 8.   Terminate.

Flowchart for the main program is shown in Fig. 1.

The choice of product to be produced was based on the computed profitability ratio $P_j = C_j/a_{ij}$, with C_j the gross contribution, and a_{ij} being the variable cost of product j. The choice rule provided a good candidate for profit maximization but does not ensure optimality.

This rule was developed after having observed the break-even concept under constant selling price and variable cost by Brown and Revelle (1978). The break-even formula

$$BE = \frac{\text{Fixed Cost} + \text{Desired Profit}}{1 - \dfrac{\text{Unit Variable Cost}}{\text{Unit Selling Price}}} \qquad (1)$$

can be transformed to

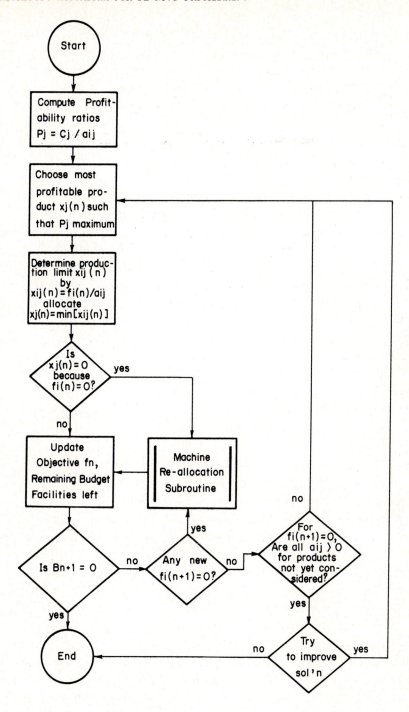

Fig. 1 Flowchart of the Main Program of De Novo Heuristic

$$BE = \frac{\text{Fixed Cost + Desired Profit}}{\dfrac{\text{Unit Selling Price - Unit Variable Cost}}{\text{Unit Selling Price}}}$$

or
$$BE = \frac{\text{Fixed Cost + Desired Profit}}{\dfrac{\text{Unit Gross Contribution}}{\text{Unit Selling Price}}} \tag{2}$$

The denominator in Eq. (2) may at times be approximated by the ratio (C_j/a_{ij}) if the product has a low profitability. Observing the formula:

$$BE \ (P_j) = \text{Fixed Cost + Desired Profit} \tag{3}$$

if instead of a bieak-even capacity, a desired capacity utilization of 100% is assumed, then the above formula shows that desired profit is directly proportional to P_j. If there are several product choices, higher P_j contributes more to profit.

ii) Machine Capacity Reallocation Subroutine

This subroutine was developed in the later part of the research to improve the solution of the heuristic when facilities limit production instead of budget. The subroutine is as follows:

Step 1. From the main program, identify the facility posing as constraint to output of $x_{j(n)}$. For every product loaded in this machine, compute return on capital per unit machine time used, i.e. $\text{Index}_j = P_j/a_{ij}$.

Step 2. List all candidate products for switching. These are the products with profitability indices less than the index of the product currently under consideration.

Step 3. Are there candidates for switching? If yes, go to Step 4. If no, go to Step 6.

Step 4. For the product $x_{j(n)}$, increase production up to the second lowest level possible from Step 4 of the main program. Compute for the corresponding decrease in the production of each candidate product for switching. This in effect re-allocates machine capacity from one product to another.

Step 5. Compute for additional profit because of the change in product mix. Choose the one with maximum profit change as the product to be adjusted against the product in the current iteration.

STep 6. Go to Step 5 of the main program.

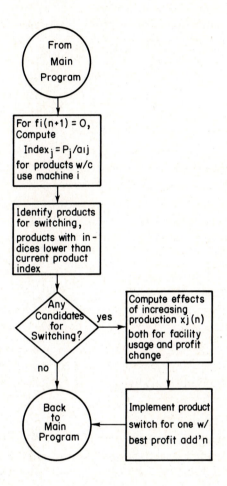

Fig. 2   Machine Time Reallocation Subroutine

Fig. 2 shows the Machine Capacity Reallocation Subroutine.

The choice of candidate product for the machine capacity reallocation subroutine is based on the index (P_j/a_{ij}).   This rule of reallocation is motivated by the following knapsack problem presented by Lawler (1976).

Suppose there are n objects, the jth object having a positive integer weight a_j and value P_j. It is desired to fine the most valuable subset of objects subject to the restriction that their total weight does not exceed b, the capacity of the knapsack. This problem can be formulated as an integer linear programming model of the form

$$\text{Maximize} \qquad Z = P_1 x_1 + P_2 x_2 + \ldots + P_j x_j \qquad (4)$$
$$\text{Subject to} \qquad a_1 x_1 + a_2 x_2 + \ldots + a_j x_j \leq b \qquad (5)$$

Solving this type of problem through the Branch and Bound Algorithm, x_j's with higher P_j and lower a_j are preferred in order to maximize the objective function without immediately going over the capacity b.

The knapsack capacity constraint in the above problem is analogous to our capacity constraint posed by the single machine in the subroutine. Benefit can be measured by profitability, or the highest contribution to desired profit P_j. The decision variable would be the choice of product to be loaded.

4. ILLUSTRATIVE EXAMPLES

4.1 Budget Constraint Problem

Suppose Chocoman (Section 9, Chapter V) has a budget constraint of $200,000 for working capital. Facility and demand limits are given in Model 1. What would be the product mix using the De Novo heuristics?

i)   Computations

Referring to Solution Table 1 of Model 1, the P_j's were first calculated for every product. For the first iteration, MS with maximum $P_j=1.24$ was chosen.

Solution Table 2 determined the maximum amount of MS that can be produced. Demand limited production of this product to 1,000. The current profit, remaining budget and facilities available were computed. The same procedure was repeated for iterations 2, 3 and 4 which involved choosing the unallocated product with the highest P_j and determining the maximum production.

At iteration 3, even if facility 6 was used up, we could still proceed because none of the other products used this facility. The problem is solved when budget was used up in 4th iteration.

Model 1   De Novo Heuristic, Illustrative Example 1

The Problem

Products	MB	MS	CB	CS	NB	NS	CY	WF	Limits
Profit Eq.	179.95	82.9	153.08	72.15	129.95	69.9	208.5	83	
1 B'get	195.05	67.1	246.93	87.85	290.05	105.1	191.5	67.1	200000
2 Cook	0.5	0.2	0.425	0.17	0.35	0.14	0.6	0.096	1500
3 Mix			0.15	0.06	0.25	0.1			200
4 Form	0.75	0.3	0.75	0.3	0.75	0.3	0.9	0.36	2000
5 Grind			0.25	0.1					200
6 WfrMkg								0.3	100
7 Cut	0.1	0.1	0.1	0.1	0.1	0.1	0.2		600
8 Pkg1	0.25		0.25		0.25			0.1	400
9 Pkg2	0.05	0.3	0.05	0.3	0.05	0.3	2.5	0.15	1500
Demand Limits	800	1000	750	800	500	800	400	1000	

Solution Table 1   Product Mix Decisions

Product	P_j	n=1	n=2	n=3	n=4	n=5	Final Solution
MB	0.92				174		174
MS	1.24	1000					1000
CB	0.62						
CS	0.82						
NB	0.45						
NS	0.67						
CY	1.09			400			400
WF	1.24		333.33				333.33

Solution Table 2   Budget, Facility Availability

		n=1	n=2	n=3	n=4	n=5
Profit			82900	110566	193966	225278
Budget		200000	132900	110534	33934	0
Facility	2	1500	1300	1268	1028	941
	3	200	200	200	200	200
	4	2000	1700	1580	1220	1089.5
	5	200	200	200	200	200
	6	100	100	0	0	0
	7	600	500	500	420	402.6
	8	400	400	366.7	366.7	323.2
	9	1500	1200	1150	150	141.3
$X_j(n)$		MS	WF	CY	MB	
Eq Limit		B 5961	B 4961	B 1622	B 174	
		D 1000	D 1000	D 400	D 800	
		2 7500	2 15625	2 2113	2 2056	
		4 6667	4 5556	4 1756	4 1627	
		7 6000	6 333.33	7 2500	7 4200	
		9 5000	8 4000	9 460	8 1467	
			9 10000		9 3000	

ii)   Results

The solution set from the heuristic

$$Z = 225,278$$

MB	=	174	CY	=	400
MS	=	1,000	WF	=	333.33

was not significantly different from the answer obtained through simplex method. Deviations were due to rounding errors. The whole procedure took less than an hour when all the data were already available.

4.2 Facility Limiting Production

Taking the same problem, suppose the budget was increased to $400,000. Would we still be able to achieve the optimal solution through the De Novo heuristics without using the machine capacity reallocation subroutine?

i)   Computations

Referring to Model 2, the solution was continued from iteration 4 of the previous Model 1. With more financial resources, more of MB can be produced. The product mix was increased by one product, CS.

At iteration 6, the entire packaging machine, facility 9 was used up. No further allocation was possible because all unallocated products had to pass through this facility.

ii)   Results

Comparing the results of the heuristics and using simplex method with respect to objective function,

Simplex method	Z = 395,588
Heuristic approach	Z = 364,382
Difference	31,206
% deviation	7.9%

The result obtained from the heuristic can be considered near optimal. The solution can, however, be improved to achieve optimality as will be shown in the next example.

Model 2   De Novo Heuristic, Illustrative Example 2

The Problem

Products	MB	MS	CB	CS	NB	NS	CY	WF	Limits
Profit	179.95	82.9	153.08	72.15	129.95	69.9	208.5	83	
Eq.									
1 B'get	195.05	67.1	246.93	87.85	290.05	105.1	191.5	67.1	400000
2 Cook	0.5	0.2	0.425	0.17	0.35	0.14	0.6	0.096	1500
3 Mix			0.15	0.06	0.25	0.1			200
4 Form	0.75	0.3	0.75	0.3	0.75	0.3	0.9	0.36	2000
5 Grind			0.25	0.1					200
6 WfrMkg								0.3	100
7 Cut	0.1	0.1	0.1	0.1	0.1	0.1	0.2		600
8 Pkg1	0.25		0.25		0.25			0.1	400
9 Pkg2	0.05	0.3	0.05	0.3	0.05	0.3	2.5	0.15	1500
Demand									
Limits	800	1000	750	800	500	800	400	1000	

Solution Table 1   Product Mix Decisions

Product	P_j	n=1	n=2	n=3	n=4	n=5	Final Solution
MB	0.92				800		800
MS	1.24	1000					1000
CB	0.62						
CS	0.82					366.67	366.67
NB	0.45						
NS	0.67						
CY	1.09			400			400
WF	1.24		333.33				333.33

Solution Table 2   Budget, Facility Availability

	n=1	n=2	n=3	n=4	n=5	n=6
Profit		82900	110566	193966	337926	364382
Budget	400000	332900	310534	233934	77894	45682
Facility 2	1500	1300	1268	1028	628	566
3	200	200	200	200	200	178
4	2000	1700	1580	1220	620	510
5	200	200	200	200	200	163
6	100	100	0	0	0	0
7	600	500	500	420	340	303
8	400	400	366.7	366.7	166.7	167
9	1500	1200	1150	150	110	0
$X_{j(n)}$	MS	WF	CY	MB	CS	
Eq Limit	B 5961	B 4961	B 1622	B 1200	B 887	
	D 1000	D 1000	D 400	D 800	D 800	
	2 7500	2 15625	2 2113	2 2056	2 3694	
	4 6667	4 5556	4 1756	4 1627	3 3333	
	7 6000	6 333.33	7 2500	7 4200	4 2067	
	9 5000	8 4000	9 460	8 1467	5 2000	
		9 10000		9 3000	7 3400	
					9 366.7	

4.3 Use of Machine Capacity Reallocation Subroutine

The effectiveness of the machine reallocation subroutine was tested using the same problem with budget increased to $500,000.

i)   Computations

Referring to Model 3, iteration 6, instead of terminating the solution process, we move to the machine reallocation subroutine because facility 9 was used up. Referring to the flowchart in Fig. 1, this answers the question, "any new $f_{i(n+1)} = 0?$".

Solution Table 3 showed how other products were evaluated for possible switching.   After computing the index, P_j/a_{9j}, CY was identified to be decreased to give way to increased production of CS, resulting into an additional profit of $20,423.

At iteration 7, no new facility was used up, however, no other allocation was possible because all products had to use facility 9. To try to improve the current solution, the next used to explore more profitable options.

The procedure was repeated for the succeeding products. The problem was considered solved when the budget left was $825.

ii)   Results

The results of the heuristic was again compared to the simplex solution. There were some slight deviations in the amounts of the different products to be produced, however, the product mix was the same.   Comparing objective function achievements,

$$
\begin{array}{lll}
\text{Simplex method} & Z = 456{,}782 \\
\text{Heuristic approach} & Z = 451{,}979 \\
\text{Difference} & 4{,}803 \\
\text{\% deviation} & 1\%
\end{array}
$$

A negligible difference was observed between the two results.

Model 3 De Novo Heuristic, Illustrative Example 3

Solution Table 1 Product Mix Decisions

Product	P_j	n=1	n=2	n=3	n=4	n=5	n=6	n=7	n=8	Solution
MB	0.92			800						800
MS	1.24	1000								1000
CB	0.62								210	210
CS	0.82				366.67	800				800
NB	0.45									
NS	0.67						800			800
CY	1.09			400			348	252	247.8	247.8
WF	1.24		333.33							333.33

Solution Table 2 Budget, Facility Availability

		n=1	n=2	n=3	n=4	n=5	n=6	n=7	n=8	n=9
Profit			82900	110566	193966	337926	364382	384804	420708	451979
Budget		500000	432900	410534	333934	177894	145682	117572	51876	825
Facility	2	1500	1300	1268	1028	628	566	523.2	468.8	382
	3	200	200	200	200	200	178	152	72	41
	4	2000	1700	1580	1220	620	510	426.8	273.2	119
	5	200	200	200	200	200	163	120	120	68
	6	100	100	0	0	0	0	0	0	0
	7	600	500	500	420	340	303	270.4	209.6	189
	8	400	400	366.7	366.7	166.7	167	116.7	116.7	114
	9	1500	1200	1150	150	110	0	0	0	0
							Sub.	Imp.	Imp.	

$X_{j(n)}$	MS	WF	CY	MB	CS	CS=800	NS	CB
Eq Limit	B 5961	B 4961	B 1622	B 1200	B 887		B 1118	B 210
	D 1000	D 1000	D 400	D 800	D 800		D 800	D 750
	2 7500	2 15625	2 2113	2 2056	2 3694		2 3737	2 1103
	4 6667	4 5556	4 1756	4 1627	3 3333		3 1520	3 480
	7 6000	6 333.33	7 2500	7 4200	4 2067		4 1423	4 436
	9 5000	8 4000	9 460	8 1467	5 2000		7 2704	5 480
		9 10000		9 3000	7 3400		9 0	7 2096
					9 366.7		Sub.	8 667
								9 0
								Sub.

Sub. - Subroutine   Imp. - Improve

Model 3   De Novo Heuristic, Illustrative Example 3 (Continued)

Solution Table 3   Machine Capacity Reallocation

Products	MB	MS	CB	CS	NB	NS	CY	WF	Candidates
P_j	0.92	1.24	0.62	0.82	0.45	0.67	1.09	1.24	
n=6									
a_{9j}	0.05	0.3	0.05	0.3	0.05	0.3	2.5	0.15	
Index	18.4	4.13		2.73			0.44	8.27	CY
Add(Dec)				433			-52		
Profit							20423		
Decision							Go		
n=7									
Index	18.4	4.13		2.73		2.23	0.44	8.27	CY
Add(Dec)						800	-96		
Profit							35904		
Decision							Go		
n=8									
Index	18.4	4.13	12.4	2.73		2.23	0.44	8.27	MS,CS,NS,
Add(Dec)		-35	210	-35		-35	-4.2	-70	CY,WF
Profit		29245		29622		29700	31271	26337	
Decision							Go		

5.   DISCUSSION OF RESULTS

5.1   Use of the Main Program, Bypassing the Subroutine

Different budget limits were tested using the De Novo heuristics main program.   The results are shown in Table 1.

Models with budget limits of $300,000 and below achieved optimality with the heuristics.   Differences were due to rounding off errors.   As budget increased and facilities limited total production, the main program alone is unable to achieve optimality.   The machine reallocation subroutine was therefore necessary to improve the solution.

5.2   Performance of the De Novo complete Heuristic

Applying the machine reallocation subroutine to the last three problems with budget limits above $400,000, the results are presented in Table 2.

The subroutine was effective in the first two cases when only one facility limited production.   Results were near optimal.   However, when two facilities were used up simultaneously as experienced in the last trial, the subroutine was not able to handle such type of problem.

Table 1   Results of Heuristic's Main Program Compared to Simplex

	Objective Function		Difference	
Allowed Budget	Simplex	Heuristic	Amount ($)	%
$100,000	$122,071	$122,040	31	0
200,000	225,304	225,278	26	0
300,000	317,562	317,592	30	0
400,000	395,588	364,382	31,206	7.9
500,000	456,782	364,406	92,376	20.2
600,000	476,285	364,406	111,879	23.5

Table 2   Results of Heuristic's Main Program Compared to Simplex

	Objective Function		Difference	
Allowed Budget	Simplex	Heuristic	Amount ($)	%
400,000	395,588	$392,317	3,271	1.0
500,000	456,782	451,979	4,803	1.0
600,000	476,285	420,717	55,568	11.7

5.3   Limitations of the Heuristic

The complete De Novo heuristics formulated in this section was found to be effective for both production limited by the budget and/or a single facility. However, the program does not ensure optimality.   In cases of excess financial resources, there is no assurance that the solution obtained is optimal.   The main program is easy to understand and apply.   The subroutine needs some practice to be able to get use to it.   Each step has a relevant interpretation making it easy to understand.

Unfortunately, when more than one machine would be used up simultaneously, there is yet no method formulated to re-evaluate machine capacity loading.

SUBJECT/AUTHOR INDEX